The State in Africa

An Analysis of Impacts of Historical Trajectories of Global Capitalist Expansion and Domination in the Continent

Tatah Mentan

Langaa Research & Publishing CIG
Mankon, Bamenda

Publisher:
Langaa RPCIG
Langaa Research & Publishing Common Initiative Group
P.O. Box 902 Mankon
Bamenda
North West Region
Cameroon
Langaagrp@gmail.com
www.langaa-rpcig.net

Distributed outside N. America by African Books Collective
orders@africanbookscollective.com
www.africanbookscollective.com

Distributed in N. America by Michigan State University Press
msupress@msu.edu
www.msupress.msu.edu

ISBN: 9956-616-12-5

DISCLAIMER

Other Titles by *Langaa* RPCIG

Francis B. Nyamnjoh
Stories from Abakwa
Mind Searching
The Disillusioned African
The Convert
Souls Forgotten
Married But Available
Intimate Strangers

Dibussi Tande
No Turning Back. Poems of Freedom 1990-1993
Scribbles from the Den: Essays on Politics and Collective Memory in Cameroon

Kangsen Feka Wakai
Fragmented Melodies

Ntemfac Ofege
Namondo. Child of the Water Spirits
Hot Water for the Famous Seven

Emmanuel Fru Doh
Not Yet Damascus
The Fire Within
Africa's Political Wastelands: The Bastardization of Cameroon
Oriki'badan
Wading the Tide
Stereotyping Africa: Surprising Answers to Surprising Questions

Thomas Jing
Tale of an African Woman

Peter Wuteh Vakunta
Grassfields Stories from Cameroon
Green Rape: Poetry for the Environment
Majunga Tok: Poems in Pidgin English
Cry, My Beloved Africa
No Love Lost
Straddling The Mungo: A Book of Poems in English & French

Ba'bila Mutia
Coils of Mortal Flesh

Kehbuma Langmia
Titabet and the Takumbeng
An Evil Meal of Evil

Victor Elame Musinga
The Barn
The Tragedy of Mr. No Balance

Ngessimo Mathe Mutaka
Building Capacity: Using TEFL and African Languages as Development-oriented Literacy Tools

Milton Krieger
Cameroon's Social Democratic Front: Its History and Prospects as an Opposition Political Party, 1990-2011

Sammy Oke Akombi
The Raped Amulet
The Woman Who Ate Python
Beware the Drives: Book of Verse
The Wages of Corruption

Susan Nkwentie Nde
Precipice
Second Engagement

Francis B. Nyamnjoh & Richard Fonteh Akum
The Cameroon GCE Crisis: A Test of Anglophone Solidarity

Joyce Ashuntantang & Dibussi Tande
Their Champagne Party Will End! Poems in Honor of Bate Besong

Emmanuel Achu
Disturbing the Peace

Rosemary Ekosso
The House of Falling Women

Peterkins Manyong
God the Politician

George Ngwane
The Power in the Writer: Collected Essays on Culture, Democracy & Development in Africa

John Percival
The 1961 Cameroon Plebiscite: Choice or Betrayal

Albert Azeyeh
Réussite scolaire, faillite sociale : généalogie mentale de la crise de l'Afrique noire francophone

Aloysius Ajab Amin & Jean-Luc Dubois
Croissance et développement au Cameroun : d'une croissance équilibrée à un développement équitable

Carlson Anyangwe
Imperialistic Politics in Cameroun:
Resistance & the Inception of the Restoration of the Statehood of Southern Cameroons
Betrayal of Too Trusting a People: The UN, the UK and the Trust Territory of the Southen Cameroons

Bill F. Ndi
K'Cracy, Trees in the Storm and Other Poems
Map: Musings On Ars Poetica
Thomas Lurting: The Fighting Sailor Turn'd Peaceable /Le marin combattant devenu paisible

Kathryn Toure, Therese Mungah Shalo Tchombe & Thierry Karsenti
ICT and Changing Mindsets in Education

Charles Alobwed'Epie
The Day God Blinked
The Bad Samaritan

G. D. Nyamndi
Babi Yar Symphony
Whether losing, Whether winning
Tussles: Collected Plays
Dogs in the Sun

Samuel Ebelle Kingue
Si Dieu était tout un chacun de nous ?

Ignasio Malizani Jimu
Urban Appropriation and Transformation: bicycle, taxi and handcart operators in Mzuzu, Malawi

Justice Nyo' Wakai
Under the Broken Scale of Justice: The Law and My Times

John Eyong Mengot
A Pact of Ages

Ignasio Malizani Jimu
Urban Appropriation and Transformation: Bicycle Taxi and Handcart Operators

Joyce B. Ashuntantang
Landscaping and Coloniality: The Dissemination of Cameroon Anglophone Literature

Jude Fokwang
Mediating Legitimacy: Chieftaincy and Democratisation in Two African Chiefdoms

Michael A. Yanou
Dispossession and Access to Land in South Africa: an African Perspevctive

Tikum Mbah Azonga
Cup Man and Other Stories
The Wooden Bicycle and Other Stories

John Nkemngong Nkengasong
Letters to Marions (And the Coming Generations)
The Call of Blood

Amady Aly Dieng
Les étudiants africains et la littérature négro-africaine d'expression française

Tah Asongwed
Born to Rule: Autobiography of a life President
Child of Earth

Frida Menkan Mbunda
Shadows From The Abyss

Bongasu Tanla Kishani
A Basket of Kola Nuts
Konglanjo (Spears of Love without Ill-fortune) and Letters to Ethiopia with some Random Poems

Fo Angwafo III S.A.N of Mankon
Royalty and Politics: The Story of My Life

Basil Diki
The Lord of Anomy
Shrouded Blessings

Churchill Ewumbue-Monono
Youth and Nation-Building in Cameroon: A Study of National Youth Day Messages and Leadership Discourse (1949-2009)

Emmanuel N. Chia, Joseph C. Suh & Alexandre Ndeffo Tene
Perspectives on Translation and Interpretation in Cameroon

Linus T. Asong
The Crown of Thorns
No Way to Die
A Legend of the Dead: Sequel of *The Crown of Thorns*
The Akroma File
Salvation Colony: Sequel to *No Way to Die*

Vivian Sihshu Yenika
Imitation Whiteman
Press Lake Varsity Girls: The Freshman Year

Beatrice Fri Bime
Someplace, Somewhere
Mystique: A Collection of Lake Myths

Shadrach A. Ambanasom
Son of the Native Soil
The Cameroonian Novel of English Expression: An Introduction

Tangie Nsoh Fonchingong and Gemandze John Bobuin
Cameroon: The Stakes and Challenges of Governance and Development

Tatah Mentan
Democratizing or Reconfiguring Predatory Autocracy? Myths and Realities in Africa Today
The State in Africa: An Analysis of Impacts of Historical Trajectories of Gobal Capitalist Expansion and Domination in the Continent

Roselyne M. Jua & Bate Besong
To the Budding Creative Writer: A Handbook

Albert Mukong
Prisonner without a Crime: Disciplining Dissent in Ahidjo's Cameroon

Mbuh Tennu Mbuh
In the Shadow of my Country

Bernard Nsokika Fonlon
Genuine Intellectuals: Academic and Social Responsibilities of Universities in Africa

Lilian Lem Atanga
Gender, Discourse and Power in the Cameroonian Parliament

Cornelius Mbifung Lambi & Emmanuel Neba Ndenecho
Ecology and Natural Resource Development in the Western Highlands of Cameroon: Issues in Natural Resource Managment

Gideon F. For-mukwai
Facing Adversity with Audacity

Peter W. Vakunta & Bill F. Ndi
Nul n'a le monopole du français : deux poètes du Cameroon anglophone

Emmanuel Matateyou
Les murmures de l'harmattan

Ekpe Inyang
The Hill Barbers

JK Bannavti
Rock of God *(Kilán ke Nyiy)*

Content

To The Victims of:

Repression

Dispossession,

Exploitation,

and Violence

by the State in Africa

List of Acronyms

AGP	(WTO) Agreement on Government Procurement
APEC	Asia-Pacific Economic Cooperation (forum)
CSR	Corporate social responsibility
EFTA	European Free Trade Association
EU	European Union
FDI	Foreign direct investment
FIPA	Foreign investment promotion and protection agreement
FTA	Free trade agreement
FTAA	Free Trade Area of the Americas
FTC	Free Trade Commission
GATS	General Agreement on Trade in Services
GATT	General Agreement on Tariffs and Trade
GCC	Cooperation Council for the Arab States of the Gulf (formerly Gulf Cooperation Council)
GDP	Gross domestic product
ICT	Information and communications technologies
IPR	Intellectual property rights
ITARs	International Traffic in Arms Regulations
LDC	Least developed country
MENA	Middle East and North Africa
Mercosur	Southern Common Market
MOU	Memorandum of understanding
NAFTA	North American Free Trade Agreement
OECD	Organization for Economic Co-operation and Development
TRIPS Agreement	Agreement on Trade-Related Aspects of Intellectual Property Rights
UAE	United Arab Emirates
WTO	World Trade Organization

Preface

This book explores several of the latest endeavours that theorize the state and globalization. The aim is to reflect further on some of the wider follies that lie within the ambition of debates on the state and globalization, especially in the case of Africa. By uniting common themes throughout the book—revolving around issues of state capacity in the post-colonial African world, the relationship between globalization and international relations, and the very meaning of globality—the book raises a series of questions for further research on the state and globalization. Most significantly, it seeks to question the future of *critical* theorizing on the state and globalization within international studies. It does so by arguing that there remain serious questions, begging assumptions about capitalism that lie at the core of present general theories of the state and globalization that, if overlooked, might also blunt the precepts of critical international theorizing.

To understand Africa in global capitalism we may view it from two perspectives. That is, there are two ways of picturing Africa in the context of global capitalism. One is from the point of view of the people living and hoping to improve their lot in Africa's fifty-four nation-states with a considerable variety of kinds of 'insertion' into the global capitalist economy, and a corresponding range of experiences of development (or the lack of it). The other is from the point of view of capital, for which Africa is not so much a system of states, still less a continent of people in need of a better life, as simply a geographic—or geological—terrain, offering this or that opportunity for global capital to make money.

Globalization is a term that has come to be used in recent years increasingly frequently and, arguably, increasingly loosely. In this book, I shall focus on the concept of globalization as the transcendence (rather than the mere crossing or opening) of borders arguing that this interpretation offers the most distinctive and helpful insight into the contemporary State in Africa, itself a creation and determination of capitalist globalization. The book goes on to explore one of the key questions raised by this trend, namely, how the growth of supraterritorial space has altered capitalism in general, and the role of the state in Africa within the given historical transformations and expansion of capitalism in the continent in particular.

My central argument about the role of the state in Africa is simple: throughout history, Western interests in Africa have been consistent: access to cheap labour, and control of the economy, markets and raw materials. The state in Africa, since its creation during the colonial era, has been shaped to meet these Western goals. The development of the state in Africa has been marked by contradictions. The colonial state was established to dominate, integrate the continent asymmetrically into the world capitalist system, and extract surplus produced by Africans for the colonizers. African independence made little or no difference to this colonial state structure in an era of capitalist expansion.

Two contradictory features have marked the development of the imploding states in Africa after decolonization. These twin features are: extreme political fragility and extreme consistency in serving the interests of international capital, be it in the neocolonial context or that of neoliberal globalization. In both cases, there is the crystallization of a common structure: a gap, a lack of connection, between African civil society and the chaotic state politics.

On one hand, the state serves mainly as a dynamic part of the structure of dependent underdevelopment, and on the other hand, governments serve as the foreman to keep civil society producing a surplus to be accumulated by foreign finance capital and parasitic native social classes that enjoy almost absolutist power. As a result, African goals such as self reliance, development, democracy, and continental unity cannot be achieved by the present state in Africa. If these needs are to be met, Africans will have to restructure the state away from its client-collaborator existential situation.

The *raison d'être* for this argument is simple. The nation-state initially arose in Western Europe and then spread throughout the world as four conditions came into being: 1) a sizable people that considered itself distinct from other peoples, 2) a sizable territory, with which the people historically identified, as its homeland, 3) a massive sentiment of affection by the people for its current or past heroic leader(s), and 4) a general patriotic belief that the people as a whole should have self-rule in their own homeland. States and empires have existed for thousands of years. New feudal states came into being with the breakup of Charlemagne's new Roman Empire in 840-43. France has generally been considered the prototype of this new feudal state. As it contended with other feudal states, especially England, heroic figures like Joan of Arc arose in France as its people identified with their homeland.

When in 1521 the Saxon Elector Frederick provided 'state' protection for Luther, a religious revolution began in Western Europe that soon spread to England, Holland and Scotland. There was a gradual transition of feudal states into bourgeois states led by the establishment of the evolving new Dutch State in 1581. It soon developed world-wide trade that made it rich despite the insecurity of its territory. During the period of English civil conflict and war of 1640-48, the state system, which had been developing since the truce between Spain and the Netherlands in 1609, officially came into being with the Treaty of Westphalia. It is that state system and the evolving nation-state idea that have since spread throughout the world. [i) the English Civil War is generally held to be 1642-51; although earlier conflict could date the beginning to 1640, the end is certainly 1651; ii) the link between the English Civil War and the 1648 Treaty of Westphalia isn't clear here – England was not a signatory.]

European imperial or colonial states established the political conduits through which colonized African societies engaged the global political economy. In many ways, this engagement was a process of simplification, reducing complex African social formations to basic national templates: the zoning of agricultural production; the reduction of varied cultures of ownership and norms of trade to 'chieftaincies' and the regulations of marketing boards; and the redirecting of local and long distance trade networks to the road and rail links to port, capital city, and customs office.

Intrinsically authoritarian, this process of colonial standardization was executed with violence and was resisted both actively and passively by Africans. This alien violence and local resistance resulted in a mosaic of complex outcomes. The colonial project might not have completed its immanent desire to produce self-contained national economies malleable to the designs of international capital, but it did mark a profound historical transition which defined the historical possibilities of independence. In spite of the vibrant African political currents of the late 1950s and 1960s, statesmen inherited repressive and exploitative political and economic kingdoms that had been structured by colonialism, whether these kingdoms were inherited through negotiations or armed struggle.

This inheritance of repressive and exploitative alien state structures explains why the political trajectory of the state in Africa since the terminal European colonial period had, by the 1990s, reduced the pertinence of the 'post-colonial' label still widely employed. The term 'post-colonial' acquired widespread currency not long after (in) dependence status in the world capitalist system in acknowledgment of the importation into these extensions of imperial states of the practices, routines and mentalities of the colonial state. These attributes served as a platform for a more ambitious form of political monopoly, whose legitimating discourse was developmentalism.

At the dawn of Africa's independence, the European colonial state legacy decanted into a patrimonial autocracy that decayed into ungovernable crisis by the 1980s, bringing external and internal pressures for economic and political state reconfiguration. But the serious erosion of the stateness of many African polities by the 1990s limited the scope for effective state transformation and opened the door for a complex web of neoliberal states bathed in novel civil conflicts; there was also a renewed saliency of informal politics, as local societies adapted to diminished 'post-colonial' state presence and service provision.

This study of THE STATE IN AFRICA was prompted by the apparent post-1980 neglect by academics of Africanist and non-Africanist origin to engage with the state and social class, in the contextual framework of the political economy, as central elements of social analysis. The broad purpose of this book is thus to investigate to what extent critical works offer analyses of social change that embrace the relationship between the state, African society and globalization and to make these perspectives available to other academics and political practitioners.

As conceptualized by Marxist structuralists in the 1960s and 1970s, the state comprises political, economic and ideological constructs that incorporate conflicting class interests, existing as a site of contestation and the manifestation of class struggle. However, within the various state apparatuses and structures, tensions and fractures exist that create, in the midst of class struggle, opportunities for agency that defy the dictates of particular class interests, be they domestic or foreign. These interests are manifested in strategic alliances of a contradictory nature, sometimes inimical to the interests of the class concerned.

This analytical perspective of the state was marginalized by post-modernism and post-structuralism during the 1980s and 1990s, with the state redefined by contemporary globalization theorists according to a notion of the 'nation-state'. This constitutes one element of an overarching configuration of power relations and networks comprising a variety of transnational 'players', who assume political and economic roles to pursue their interests. This designation of 'players' detracts from the centrality of class as an analytical tool, preferring to dwell on notions of power and conflict without pursuing the analysis to its fundamental origin in a system of control and ownership of resources by dominant transnational corporations.

An abandonment of the state as the central conceptual tool has coincided with changes in the way the role performed by academics and other researchers as well as political practitioners is conceptualized, foregrounding symptoms of an ideological intrusion by neoliberal discourse concerning the role of academics, rather than locating the cause. Hence, the greater struggle for ideological hegemony that occurs within society, waged by the mass media, as a mouthpiece of implementation by agents of transnational financial capital, and propagating a neoliberal discourse, seems to have been overlooked.

Nonetheless, the critical perspectives threaded out in this book are intended to: continue to recognize the centrality of the state and social classes in conducting social analysis; challenge dominant ideology of capitalist globalization and propose social alternatives; identify the relationship between the chaotic and weak neoliberal state in Africa with 'mafia' characteristics and dominant sectors of the national and transnational bourgeoisie, concomitant with the intrusion of market ideology and its insertion into the state and society; and encourage further engagement with the state and social classes as analytical points of departure.

In summary, the seemingly chronic inability of most African countries to overcome poverty, debt, and bad governance has inspired a growing literature for readers that apply diagnostic and prescriptive approaches on a continental scale. Each author adopts a spin that allots responsibility for Africa's problems primarily to external or internal causes, then offers solutions that can range from the technocratic through the hard-nosed political ones into the realm of the spiritual and cultural.

For instance, the political crisis that culminated in radical land reform in Zimbabwe has brought about a new round of enquiry regarding the nature of state-society relations. There are several critics of left nationalism that have focused their analyses on this issue. However, as we will see, they have operated without a coherent theory of the state and civil society. The result is that the neocolonial situation is obscured, and the national and agrarian questions are replaced by a formalistic defence of civil society and procedural democracy.

Historical-materialist analyses of the state and civil society in Africa went into long decline with the onset of structural adjustment. During this time, liberal theories led the way, in support of 'getting the prices right', while a new breed of Weberian approaches trailed closely behind. In the 1990s, these streams of theorizing converged towards the new objective of 'getting the politics right'. It is clear that these approaches have weighed heavily on debates in Zimbabwe, infiltrating and emptying out historical-materialist approaches, to the ultimate effect of converging programmatically on the issue of 'régime change'.

These books blame Africa's economic woes mainly on weak and corrupt African leaders and prescribe a return to the foundations of pre-colonial culture. The only solution to economic failure is radical political reform to rid Africa of its vampire states in league with the transnational capitalist state and restore the accountability and democracy said to be characteristic of African political tradition. The agents of this transformation must be Africa's intellectuals, particularly those who are not ready to sell their services to immoral regimes.

Why Political Economy?

An economic analysis of the failure of the developmental state in Africa confined to the narrow framework of economic science can offer only very limited results. Economic science relies on a threadbare concept of 'agents of economic change,' limited to the abstract categories of the 'dynamic entrepreneur,' the 'consumer' and when needs must, the state, but in the latter instance in a cut-down version of the 'economic functions of the state' (economic legislation and regulation).

Political economy looks wider by taking into account the collective agents in the social classes and the state perceived less narrowly. But this is far from being enough. For the whole problematic of peripheral capitalism and the bifurcated state in Africa raises the theory of 'subjects of historical change' and challenges the simplifications drawn by extrapolation from European experience. It has been possible to identify a series of questions about the state, the nation and ethnicity, the character of the categories called social classes in classical Marxism, the manifestations of social movement and culture.

These issues may be summarized as follows:

(1) Is the state in Africa an historical subject in itself, overriding social classes? In the currently existing centres of global capitalism, the state does appear to be so. But here a concomitance can be observed between the active role played by the states in the inter-state -primarily European - world system (at the level of national economic policies as well as diplomacy) and the crystallization of that other social reality known as 'nation.' It looks very much as if this concomitance is missing in the Third World and in Africa particularly, to the advantage of so-called 'ethnic' forms otherwise defined and undoubtedly diverse. Is the result a series of particular handicaps interfering with the state's manifestation as an active historical subject? What is the role of African nationalist ideologies in this context?

(2) Transnationalization sets limitations on the state in Africa. These limitations are to such an extent that the state may nowadays seem powerless against the forces operating in a worldwide economic environment, in the developed centres and *a fortiori* in the vulnerable

African peripheries. What is the character of this contradiction and how are the 'adjustments' forced by transnationalization made? Are these 'adjustments' similar or different for the developed and the underdeveloped (African) societies?

(3) The social movement in modern history has appeared in two principal shapes: organization of so-called 'class struggle' (particularly of the working class-under trade union and partisan form--and *of* some peasantries), and organization of the so-called 'national struggle' (notably the national liberation movement in Africa and Asia). These two principal organizational forms of social movement seem to have run aground, whereas the wind seems to be in the sails of other social forms, whether trans-class (the feminist movement for example) or with an ethnic, religious, linguistic or provincial basis. To what extent does this evolution call into question the concepts of classical Marxism defining social classes as subjects of history?

(4) Study of the cultural aspect of societies has scarcely been brought into any theory of global social change. The implied hypothesis here was that economic change makes itself felt and thus causes a subsequent 'cultural adaptation'. It is a hypothesis that must be questioned.

We shall go on to consider some of these issues in order to highlight the specific character of the African situation. Our era is certainly characterized by an awakening--or reawakening—of collective social identifications other than those attributable to national and class affiliation. Regionalism, linguistic and cultural adherences, 'tribal' or 'ethnic' loyalties, devotion to a religious institution, attachment to local communities, are among the many forms of this awakening.

In the West and the East or in the Third World, the catalogue of these 'new' movements, or old ones with a new lease of life, is extensive. These movements are a significant aspect of the crisis of state, and more precisely of nation-state, whether the nation in question has greater or lesser reality or is merely imaginary. This crisis of state must be viewed as a manifestation of the increasing contradiction between the transnationalization of capital (and behind this of the economic life of all countries in the capitalist world) and the persistence of the Westphalia state system as the exclusive political pattern in the world. The questions that arise here are: if capital is becoming more international, why do the peoples not respond with more internationalism, or by asserting their class identity? Why, instead of class consciousness coming to the fore over the diversity of 'alternative' aspects of social reality, does this consciousness lose ground to 'racial', 'ethnic' or religious identity?

It is certainly not our aim to offer a reply to this question, but more modestly to contribute to clarifying the analysis through offering an ideological critique of two of the main social 'realities' at issue: nation (or the supposed nation) and ethnicity (or the supposed ethnicity). The state system in which we live is a system of genuine states or those allegedly being built, to such a degree that in some languages, such as English, the distinction between the two concepts is diminished by synonymous usage of the two expressions: the United Nations body is in fact an organization of states.

The 'ethnicity' concept which must in turn be open to question - is advanced by opponents of the nation-state. The first half of the question (the nation state and the ideology of the nation in crisis) revolves around what we believe to be the main issue, the crisis of the modern state as a consequence of the increasing worldwide expansion of capital. This general crisis affecting even states outside the capitalist system (the socialist countries) hits the states of the African periphery more severely than those of the centre.

There are two reasons for this. The lesser reason is that the 'national question,' in the sense of the nation we know as the creation of the central capitalist state, is a social reality of a particular time and space. It is the product of particular historical circumstances and this crystallization has given rise to an ideological frame, and more seriously to the export of this ideology on a world scale, including to the peripheries of the system where circumstances did not allow the nation to take shape. The greater reason is that these very (economic and political) circumstances prevent the crystallization of the autocentric (and potentially national) bourgeois state at the African periphery.

The current phase, typified by the offensive of transnational capital to 'recompradorize' the states of the periphery and dismantle the attempts at crystallization that were underway in the previous phase, makes all too apparent the character of these unfavourable historical 'conditions'. The threat to the Third World, especially African peoples, of unlimited fragmentation (on ethnic or pseudo-ethnic bases, or when the national factor is wanting or unsound) exactly in line with the aims of compradorization, can be countered only by a dual objective: organization into states as large and powerful as possible (while continuing to respect diversity) and 'delinking'.

The second half of the question (ethnicity: myth and reality) complements the analysis by considering forms of social organization in the absence of the bourgeois nation. These are pre-capitalist forms that beyond their variety sometimes establish a so-called 'ethnic' crystallization but more often prevent it. We also have peripheral, especially colonial, forms of capitalism that are ranged about the objective of dominant capital (unity through destruction) and are the origin of the ideological illusions of ethnicity. We go on to consider the cultural aspects of the problem and their effects on the social movement.

This book was improved by the incisive ideas of a large number of people that helped debug it and helped develop the analysis that proceeded from their works. In fact, it could not have come this far without insightful ideas from these eminent scholars. I shall name only a few so that the long list should not take an enormous toll on space. Particular thanks to: Giovanni Arrighi, Christopher Chase-Dunn, André Gunder Frank, James Petras, Samir Amin, Thomas D. Hall, Immanuel Wallenstein, William I. Robinson, Michel Chossudovsky, George Ayittey, Lena Wallenstein, Claude Ake, Steve Biko, Amilcar Cabral, Cheikh Anta Diop, Frantz Fanon, Kwame Nkrumah. I owe them a huge debt of gratitude. My thanks also to Professor Francis Nyamnjoh whose corrections and clarifications brought a kind of literacy to the manuscript I could not have achieved on my own.

I stand like a sailor stranded on islands sending messages for help, or putting my heartfelt wishes into bottles, hoping the messages will survive and carry on my memory and message to my loved ones under the grinding heels of The State In Africa, if I should perish. My message has been carried thanks to those who brought me to teach and research on this subject at the University of Minnesota: Evelyn Davidheiser (Director of the Institute for Global Studies) and Robert Jones (Senior Vice President in charge of Systems Administration). I owe them immeasurable gratitude for their unrelenting search for financial resources for my employment contract despite the difficult financial situation of the University of Minnesota.

To my family (Charity, Yiefon, Keleghai, Mbiylufeyin, Kefeyin and Berinyuy) I say give God praise. "Be careful for nothing; but in everything by prayer and supplication with thanksgiving let your requests be made known unto God. And the peace of God, which passeth all understanding, shall keep your hearts and minds through Christ Jesus.' '(Philippians 4: 6-7).

Despite this immense debt I am solely responsible for all the errors in this book.

Tatah Mentan

Section One

Introduction and Framing the Problem of the State in Africa

Preview

Globalization, that I define here as capitalist expansion, confronts humanity as a range of processes, as competing discourses and as a contested project. As such, it challenges researchers both to distinguish between its different forms and to comprehend the interplay between them. Whilst containing a universal dynamic, the impact of globalization has been uneven and responses to it varied, and this has exacerbated the complexity of its conceptual challenge.

Early enthusiasm for globalization as an overwhelmingly beneficial set of processes has yielded to an understanding that the phenomenon is equally associated with increasing social inequality within and between countries and changing forms of political and economic relations as well as instability and conflict. Just as it has generated a new international system of economic regulation and super-imposed institutional and policy reforms particularly on Africa, simultaneously it has given rise to new social movements and local responses, all of which have begun to affect the character of globalization itself.

The focus area is concerned with furthering our understanding of the social, economic and political consequences of globalization on THE STATE IN AFRICA. It is also interested in developing an understanding of the implications contemporary economic processes, new technologies, and social and political relations have for the future course of globalization. Further, it seeks to better theorize the global and thereby the contemporary world in order to bring the insights of this knowledge to bear on the old and new challenges that confront African people and societies, as well as the knowledge systems they are part of. While THE STATE IN AFRICA is the primary focus for research on the impact and shaping of globalization, local problems and possibilities cannot be understood in isolation. Comparative research will be supported.

Chapter One

Introduction

Overview

The state is a tool for preserving class rule. And, "THE EXECUTIVE of the modern state," wrote Karl Marx and Frederick Engels in the *Communist Manifesto*, "is but a committee for managing the common affairs of the whole bourgeoisie." The state in an era of globalization is the state of the dominant class—the big capitalists. In fact, as articulated by Ernest Mandel (1969), Engels argues that the state, ever since its origins, was always the state of the dominant class, and its main purpose was to secure the rule of that particular class: As the state arose from the need to keep class antagonisms in check, but also arose in the thick of the fight between the classes, it is normally the state of the most economically powerful, ruling class, which thereby becomes also the politically ruling class, and so acquires new means of holding down and exploiting the oppressed class.

The ancient state was, above all, the state of the slave-owners for holding down the slaves, just as the feudal state was the organ of the nobility for holding down the peasant serfs and bondsmen, and the modern representative state is the instrument for exploiting wage labour by capital. Unfortunately, this is not the view taught in school. There, students learn that constitutional government, with its elections, 'interest groups,' political parties and different branches of government are all there so that the opinions of the competing groups can be weighed and balanced. These views of the state, peddled in sociology and political science departments, assume society to be nothing more than a jumble of competing interest groups, the aggregate of which constitutes 'the people.'

This approach is typical of the so-called liberal 'social sciences,' where analysts rarely go beyond the surface appearance of things in society to discover the more fundamental relations governing human behaviour. There are also those who argue that human behaviour is rooted in our biological nature, and on those grounds come to a similar conclusion: since people are by nature nasty, violent and competitive toward each other (an assumption they make simply by skimming the surface of existing society), the state exists to regulate those tendencies, so that society does not pull apart into a war by each against all.

For Marxists, the state has roots in the material and historical development of human society. It arose as soon as society began to produce a surplus—usually based on the adoption of cultivation—but where the surplus was still insufficient to do more than release a tiny minority in society from hard daily toil. In other words, the state arose as a result of, and in conjunction with, the rise of class divisions. The state arose to help sustain and develop the conditions most suitable for pumping the surplus out of the producers, be they peasants, slaves or wage workers. That meant both an economic role (such as building roads), an ideological role (developing religion that justifies the divine rule of kings, for example) and a coercive role (maintaining an armed force standing above or outside society that can be called on to restore 'order' when necessary).

Prior, therefore, to the rise of class—when human beings lived in small bands and foraged for food—there was no need for a state. "The state, therefore, has not existed from all eternity," writes Engels. "There have been societies which have managed without it, which had no notion of the state or state power. At a definite stage of economic development, which necessarily involved the cleavage of society into classes, the state became a necessity because of this cleavage." The formality of voting, say, in the United States doesn't alter the fact that the state is the state of the economically dominant class. Most people have some vague idea that it is the rich who call the shots, and they are right. Engels once described the U.S. political system as consisting of "two great groups of political speculators, who alternately take possession of the state power and exploit it by the most corrupt means and for the most corrupt ends—and the nation is powerless against these two great cartels of politicians, who are ostensibly its servants, but in reality exploit and plunder it."

It's as though Engels wrote this passage yesterday. We should add, however, that the two great gangs of speculators are in every way tied in with the gangs of speculators known as investors, bankers and industrialists. It is they who hold the government's purse strings, and who the government answers to. It isn't simply that politicians get the bulk of their campaign funding and other forms of financial backing from wealthy capitalists; that the most powerful lobbyists are corporate lawyers; or that it requires millions of dollars even to consider running for high office; it is that the entire economic structure of society shapes the way the state functions.

Take, for example, the question of government debt. Doug Henwood (2003) noted that public debt is a powerful way of assuring that the state remains safely in capital's hands. The higher a government's debts, the more it must please its bankers. Should bankers grow displeased, they will refuse to roll over old debts, or to extend new financing on any but the most punishing terms, if at all. On top of all this, the whole structure of democracy is designed to reduce the democratic factor to a minimum.

The electoral process by which presidents are chosen is not direct: between voters and the final decision stands the Electoral College, a holdover from the days of slavery. Most government institutions, such as the various state agencies and the military, are not subject to any electoral control; massive bureaucracies, whose upper echelons are closely intertwined with the wealthy elite, run them.

The evidence that the state serves capitalism and, in particular, wealthy capitalists is revealed in many ways: how the judicial system punishes 'white collar' crime far less severely than crimes normally committed by poorer people; how wealthier individuals and corporations bear a lower tax burden than poor and working-class people; how social welfare is always dwarfed by corporate welfare and military spending. Ultimately, the state asserts itself as the defender of the capitalist system in that its various armed forces are used to prevent any challenge, whether by intervening against strikers, pummelling peaceful protesters, or imprisoning and murdering dissidents and left-wing organizers.

Other things being equal, socialists prefer a democratic republic over a monarchy or a military dictatorship, because a democratic republic affords better conditions (freedom of the press, of speech, and of organization, within certain limits, are permitted) to organize and fight the capitalist system. However, we understand that even the most democratic republic—with its bloated bureaucracy, police and military—is still an instrument for the maintenance of the exploitation of the many by the few. That is why Lenin (1970[what does this date refer to?]; 1917) wrote that the essence of bourgeois democracy is "to decide once every few years which member of the ruling class is to repress and oppress the people through parliament—this is the real essence of bourgeois parliamentarism."

Introduction

One of the main problems of studying the state is that of denialism. This statement is typical: "There can be no 'general state theory.' There can only be state structures formed by the contingencies of social developments."[1] This denialism claims the absence of any standard definition or theory that can serve as base for building a general hypothesis about the state. Anyone who is interested in studying the state therefore finds himself before a mass of theories and definitions that reflect in some part the author's own perspective, and in part the empirical reality of the case under investigation.

Another problem in studying the state is related to the history of state formation, or to when the state emerged. This problem is basically connected to the first one. The lack of consensus among scholars as regards what the state is has led to the emergence of different histories of state formation. Some authors claim that the state had already emerged several thousand years ago, while others claim that the state in its current form emerged in the 19th century with the full blooming of capitalism at the expense of the land-based feudal system.

These authors assert that the full bloom of capitalism, marked by the rapid development of trade and communications and emergence of a market economy, gave rise to new social forces such as the bourgeoisie, merchants, bankers, and civil servants. These socio-economic developments manifested themselves politically and led to increasing demands for extending political, civil, and social rights, phenomena which made it necessary to re-conceptualize the relationship between society and political authority.[2]

Accordingly, a new form of politics emerged. The nation-state as a relatively autonomous, differentiated, centralized, and separate association came into existence for the first time. Such a state gradually expanded the ranks of citizenship to include all the excluded social groups, and made it possible for an individual to stand in direct relationship with the sovereign political authority, a fact which contrasted with the feudal system, where such direct relationship was limited only to specific social groups (groups of nobles and clergy, for example).[3]

The impact of the 19th century's socio-economic developments was not limited to these realms, but also extended to include other realms of thought, particularly political thought. That century's socio-economic developments had shifted the political focus from the individual (for example, the political thought of Hobbes, Locke, and Rousseau) to the structure of society. This shift in political thought expressed itself in the political ideas of Karl Marx (1818-1883), Friedrich Engels (1820-1895), Emile Durkheim (1858-1917), Max Weber (1864-1920), and others.

These thinkers had basically devoted themselves to the study of the new socio-economic transformations in Europe, and their political manifestations, in particular the newly emerging political identity (the capitalist state) and its relationship to society. It is not the aim here to review the ideas of these thinkers on the state, as that goes beyond the scope of this book, but it is worth mentioning Karl Marx's and Max Weber's contributions to theories of the state, as their ideas formed the departure point for most of the 20th century's theories of the state.

Changing Notions of the State in General

The state has recently been rediscovered as an object of enquiry by a broad range of scholars as well as by development practitioners. Social anthropologists have contributed with studies of what the state looks like to those seeing it from a variety of local vantage points (Nugent 1994; Blom-Hansen and Stepputat 2001). These studies, focusing on the micro-politics of everyday state-making, examine the mythologies, paradoxes, and inconsistencies of the state. They show that the authority of the state is constantly challenged from the local as well as the global and that growing demands to confer rights and recognition to ever more citizens, organizations, and institutions also undermine the idea of the state as a source of social order and an embodiment of popular sovereignty (Trouillot 2001, Shore 2001). Many of these studies are inspired by Abrams' (1988) important unpacking of the state theoretically, rejecting the dominant view of the state as a distinct social unit separated from and 'located' over and above the social, which has been a common way to conceptualise the state both by Marxists and political sociologists. The following quotation summarises his concept of the state:

> The state is a state-system in Miliband's sense; a palpable nexus of practice and institutional structure centred in government and more and less extensive, unified and dominant in any given society. And its sources, structure and variation can be examined in a fairly straight-forward way. There is, too, a state-idea, projected, purveyed and variously believed in different societies at different times. And its modes, its effects and variations are also susceptible to research.' (Miliband, R. (1969). The State in Capitalist Society.New York: Basic Books, *ibid.*p.71).

Abrams emphasises the ambiguity of the state. This idea of the ambiguity is central in the perspective developed by Blom Hansen and Stepputat in their book with the suggestive title of *States of Imagination* (2001). They argue for a broad perspective embracing the ambiguities of the state as both illusory as well as a set of concrete institutions, as both distant and impersonal ideas as well as localized and personified institutions, as both violent and benevolent and productive. Modern forms of state are in a continuous process of construction, they argue, and this construction takes place through invocation of a bundle of widespread and globalised registers of governance and authority (p.5). To understand the modern state we need to look behind the facade of its formal institutions (although these should not be ignored either) and explore the more diffuse ways that 'power' and 'governance' work – including the everyday rules and normalising technologies that govern conduct and render populations governable in the first place (Shore 2001:30).

The study of the migration trajectory referred to above, may help in understanding the multifaceted character of state-society relations. What does it mean for people to be citizens of a state that, more or less explicitly, suspects them of opposing its authority? And what happens when they learn that they have rights, as human beings, as refugees and indigenous people? To answer these questions, consideration must be given to the subtle, non-violent techniques of social domination, focusing on the way power works through everyday state and non-state agency; how it arises from routinized practices of government operating at the level of the individual and local community. I will also explore in what conditions institutional authority is accommodated, and when, why and how it is opposed.

Symptomatic of individual's encounters with state and other powerful institutions is the ascription to people of labels which have implications for various levels of social interaction. The most conspicuous labels carry negative meanings, such as 'illegal migrants,' 'subversive' or 'terrorists,' but seemingly positive or neutral labels such as 'returnee' or 'repatriated' may be equally forceful in this process. Moreover, people also label themselves, and by so doing invest labels with their own meanings. When power is mediated and contested by particular social groups, domination involves both control and conviviality; it is about the wielding and yielding of power. In this regard I am particularly interested in how people draw upon their experiences of migration, transnational communication and networks to generate alternative forms of organisation which attempt to shape policies and change the relations between state and society.

The Marxist Perspective Versus the Weberian One

More than a quarter century after the Miliband-Poulantzas debate renewed interest in Marxist political theory, there is still no agreement on what constitutes a Marxist theory of the state. The state theory debate has produced a range of competing theories including instrumentalism (Miliband), structuralism (Poulantzas), derivationism (Altvater), systems analysis (Offe), and organizational realism (Skocpol). Each of these theories is grounded in a conception of the Marxist tradition, but each theory diverges in its definition of what counts as Marx's political writings. Efforts to arbitrate between competing theories of the state by returning to the Marxian classics are futile; firstly because the classical texts are incomplete,, and secondly because they are ambiguous and often self-contradictory. Hence, as long as Marx's writings remain a key referent for the development of state theory, it will be necessary to recognize that a range of positions is defensible from within the intellectual canon and that the canon itself provides no basis for arbitrating among the competing theories.

However, a brief survey of Marxist and Weberian political thought will show clearly how such thought is developmental, and conceives history in a dynamic way. This dynamic vision of history had, in fact, shaped both Marx's and Weber's notion of the state. The state for both Marx and Weber is the apparatus of government, administration, and an instrument of coercion, and is in a continuous developmental process.

Marx considered the society's mode of production, more specifically the production relations, as the basic foundation on which the political and other institutions arise.[4] Accordingly, the state as a political institution is, for him, a manifestation of the dominant mode of production within the society, and varies according to variation in this mode of production. The state in this sense serves the interest of the economically dominant class, which manages to control the civil bureaucracy as well as the military and police apparatus. Therefore, the state in pursuing its policy becomes fully guided (not autonomous) by the interests of this class. State policy is the political expression of such interest.

On the other hand, Weber believes that the state has its own interest totally separate from the interest of any social group within the society. The state, according to him, emerges as part of a general trend toward rationalizing the society according to impersonal, universal, and general rules. In this sense the state is understood as a rationalized bureaucratic organization working according to general, universal, and impersonal rules that are devoted to specific ends established by the state itself. These rules make the state immune from the influence of society. In implementing these rules the state tends to monopolize the means of coercion within well-defined territories.[5] The state according to this concept is fully autonomous in pursuing its own policy and is not subject to the influence of any social force/class within the society, as in the case of the Marxist concept.

Clearly, the two notions converge on what the state is, but they separate when it comes to the relationship between state and society. While the Marxist notion reduces the state to a specific social force/class within the society, and identifies coercive force as the essence of the state for protecting the interest of the said social force/class, the Weberian one regards the state as neutral. It emerges within the context of a general sociological process rationalizing society according to legal rules and principles. Such rules and principles constitute the essence of the state, and coercive force comes as a necessity to preserve these means of protecting society's welfare.

20th Century State Theories

Most of the 20th century's theories of the state are built on either Marx's or Weber's notion of the state. Antonio Gramsci (1891-1937), drawing on Marx, conceived the state as an instrument in the hands of the dominant class and for the serving of it, but he expanded the means of social control to include ideological means alongside the coercive ones. Accordingly, Gramsci introduced us to his concept of 'Hegemony', by which he meant "A mode of social control through which one group exerts its dominance over others by means of ideology."[6]

For Gramsci, coercion secures state domination over society, but it does not secure state hegemony. To achieve hegemony over society, coercion should be complemented by ideological means of domination. Only this would enable the state to gain the cultural and political support of the subordinated groups. Consequently, Gramsci provided the state as, "the entire complex of practical and theoretical activities with which the ruling class not only maintains its dominance but manages to win the consent of those over whom it rules." Thus, state is "political society plus civil society" or in other words, "hegemony protected by the armour of coercion."[7] Gramsci did not discuss how such a capitalist state comes into being. He was more interested in analysing the relationship between state and society, than in explaining the process by which this state comes into being.

Paul M. Sweezy, too, in his *Modern Capitalism and Other Essays* argued that the state is an instrument in the hands of the economically dominant class. In this regard he wrote:

> 'The continued existence of monopoly capitalism depends on the existence or creation of sufficiently strong counteracting forces to permit the system to operate at a politically tolerable level of production and employment...; this therefore becomes increasingly the responsibility of the state, which, as noted above, has its primary task in assuring the smooth functioning of the accumulation process."[8] (Paul Sweezy, "Marxian Value Theory and Crisis," Monthly Review, July-August 1979; reprinted in Ian Steedman, et. al., The Value Controversy (London: Verso, 1981).

Like Gramsci, Sweezy was not interested in studying the process through which the capitalist state emerges. His interest was in the international capitalist system, and in how such a system had developed during the 20th century.

Charles Tilly, in his distinguished essay entitled *Reflections on the History of European State Making,*[9] focused on the process through which the state comes into being. According to him, the main engine of building the state is tax extraction for military purposes. Military purposes necessitated the process of tax extraction, which in turn necessitated the process of establishing bureaucratic staff to extract tax, and to manage and coordinate the flow of revenue to the state. Army establishments are crucial in this context. They produce the means to support government control over the population, to promote territorial consolidation, centralization, differentiation of the governmental apparatus from other organizations, and monopolization of the means of coercive force. Accordingly, Tilly, based on Weber, introduced the state as:

> 'an organization which controls the population occupying defined territory is a state in so far as (1) it is differentiated from other organizations operating in the same territory; (2) it is autonomous; (3) it is centralized; and (4) its divisions are formally coordinated with one another.'[10]

Theda Skocpol in her *Theory of Revolution* agreed with Tilly on tax extraction as the main motor of state building, and strongly emphasized, in this regard, the administrative and coercive organization as the most important aspects of any state. The state, she declared, is:

> 'A set of administrative, policing, and military organizations headed, and more or less well coordinated by, an executive authority. Any state first and fundamentally extracts resources from society and deploys these to create and support coercive and administrative organizations.'[11]

Michael Mann accepted the coercive force as an aspect of the state, but he refused to consider it, as was the case with Skocpol, as the basis of the state. Instead, he highly emphasized the monopoly of making binding rules, and the centralized functional institutions, as the most important foundations of any state. The state, he wrote, is:

> A *differentiated* set of institutions and personnel embodying;
> *Centrality* in the sense that political forces radiate outwards from a centre to cover;
> A *territorially* demarcated area, over which it exercises;
> A monopoly of *authoritative, binding rule-making*, backed up by a monopoly of the means of physical violence.[12]

Joel S. Migdal emphasized also these binding rules as the base of any state. In this regard, he cited the state as an organization that had as its major function "...To make and implement the binding rules for all the people as well as the parameters of rule making for other social organizations in a given territory, using force if necessary to have its way."[13]

Clearly, the underlying assumption of the Weberian perspective is that the state is differentiated, distinctive, separate from society, and strong enough to lead it. There is no space within this perspective for society to influence state. Society is always seen as a dependent variable while state is an independent one. In other words, the state is the entity that is responsible for solving the crucial questions concerning society, and in creating historical changes.

Towards an 'Advanced' Definition of the State

The above brief survey of state theories shows the basic conditions of any modern state. Evidently, any organization which controls a given population in a well-defined territory, and has the ability to issue binding rules for its population and to monopolize the levers of coercion, is called a state. Given those basic features of a state, scholars might vary in their perception of the relationship between state and society. The Marxist perspective is extremely reductive in the sense that it conceives the nature of the state-society relationship to be rooted in the economic structure. At the same time, the Weberian perspective is extremely static in the sense that it conceives the state to be an undifferentiated entity with an homogenous interest.

Both Strath and Rolf Torstendahl in their *State Theory and State Development*[14] rejected the Marxist and Weberian perspectives on the state-society relationship, and developed a new perspective on that relationship. In doing so, they traced how the state had developed since 1800, from the early capitalist state until it reached its current form of the modern welfare state. After explaining how the state had developed to its current form, they arrived at a more holistic, reciprocal, and dynamic vision of the state-society relationship.

According to them, the form of any state is not the outcome of the interest of a specific social force/class, or the state agents' interest. The state cannot be reduced to a specific social force/class, nor yet can it be reduced to the interest of state agents. Rather, the state's form is the outcome of the reciprocal influences of social forces/classes and state agents. In other words, the state is influenced by the interests of different social forces/classes within the society, but it is not a mirror of such interests, since it reflects also the interest of state agents. In this sense the state is autonomous but, at the same time, influenced by the society.

Charles Bright and Susan Harding highlighted also the influence of social forces on the state, as they consider state building to be a question of state agents' initiatives, as well as of social forces reacting to such initiatives. But, they added the competition between the politicians and bureaucratic agents, who can develop and defend their own interest in the face of the politicians, as another factor that influences the form of a state. The state, according to them, is:

> 'A distinct realm of structural political relations that is defined by contentions along its boundaries and among politicians and bureaucrats who, in competing for office and influence, rework social and economic conflict into political terms. These contentions both define the state vis-à-vis other social and economic institutions and continually re-make the state.'[15]

Although Charles Bright & Susan Harding highlighted the state as a differentiated organization that formed two competitive parts, the bureaucracy and the politicians, they remained unable to explain how these two parts might be influenced in different degrees by different social groups or forces, an issue which is heavily emphasized by Joel S. Migdal in his *State in Society: an approach to struggle for domination.*[16]

Migdal went a step further and regarded the state as an organization formed of not just two parts, but of many different parts with different interests. These parts, according to him, are in a continuous competitive engagement with other social forces. Such engagement includes the top policy makers, legislators, law enforcement personnel (executive bodies), the state's policy implementation structure (bureaucracy system), and so on. The new contribution of Migdal is his assertion that through such engagement the different parts of the state, according to the different interests they encompass, react and respond differently to the pressures they are exposed to.

The overall reactions of different parts of the state and different social forces resulting from such competitive engagement decide the pattern of domination in the society. It decides the extent to which the state can assume a full coherent domination and complete control over society, and thus act in a coherent fashion (integrated domination or centralization), or to which neither the state nor any other social forces have full domination in the country (non-integrated or dispersed domination or decentralization).

Generally speaking, the state is seen as an organization that monopolizes coercion as a means to support its major function of issuing binding rules for a given population occupying a given territory.

For Charles Bright and Susan Harding (1984) and Bo Strath and Rolf Torstendahl (1992) the state must not be seen in a static way. Rather, the state is placed in a social context that influences and is influenced by it, and therefore affects the state's form. Also the state must be placed within its international environment, which also influences its form. For Migdal (1994), moreover, the state must be seen not in a coherent, but in an heterogeneous fashion, in which its different agencies exhibit different interests and continuously interact with other social forces in the society.

Accordingly, and drawing on the above-mentioned scholars' discussion, it's possible to perceive the state as an organization that,

- Monopolizes coercive force and has extractive capacity (tax collection).
- Constitutes the ultimate source of the legally binding rules for the population.
- Works in a well-defined territory.
- Controls the population that occupies this territory.
- Forms agencies with different interests.
- Locates within a social context which it influences and by which it is influenced.
- Engages in international activities.

Conceiving of the state according to the above-mentioned paradigm sheds light on issues that lie at the heart of any state itself. Issues such as state differentiation, state agency coordination, autonomy, and centralization seem to be, as Tilly emphasized, a major criterion by which one can judge the degree of statehood in any country.[17]

The process of statehood necessitates the establishment of well-coordinated agencies (legislative, executive, judicial agencies) that are differentiated from other economic or social organizations within the society, a task that is heavily connected with state autonomy. State autonomy seems to be an extremely vague concept. For example, Charles Bright and Susan Harding stressed that state autonomy lay in its ability to self-regulate, in the sense that it was governed by its own law, and not influenced by other internal or external forces.[18]

Joel Migdal sheds light on the actions of state officials, considering the state to be autonomous when state officials have the capacity to act upon their own preferences.[19]

Bo Strath and Rolf Torstendahl refused to consider state autonomy as an empirically-oriented concept, rather asserting that state autonomy is an 'amorphous' concept.[20] Theda Skocpol rejected such an idea, asserting that the state can be, to some extent, autonomous, and this can be measured by looking at the administrative and military institutions of the state. These institutions, she emphasized, are the basis of state power (as the resources in the society are extracted for them), and have the potential of being autonomous (in their relationship to the social forces, and in their relationship to other states). To what extent they are autonomous can be explained .'..in terms specific to particular types of socio-political systems and to particular sets of historical international circumstances.'[21]

The concept of state centralization seems to be strongly related to the concept of state autonomy. State centralization, in the sense of its ability to get its people to obey its rules and to absorb and monopolize them toward its legal and moral framework, seems to be the normative foundation of state power, or what Michael Mann called the 'infrastructural power.'[22] According to Mann the source of the state's real power is to be found not in its ability to monopolize the sources of coercive force, but in its ability to penetrate the society and to implement its authoritative legal rules throughout the whole society, in a way that secures the dominance of such rules over any other rules within the society. The state's authoritative legal rules must triumph over any ethnic, clan, familial, or any other social-force-based rules (primacy).

References

1. Bo Strath & Rolf Torstendahl (1992) ' State Theory and State Development: States as Network Structures in Changes in European Modern History,' in Rolf Torstendahl (ed.). *State Theory and State History*. London, Newbury Park, & New Delhi: Sage Publications, p.12.
2. *Ibid.* See also Tilly, Charles (1975) ' Reflections on the History of European State Making. In Charles Tilly (ed.) *The Formation of National States in Western Europe*. Princeton & London: Princeton University Press. See also Charles Bright & Susan Harding (eds.) *Statemaking and Social Movements: Essays in History and Theory*. US: The University of Michigan Press (1985).
3. Reinhard Bendix(2002) *Nation-Building & Citizenship: Studies of Our Changing Social Order*. New Brunswick/US & London: Transaction Publishers, 2nd edition, pp. 39-96.
4. Theda Skocpol (1979) *States & Social Revolutions: A comparative Analysis of France, Russia & China*. Cambridge: Cambridge University Press, pp. 24-28.
5. Max Weber(1947) *The Theory of Social and Economic Organization*. Talcott Parsons (eds.) New York: Oxford University Press, pp.8-86.
6. James Martin (1998) *Gramsci's Political Analysis: A Critical Introduction*. Basingstoke: Macmillan Press, p. 66.
7. Quoted in Roger Simon (1982)*Gramsci's Political Thought*. London: Lawrence & Wishart, p. 71.
8. Sweezy, Paul M (1972) *Modern Capitalism and Other Essays*. New York & London: Monthly Review Press, pp. 8-9, 34.
9. Tilly *op.cit.*

10. *Ibid.*, p. 70.
11. Skocpol *op.cit.* p. 29.
12. Michael Mann (1988) *States, War and Capitalism: Studies in Political Sociology.* Oxford UK & Cambridge USA: Blackwell Publishers, p. 4.
13. Joel S. Migdal (1988) *Strong Societies and Weak States: State-Society Relations and State Capabilities in the Third World.* Princeton & New Jersey: Princeton University Press p. 19.
14. Strath & Torstendahl *op.cit.* pp. 12-37.
15. Bright & Harding *op.cit.* p. 4
16. Joel Migdal (1994) 'The State in Society: an approach to Struggle for Domination.' In Joel Migdal & others (eds.) *State Power and Social Forces: Domination and Transformation in the Third World.* Cambridge: Cambridge University Press pp. 8-34. See also Migdal *op.cit.*. pp. 10-41.
17. Tilly *op.cit.* pp.. 34-35.
18. Bright & Harding *op.cit.* p.. 4.
19. Migdal *Strong Societies, op.cit.* pp.. 18-19.
20. Strath & Torstendahl *op.cit.* p.. 15.
21. Skocpol *op.cit.* p. 30.
22. Mann *op.cit.* pp. 5-30.

Chapter Two

Framing the Problem of the State in Africa

Overview

THE STATE IN AFRICA is today the most demonized social institution, vilified for its weaknesses, its over-extension, its interference with the smooth functioning of the markets, its repressive character, its dependence on foreign powers, its ubiquity, its absence, etc. The state—once the cornerstone of development—is now the millstone around otherwise efficient markets. It is now the 'rentier state,' the 'overextended state,' the 'parasitical state,' the 'predatory state,' the 'lame leviathan,' 'the patrimonial state' the 'prebendal state,' the 'crony state,' the 'kleptocratic state,' the 'inverted state,' (Mbaku and Ihonvbere 1998; Mkandawire 1998).

Theories of international relations, assumed to be universally applicable, have failed to explain the creation and sustenance of the African state. Why? The state in Africa is an external creation and external determination by foreign capital. And the interaction of power and space of the alien state is dramatically different from African cultures and expectations.

Why The State In Africa?

What 'nation state' in Africa is one talking about? The present 'nation-state' structures in Africa are the creations of the imperialist powers. It is essential to clarify the meaning of 'nation-state' as used in our study of THE STATE IN AFRICA before we proceed. The hyphenated term 'nation-state' reflects a linking of two historically related but separable social phenomena. The term 'nation' refers to an interconnected population that has a sense of their common unity. A nation exists both objectively in its compatriots' interdependence and subjectively in the consciousness they share. The term 'state,' on the other hand, refers to the political institutions that rule over the population of a certain territory or country where the members of one (or more) nation might live. The people are the nation; the political institutions are the state.

Historically, the rise of bourgeois society saw the linking of nation and state to the extent that in many minds the nation-state came to be thought of as a single (although complex) entity. To be a Nigerian, for example, was thought of as being at the same time a citizen of a state and a member of a people. The resulting identification with such a nation-state as a single entity became an important source of identity. Who one *was* came in no small measure from the people with whom one shared a culture and a history. And in so far as the nation became linked to a state, subjection to its rule also became a part of one's identity. Thus, one's identity as a Nigerian meant at one and the same time to be *in* a nation and *under* a state. Thus did the nation-state become an essential element in modern personal identities?

Nevertheless, a nation has its own interests and a state also has its own, often different, interests. It was the convergence of these two sets of interests that lent credibility to their conflation into a single entity called the nation-state. What I want to suggest is that in the present historical stage of capitalism known as globalization, the interests of nations and those of states are diverging and thus the two parts of this hyphenated term are becoming detached. Not only are they moving in different directions, but also globalized states are often pitted *against* the nations over which they rule. The evidence is abundant in the possible implications of this antagonism for the intractable African social struggles of this era. This explanatory note reveals clearly why THE STATE IN AFRICA cannot be the vehicle for the liberation of the African masses from its domination. But on this, as on any other question, basic class issues are raised. While the post-colonial states have been the vehicle for the suppression of the masses and their subordination to imperialist finance capital, these structures have been eagerly grasped by the African bourgeoisie as the means for its own survival and advancement.

Within Fourth World theory, a State represents a centralized political system with a recognised civilian and military bureaucracy established to enforce one set of institutions, laws and sometimes language and religion within its boundaries (see Hyndman 1994; Nietschmann 1987). The modern state in Africa grew from 'European kingdoms, overseas colonialism, and the division of large colonial empires into smaller and smaller neo-colonial pieces' (Nietschmann 1994:227). It was not an African creation, thus not an African state. The State, as a political entity, is a legal creation which comes into being on a specific date (see Nietschmann, 1994), is comprised of a 'set of internationally recognised boundaries that comprise greater than one (1) nation' (Griggs 1994 b:260; see also Nietschmann 1994; Spicer 1992), and is acknowledged by other States.

It is very easily forgotten that the state of the underdeveloped world today is the result of a history of colonial atrocities perpetrated by Europeans. Previous invasions of non-Western lands, say in Africa, by European imperialists allowed them to conquer and gradually institutionalize the global dominance of their Westphalia nation-state system, brutally wiping out existing African Kingdoms and Empires as viable forms of governance.

Overview Of Pre-colonial African Systems Of Governance

Some African societies were large empires (Cheikh Anta Diop 1987) governed by kings who had near absolute power (Godelier 1970). The empires of ancient Egypt in North Africa, of Nubia and Axum in North East Africa, of Ghana, Mali and Songhai in West Africa, and Zimbabwe in Southern Africa are examples of large kingdoms or empires that developed a complex system of government. These political systems of African kingdoms shared similarities with European kingdoms. The king, such as Mansa Musa of Mali and Sonni Ali of Songhay, had near absolute power and there was no ***separation of powers.***

The king and his councillors and advisors carried out executive, legislative, and judicial functions. The king's power was often based on his ability to collect revenue and tribute, usually through the control of trade, and to control and use an army to defend his ***sovereignty***. Moreover, there were no independent judicial systems. Officials appointed by the king were responsible for criminal justice. In short, the king was chief executive, chief law-maker, and chief judge. Many factors explain the development of strong kingdoms in Africa:

1. Expansion of agricultural production.
2. Development of new metal technology.
3. Expansion of trade.

Just as in Europe, Asia, and the Americas, large and powerful kingdoms in Africa did not last forever. At times, a powerful kingdom was conquered and overthrown by a new group of rulers who established a new kingdom, as was the case when the Kingdom of Mali replaced the Kingdom of Ghana. In other situations, a kingdom may have become less powerful due to a combination of factors such as poor leadership or the loss of an important source of power. For instance, one of the reasons why the Kingdom of Songhai declined in strength had to do with the lessening of the importance of the trans-Saharan trade.

As was true in Europe, Asia, and the Americas, not all African peoples lived in large kingdoms. There were a variety of social and political systems in Africa. In addition to the large kingdoms, there were smaller centralized political units. These geographically smaller states shared much in common with the larger African kingdoms. The primary difference was size. The system and practice of governance that centralized power in the hands of a king and a supporting *caste* of political advisors and elites in these smaller kingdoms was similar to that of larger kingdoms. Moreover, control of trade and a strong military were also important factors in the development and maintenance of these smaller states. Oyo, Ife, Illorin, and Ibadan are examples of West African city-states. Sofala, Kilwa, Mombasa, and Lamu are examples.

African economies featured a case study of the Yoruba (Oyo, Ife, Illorin, Ibadan). The economic specialization was evidenced through the cotton and textile industries. Economic specialization and political centralization assisted each other. Economic specialization increased wealth and revenues that were used to support ruling elites and standing armies. In turn, the kings and ruling elites, along with the military under their control, provided stability and protection necessary for economic growth and productivity. There were many African societies which have been classified as stateless or de-centralized. These terms are used to describe societies that did not have well-defined and complex or centralized systems of government, such as political systems of Ghana, Oyo or Zimbabwe. Although they cannot be certain, as many as a third of the people of Africa on the eve of colonial rule lived in ***stateless*** or ***decentralized*** *societies.* There are a couple of reasons why the decentralized societies in Africa have not been well studied by historians.

As the brief case study on the Igbo speaking peoples will show, decentralized and stateless societies can develop economically, culturally, and socially, even if they don't have a centralized system of government. Decentralized or stateless political societies in Africa were often made up of a group of neighbouring towns or villages that had no political connection with a larger kingdom or nation. Most stateless and decentralized societies did not have a system of chiefs. However, some of these societies had chiefs. In these societies the position of chief was weak and was often not ***hereditary***. Do you remember what this term means? Chiefs were usually selected by a group of elders. In such a system, chiefs were selected not based on their family connections, but on their reputation as a person who contributed to the welfare of the group.

Some decentralized societies did not have chiefs. They were governed by a council of elders that was composed of many of the elderly people in the community. In most decentralized societies in Africa, the elders held social, economic and political power. Elders were so important that some historians have defined decentralized societies as ***democracies of age***. There is a set of stereotypes that many use when thinking of stateless or decentralized societies. Stateless societies are thought to be small in terms of population and geographic area. They are often thought of as being nomadic or semi-nomadic, or as comprising small bands of hunters and gatherers. These hunter and gatherer societies were politically decentralized. Most decentralized societies are agriculturally-based and are not nomadic. Moreover, many of these societies are as complex as their more centralized neighbours.

Another, and perhaps more representative, example of decentralized society in Africa are the Igbo speaking peoples. The Igbo speaking peoples live in the south eastern part of contemporary Nigeria. The Igbo are neighbours of the highly politically centralized Yoruba, but their political system is much different. Instead of centralized kingdoms headed by powerful kings, chiefs, and their advisors, the Igbo had no centralized system of governance. Rather they lived in ***politically autonomous villages***. That is, each village was politically separate and was not politically connected to neighbouring villages. Within the villages there was not a system of hereditary chiefs. Village decisions were made by a ***headman*** and a council of elders that selected the headman.

The absence of a centralized system of government did not mean that there was no system or institutions of governance among the Igbo speaking peoples. In addition to a village based council of elders, there were religious organizations, structures of kinship ties—***lineage groups***, and ***secret societies,*** that provided regulations that governed people's lives. These organizations guaranteed that no one group or institution gained too much power—a system of ***checks and balances.*** Colonialism changed all this.

Colonial Connection

The changes engendered by European colonialism explain why the history of Africans is integrally connected with the history of colonialism. European colonialism represents the imposition of the power of one State or nation over the territories of another in order to gain economic and/or political advantage (Brough, 1989). Thus, colonialism is about the spatial expansion of one people and the corresponding constriction of another; colonialism is about the discovery and exploitation of 'frontiers'. By calling indigenous territories, 'frontiers', colonialists debased any prior political attachments to that territory and denied the existence of the original owners of those territories. Frontiers were seen as abstract spaces devoid of human connections; they were wildernesses which required 'taming'. Indigenous nations and their territories become conceived in economic terms, as 'untapped natural resources' (Tauli-Corpuz 1993:7) waiting for the taking. Indigenous nations' natural resources became 'national and transnational resources' (Hyndman 1988:281).

Colonialism also established the foundations for all future relations between colonizers and colonized. The fact that indigenous nations continue to be marginalized (in a comparative sense) is testament to this ongoing problem. Further, colonialism is a globalizing process through time and space, and, as such, indigenous nations have not only been dispossessed of their lands but also of their histories (see Brough 1989).

The history of indigenous nations was often portrayed as 'peripheral', 'backward', and 'doomed to extinction', 'by the dogma of colonialist notions of the 'progress' of 'civilisation'' (Tauli-Corpuz 1993:10; see also Wilmer 1993). Indigenous nations are not only resisting the spatial relationship, the 'ever expanding space' (Brough 1989:24) that advances their lands as underdeveloped frontiers, they are resisting an augmented sense of time: [close this gap]...the expansive, aggressive, and oppressive societies, which we collectively and inaccurately call the West, needed Space to occupy. More profoundly and problematically, they required Time to accommodate the schemes of a one-way history: progress, development, modernity (and their negative mirror images: stagnation, underdevelopment, tradition) (Fabian 1983:144). Thus time and space became 'ideologically construed instruments of power' (Fabian 1983:144; see also Brough 1989). These trends continue today to marginalize indigenous nations in both colonial and neo-colonial situations, resulting in clashes between ideas and philosophies.

The wars of national liberation were inevitable and indispensable for African societies to regain their humanity and historical agency so cruelly seized by European colonialism. Contrary to conventional opinion, the Western powers have managed to maintain this global dominance and influence on the affairs of non-Western nations despite a process of apparent decolonization, thereby continuing to exploit their wealth and resources to this day. The prime legacy of colonialism was the integration of colonies into the international capitalist economy. The main force keeping economies in the global system and sustaining imperialism is the market itself mediated by the state.

The interest in state theory that swept academic circles following the Miliband–Poulantzas debate waned considerably in the late 1980s and 1990s so that much of the previous decades have been notable for the impoverishment of state theory. Indeed, during this time, there was a never-ending litany of books and articles on the crisis of the nation-state, the eclipse of the state, the retreat of the state, and even the end of the nation-state. The central theme in these eulogies was that nation-states had lost control of their national economies, currencies, territorial boundaries, and even their cultures and languages and that macroscopic forms of power were shifting from the nation-state to the global market, transnational corporations, and globalized channels of communication. However, this article re-examines the relationship between globalization theory and state theory to argue that nation-states are the principal agents of globalization as well as the guarantors of the political and material conditions necessary for global capital accumulation.

A controversial debate in the field of political science persists over how globalization affects the authority of the state in Africa. The prevailing wisdom is that globalization, measured by increased cross-border flows and the concentration of power in international financial institutions, such as the International Monetary Fund and the World Bank, is breaking down states in Africa as structural adjustment programmes undercut patronage networks and unregulated global economic avenues permit violent non-state actors to accrue weapons and financing. As the state is weakened, rebel groups are empowered, which escalates and provokes state failure and, perhaps, prolonged civil wars and economic collapse. This concrete reality explains why African warfare, most often intra-state in nature and symptomatic of political collapse, is intermingled in civilian life, involves child soldiers, militias and warlords, and is sustained over long periods by the illegal trade of mineral resources, drugs and arms.

Today, many Western analysts have come to associate Africa with egregious examples of failed states (Rotberg 2002). When extrapolated and explained, the term depicts a polity where political, economic and social institutions have crumbled, as a result of longstanding and protracted crises like intra-state conflict, war, maladministration, corruption, mismanagement, economic distress, deepening poverty, violence, crime, social chaos, anarchy, and so on.

In the 1960s, 1970s and 1980s, most of Africa was battling with the destabilizing and debilitating forces of colonialism, neo-colonialism (imperialism), apartheid, the Cold War and political authoritarianism. With the disappearance of these centrifugal forces, except neo-colonialism and political authoritarianism, several African countries started to recover their souls and move towards normality until the introduction of gunboat democracy--democracy given through the mouth of the cannon or through threats of aid cuts.

For example, since the Cold War-inspired brutal armed conflicts in Southern Africa (Mozambique and Angola) and the Horn of Africa (between Ethiopia and Somalia) ceased, the post-apartheid South Africa has made sufficient progress towards becoming the economic and techno-industrial powerhouse of sub-Saharan Africa. In some states such as Ghana, Mali, Nigeria, Niger, Benin Republic, Togo, Cote d'Ivoire, Chad, Guinea, Equatorial Guinea, Malawi, Zambia, Zimbabwe, Kenya, Cameroun, Gabon and others, the process of democratization has been captured under the guise of competitive elections (sometimes bitter and divisive), by the authoritarian groups already in control of power (Clark 2005; Mentan 2009).

Despite the hopes and dreams brought by the end of the Cold War and apartheid in Africa, the new era could well be described as tumultuous times on the continent. Capturing this development that seems like taking one step forward and two steps back are the enduring dilemmas of political, social, and economic crises in many African countries today. These crises include maladministration, political repression and instability, electoral fraud, virulent ethnic nationalism, religious fundamentalism, civil unrest, armed conflict, proliferation of illicit arms, violent crimes, economic crunch, famine, hunger, poverty, emerging and re-emerging infectious diseases (AIDS, Ebola, malaria and tuberculosis), environmental degradation and underdevelopment.

Conflicts Of Globalization

Let us turn to one area where African policy makers, civil society, and intellectuals need to appreciate more keenly the horrendous costs of Africa's violent conflicts, to focus squarely on the causes and costs of these conflicts and devise effective mechanisms of conflict resolution and strategies of post-conflict reconstruction. Africa's yawning developmental and democratic deficits can in large part be attributed to the continent's violent conflicts. At the dawn of the twenty-first century, Africa was already hurting badly, in that most parts of the continent were embroiled in independence wars, ethnic conflicts, violent wars for political and resource control, and cross-border conflicts. In fact, of 33 countries at high risk for instability in the world in the year 2001, 20 were in Africa. For example, Somalia is a profile in the crisis of instability in contemporary Africa. Since after the popular upheaval that snowballed into the overthrow of the oppressive regime of Mohammed Siad Barre by various notorious clan warlords and their militias, this Horn of African country has been in turmoil and fragmented into self-recognised independent republics of Somaliland, Puntland, and South West Somalia.

Owing to the current civil war, chaos, anarchy, bloodshed, horror, barbarism and devastation in Somalia, many watchers of African politics have seen the country as a clear indication of the extreme difficulty of state building in Africa. Somalia is the only political society on the continent that is a nation in the real sense of the word because of the ethnic, religious and cultural homogeneity of her people, yet, she is atomised across the fault line of clan. In the light of this, many Western analysts have come to associate Somalia with an egregious example of a failed state.

This is exemplified by the scenario of a failed state presented by Somalia and is being replicated by other African countries, namely Ethiopia, Eritrea, Djibouti and Sudan, which are plagued by disastrous armed conflicts that have caused catastrophic breakdown of law and order and opened the floodgates of carnage, social dislocation, hunger and famine. Mindful of the political and communal turmoil in Rwanda, Burundi, Democratic Republic of Congo, Congo-Brazzaville, Central African Republic, Liberia, Sierra Leone, *Côte d'Ivoire* and a host of others, one can surmise that these countries are equally failed states *à la* Somalia. Rwanda and Burundi have been bogged down by the vicious cycle of revolt by Hutus and repression by Tutsis. In Rwanda, the communal feud led to the world-shaking genocide of April—June 1994, in which about 800,000 Tutsis, along with moderate Hutu politicians, were slaughtered by Hutu extremist militias (the *Interahamwe*) and members of the former Hutu-led national army (Horowitz 1985).

The Democratic Republic of Congo (formerly Zaire) is not immune to the widening battlefields in the Great Lakes or Central African region. At present, the country is recovering from a devastating civil war that orchestrated the violence and unrest that led to the downfall of the corrupt, despotic and tyrannical regime of Mobutu Sese Seko in May 1997. The war, seen as Africa's 'First World War,' on account of the involvement of Uganda, Rwanda, Burundi, Zimbabwe, Namibia, Angola and Sudan on the side of different groups in the country, claimed an estimated five million lives and depleted vast mineral resources there.

From the sombre and dire picture of catastrophic armed conflicts in Africa's Great Lakes region, one cannot dismiss suggestions that the pernicious ideologies of Hutu supremacy (or power) and Hima-Tutsi empire, which have found vent in the fierce communal rivalry in the putative states of Rwanda and Burundi, could have convulsive impact on the region and beyond. Noticeably, the seemingly intractable crisis has already spawned a culture of xenophobia, deep-seated resentment, extremism and ethnic cleansing in the neighbouring DR Congo, where the *Banyamulenge* (Tutsi of Rwandan extraction) who provided the bulk of the fighters that ousted the Mobutu regime in 1997, are restive.

In Congo's Northeastern lturi region, the Hema and Lendu tribesmen have been entangled in mutually assured killings and destruction. Another anxiety over Hutu-Tutsi animosity is that the conflict in Rwanda and Burundi could seep into the laps of Uganda and Tanzania, which have a sizable population of the two antagonist ethnic nationalities as immigrants. So far, Uganda is struggling to contain the atrocious rebellion of the millennial cult guerrillas of the Joseph Kony-led Lord's Resistance Army (LRA), which is operating in the North from Sudan. In Congo-Brazzaville and Central African Republic, the nefarious activities of heavily armed militia groups, supported by insurgents from DR Congo, have paralysed governments and institutions in the two countries, just as the insurrection of the rebels in Chad.

In Côte d'Ivoire, formerly seen as havens of peace and economic stability in the emerging volatile Africa--as observed in the chaos and madness of the horrific civil wars of the recent past in Liberia, Sierra Leone and Guinea Bissau—political intolerance, the nationality question and xenophobia have ignited a divisive civil war and the 2007 post-election massacres in Kenya.

Nudging other states in Africa towards the precipice of a failed state is the new potentially grave danger of religious extremism, that has gathered sheer momentum on the continent since the end of East-West rivalry (the Cold War) in 1989. In Egypt and Algeria, wild, bearded Islamic zealots with AK-47 assault rifles and bombs have been waging vicious campaigns to wrest power from their secularist governments. Kenya and Tanzania have become the centres of Al-Qaeda inspired anti-Western, anti-Israeli struggles in Africa, buttressed by the spate of suicide bombings by hardline Islamic militants in the East African countries in the recent past.

In sum, the advent of colonial globalisation was tsunamic for Africa. Chinua Achebe captured this well in *Things fell apart!* Africa and her centre could no longer hold. She became embroiled in a dynamic that would change her structure, her culture and her future forever. The former league of tribes coagulated into pseudo-states, as a result of colonialism. Strange bedfellows became fellow citizens over night. Consanguine relatives found themselves facing each other as citizens of different countries.

The African psyche was ripped apart. These changes were too radical, as African cultures were demonized and labelled as inferior. The African had to forfeit his language in many cases. He was equated to a dog, since, when he sought admittance into drinking parlours, like dogs he was not admitted. There arose a miseducation on the socio-cultural level, as colonialism deformed the collective African psyche, something from which it is yet to recover.

To carve up Africa, drawing boards were built in 1885 Berlin. Africa was scrambled up among the occupying powers. The aim was to ensure each power an unimpeded and unmonitored freedom to loot as much as they could in their area of influence. The Belgian-Congo became an abattoir, where King Leopold's polymorphous perversity, sought and obtained unrestrained ventilation. For the sake of rubber, Leopold's men sacked villages, decimated cultures, and harvested a pyramid of chopped hands, in an orgy of brutality, unmatched even by Hitler's men. Congo bled, and haemorrhaged her resources into Belgian coffers. The Germans tried the annihilation tactics on the Herero of Namibia. British piratical treachery blossomed in Nigeria and her other territories. Africa bled so that Europe could have a river of wealth flowing through her.

In order to effectively continue this robbery and butchery when their various suns must have set, they created states that were simply neo-colonial dependencies. And to run these states, they mass-produced a semi-literate, middle-class of yes-men, to complement the paucity of men they had to put on the ground. This crop of creatures became the collaborative vehicle of colonial exploitation. Hatred for them, which was a rampant phenomenon, sometimes took deadly proportions, as was mirrored in Achebe's *Things Fall Apart*, where Okonkwo had to kill a court messenger, to vent his anger on an invading establishment that has despoiled the land of his fathers, and insulted his culture.

Almost all the modern states in Africa today were built on political ontologies, [is this the best word? If used in the sense of 'metaphysics' it means that the sentence repeats itself; perhaps better to say: 'Almost all the modern states in Africa today ooze from this engineered political metaphysic'?]oozing from this engineered political metaphysic. The people never dialogued their differences as a basis for federating. They never talked to each other about a political union. They woke up one morning, and saw themselves conscripted into geopolitical constructs they neither chose nor bargained for. For the natives, it was a bazaar of unfunny jokes, and for the colonial officers, a duty for country and monarch.

These collapsing states in Africa were created to facilitate and ease the efficiency of rapid colonial exploitation. That was their *raison d'être.* They were never designed to be independent, or to cease being a source of cheap raw materials and slave labour for colonial industries. They were equally meant to be a cheap market to cushion the inflationary effects of mechanized mass production. The colony was a laboratory of caprice. Every socio-economic, geopolitical or cultural hypothesis was subjected to clinical trials on the hapless colonies. This accounts for the fact that every discredited socio-political, economic or eugenic theory was once tried out in Africa.

Globalization And New Nationalisms

Ethnic/micro nationalisms (Adekanye, 1996) are also a potent force to reckon with in the crisis of instability in Africa. In this regard, Nigeria is, in recent years, becoming volatile, a kind of powder keg, on account of frequent nasty inter-ethnic and religious riots, fuelled by years of bubbling communal discontent and frustration across the country. In Western Sahara, Sudan (in the South), Senegal (in Casamance), Angola (in Cabinda), Ethiopia (in Oromoland, Ogaden and Haud), Comoros (in Anjou an), Niger (in Agadez) and Mali (in Alawak), disaffected ethnic nationalities have been waging armed separatist struggles for autonomy or outright independence. In recent years, Namibia and Cameroun have increasingly become volatile since the beginning of the agitation for national self-determination by San people of the Caprivi Strip and English-speaking Cameroonians respectively.

Inter-state conflicts have added to the sources of violence and instability in Africa. Such conflicts include the long time standoff between Nigeria and Cameroun over the oil-rich Bakassi Peninsula and the continued tension between Ethiopia and Eritrea over the Badme territory. Such conflict has often had the ominous implication of undermining African unity. There is no question that political and social crises that inform the unfolding failed state syndrome in Africa are partly responsible for Afro-pessimism, the notion by western scholars and commentators that the future of the continent is bleak, gloomy and depressing because of multiple and endless crises. Karl Maier, in his book *Midnight in Nigeria, This house has fallen*, has captured such pessimism, painting a gory picture of the uphill task of nation-building in Nigeria, bedevilled by a medley of political, ethnic and religious turbulence.

In a similar vein, Robert D. Kaplan, in his widely read but controversial essay *The Coming Anarchy* (1994), has gazed into the crystal ball and predicted the fragility of many African territories because of political and social chaos and instability. Currently, Zimbabwe, Swaziland, Malawi, Togo and Guinea encapsulate such grave assumptions of doom and gloom about the continent, considering the dire prospects of political and social implosions in these countries owing to creeping dictatorship and violation of the basic tenets of democracy and constitutionality. In South Africa, despite the routing of the tangential forces of apartheid, the subversive rise of white Afrikaner nationalism, under the aegis of the Boeremag (or *Warriors of the Boer Nation*) and Zulu militancy, reminiscent of those of the 1980s and early 1990s, has ignited fears about the return of the terrible racial tension and divisions of the apartheid years.

Economically, the outlook for some of the African states is bleak, as some of them are being relegated in international finance and trade in the post-Cold War era, as well as in the emerging order of globalization and information and communication technology (ICT). Oddly enough, except, to some extent, South Africa, Egypt, Tunisia, Libya, Botswana, Mauritius, Senegal and Uganda, the economies of many political configurations on the continent are not dynamic and booming.

Efforts to combine the requirements of Western-induced reforms with the demands of democratization in some of the countries have also met a brick wall (Bangura, 1998). Worse still, the United States and countries of the European Union (EU) have been tempted to reduce their level of official development aid for African countries because of doubts about their efficacy, and this is more so in the post East-West rivalry when Russia is no longer a diplomatic player in Africa.

Consequently, loans and grants by these Western countries to African states are tied to conditions like inauguration of Western style democracy and market reforms, human rights and support for 'war on terror'—a situation that has impinged on the national sovereignties of such states. Not helping matters are the literal kleptocracies in some African countries, which, sometimes, have taken the form of a veritable economy of loot and plunder of Mobutuesque proportions. And this development has contributed to serious problems of sluggish economy, debt overhang, human suffering, social unrest and political quagmire in some of the states, especially those in sub-Saharan Africa.

In the face of the unmitigated political, social and economic crises and woes that have made many African countries face an uncertain future, the immediate task before African leaders is how to use the opportunities offered by the end of the destabilizing Cold War and apartheid to confront the harsh realities of independence, reinvent their national entities and satisfy the welfare demands of law, social justice, peaceful coexistence, economic reconstruction, human welfare and African brotherhood. Interestingly, former President Nelson Mandela (the Madiba) of South Africa and his successor, Mr. Thabo Mbeki, are today championing the 'idea of African renaissance, a project of renewal to bring the continent' back from the brink, strengthen its possibilities, raise hope and optimism and reposition it as an important centre of human civilization.

Therefore, there is a growing sense of urgency to transform the 'failed states' of Somalia and DR. Congo into stabilized, modernized and pro-active states, guided by justice, peace, security and development. The same is required from other war-subsidies. Coupled with the African Union (AU)'s agenda for [a?]federal African state, conflict resolution, peace building, security, good governance, human rights, the rule of law and sustainable development, there is hope that, with commitment, courage and dedication, a stable Africa will emerge out of the chaos and rubbles of crises. No doubt, the pressure and onus for the realization of these Afro-optimistic expectations are on African leaders and the stakes are too high for them to fail in helping provide certainty and stability to the distraught continent. In fact, Africa has been paying the expensive price as European empires change gear.

World capitalism has been undergoing a profound restructuring in Africa since the colonial era. Many have come to refer to this process as globalization, although what this concept exactly means, the nature, extent and importance of the changes bound up with the process, is hotly debated. In my view, globalization is a concept useful intellectually and enabling politically. It helps us to organize empirical information on the restructuring of capitalism in such a way as to provide an explanation of the nature and direction of world social change at the dawn of a new millennium, and therefore to gain a better grasp of the prospects for emancipatory social action.

Why Globalization Matters: Whose Capital? Whose State?

It is certainly true that the economy of Africa remains trapped within poverty and backwardness. But this backwardness is not a national phenomenon. It is the outcome of the highest stage of capitalism—the domination of the world economy by global capital. Furthermore, while its economy is backward, there is a powerful working class throughout the African continent whose potential political power is far beyond its numerical strength. However, one might conclude that while such a perspective may be all very well for the future, a seemingly more realizable programme needs to be advanced. Should not the national state be strengthened against the depredations of global capitalism?

What has globalizing capitalism implied for the state in Africa? The first point to emphasize is that not all states have been affected by and responded to transborder capitalism in the same way. Individual states have, of course, faced globalization with different levels and kinds of resources, different histories and cultures, different policy options and choices. Moreover, the globalization of capital has on the whole proceeded much further (in aggregate terms) in Australasia, East Asia, North America and Western Europe than in the rest of Asia and Europe, Africa and Latin America. That said, contemporary globalization has left no country untouched, and even relatively small concentrations of transborder capital have had far-reaching effects in various countries of Africa (as the debt crisis has demonstrated, for example). In other words, the relation between capital and the state is central to an understanding of developments in the world today, Africa notwithstanding. It is thrown up in a whole series of apparently different discussions: on the future for the Third World, on the relations between the superpowers in the aftermath of the Cold War.

Amid the diversity, several major themes in the relationship between global capital and the state in the late twentieth century are common. One is that the state survives and shows precious little sign to date of dissolving in the face of globalizing capital. Second, transborder capitalism has, together with other aspects of globalization, deprived contemporary states of sovereignty. Third, transborder capital has given present-day states certain supraterritorial constituents in addition to their traditional domestic citizenry. Fourth, transborder processes of surplus accumulation have arguably created major disincentives to warfare between states. Fifth, supraterritorial capitalism has in general encouraged contemporary states to reduce many social welfare or social security provisions. Sixth, globalizing capital has promoted an unprecedented growth in multilateralism among states. Seventh, the foregoing trends in sum have created major difficulties for the realization of democracy through the state.

By way of explanation, the relation of the national state to capital is a relation of a nationally fixed state to a globally mobile capital (Robinson 2004). This makes it impossible to establish any simple relation between a national state and any particular part of world capital. In effect, the political as a moment of the capital relation is a moment of a global totality in which the absolute contingency of space is epitomized in the existence of capital as money (Hilferding 1981;1910). The political finds expression in a plurality of territorially distinct national states. Historically, the liberation of the relations of exploitation from spatial constraint was accompanied by the development of a new territoriality in the form of the nation state. The state form in Africa is therefore a specific mode of existence of the class relation, the moment of coercion, without which no class-divided society, with its attendant inequalities, can exist.

Let us take a look at Sub-Saharan Africa's overall economic growth rate in 1998 that fell to between 2.1 per cent and 2.4 per cent, down from 3.5 per cent the year before, the World Bank reported in early December that year. Given the region's rapidly growing population, this means that its per capita gross domestic product (GDP) turned a negative 0.5 per cent, after several years of positive growth. The World Bank estimate was significantly below the 3.7 per cent figure released in early October by the International Monetary Fund, which used different methods for projecting economic growth.

According to the World Bank's *Global Economic Prospects and the Developing Countries, 1998/99*, a variety of factors were involved in Africa's slowdown, including a resurgence of armed conflict and the effects of the El Niño weather phenomenon. But the dominant factor was the impact of the global economic crisis that began last year in East Asia, which buffeted Africa's vulnerable economies 'through all three of the main transmission channels—private capital flows, terms of trade, and export market growth,' says the report. However, if the Bank's assumptions about trends in the world economy are borne out, then 1999 should bring a resumption of positive growth, at around 3.2 per cent, rising further to 3.8 per cent in 2000. Indeed, the promises of neoliberal globalization had failed.

Many of these crises reflect and are spawned by the lingering structural deformities bequeathed by European globalization from colonialism till today, some are fuelled by postcolonial Africa's staggering failures to achieve the enduring dreams of *Uhuru*, and others are fanned by new forms of imperialism, often cloaked in the giddy rhetoric of globalization, that are engendering new contexts and excuses for imperialist adventures, which are stoking local and regional conflicts across the world. A particularly egregious recent example of this is the so-called U.S.-led 'war on terror,' a crusade that has already left a trail of wanton destruction in Somalia, Iraq and Afghanistan, and shattered the shaky scaffolding of global order.

Significant changes in the global political climate during the late 1980s sparked off dramatic enthusiasm for democratization which swept across much of Africa. Previously authoritarian governments, through the combined pressures from both external and internal arenas, began to topple, to be replaced by regimes organized along liberal democratic lines. Internally, the public reacted to the corrupt and repressive tactics of predatory patron-client state systems that had continually failed to operate in accordance with societal needs, with street riots, strikes and other outbursts of discontent. Such events played a major part in introducing multi-party politics by demanding accountability from those in power. Such dramatic changes were also a product of marked changes in the external environment, with governments no longer able to rely on uncritical donor support to secure a bulwark against communism.

Furthermore, excessive state repression and intervention, in terms of human rights violations were no longer deemed to be acceptable behaviour. This was mirrored by a clear policy change as evidenced by the British Government's White Paper (1997) which clearly outlined the need for a more enabling, effective and strengthened role for governments in the developing world which enabled them to become more dedicated to promoting the interests of the most disadvantaged sectors of society. Only governments that demonstrate a commitment to good governance could receive funding and not adhering to these policy dictates could have drastic consequences in terms of future levels and types of support.

The decision came at a time when corporate-led globalization entailed very high costs for the African continent, as a result of the acceleration of trade and financial liberalization and privatization of national assets to the benefit of multinational corporations. Trade liberalization, combined with western countries' disguised or open protectionism and subsidies, resulted in the deterioration of sub-Saharan Africa's terms of trade. Trade liberalization alone cost the region more than $270 billion over a 20-year period, according to Christian Aid (2005). An illustration of these costs is Ghana, which lost an estimated $10 billion. According to Christian Aid, it is as if the entire country had stopped working for 18 months! Capital flight, fuelled by trade and financial liberalization, reached alarming proportions, estimated at more than half of the continent's illegitimate external debt, according to the United Nations Economic Commission for Africa (2005).

The privatization of state-owned enterprises and public services resulted in a massive transfer of the national patrimony to foreign hands, precisely to western multinational corporations. This, combined with the illegitimate and unbearable external debt, deepened external domination and increased the transfer of wealth from Africa to western countries and multilateral institutions, as acknowledged by the Commission for Africa (2005), put together by then British Prime Minister, Tony Blair. And members of the Commission had reliable sources to back up their claim, since Britain is one of the main beneficiaries of this transfer of wealth. Quoting a study published in 2006 by *Christian Aid*, Archbishop Ndungane (2006) indicated that:

Britain took away far more money from sub-Saharan Africa than it gave in aid and debt relief last year, despite pledges to help the region. In all, it took away £27 billion from Africa. In the 12 months since an annual Group of Eight (G8) summit in Scotland last July, the British economy gained a net profit of more than £11 billion ($20.3 billion) from the region. The charity calculated that almost £17 billion had flowed from Britain to sub-Saharan Africa in the past year, including donations, remittances from salaries earned by Africans in Britain and foreign direct investments. At the same time, more than £27 billion went in the opposite direction, thanks to debt repayments, profits made by British companies in Africa and imports of British goods and capital flight.

This is just one example of the financial haemorrhage hurting Africa because of globalization.

Global Capitalism and the State in Africa

What is the relation between global capitalism and the state in Africa? Global capitalism has contributed to: (a) the end of sovereign statehood; (b) a rise of supraterritorial constituencies; (c) possibly, a decline in interstate warfare; (d) increased constraints on state provision of social security; (e) a growth of multilateralism; and (f) the impracticability of achieving democratic governance through the state alone. In sum, then, although the state survives under globalizing capitalism, it is in at least six important respects a different kind of state.

Evidence is not far to seek. The United Nations Development Programme's (UNDP) 1997 *Human Development Report* points out that the term globalization both describes and prescribes the system of economic relations in the world today. (UNDP 1998, p.82). The descriptions refer to the fact that international flows of trade, finance and information are being integrated into a single global market. Globalization, therefore, is a process that is aimed at integrating the world market where national commodity capital, financial and currency markets are joined together into a single market that operates according to a set of rules that apply universally. Transnational corporations, multi-lateral institutions and governments of advanced industrialized countries are driving globalization. This is happening in a context where there are major advances in technology, particularly in the information and communication industries.

Eric Hobsbawm outlines the differences between international and transnational ways of operating in the world economy. During what he calls the 'Golden Age' (between the end of World War 2 and the late 1960s), Hobsbawm argues that although countries traded with each other to a growing extent, most of their economic activities 'remained home-centred' and the basic way in which the world economy operated was international. But from the late 1960s on, an increasingly 'transnational economy began to emerge.' This transnational economy was characterized by 'a system of economic complicating factors.' And from the early 1970s, this transnational economy became a global force and grew more rapidly.

It is this transition from an international economy to a transnational world economy that defines the present phase of globalization. Globalization has been facilitated by the introduction of new information and communication technologies. These technologies have made capital, financial and commodity flows much quicker. But globalization cannot be reduced to technicist changes alone. Globalization is much more fundamentally a process of restructuring the entire way in which global capitalism works.

Globalization has transformed the way in which dominant forces in the global economy have defined their interests in the world outside of their own home base. In earlier economic phases, these forces were focused on ensuring access to cheap raw materials in the periphery as well as whatever access they could get to foreign commodity markets that was compatible with ensuring protected access to their economies at home. They are no longer focused on this. The agenda now of transnational capital is to look for a much broader and far-reaching breakdown of barriers to the free movement of commodities and capital across national borders, as well as removing obstacles to setting up production processes in any part of the world.

Globalization has therefore come together with the demands for removing regulatory and other barriers in national states. These barriers are seen as obstacles to the freer movement of commodities, finance and capital, but not of labour, across the world. National states have been pressured by the rules of the World Trade Organization (WTO), the conditionalities of international financial institutions (IMF—International Monetary Fund—and World Bank), and the impact of globalised currency and capital markets (that react with frightening speed against any country that does not conform).

At the same time, as there is deregulation at a national level, there is more regulation at a global level. The Uruguay Round of the General Agreement on Trade and Tariffs (GATT), and the setting up of the WTO, were important steps in this process. The Marrakesh Agreement coming out of the Uruguay Round negotiations introduced tariff reductions and other aspects of the agreement. A key feature of the process from Uruguay onwards has been the extension of the agenda to cover much more than the regulation of developed countries. This is seen in Trade Related Investment Measures (TRIMS) and Trade Related Intellectual Property Measures (TRIPS). These measures extended international regulations to areas such as investment policy, the financial sector and patent law enforcement. Another issue that became clear was the desire of advanced industrialized countries for further rounds of negotiations for reducing tariffs and a broadening of the WTO agenda to include matters such as a Multilateral Investment Agreement.

Uneven Impact of Globalisation

The term globalization describes the contradictory economic, political, and cultural processes of world capitalist integration. Although capitalism has been of a global character since the 1400s, the current phase of globalization is manifest by emergent transnational institutions, changing relations between multinational corporations and sovereign nation-states, and the development of a global monoculture of consumption. The above processes can be seen as real and objective changes in the way that the capitalist mode of production operates. The UNDP has, however, also said that globalisation is 'prescriptive..' 'The prescription,' according to the UNDP, 'is to liberalise national and global markets in the belief that free flows of trade, finance and information will produce the best outcome for growth and human welfare.''All is presented,' says the UNDP, 'with an air of inevitability and overwhelming conviction. Not since the heyday of free trade in the 19th century has economic theory elicited such widespread certainty' (UNDP, 1997: 82). There are, however, a number of problems with this kind of ideologically driven policy prescription. Some of the problems include liberalization associated with globalization. The fact is that liberalization is being applied selectively in that free movement of unskilled labour is not part of the agenda.

In addition, while global negotiations are moving rapidly towards free markets in foreign investment and services, developed countries intervene in textile and agricultural markets to create obstacles for exports by developing countries in areas where they are currently competitive. The ideology of neo-liberalism says that the maximum liberalization of tariff and regulatory controls is as good for the party taking these measures as it is for the potential entrants into a newly liberalized domestic market, but, in practice, globalization is a highly uneven and unequal process of liberalization. Developing countries have been pressured into significantly 'opening up' their national economies and substantially reducing real levels of protection, only to encounter continuing real protection, taking various forms, in advanced industrialized countries.

According to the UNDP, non-tariff barriers in at least 20 industrialized countries became more rather than less restrictive in the decade 1982-1992. By 1992, these 'global market restrictions and unequal partnerships' were costing developing countries about $500 billion—an amount equal to about 20% of the their combined Gross National Product (GNP) and more than six times their total amount spent on development priorities, such as basic education, primary health care, safe water and the elimination of malnutrition (UNDP, 1992: 6).

Although the implementation of the Marrakesh Agreement is leading to the removal of some of these non-tariff barriers (while converting others into tariffs), its effects too are highly uneven. A study by the OECD has suggested that those who benefit the most from the Uruguay Round will be North America and Europe. It further says that Africa, including South Africa, will be net losers at least in the short and medium term (see *Third World Economics*, 15/11/1993).

In agriculture, in particular, non-tariff barriers and subsidies in developed countries and regions, many of which were justified as a price that had to be paid in order to secure the Marrakesh Agreement, have resulted in a playing field that is far from level. For example, the producer subsidy equivalent for European Union agricultural products is 15% in South Africa. These subsidized EU products compete with those from South Africa and other developing countries not only in the EU market, but also in third country export markets and even the domestic South African market.

The UNDP concludes that 'in the real world, as distinct from the imaginary one inhabited by free traders, survival in the agricultural market depends less on comparative advantage than on comparative access to subsidies. Liberalising local food markets in the face of such unequal competition is no prescription for improving efficiency, but a recipe for the destruction of livelihoods on a massive scale' (UNDP, 1997: 86). Thus while globalization has been seen as potentially raising world GDP by between $212 billion and $510 billion, it needs to be recognized as highly uneven process that has produced losers as well as winners.

Globalization has been linked with the widening of differences in income and wealth both within and between countries. The UNDP points out that liberalization has demanded the 'shrinking of state involvement in national life, producing... privatisation of public enterprises and, generally, job cuts.' The UNDP further states that 'the opening of financial markets has limited government's ability to run deficits - requiring them to slash health spending and food subsidies that benefits poor people.' (UNDP 1997: 88). Liberalisation has sometimes come together with greater inequality and a 'falling share of income for the poorest 20%' (UNDP 1997: 88-89).

Similar thinking also underlies concerns repeatedly expressed about the marginalization (actual or potential) of a number of the least developed countries. In forums such as UNCTAD, it has been argued over and over that while the process of globalization has the potential to raise growth and living standards across the globe, it also has the potential to marginalize a number of countries and peoples who lack the basic requirements to integrate effectively.

Former President Benjamin Mkapa of Tanzania told the Mozambican parliament during an official visit in April 1996, '..we face pressure to prepare ourselves for liberalised world trade... With our low capacities for science and technology, productivity and hence competition, coupled with our indebtedness and ever deteriorating terms of trade, we stand to lose rather than gain from this new trade regime' (Southern Africa News Features, 16/5/1996).

Linked to this perception of the threat of marginalization and the need for 'development' to feature more prominently in trade negotiations, is an increasing questioning of the whether the neo-liberal policy response to the objective reality of globalization is appropriate and correct or not. As indicated earlier, the 'Washington consensus' says that globalization requires the same kind of policy response everywhere, which includes that:

- National economies should open themselves to the global economy by implementing widespread tariff reductions and removing other non-tariff barriers to the movement in or out of commodities or capital.

- Firms and enterprises should be subjected to the full force of competition by removing subsidies and deregulation.
- Budget deficits should be slashed, through reducing the amount spent by the state, and state and parastatal entities should be privatized.
- In this way, 'distortions' will be eliminated and appropriate price signals carried through market forces.

Ethan Kapstein (1996) has argued that such policies have had an impact of contracting the world economy. He writes, 'The global economy is leaving millions of disaffected workers in its train. Inequality, unemployment, and endemic poverty have become its handmaidens.' Kapstein blames ...'the current obsession with balanced budgets in the United States and the Maastricht criteria in Europe.'

The failure of many developing countries to achieve East Asia style export-led industrialization, despite years of IMF and World Bank recommended Structural Adjustment Programmes (SAPs), has also led to some reflection on whether or not they are correct as a strategy, even among economists who encourage their integration into a globalizing world economy. In a paper presented to the North-South Round Table on Africa held in Johannesburg, Sanjaya Lall and Frances Stewart (1995) argued that protectionist policies had one-sidedly emphasized efficiency. The real challenge, they suggested, was to steer a delicate balance between the two.

In this vein, the thinking goes:

> There is no definitive guide on how to do so,' they write, 'though the experience of Taiwan, South Korea and, in the African context, Mauritius, provide some pointers. These countries first built up strong human capabilities through... and, once industrial capability was established, they changed the incentive system to favour manufacture of exports based on simple labour intensive technologies (mainly textiles and garments). They did not abandon the protection of domestic industry, but provided incentives for efficiency through domestic competition and government pressure on firms, including pressures to enter export markets and thus face competition from international markets after a predetermined number of years.

The threats come from the fact that globalization has increased competitive pressures. No country can maintain protective tariffs and regulatory barriers at the levels they were in the past—unless it is prepared to cut itself off entirely from the global trading system. As protective barriers are lowered, producers directed at domestic markets will face increased competition from potential imports. At the same time, taking advantage of the opportunities available through engaging in export trade has become an objective of many countries.

Unlike the East Asian Newly Industrialized Countries (NICs) who began their drive for export-led growth at a time when most other developing countries were following import substitution industrialization (ISI) policies, Africa faces the prospect of having to attempt to realize its objectives in this regard at a time when many other countries are trying to do precisely the same. In both export and domestic markets, globalization is thus increasing competitive pressures. Africa has strengths it can build on in developing a proactive response to globalization. It has a significant natural resource base, has a geographic location closer than the advanced industrialized economies of 'the North' to the faster growing economies of Asia and Latin America, has human resource potential and is undergoing a political transition from authoritarianism to western engineered democracy.

At the same time, Africa has clear weaknesses and vulnerabilities that need to be identified and overcome. Much of the inherited productive economy and the manufacturing sector in particular, are relatively uncompetitive. Years of isolation under neocolonial misgovernance, repression and graft, and policies of import substitution industrialization have left much of the manufacturing sector, in particular, vulnerable to foreign competition. These actual or potential weaknesses are made worse by the unevenness and selectivity of globalization today.

Africa's level of development means that it is seen as a potential competitor, at least in some sectors, to developed countries. Fears about the impact of our products in sectors where we are currently competitive, e.g. processed agricultural products, clearly exist in influential circles in developed countries. We have discovered that we are unlikely to receive much more than we already have by way of preferential non-reciprocal access to major developed country markets. Any further benefits in terms of access to such markets are likely to require that we grant reciprocal favourable access to our own market through the negotiation of Free Trade Agreements.

Our policy stance requires that a number of elements are put in place at the same time. First, there is a need for a clear trade strategy aimed at identifying countries and regions where we can most beneficially increase our trade. The Department of Trade and Industry (DTI) has identified the fast growing regions of the Indian Ocean Rim and Latin America, as well as the Southern African region and West Africa, as particularly important in this regard. Second, we need industrial and sectoral policies aimed at raising the overall level of competitiveness, identifying sectors where we have potential and those where there are vulnerabilities that need to be overcome.

Africa must be willing to learn from international experience, and identify international best practice. But the continent must protect and defend the integrity of its original policy formulation. It must not succumb to ideologically driven or self-interested policy prescriptions that come from elsewhere. Protectionism of the sort applied in previous years is no longer an option. A minimalist approach to tariff reform can create a false sense of complacency. But we must recognize that being more free trade than the norm is unlikely to bring us real benefits. The main thrust of our domestic policy response must involve recognizing that change is certain and we must therefore proactively promote appropriate restructuring that serves our growth and development objectives.

Globalization also requires of us that we introduce concrete measures to counter its polarizing and marginalizing tendencies. In a context where globalization has been accompanied by a widening of inequalities within countries and where jobless growth has become a global norm, active policies to promote employment, including by focusing on services and other non-tradable sectors, human resource development and basic needs provision, are all essential.

Finally, the academic challenges of globalization cannot be ignored by scholars. Scholars should actively engage in wide trade research while politicians pursue wide trade diplomacy. A process which is continuing to reproduce a division of the world into 'winning' and 'losing' nations, particularly in a situation where many states in Africa seem doomed to remain 'losing' nations cannot be one to which scholars are simply indifferent. Africans need to recognize that globalization and liberalization have created an imperative to, on the one hand, struggle to find new ways to protect the integrity of domestic policy formulation and sovereignty, while, on the other, actively engaging in the international arena both to maximize opportunities within existing norms and structures, and at the same time striving to become an active force seeking to bring about changes in the global environment that will benefit states in the continent. In circumstances where there are powerful pressures merely to conform, this will need to be constantly based on an informed and critical analysis of the emerging global environment and of the balance of forces within it.

To sum up, capitalist globalization has provided some of the main spurs to, and has figured centrally in, some of its chief impacts. With the rise of supraterritoriality, much surplus accumulation has come to occur through the sale of global articles whose markets develop largely irrespective of distances and borders. In transborder production processes, inputs are sourced pretty well anywhere in the world. The growth of supraterritorial production and markets has been achieved *inter alia* through a proliferation of global business organizations: companies, strategic alliances and corporate lobbies whose networks transcend borders. The emergence of global capitalism has prompted many mergers and acquisitions, a trend that has increased concentration in many industries both within countries and on a world scale. Globalization has also brought a major delinkage of money and financial instruments from territory and has created major new spheres of accumulation: telecommunications, information technology, electronic finance, and so on.

These various developments have had far-reaching implications for contemporary states. Contrary to many assertions, global markets have not erased the state. Instead, states have developed strong relationships of mutual dependence and support with other agents of global capitalism. That said, these adjustments have yielded a different kind of state. Largely owing to globalizing capital, states of the late twentieth century have on the whole experienced declining sovereignty, acquired supraterritorial constituents, retreated from interstate warfare (for the moment), frozen or reduced social security provisions, multiplied multilateral governance arrangements and lost considerable democratic potential.

The last of these observations provides an important starting point for further critical investigation. Contemporary globalizing capital presents a challenge not to the survival of states in Africa, but to the realization of democracy. Transborder processes of surplus accumulation have to date generally incorporated the state but marginalized democracy. The obvious question to ask is whether growing inequality and declining democracy in the contemporary era of globalization are not connected, and whether more democratic global governance and greater global distributive justice could not go hand in hand towards a more equitable future.

Summary and Conclusion

The changes associated with the globalizing international capitalist economy have had significant effects on the nature and functions of states in Africa since their creation by European colonization. Rather than being in a process of decline in both relevance and effectiveness, the state in Africa remains central to the study of International Political Economy and to processes of transformation at the national, regional and global levels. The process of globalization has created a situation which we can call the 'paradox of state power,' in which the state in Africa is simultaneously weakened and strengthened. In the African case, the 'internationalization of the state' was engineered very consciously by European capitalist and government elites as a means of using international constraints to overcome domestic constraints. As a result of the location of significant decision-making authority at the global levels, and also as a result of the changing policy environment associated with financial globalization, the policy-making options available to African governments were significantly diminished.

On the other hand, the 'internationalization of the state' provided precisely the conditions in which the state was able to recompose itself and recover its coherence *vis-à-vis* societal interests following the conditions of economic and political collapse which characterized the African region at the end of the 1980s. In this way, state power in Africa was simultaneously weakened at the global level, as a result of the changing structures of rewards and punishments in the international economy, and strengthened at the domestic level as a result of the space created by the internationalization of the state for the consolidation of economic and political reform in favour of capitalist globalization.

Chapter Three

Historical and Theoretical Context

Overview

One of the oldest social practices is the conduct of international relations. However, the history of relations between peoples is punctured with 'new beginnings, collapsed old orders and proclaimed new arrangements' (Ryser 1996:139). The present political order was instituted at the Congress of Munster and Osnabrug in 1648 and is known as the Peace of Westphalia. During the seventeenth century a series of religious and political wars spread across Europe. It started as a conflict between Roman Catholics and Protestants in the Holy Roman Empire, but it eventually became a general struggle for territory and political power.

This treaty brought an end to the Thirty-Years War between the keepers of the flame for the Holy Roman Empire in Austria and Spain, and the monarchies of France and 'Swedeland.' At the same time, the peace treaty created new structures between emerging 'European Christian States,' established monarchs as sovereigns in their own right, formalised borders between separate sovereigns, affirmed that all states would be ruled under the guiding hand of the Catholic Church and established mutual recognition of sovereignty as the basis for state legitimacy (Westphalia 1648; see also Ryser 1996:140.

Instead of an individual or family unit being the focus of sovereign authority, the Peace of Westphalia established a new political order typified by the distribution of sovereignty between states (see Wilmer 1993). Exercising governmental power within the framework of a state evolved into a 'generally accepted system predicated on the principles of legal universality and of individual rights' (Ryser 1994: NET). Initially only affecting Western Europe, as a result of global colonization by a few European states, the Westphalian political order spread across the world: 'Independent states loosely connected to each other and supported by international and regional organizations defined the new international political order of the 19th and 20th centuries' (Ryser 1996:142-143).

The Westphalian system of states has functioned for close on four hundred years on a basic premise: 'Universal standards for political sovereignty and political organization would ensure peaceful relations between peoples and promote global stability' (Ryser 1996:145). However, just as smaller political units (states) contested and eventually supplanted empires, even smaller units of human political organization as well as transnational corporations have arisen to challenge the sovereign power and legitimacy of modern states.

These smaller units (sometimes much larger than many individual modern states) are the world's more than five thousand nations; the original peoples whose cultures distinguish them one from the other. The peoples and territories that are these nations are the building blocks from which virtually every state is made (Ryser 1996:145).

Historically, the sovereignty of states is a concept that has always been challenged. In its post World War II, United Nations construction, it embodied three contradictions that have been the source of subsequent derogations, revisions, and expansions: 1) that the power of the state is unlimited within its own territory but limited within the international system; 2) that all states are equal; and 3) that both the state and the people are sovereign. The most spectacular re-interpretation of sovereignty in the post Cold War period has been the growing association of sovereign legitimacy with democratic principles, that is, a populist approach to sovereignty, based on a universal and secular political doctrine, which impacts conceptions of sovereignty in all three sites of contradiction.

The Repressive State

'Bedrock nations' (Griggs ND:NET 1992) existed prior to all states (see Nietschmann 1994; Ryser 1996). War became, and remains, the vehicle by which states appropriate ('state-building') the territories and peoples of bedrock nations. State governments tend to share and reproduce state-building strategies, and since 'the common underpinnings of such strategies are force and tyranny, most are repressive and are reeled out with but minor variations' (Nietschmann 1994:234). The 'theory of the repressive state' proposes that because no indigenous nation cedes its independence freely, state-building proceeds through 'various military and legal mopping-up stages,' many of which may exist simultaneously 'creating a single historical geographic process' (Nietschmann 1994:234). Viewing state-building as a historical-geographical sequence facilitates the defence of nations and understandings of state build-up and breakdown.

While nations predate states, all states attempt to erase the histories and geographies of the nations they occupy, through programmes commonly referred to as 'nation-building': programmes which are 'based on political, cultural and territorial integration and development and education' (Nietschmann 1994:229) through the creation of common symbols (flags, national anthems, history and school-map geography). However, when states speak of nation-building they are, in most cases, undertaking 'state-building by nation-destroying' (Nietschmann 1986:2,

1994:229; see also Connor 1978). Does nation-building even matter? Nation-building matters to intractable conflict because of the theory that a strong state is necessary in order to provide security, that the building of an integrated national community is important in the building of a state, and that there may be social and economic prerequisites or co-requisites to the building of an integrated national community.

Statehood By The Treaty Of Westphalia – 1648

The Westphalian state model shaped what we call 'realism' today. States were sovereign entities that could apply their own laws to their people. They were equal to other states, and the principle of non-intervention between states was upheld as a goal (if not put into practice). This model still exists today, although the trends towards globalization have started to diminish the concept of absolute sovereignty.

The specific definitions of Wesphalian sovereign statehood frequently cited include a political entity which: (1) exercises independent sovereignty (Article 73), (2) is recognised by other states (Article 76), (3) has the capacity to defend specific boundaries or lines of demarcation within which it exercises absolute power, and (4) maintains the Catholic religion (Article 77: 'The most Christian King shall, nevertheless, be obliged to preserve in all and every one of these Countries the Catholic Religion, as maintained under the Princes of Austria, and to abolish all Innovations crept in during the War.'(Westphalia, 1648; see Ryser, 1996:143).

This definition of statehood has been punctured by current historical evidence. Global and transnational forces increasingly usurp the power of states to determine their own fiscal and economic policies. Some countries peg their currency to the dollar to maintain exchange rate stability, but dollarization eliminates the possibility of independent national monetary policy and exposes countries to policies set in Washington. In the interests of attracting foreign investment, some states set up Export Processing Zones that turn sovereignty over to corporate investors, undermining national tax and regulatory systems.

In many countries, the US dollar has become the national currency. In others, the national currency has been pegged to the US dollar. In still others, major transactions like real estate usually take place using the dollar. Dollarization therefore eliminates the possibility of independent national monetary policy and it exposes countries, especially African ones, to policies set in Washington.

Furthermore, with the rising concentration and globalization of corporate power, Transnational Corporations (TNCs) gain increasing power over states. TNCs influence states' economic policy, exploit workers, and often endanger the environment. As privatization and deregulation expand into public services, states are left with less control over their economies and little recourse in times of trouble.

States Breakup or Breakdown

As states are 'artificial creations' (Nietschmann 1994:238), they break down and break up as a part of their life cycle. State breakdown results when new internal boundaries permit greater autonomy for nations within a state (Griggs 1994b:260). State boundaries are generally subject to reorganization when 'the political and economic costs of occupation exceed returns, and the empire becomes too expensive to maintain' (Nietschmann 1994:238). Spain's post-Franco development of 17 Autonomous Communities is an example of state breakdown (Griggs 1994b). State breakup refers to 'the breakup of a state into 2 new ones' (Griggs 1994b:260). Recent examples of state breakup include Czechoslovakia, Yugoslavia, and the Soviet Union.

State-building by nation-destroying 'sows the seeds' (Nietschmann 1994:238) for the state's eventual breakup or breakdown. Particularly significant is the notion that state breakup and breakdown occurs most commonly along the boundaries of historic nations (see Griggs 1994b; Ryser 1992, 1993). Griggs (1994b:260) states that '[t]hese old nation boundaries can be considered cultural fault lines since nations often persist in cultural form centuries after their legal boundaries have been absorbed by expansionist states or nations.' When confronted with the reality of internal disintegration due to political turmoil, economic stagnation, and environmental devastation, states typically facilitate their own demise.

They may expand further (e.g., the USSR's movement into Afghanistan, Argentina's into the Falklands, Morocco's into Saharawi Republic); apply more repression (e.g., Ethiopia, Nicaragua, Guatemala, and Sri Lanka in the 1980s and Burma in the 1980s and 1990s); loosen up economic control but maintain the political and military occupation of nations (e.g., the USSR in the later 1980s); try to decentralize as little as possible within the existing state system (e.g., Canada and Quebec and home rule for indigenous peoples in the north); or develop a new method of international governance based on federations or confederations of nations that run their own affairs domestically and loosely unite to run the affairs of regions (trade, pollution, communications, defence and illegal drugs) (Nietschmann 1994:238-239). Griggs (1994a, 1994b) and Ryser (1994) offer an example of a new method of international governance based on confederal organizing along national and regional lines; the emerging Europe of Regions (ER) movement (state breakdown). Encompassing

130 nations inside the boundaries of 35 states, discussions are taking place within the framework of the European community (see Griggs 1994a, 1994b; Ryser 1994).

The central goal is to create a European Union (EU) (state breakup) that more closely aligns with geographic realities. For instance, the physical geography of Europe does not always fit well with economic dominance by state capital. Malmo, the capital of Skaneland, is hundreds of kilometres closer to Copenhagen than it is to Stockholm but politics rather than local geography dictates that Skaneland make its trading hub the latter rather than the former (Griggs 1994b:263).

The EU seeks to encourage trade and free regional economies by reinvigorating old trading regions that emulate geographic logic rather than politically bounded spaces: 'One example is the European Union-sponsored Atlantic Arc that renews the ancient trading line among Cornwall, Brittany, Galicia, and Portugal' (Griggs 1994a:6, 1994b:263). This new international endeavour places states under serious pressure, as do international conflicts which contribute to the breakdown or breakup of states.

Raping The World: 'Modernization And Development?'

The needs and interests of political states and indigenous groups are in many ways diametrically opposed to one another. Political states view uncontrolled growth and progress as the highest idea, while indigenous groups regard balance and limited growth essential to their livelihood. From all appearances these ideas cannot be reconciled. We must reconcile the differences or a great deal of humankind will not survive (World Council of Indigenous Peoples (WCIP) 1979:NET).

In the globalized world, industrialization, capitalism and modernization have increasingly alienated peoples (indigenous and non-indigenous) from land and nature in differing ways. The past few decades have witnessed a massive acceleration in the rate at which indigenous peoples have been deprived of their lands and livelihoods by imposed development programmes. Characterized by unchecked resource exploitation, these development programmes have increasingly been brought to international attention; especially at a time when it has become apparent that they pose grave and irreversible threats to the earth's bio-cultural diversity.

The New Wave of Colonialism

The breakup of Serbia or the attempt by Ogadenia calls into question whether the concept of Westphalian sovereignty remains extant. Shall Burgundy go back to the Burgundians, if they so desire? Will Wales and

Cornwall exit from Great Britain? Can Texas declare its independence? More pragmatically, are we seeing a return to the micronationalism that generated numerous wars on the European continent over the centuries before Westphalia?

This occurs in the shadow of the struggles in Africa and the Middle East over nationalism, sovereignty, and statehood. Just as we want to solidify the boundaries between nations in these regions to produce more stability, we seem to be supporting the breakdown of the exact same system in Europe. The end of the Age of Empire has left civilization struggling for a new model of political stability for almost a century—and the struggle continues today in Kosovo.

Third World colonialism has replaced European colonialism as the main global force threatening indigenous nations' survival today. The wave of post-WWII decolonisation created the boundaries of Third World States 'largely on the artificial outlines of the vanquished colonial empires' (Nietschmann 1986:2). As the notion of decolonization was not extended to indigenous nations, Fourth World nations are now the subjects of recolonization and internal colonialism. In artificial Third World states, like the Philippines, Papua New Guinea (PNG), Indonesia and Bangladesh, economic development is used to invade Fourth World nations (see Duhaylungsod and Hyndman 1993; Hyndman 1994a; Nietschmann 1986).

For example, the mining frontier expands in Indonesia and PNG by dispossessing indigenous nations from their land and resources and degrading the environment. Nations manage resources and states consume them. Melanesian indigenous nations maintain the quality of their lands, waters and resources but Third World states like Indonesia and PNG do not. A system that does work is being destroyed to maintain a system that does not work (Hyndman 1994a:177-178).

The strategy that many states like Morocco, Indonesia, and Bangladesh employ to annex indigenous nations' lands, territories and natural resources is termed 'transmigration'--the resettlement of people loyal to, or dependent on, a central government, backed by military force, '...with almost all expenses lobbied for by transnationals and provided by international development agencies' (Nietschmann 1986:6). In Indonesia, the Jakarta government lists seven goals for its transmigration programme: 'to promote national unity, national security, an equal distribution of the population, national development, the preservation of nature, help to the farming classes and improvement of the condition of local peoples' (Nietschmann 1986:7). The reality is the spread of poverty; forced displacement of indigenous peoples from their homes, communities and lands; deforestation and social damage at the rate of some 200,000 hectares per year...destruction of local governments, economies, means of sustainable resource use; forced assimilation programmes; wide-spread use of military force to 'pacify' areas and to break local resistance by bombing and massacring civilians (Nietschmann 1986:7).

It is obvious that the fallacy of 'nation-building' disguises the real situation of 'nation-destroying' by state expansion: 'Capture and control of resources, not extension of politics or economic philosophy, is behind the plunder and confrontation for control'(Duhaylungsod and Hyndman 1993:141; see also Hyndman 1994a; Nietschmann 1986) of indigenous nations' frontiers.

Social And Political Issues: Challenging Notions Of Sustainable Development

Like the fallacy of 'nation-building', technical definitions of 'sustainability' also deny the social and political issues implicit in the notion of sustainability (and by extension conservation movements). Colchester (1994:70) notes succinctly that as the World Commission on Environment and Development (WCED) study acknowledges, achieving sustainability implies a radical transformation in present-day economies. It requires a fundamental change in the way natural resources are owned, controlled and mobilized. To be sustainable, development must meet the needs of local people, for if it does not, people will be obliged by necessity to take from the environment more than planned. Sustainability is fundamentally linked to concepts of social justice and equity, both within generations and between generations, as well as both within nations and between nations. Achieving sustainability thus implies major political changes. Even when government policies are nominally designed to discriminate in favour of indigenous communities, rights to traditional lands and to control of development are systematically denied; disenfranchising policies are underpinned by deeply held prejudices.

One example (of many worldwide) is illustrated by Colchester (1994:73). These disenfranchising policies have been most explicitly stated in Indonesia, where so-called *suku suku terasing* ('isolated and alien peoples') are defined by the government as 'people who are isolated and have a limited capacity to communicate with other more advanced groups, resulting in their having backward attitudes, and being left behind in the economic, political, socio-cultural, religious and ideological development process'.

It is clear that implicit in the Indonesian government's formulation of development is the notion that societies or nations may be placed on a social Darwinist evolutionary scale; 'developed' states (i.e. Indonesia) are the most advanced and the so-called 'underdeveloped' indigenous nations are those that have not yet undergone the necessary transformations towards prosperity and economic growth (they are in a 'backward' state). Government directed development initiatives are often justified as being 'in the national interest' (national security and identity) and the state is therefore exercising its power of 'eminent domain' in denying local peoples' rights (see Colchester 1994; Nietschmann 1986; Tauli-Corpuz 1993).

Indonesia is just one example of a state which considers development to be a transition from one type of economic system to another; a transition that implies both economic growth (increased production and increased per capita income) and socio-cultural change for the better. Intrinsic to the historical development of the capitalist system of production is the tendency to expand frontiers of economic activity in order to amass surplus value.

Historically, capitalism is thus an expansive or predatory system, constantly in search of new fields of operation. Thus the phenomena of imperialism, colonialism and neo-colonialism may all be interpreted not only as phases in the development of a capitalist productive system, but also as expansions that are necessary in developed countries. (Seymour-Smith 1986:31).

With capitalist expansionism has come exploitation of indigenous nations and their environments; both ecological exploitation of resources in the environment and economic exploitation with the extraction of surplus value from producers. The capitalist ideologies of expansion and growth also entail the expropriation of indigenous lands; generally carried out by the state as part of programmes of land reform or as part of nationalization schemes affecting foreign or national private capital enterprises.

Colchester (1994:75-76) again provides one of many examples. The most severe problem that forest peoples face throughout south and south-sast Asia is the lack of recognition of their customary rights to their land. The main result of this lack of land security has been the massive take-over of forest peoples' lands by expanding lowland populations and enterprises. The denial of communal land rights and their fragmentation into individually owned plots has undermined traditional systems of resource management, shifting cultivation in particular.

Nation and State Conflicts

States and nations represent two seemingly irrepressible forces in collision: states, with their large armies, expansionist ideologies and economies, and international state-support networks, and nations, with their historical and geographic tenacity anchored by the most indestructible of all human inventions—place-based culture (Nietschmann 1994:236-237).

Nation versus nation and state versus nation conflicts since World War II (WWII) have produced the most extended and abundant wars, inflicted some of the most extreme measures of genocide on civilians, created the greatest number of refugees, and, unfortunately, have the fewest peaceful solutions (see Nietschmann 1987, 1994). Ryser (1996) calculates that of the 250 wars waged since the end of WWII in 1945 until the end of 1994, 145 or 58% are wars between nations and between nations and states - Fourth World wars. Broken down further, 111 or 77% of all Fourth World wars are nation versus state wars and 22 or 15% are nation versus nation wars (see Ryser 1996). Of these Fourth World wars, 85 or 59% continue today (see Ryser, 1996), and many will continue into the next century. According to Ryser (1996:25), 'intimidation by the use of state power is the single most common explanation for violent contention between nations and states.' While these violent confrontations tend to be multi-faceted, most are rooted in territoriality and political status issues with the major secondary component being economics (see Ryser 1996). These wars by bedrock nations are essentially about their self-determination.

These conflicts include wars of environmental destruction where groups on behalf of the state (usually economic developers) generate death and devastation in Fourth World nations: 'The act of development instils terror, causes psychological and somatic trauma and produces death either as a result of direct combat or as a consequence of destroyed habitat' (Ryser, 1996:18; emphasis in original[emphasis not noted]). Wilmer (1993:193) refers to the psychological trauma experienced by many indigenous peoples ('captive cultures') as a form of 'post-traumatic stress disorder'; a disorder that is historical in nature and firmly based in tribal, community and personal histories.

Wilmer (1993:193) acknowledges that at a very personal level, meaning cannot be created and maintained until, and only as long as, an individual is able to locate herself or himself within a cultural universe of meaning and continuity. The destruction of culture inflicts real harm on individual human beings. One culture cannot simply be removed and another transplanted in an individual without committing a violation of the dignity and integrity of that individual.

The irony is that in most cases these developers and their states suffer no casualties. More than three-fourths of the Fourth World wars studied were of the nation *versus* state type, suggesting that it is the failed capacity of the state to accommodate the nation that creates contention in the first place (Ryser 1996:38). Much of the violence perpetrated against indigenous nations is hidden by common consensus between states to transform the terminology of conflict: 'aggressive conflict between states is called war; a nation's defence against aggression by a state is called terrorism; and the aggressive invasion and occupation of a nation by a state is called development' (Nietschmann 1986:2, 1987).

Additionally, despite the fact that so many of the world's wars, refugees and genocide are the result of conflict over territory, resources and political status between states and nations, they do not come under international laws, rules, instruments, conventions or agreements: 'States make international laws...From the point of view of the state, only 'terrorists' resist state takeover' (Nietschmann 1987:1, 1994:237; see also Ryser 1996). Without new international laws, policies and multi-lateral institutions that recognize nations and their claims, many of these wars will continue, as will the deaths resulting from these nation-state conflicts.

Alternatives: Interdependence of Biological and Cultural Diversity

Since the late 1980s, 'sustainable development' (popularized by the United Nations' WCED) has become a major catch-phrase associated with development (and allied to conservation issues); referring 'to the means by which 'development' is made to meet the needs of the present without compromising the ability of future generations to meet their needs' (Colchester 1994:70). However, many development institutions have adopted technical definitions of sustainability—'ecosystems' continued production of goods or services or the maintenance of biodiversity—without any emphasis on human needs or sustaining livelihoods' (Colchester 1994:70). These types of definitions, in their search for ecologically sound production systems, effectively divorce technologies from their wider context; contexts that encompass social, economic, physical, technical and political environments (see Chapin 1991). Any search for ecologically sound production systems must take into account both human cultural resources (for example, applied traditional knowledge and resource management strategies) and biological resources; both are necessary for the maintenance of the dynamic evolutionary processes involved in plant-human interactions (see Oldfield and Alcorn 1991).

To date, technical definitions of sustainability deny the interdependence of cultural and biological diversity. Nonetheless, concern about the loss of cultural and biological diversity has increased significantly over the past decade (see Hitchcock 1994). The earth's biological diversity, its ecological diversity, 'is mirrored by the diversity of cultures humans created over great lengths of time' (Ryser 1996:6; see also Tauli-Corpuz 1993). Biological diversity refers to the variety of species, genes, and environments of the world (see Hyndman 1994b; Nietschmann, 1994). Cultural diversity refers to the variety of human life ways, knowledge, and landscapes (see Hyndman 1994b; Nietschmann 1994). Biological and cultural diversity are mutually dependent, they are also geographically codeterminant (see Elford's maps 1995).

In Nietschmann's (1991:373) clarification, in 'Central America...as in other regions of the world, most remaining wildlife and wildlands exist where indigenous peoples exist. In non-indigenous areas, the same forces that degraded and destroyed biodiversity and environments did the same to indigenous peoples. Where indigenous people survived, biologically rich environments also did. This means that the best guarantee for the survival of nature is the survival of indigenous peoples, and vice versa.'

By applying the theory of Fourth World environments two rules can be elicited: (1) 'The Rule of Indigenous Environments'—'where there are still indigenous peoples with homelands there are still biologically rich environments' (Nietschmann 1992:3, 1994:239); and conversely, and strikingly, (2) 'The Rule of State Environments' - non-indigenous environments are almost always destructive of generic and biological diversity (see Nietschmann 1994).

Indigenous Nations Fight Back

To indigenous peoples, sustainable development means meeting the basic needs for subsistence in partnership with nature. It means maintaining a spiritual and reciprocal relationship with nature and all living creatures and non-living things in it. They cannot abuse nature because it is tantamount to abusing themselves or abusing their mothers but also because their needs are very simple and the indigenous technologies, skills and processes they have developed are appropriate and in harmony with nature (Tauli-Corpuz 1993:12).

For centuries indigenous peoples have been actively manipulating, modifying, utilizing and caring for their homelands, turning their environments into humanized, cultural landscapes and seascapes (see Chapin 1991; Hyndman 1994b) ecologically maintained through established forms of sustainable resource-management. An example of ecologically sustainable resource-management strategies (once again from thousands all over the world) is given by Clarke (1990:24), 'polycultural agricultural systems' in some Pacific communities. He states that 'Recognizable orchards have been described for many Pacific communities, for example, on Santa Cruz by Yen (1974) or the highland fringe of New Guinea by Clarke (1972). Often, too, what looks at first glance like wild forest is really a humanized orchard in which almost all species are useful and many trees and shrubs may have been planted or encouraged. Rather than being a compartmentalized sector of the economy as forestry is today, traditional arboriculture was an integral part of agriculture, housing, medicine, and the production of a wide range of material goods, while at the same time providing ecological services such as shade, erosion control, watershed protection, and habitats for wildlife.'

It is fair to surmise that most of the world's states are essentially governments without environments or resources as they are actually located within the lands and territories of indigenous nations; pre-existing nations who have successfully maintained, and stewarded for future generations, their lands, territories, waters and resources. Most states have come to exist because of their invasion and take-over of indigenous resources and environments; military force is often resorted to in the face of non-consent. However, the intimate association between indigenous peoples and their land, and their determination to maintain their way of life, is most obviously expressed in their worldwide opposition to imposed destructive change.

For example, the Dayak peoples of Sarawak have been struggling against loggers and the resultant deforestation of their homelands .'..denied legal or political means of defending their lands, [the Dayak] have resorted to setting up human barricades across the logging roads to defend the forests around their longhouses. The government has responded with mass arrests and with a new law making all interference with logging roads a criminal offence. Yet despite the intimidation and threats, the blockades have been persistently re-erected, halting timber extraction on the concessions of prominent politicians such as the Minister for Environment and Tourism.' (Colchester 1994: 82).

Not all resistance has been subtle, but whether violent or not, and whether successful or not, 'the most important and enduring outcome of these conflicts over natural resources has been the local, national and international mobilization and organization that has resulted' (Colchester 1994:85).

Conservation by Self-determination and Self-determination by Conservation

Fortunately, in more recent years it has become increasingly clear to some conservationists that biodiversity cannot be sustained without cultural diversity and the preservation of traditional environmental knowledge; 'symbiotic conservation' (Hyndman 1994b:300) is essential. However, what still remains contestable is how best to integrate traditional resource management knowledge, and associated customs and techniques, into effective and useful national development and conservation endeavours involving sustainable resource management and protection.

As Nietschmann (1991:372; see also Colchester 1994) points out 'Most indigenous peoples are not simply interested in economic alternatives to resource use, but in re-establishing or reinforcing their control and self-determination over their territory so that they can effectively use their own time-proven and culturally based conservation and resource management systems—sometimes augmented by incorporating the best knowledge and planning from Western societies.'

One recent development, the Miskito Coast Protected Area (MCPA) (which has recently been incorporated into the Windward Project of central American nations) represents a grassroots endeavour which provides an alternate model for protecting environments and wildlife; 'it is... forging a different example because its starting point is that indigenous self-determination and environmental protection are interdependent and mutually reinforcing' (Nietschmann 1991:373; see also Elford 1995; Houseal, MacFarland, Archibald and Chiari 1985 for information on a similar project under the Kuna Yala). Elford (1995:109), in her study of conservation by self-determination in Central America, concludes that 'conservation by self-determination has potential as a theoretically grounded programme of action capable of changing conditions, engendering new understandings, and contributing to the emancipation of the oppressed nations of the Fourth World.'

Nation self-determination by conservation and conservation by nation self-determination, is increasingly (and ironically, since most indigenous societies were sustainable before capitalist invasion and expansionism) being recognized by conservationists and protected-area specialists who are now working more and more with indigenous nations. Similar notions of ethnodevelopment and ecodevelopment as alternatives to capitalist economic development projects are also being put forward by some indigenous nations and planners as ways to maintain cultural and biological diversity.

It should not be concluded naively that all established indigenous systems of resource use are undisputedly 'sustainable' and above criticism, but rather that they are far more diverse, complex and subtle than outsiders realize (see Colchester 1994). The social, cultural and institutional strengths inherent in established indigenous systems of resource use need to be built on to achieve sustainability. While states continue to dismiss indigenous resource-management strategies as 'backward' and 'wasteful', environmental and biological devastation will continue at a rapid speed: State environments will remain dominated by state people, 'centrifugal economies' and biological impoverishment, while important nation environments—characterized by ecologically adapted and long-standing resident peoples, 'centripetal economies' (Nietschmann 1992:3; 1994:259-260; see also Hyndman 1994b) and the world's surviving biological diversity (both landscapes and seascapes)—will continue to be destroyed to the detriment of all.

While it is clear that state-building by nation-destruction is unsustainable, the challenge for the immediate future is how to achieve global environmental security through joint indigenous nation/state co-operation programmes (see Hyndman 1994b; Menchu 1994) 'If we manage to establish some sort of mutual respect and understanding, and in the process learn to work together toward a set of common goals, we may just succeed in salvaging some of the earth's precious biological and cultural diversity.' (Chapin 1990:3).As the environment of the planet we all share, the source of life which many indigenous people call Mother Earth, continues to deteriorate after centuries of abuse, a philosophy that incorporates all living and nonliving things in its vision is being sought...Long proud of our tradition as 'caretakers of the earth,' indigenous people are combining energies to raise awareness of the need for everyone to become active defenders of the remaining wildlife and wilderness—a part of the world that has now become totally dependent on human generosity and sensitivity for its continued survival (The Native American Council of New York City 1994:19).

Summary and Conclusion

Much of the political activism of indigenous nations is directed towards the rhetorical issues that underpin their on-going marginalization as the epiphenomenon of capitalist globalization. Their demand for inclusion in 'global civic discourse' (Wilmer 1993:36) directly challenges and deconstructs the meaning of normal international assumptions and values surrounding the concepts of modernization, progress and development advanced by the imperialist culture of states.

In other words, in confronting and challenging the legitimacy of policies resulting in forced assimilation, relocation, the introduction of deadly alien epidemics, and the sanctioning of private violence by settlers, indigenous peoples have targeted the source - the meaning of development itself. For instance, representatives of the indigenous Yanomamo people in Brazil travelled to the World Bank in the 1980s and argued before officials that 'development can have many meanings. Your interpretation of development is material. Ours is spiritual. Spiritual development is as legitimate as material development.' (Wilmer 1993:37; see also Dallam 1991).

Indigenous nations do not simply oppose modernization or progress. Instead, they assert the right to define and pursue development and progress in a manner compatible with their own cultural contexts. They champion the right to choose the scale and terms of their interaction with other cultures. In order to achieve and secure cultural, political and economic rights, sovereignty and self-determination have become some of the most important values sought by the international movement of indigenous nations. The rise of Fourth World theory offers one of the greatest challenges theorists will have to contend with this century.

Chapter Four

The State in Africa in an Era of Capitalist Globalization: A Theoretical Exploration

Overview

The question of the state is at the heart of the globalization debate. But this debate has been misinformed by the persistent conflation of the nation-state and the state. The two are not coterminous. This conflation is grounded in a Weberian conception of the state that informs much analysis of this subject. For Weber, the state is a set of cadre and institutions that exercise authority, a 'legitimate monopoly of coercion,' over a given territory.

In the Weberian construct, the economic and the political (in Weberian terms, 'markets and states') are externally related, separate and even oppositional, spheres, each with its own independent logic. Nation-states interact externally with markets. Consequently, globalization is seen to involve the economic sphere while the political sphere may remain constant, an immutable nation-state system. State managers confront the implications of economic globalization and footloose transnational capital as an external logic. This has become the dominant framework for analysis of globalization and the state, especially prevalent in realist approaches to international relations, ever since Raymond Vernon published his seminal *Sovereignty at Bay* in 1971. In the globalization literature this approach emphasizes the increasing impotence of nation-states in the face of world market forces.

Antinomies of State—Market Dualism

The state-market dualism is closely related to the global-national dualism. Globalization is said to be overstated since nation-states 'have more power' than is claimed, or because there are 'national' explanations that explain phenomena better than globalization explanations. Some point to the continued relevance of nation-states to claim that globalization is overstated or even imaginary. In this construct, what takes place 'within' a nation-state becomes counterposed to what takes place in the global system.

In these recurrent dualisms, economic globalization is increasingly recognized but is analysed as if it is independent of the institutions that structure these social relations, in particular, states and the nation-state.

The problem is manifest, for instance, in the notable work of sociologist Christopher Chase-Dunn (1989), *Global Formation: Structures of The World-Economy*. This is a major theoretical synthesis and restatement of the world-systems approach to the study of social change. Breaking free from what is often seen as the dogmatism of scholars working in the world-systems tradition, Chase-Dunn takes a pragmatic approach to understanding the structure of the modern world-economy and its evolution over time. This means that he incorporates data and appropriates theoretical models from a variety of sources, including the work of scholars not associated with the world-systems tradition. As a result, *Global Formation* has become a standard reference work for world-systems scholars, even though they may not always agree with Chase-Dunn's approaches to the problems they study.

Global Formation argues from a world-system perspective for a dual logic approach. At the economic level, the global logic of a world economy prevails, whereas at the political level a state-centred logic of the world-system prevails. Relatedly, much has been written about 'global governance,' an approach that assumes as well the duality of a nation-state system with its own logic alongside a global economy. Nation-states are to cooperate in coordinating expanding international activity and in confronting the problems of the new age.

The way out of these antinomies is to move beyond Weber and return to an historical materialist conception of the state. In the Marxist conception, the state is the institutionalization of class relations around a particular configuration of social production. The separation of the economic from the political for the first time under capitalism accords each autonomy—and implies a complex relationship that must be problematized—but also generates the illusion of independent externally-related spheres. In the historical materialist conception, the economic and the political are distinct moments of the same totality. An internal relation is one in which each part is constituted in its relation to the other, whereas an external relation is one in which each part has an existence independent of its relation to the other. The relation between the economy, or social production relations under capitalism, and states as sets of institutionalized class relations that adhere to those production relations, is an internal one. It is not possible here to address the theoretical debates that have raged since the revival of interest in the state in the 1960s,that have remained inconclusive and open-ended.

Note, however, that: 1) Marxist theories on the relative autonomy of the state, whether emphasizing a 'structuralist' or 'instrumental' subordination of the state to economically dominant classes, do not posit an independent state as a separate sphere with its own logic (in Marx's words, there is no state 'suspended in mid-air'). The task of the analyst is to uncover the complex of social processes and relations that embed states in the configuration of civil society and political economy; 2) there is nothing in the historical materialist conception of the state that necessarily ties it to territory or to nation-states.

Nation-states are geographic and juridical units, and sometimes cultural units. States as coercive systems of authority are class relations and social practices congealed and operationalized through institutions. In Marx's view, the state gives a political form to economic institutions and production relations. Markets are the site of material life while states spring from economic (production) relations and represent the institutionalization of social relations of domination. It is crucial to analyse the composition of social forces that congeal in state structures and practices in particular historical periods.

Consequently, the economic globalization of capital cannot be a phenomenon isolated from the transformation of class relations and of states (Christopher Chase-Dunn, 1981). In the Weberian conception, states are by definition territorially-bound institutions and therefore a transnational state (TNS) cannot be conceived so long as the nation-state system persists. Weberian state theory reduces the state to the state's apparatus and its cadre and thereby reifies the state. States are not actors as such. Social classes and groups are historical actors.

States don't 'do' anything per se. Social classes and groups acting in and out of states (and other institutions) 'do' things as collective historical agents. State apparatuses are those instruments that enforce and reproduce the class relations and practices embedded in states. The institutional structures of nation-states may persist in the epoch of globalization, but globalization requires that we modify our conception of these structures (Chase-Dunn and Sokolovsky 1983).

Emergence of Transnational State (Tns) Apparatus

A TNS apparatus is emerging under globalization from within the system of nation-states. The nation-state system, or inter-state system, is an historical outcome, the particular form in which capitalism came into being based on a complex relation between production, classes, political power and territoriality. The nation-state system is the outcome of the historically-specific correspondence between production, social classes and territoriality—a correspondence which led to a given political form that became the nation-state (Volker Bornschier, Christopher Chase-Dunn and Richard Rubinson 1978). The material circumstances that gave rise to the nation-state are presently being superseded by globalization (Robinson 2004). If capitalism's earlier development resulted in a geographic (spatial) location in the creation of the nation-state system then its current globalizing thrust is resulting in a general geographic dislocation.

Robinson's argument here is that globalization is a new era characterized by the rise of transnational capital. The transnational economy is based on global assembly lines where production is coordinated across borders and where capital flows unrestricted from one country to another. Information technologies laid this foundation by giving capitalism greater mobility that allowed it to establish a worldwide command and control structure. These changes led to key differences between the old national industrial economy and the new global economy. The old international system was based on national production linked to the world through export trade. But today's world system is based on 'the rise of globalized circuits of production and accumulation' (*ibid.*, p.11). This means transnational corporations produce anywhere, employ everywhere and sell in markets spanning the entire world. Transnational capitalists coordinate this vast network of relationships assuming leadership in the world economy from which they dictate global patterns of accumulation.

What is required is a return to an historical materialist theoretical conceptualization of the state, not as a 'thing' but as a specific social relation inserted into larger social structures that may take different, and historically determined, institutional forms, only one of which is the nation-state. Nothing in the current epoch suggests that the historic configuration of space and its institutionalization is immutable rather than itself subject to transformation.

The state as a class relation is becoming transnationalized. The class practices of a new global ruling class are becoming 'condensed' in an emergent TNS. This TNS comprises those institutions and practices in global society that maintain, defend, and advance the emergent hegemony of a global bourgeoisie and its project of constructing a new global capitalist historical bloc. A TNS apparatus is an emerging network that comprises transformed and externally-integrated national states, together with the supranational economic and political forums and that has not yet acquired any centralized institutional form.

The rise of a TNS entails the reorganization of the state in each nation. I will henceforth refer to these states of each country as national states— and it involves simultaneously the rise of truly supranational economic and political institutions. These two processes—the transformation of nation-states and the rise of supranational economic and political institutions—are not separate or mutually exclusive. In fact, they are twin dimensions of the process of the transnationalization of the state. Central to my argument is that under globalization the national state does not wither away but becomes transformed with respect to its functions and becomes a functional component of a larger TNS.

Professor Robinson challenges the idea that states by nature have a national form, arguing that nation-states arose from a particular epoch of capitalism with historically determined capital-labour relations. These relations, when replaced by new forms of accumulation, produce new institutions through which class power is expressed. Robinson links three key ideas: first, that the Transnational Capitalist Class (TCC) has brought into existence institutions that express their authority; second, that the nation-state is being transformed and absorbed into larger global structures; and lastly that the transnational state 'institutionalizes the new class relation between global capital and global labour.' (p. 88). As Robinson shows, the transnational state is not a 'fully functioning political, administrative and regulatory structure…there is no clear chain of command and division of labour' (p.117). Rather it is emerging from the 'political consequence of the social practice and class action of the TCC' (p. 121) as it attempts to build a new economic, social and political framework. It takes form not as a preconceived plan, but from the process of historic change itself.

The TNS apparatus is multilayered. The supra-national organizations are both economic and political, formal and informal. The economic forums include the International Monetary Fund (IMF), the World Bank (WB), the World Trade Organization (WTO), the regional banks, and so on. Supranational political forums include the Trilateral Commission, the Group of 7 (G-7), the World Economic Forum, and the recently formed Group of 22, among others, as well as more formal forums such as the United Nations (UN), the Organization of Economic Cooperation and Development (OECD), the European Union (EU), the Conference on Security and Cooperation in Europe (CSCE), and so on. They also include regional groupings such as the Association of South East Asian Nations (ASEAN), and the supranational juridical, administrative and regulatory structures established through regional agreements such as the North American Free Trade Agreement (NAFTA) and the Asia-Pacific Economic Cooperation (APEC) forum.

These supranational planning institutes are gradually supplanting national institutions in policy development and global management and administration of the global economy. The function of the nation-state is shifting from the formulation of national policies to the administration of policies formulated through supra-national institutions. However, it is essential to avoid the national-global duality: national states are not external to the TNS but are becoming incorporated into it as component parts. The supranational organisations function in consonance with transformed national states. They are staffed by transnational functionaries that find their counterparts in transnational functionaries who staff transformed national states. These transnational state cadre act as midwives of capitalist globalization.

The TNS is attempting to fulfil the functions for world capitalism that in earlier periods were fulfilled by what world-system and international relations scholars refer to as a 'hegemon,' or a dominant capitalist power that has the resources and the structural position which allows it to organize world capitalism as a whole and impose the rules, regulatory environment, etcetera, that allows the system to function.

One issue worthy of note is Robinson' transnational state theory and the role of military force, a key element of state power. His argument is that since the TCC controls the US government it follows that all policies are on behalf of the global TCC, including US military goals. This fails to see a split between national and transnational factions of US capitalism and fails to recognize unilateralism as the counter hegemonic project of the nationalist wing of US capitalism. If history proceeds by two steps forward and one step back, then Bush is certainly one step back from globalism.

This is easy to see in the widespread rejection of the war in Iraq by globalist regimes throughout the world that certainly do not see US leadership on their behalf. The problem is that no functioning definition for translateral politics has been developed. There are clear lines of difference between transnational and national economic practices. In the transnational economy global capitalist share leadership and control and have many institutions through which they set goals and settle disputes. But transnational capitalists outside the US have no institutional means to affect US military policy. There are multilateral links developed in the old international system, but these lack the deep integration seen in the economic realm. The US state still maintains sole leadership of the US military (Gowan 1999).

But wouldn't a transnational state by nature have integrated and translateral political governance where global military policy would be worked out in such world institutions as the UN? [end of this sentence missing?]It seems there is still a disconnect between the advanced state of economic global integration and the emergence of a fully developed world political structure (Christopher Chase-Dunn and Richard Rubinson 1977).

This disconnect explains why the world is witnessing the decline of U.S. supremacy and the early stages of the creation of a transnational hegemony through supra-national structures that are not yet capable of providing the economic regulation and political conditions for the reproduction of global capitalism. Just as the national state played this role in the earlier period, the TNS seeks to create and maintain the preconditions for the valorization and accumulation of capital in the global economy, which is not simply the sum of national economies and national class structures and requires a centralized authority to represent the whole of competing capitals, the major combinations of which are no longer 'national' capitals.

The nature of state practices in the emergent global system resides in the exercise of transnational economic and political authority through the TNS apparatus to reproduce the class relations embedded in the global valorization and accumulation of capital. Unfortunately, much of the previous decades concerning the state in Africa have been notable for the impoverishment of state theory. Indeed, from 1970-1990, there was a never ending litany of books and articles on the crisis of the nation-state, the eclipse of the state, the retreat of the state, and even the end of the nation-state.

The central theme in these eulogies was that nation-states had lost control of their national economies, currencies, territorial boundaries, and even their cultures and languages and that macroscopic forms of power were shifting from the nation-state to the global market, transnational corporations, and globalized channels of communication. However, this chapter re-examines the relationship between globalization theory and state theory to argue that African nation-states are the principal agents of globalization as well as the guarantors of the political and material conditions necessary for global capital accumulation.

In contrast to those who see a nebulous logic of empire, a network state, or even a global state as the repositories of a new sovereignty, this book suggests that globalization, in its current form, is actually a new form of capitalist expansion or imperialism. And the state in Africa, in its present form, is the creation and agent of this expansion, not an instrument for Africa's emancipatory development.

Conceptualizing Africa Within a Transnational State Apparatus

Long-term, large-scale changes across continents seldom take place without profound processes of cumulative, heterodox changes at the level of class relations at the local, regional, and national level. The spread of new ideas, organizations, struggles and policies across national boundaries is similarly not merely a process of a 'communication' or a 'technological revolution' but the result of emerging political organizations that already share basic outlooks and interests with the 'lead actors'.

Globalization or imperialist expansion is not merely the 'spread' of an ideology and its imposition by force or persuasion. There is a prior condition—the existence of political and bureaucratic elites and important sectors of the ruling class who have a common political and economic interest and capacity to articulate the ideology and implement pro-imperial policies.

The link between the 'global' or imperial power and its control of national economies, natural and financial resources, markets and treasuries is through the ascendancy of national political-economic configurations of power. The basic 'link' in the imperial chain—what now is mistakenly called 'globalization'—is based fundamentally on the outcome of class struggle. Without a successful outcome to the class struggle, there is no political elite or dominant class capable of linking to the imperial project. Without a national 'link' the imperial powers cannot expand, or 'globalize' the world. Unable to globalize or expand, the imperial powers must intervene directly, that is, militarily to shift the balance in the national class struggle, via invasions, coups and colonization.

Imperialist expansion, almost everywhere, takes place in the first instance through force. The imperial imperative is to conquer the national resistance, in order to destroy the class adversaries of their imperial-linked dominant class. Subsequently, force is used to impose and defend the dominant class, ruling families, political clients, financial groups, and so on, who form the political elite. Force is used to defend military and paramilitary formations, police and judicial officials who will be defenders of the economic linkage groups to the empire (Christopher Chase-Dunn 1975).

Imperial 'hegemony' (Gowan 2003) is established over the ruling class and its state apparatus not simply through ideological persuasion as most so-called 'Neo-Gramscians' argue, but through shared economic interests and common enemies. Without the economic rewards and privileged access to the public treasury and financial loans, it is questionable how effective imperial ideology would be in influencing ruling class behaviour. Given the historical violence and exploitation induced by imperial intervention and the concentration of wealth in the hands of the imperial collaborators, imperial ideology does not exercise hegemony over the masses of the people. In every instance the introduction of imperial policies—privatizations, structural adjustment policies, 'free markets'—is rejected by the great majority of the populace. The exercise of imperial power is not based on 'hegemony' but rather on 'force' and 'political-organizational' control and manipulation by the local imperial-linked political-economic elites.

Power of States in Africa Versus Transnational Capital

As class formation proceeded through the nation-state in earlier epochs, the world-wide class struggle unfolded through the institutional and organizational logic of the nation-state system. During the nation-state phase of capitalism, characterized by national circuits of production ('autocentric accumulation') linked to the larger system by international market and financial flows, national states enjoyed a varying but significant degree of autonomy to intervene in the phase of distribution and surpluses could be diverted through nation-state institutions.

Dominant and subordinate classes struggled against each other over the social surplus through such institutions and fought to utilize national states to capture shares of the surplus. As a result, to evoke Karl Polanyi's (1944) classical analysis, a 'double movement' took place late last century. As capitalism developed the unregulated market unleashed its fury on the social bonds and institutions that allowed for individual survival and social reproduction. The social upheaval that ensued forced a measure of social regulation on the system that curtailed some of the most deleterious effects of capitalism.

This 'double movement' was possible because capital, facing territorial, institutional and other limits bound up with the nation-state system, faced a series of constraints that forced it to reach an historic compromise with working and popular classes. These classes could place redistributive demands on national states and set some constraints on the power of capital (these possibilities also contributed to the split in the world socialist movement and the rise of social democracy). Popular classes could achieve this because national states had the ability to capture and redirect surpluses through interventionist mechanisms. The outcome of world class struggles in this period were Keynesian or 'New Deal' states and Fordist production in the cores of the world economy and diverse multiclass developmentalist states and populist projects in the periphery ('peripheral Fordism'), what Lipietz (1982) and others have called the 'Fordist class compromise.'

In each of these cases, subordinate classes mediated their relation to capital through the nation-state. Capitalist classes developed within the protective cocoon of nation-states and developed interests in opposition to rival national capitals. These states expressed the coalitions of classes and groups that were incorporated into the historic blocs of nation-states. There was nothing transhistoric, or predetermined, about this process of class formation worldwide. It is now being superseded by globalization. The global decentralization and fragmentation of the production process redefines the accumulation of capital, and classes, in relation to the nation-state.

What is occurring is a process of transnational class formation, in which the mediating element of national states has been modified. Social groups, both dominant and subordinate, have been globalizing through the structures, institutions, and phenomenology of a nation-state world, the atavistic historical infrastructure upon which capitalism is building a new transnational institutionality. As national productive structures now become transnationally integrated, world classes whose organic development took place through the nation-state are experiencing supra-national integration with 'national' classes of other countries. Global class formation has involved the accelerated division of the world into a global bourgeoisie and a global proletariat, and has brought changes in the relationship between dominant and subordinate classes.

By making it structurally impossible for individual nations to sustain independent, or even autonomous, economies, political systems, and social structures, globalization reconfigures world social forces in a very dramatic way. Specifically, by redefining the phase of distribution in the accumulation of capital in relation to nation-states, the global economy fragments national cohesion around processes of social reproduction and shifts the site of reproduction from the nation-state to transnational space (Christopher Chase-Dunn and Thomas D. Hall eds. 1991).

The consequent liberation of transnational capital from the constraints and commitments placed on it by the social forces in the nation-state phase of capitalism has dramatically altered the balance of forces among classes and social groups in each nation of the world and at a global level towards the transnational capitalist class and its agents. If in the earlier history of capitalism the nation-state was a necessary condition for the development of the system, the institutional and spatial constraints of the nation-state became fetters to accumulation in the latter decades of the 20th century.

Indeed, the restraints on accumulation imposed by popular classes worldwide in the nation-state phase of capitalism were what drove capital to transnationalization in the first instance. This is crucial because many accounts of globalization attribute the process to technological innovation. However, technological change is the effect of social forces in struggle, which is causal to historical change. The nation-state went from being a particular historical form that made possible the development of capitalism to one that fettered its further development. Let me explain. The declining ability of the nation-state to intervene in the process of capital accumulation and to determine economic policies reflects the newfound power that transnational capital acquired over nation-states and popular classes.

Different classes and groups contest (national) state power but real power in the global system is shifting to a transnational space that is not subject to 'national' control. This structural power of transnational capital over the direct power of national states has been utilized to instil discipline or to undermine policies that may emanate from these states when they are captured by popular classes or by national fractions of local dominant groups, as popular forces that won state power in Haiti, Nicaragua, South Africa, and elsewhere in the 1970s-1990s discovered. This appears as an institutional contradiction between the structural power of transnational capital and the direct power of states.

Some critics of globalization for whom the capitalist system per se is not the source of the social contradictions they analyse, only its current global stage, see the contradiction in globalization as between national states and global agents. But this is a structural contradiction internal to an evolving capitalist system, at whose core are class relations, as the inner essence of a condition whose outward manifestation is an institutional contradiction. One set of social relations reflects a more fundamental set of social relations. On the surface, the structural power of capital over the direct power of states is enhanced many times over by globalization.

In its essence, the relative power of exploiting classes over the exploited classes has been enhanced many times over, at least in this momentary historic juncture. The newfound relative power of global capital over global labour is becoming fixed in a new global capital-labour relation, what some have called the global casualization or informalization of labour, or diverse contingent categories, involving alternative systems of labour control associated with post-Fordist 'flexible accumulation.' These systems rest in my view, in part, on the disjuncture between nation-state institutionality and capital's new transnational space. They include subcontracting and contract labour, outsourcing, part-time and temp work, informal work, home-work, the revival of patriarchal, 'sweatshop,' and other oppressive production relations.

'Downward levelling,' deunionization, 'ad hoc' and 'just-in-time' labour supply, the superexploitation of immigrant communities as a counterpart to capital export, the lengthening of the working day, the rise of a new global 'underclass' of supernumeraries or 'redundants' subject to new forms of social control and even to genocide, new gendered and racialized hierarchies among labour, are well known trends associated with the restructuring of the labour-capital relation taking place under globalization and point to the rise of a global proletariat stratified less along national than along social lines in a transnational environment.

These new relations have been broadly discussed in the globalization literature. What interests us here is the larger social and political context in which they are embedded, and the extent to which states and nation-states continue to mediate these contexts. State practices and the very structure of states are negotiated and renegotiated in specific historic periods through changes in the balance of social forces as capitalism develops and classes struggle. The current epoch is not the first time that capital has broken free of reciprocities with labour expressed in state practices. This happened in the late nineteenth century as the epoch of competitive capitalism was coming to an end and monopoly capital was emerging. Capital began to abandon earlier reciprocities with labour from the 1970s onwards precisely because the process of globalization has allowed to it break free of nation-state constraints.

These new labour patterns are facilitated by globalization in a dual sense: first, capital has exercised its power over labour through new patterns of flexible accumulation made possible by enabling 'third wave' technologies, the elimination of spatial barriers to accumulation, and the control over space these changes bring; second, globalization itself involves the culmination of the primitive accumulation of capital worldwide, a process in which millions have been wrenched from the means of production, proletarianized, and thrown into a global labour market that transnational capital has been able to shape. In this new capital-labour relation, labour is increasingly only a naked commodity, no longer embedded in relations of reciprocity rooted in social and political communities that have historically been institutionalized in nation-states.

The notion of responsibility, however minimal, that governments have for their citizens or that employers have towards their employees is dissolved in the face of this new class relation. In this age of savage capitalism unleashed from social constraints there is a veritable rollback on the 'historical' or 'moral' element in wage labour, driven by a culture of competitive individualism at whose fringe is a resurrected Social Darwinism in which collective norms and values have all but disappeared.

The dissolution of the 'welfarist' or Keynesian 'class compromise' rests on the power acquired by transnational capital over labour which is objectively transnational but whose power is constrained and whose subjective consciousness is distorted by the continued existence of the system of nation-states. Here we see how the continued existence of the nation-state serves numerous interests of the transnational capitalist class.

For instance, central to capitalism is securing a politically and economically suitable labour supply, and at the core of all class societies is the control over labour and disposal of the products of labour. Under capitalist globalization, the linkage between securing labour and territoriality is changing, and national labour pools are merging into a single global labour pool that services global capitalism. The global labour supply is, in the main, no longer coerced (subject to extra-economic compulsion) owing to the ability of the universalized market to exercise strictly economic discipline, but its movement is juridically controlled. Here, national borders play a vital function.

Nation-states are about the configuration of space, what sociologist Philip McMichael (2000) has called 'population containment zones' But their containment function applies to labour and not to capital. For example, north of the border, the U.S. consumer economy depends on low wage immigrant labour from Mexico and Central America as well as cheap, labour intensive goods imported from those low wage areas. What keeps the wages of immigrants low is not only the large supply of workers desperate for work, but also the fact that many of them are illegal and thus highly vulnerable and unable to make demands on their employers.

This brings into focus one of the important functions of a territorial border such as that between the U.S. and Mexico: by limiting the mobility of labour at the same time that capital enjoys high mobility, wage levels are kept low on both sides of the divide that the two states enforce. The territories controlled by states might thus be thought of as 'population containment zones,' to use an apt phrase of sociologist Philip McMichael. This has led one analyst to comment, 'the nation-state system boxes in and controls populations within fixed physical (territorial) boundaries so that their labour can be more efficiently exploited and their resistance contained.' (Robinson 2004: 106).

Globally mobile capital is not regulated by centralized national political authorities but labour is. The inter-state system thus acts as a condition for the structural power of globally-mobile transnational capital over labour which is transnational in its actual content and character, but is subjected to different institutional arrangements and to the direct control of national states. National boundaries are not barriers to transnational migration but are mechanisms functional for the supply of labour on a global scale and for the reproduction of the system.

How then is the newfound relative power of global capital over global labour related to our analysis of the transnationalization of the state? Out of the emerging transnational institutionality the new class relations of global capitalism and the social practices specific to it are becoming congealed and institutionalized. For instance, when the IMF or the WB condition financing on enactment of new labour codes to make workers more 'flexible,' or on the rollback of a state sponsored 'social wage' they are producing this new class relation. But more importantly, the types of practices of national states that became generalized in the late 20th century—deregulation, fiscal conservatism, monetarism, tax regressivity, austerity, and so on.—produce this relation.

The shift in the 1980s from firm- to state-financed research and development and from the state as a provider of social subsidies to a subsidizer of private business, state withdrawal from social reproduction through deregulation/re-regulation (from 'rigidity' to 'flexibility'), the privatization of collective needs, the lifting of rules and regulations that hinder market forces, all resulted in an increase in state services to, and subsidization of, capital, and underscored the increased role of the state in facilitating private capital accumulation. With this comes a shift in income and in power from labour to capital. These outcomes generate the broader social and political conditions under which the new capital-labour relation is forged.

But now we need to specify further the relationship of national states to the TNS. Capital acquires its newfound power *vis-à-vis*, as expressed within, national states. The transnational bourgeoisie exercises its class power through the dense network of supranational institutions and relationships that increasingly bypass formal states, and in conjunction, through the utilization of national governments as territorially-bound juridical units (the inter-state system), that are transformed into transmission belts and filtering devices. But national states are also transformed into proactive instruments for advancing the agenda of global capitalism.

This assertion that transnational social forces impose their structural power over nations and the simultaneous assertion that states, captured by transnational fractions, are proactive agents of the globalization process, only appear as contradictory if one abandons dialectics for the Weberian dualist construct of states and markets and the national-global dualism. Governments are undertaking restructuring and serve the needs of transnational capital not simply because they are 'powerless' in the face of globalization, but because a particular historical constellation of social forces now exists that presents an organic social base for this global restructuring of capitalism.

Hence, it is not that nation-states become irrelevant or powerless *vis-à-vis* transnational capital and its global institutions. Rather, power as the ability to issue commands and have them obeyed, or more precisely, the ability to shape social structures, shifts from social groups and classes with interests in national accumulation to those whose interests lie in new global circuits of accumulation. These latter groups realize their power and institutionalize it in emerging TNS apparatuses that include supra-national organizations and also existing states of nation-states that are captured and reorganized by transnational groups and become, conceptually, part of an emergent TNS apparatus.

The contradictory logics of national and global accumulation are at work in this process. Class fractionation is occurring along a new national/transnational axis with the rise of transnational corporate and political elites. The interests of one group lies in national accumulation, including the whole set of traditional national regulatory and protectionist mechanisms, and the other in an expanding global economy based on worldwide market liberalization. The struggle between descendant national fractions of dominant groups and ascendant transnational fractions has often been the backdrop to surface political dynamics and ideological processes in the late 20th century.

These two fractions have been vying for control of local state apparatuses since the 1970s. Transnational fractions of local elites have ascended politically in countries around the world, clashing in their bid for hegemony with nationally-based class fractions. In the 1970s and the 1980s incipient transnationalized fractions set out to eclipse national fractions in the core capitalist countries of the North and to capture the 'commanding heights' of state policymaking.

From the 1980s into the 1990s, these fractions became ascendant in the South and began to vie for, and in many countries, to capture, state apparatuses. They increasingly captured local states or key ministries and bureaucracies in the policymaking apparatus. They utilized national state apparatuses to advance globalization and established formal and informal liaison mechanisms between the national state structures and TNS apparatuses. Numerous supranational mechanisms, such as free trade negotiations, in turn, tie each national state to others in transnationalized networks. These emergent institutional configurations need to be studied.

Diverse nationally-based social forces in struggle produce different national state configurations that make for complex and multidimensional political dynamics and international relations. But, gradually, transnational blocs have become hegemonic in the 1980s and 1990s within nation-states. From the state, transnationalized factions and fractions are thoroughly transforming the vast majority of countries in the world, ranging from Sweden and New Zealand, to India, Brazil, Mexico, Chile, South Africa, and the United States.

Moreover, transnational fractions in the North have utilized the superior structural and direct power that core national states exercise in the global system not to advance 'national interests' in rivalry with other nation-states, but to mould transnational structures. Hence, national states do not disappear or even diminish in importance and may still be powerful entities. But these states are captured by transnational social forces that internalize the authority structures of global capitalism. Far from the 'global' and 'national' as mutually-exclusive fields, the global is incarnated in local social structures and processes.

The disciplinary power of global capitalism shifts actual policy-making power within national states to the global capitalist bloc, which is represented by local social forces tied to the global economy. The new managers of the neo-liberal national states, from Clinton and Blair, to Cardoso and Mbeki, from Mohathir to Zedillo, are part and parcel of a new global ruling class and represent some of the more charismatic executive functionaries of a TNS.

By the 1990s the transnational capitalist class had become the hegemonic class fraction globally. This denationalized bourgeoisie is class conscious, and conscious of its transnationality. At its apex is a managerial elite that controls the levers of global policymaking and exercises transnational state power through the multilayered configuration of the TNS. But this transnational bourgeoisie is not a unified group. The same conditions, the same contradiction, the same interests necessarily called forth on the whole similar customs everywhere were noted by Marx and Engels in discussing the formation of new class groups. But separate individuals form a class only insofar as they have to carry on a common battle against another class; otherwise they are on hostile terms with each other as competitors.

Fierce competition among oligopolistic clusters, conflicting pressures, and differences over the tactics and strategy of maintaining class domination and addressing the crises and contradictions of global capitalism make any real internal unity in a global ruling class impossible. In sum, the capturing of local states by agents of global capitalism resolves the institutional contradiction discussed above between transnational capital and national states; that is, local state practices are increasingly harmonized with global capitalism. But this only intensifies the underlying class contradictions. Before discussing these contradictions, let us reconstruct in brief the emergence of a TNS in the latter decades of the 20th century.The current challenge for Africa is to develop the considerable social mobilization against neoliberal globalization already in place into a Pan-African, why not, global movement and to overcome the social atomization that is the key resource of Western capital and its state and global apparatus. Why such a challenge? Back in the early seventies, Walter Rodney (1974: chapter one) raised the intriguing question of Africa's paradox and predicament: In order to understand present economic conditions in Africa, one needs to know why it is that Africa has realized so little of its natural potential, and also one needs to know why so much of its present wealth goes to non-Africans who reside for the most part outside of the continent (p.20). For instance, Africa covers only 20% of the world's landmass but is estimated to have 90% of global reserves of platinum and 65% of diamonds. It also has an estimated 40% of gold and 60% of manganese and cobalt, while South Africa lays claim to 80% of the world's chromite. Indeed, why is it that a continent, so richly endowed with natural resources and minerals, is consistently rated as the poorest in the world? Why is it that, contrary to what pertains in the rest of the world, Africans are still struggling for their basic human, political, economic and social rights to guarantee their human security?

The state has been the dominant mega-form of political association in the world for several centuries. The state is particularly not so in Africa today. The decline of the nation-state has taken hold around most of the world and its future has become the focus of heated debates as to whether the state is a paragon or a paradox. The disintegration of the Soviet Union and Yugoslavia gave birth to many new nation-states. Continuing ethnic violence, identity crisis and repression around the world will likely precipitate the failure and recreation of more states. On the other hand, the ever-closer integration of the expanding European Union signals a movement away from the nation-state. Steps toward an African Union are also another movement away from the nation-state system in the continent. These unions are challenges to the state in Europe as well as in Africa.

A whole set of global and domestic players challenge the authority of the state in Africa. This challenge goes from its economic and military power to its ability to provide social services and education. The boom in information and biological technologies further impedes the state's ability to control its population. Even if in the near future the state remains the only form of political organization in Africa, it will certainly undergo transformations. Late 20th century perceptions of state-sovereignty, citizenship, nation, and inter-state relations in Africa are changing and adapting to these new forces of rampaging neoliberal capitalism.

However, states are still emerging in Africa today. Eritrea is a current case. What moves people to claim the right to form a new state, and what leads to a successful outcome (i.e. independence)? In a globalizing world, with decreasing national sovereignty and closer ties between people everywhere, what is the attraction of forming or retaining other independent states? Repressive governments, denying minority populations their rights, seem to be the main impetus for independence movements.

Failed states in Africa can no longer perform basic functions such as education, security, or governance, usually because of factious and fractious violence or extreme poverty. Indeed, the state in Africa has: a) retreated as the commanding force of political loyalty and identity for many of its citizens; b) declined as a source of nationalistic identity for globalizing elites; and, c) increasingly failed to address acute problems of social and economic inequality and secure the inclusion of its marginalized and excluded populations into the global community.

Within this power vacuum, people fall victim to competing factions, fractions and crime, and sometimes the United Nations or neighbouring states intervene to prevent a humanitarian disaster. However, states fail not only because of internal factors. Foreign governments also knowingly destabilize a state by fuelling ethnic warfare or supporting rebel forces, causing it to collapse. The Democratic Republic of Congo and Côte d'Ivoire are living cases.

Corruption and money laundering drain African states of billions of dollars every year, lining the pockets of officials, business leaders, and the already super-rich, leaving less revenue for social and economic services. Systematic official corruption runs rampant in many countries, often leaving citizens in poverty. Wealthy individuals and corporations evade taxes, which could be used for social programmes, by setting up accounts in tax havens.

Change and Confusion

'Times of change,' remarks John Ruggie, 'are also times of confusion. Words lose their familiar meaning, and our footing becomes unsure on what was previously familiar terrain' (1994: 553). This dictum is no less true of the erstwhile meaning of the state in Africa.

Nick Beams once asked in dismay: 'What state are we talking about? The present 'nation-state' structures in Africa are the creations of the imperialist powers' for its transnational capital to capture, dominate and exploit. These states cannot be the vehicle for the liberation of the masses from its domination. 'But on this, as on every other question, basic class issues are raised. While the post-colonial states have been the vehicle for the suppression of the masses and their subordination to imperialist finance capital, these structures have been eagerly grasped by the African bourgeoisie as the means for its own advancement.' (Online: http://www.wsws.org/articles/2002/feb2002/corr-f18.shtml).

'The profound hypocrisy and inherent barbarism of bourgeois civilization,' Karl Marx once said, 'lies unveiled before our eyes, moving from its home, where it assumes respectable form, to the colonies, where it goes naked.' Marx's (1853) statement is telling and relevant. Where lies its relevance?

Capitalism has always acted as a global system, working across or between nation states. The ever-present imperative to produce profit pushed capital from its historic heartlands in northern Europe to all societies. But as Marx implies, the process of expansion has not been a homogenizing one: the bourgeoisie has double standards, or perhaps multiple standards, as it negotiates its presence in a wide variety of locations.

The standards that most would define as minimally acceptable (social democracy) have been a product of specific historical and material conditions: a result of the emergence of institutionally robust and interventionist states and the political demands of working classes.

But these historical conditions are part of the same conditions that produced very different states in Africa, in that the colonial states arising from the scramble for colonies of the late 1880s are themselves part of the same capitalism which produced the bourgeois civilization that Marx ironically attributes to late Victorian England. The hypocrisy is that civilization in Europe, plus plunder, primitive accumulation, and famine in the colonial world were part of the same overarching package of 'liberal ideals.'

Colonial states established the political conduits through which African societies engaged the global political economy. In many ways, this engagement can be seen as a process of simplification, reducing complex social forms to basic national templates: the zoning of agricultural production; the reduction of varied cultures of ownership and norms of trade to 'chieftaincies' and the regulations of marketing boards; and the redirecting of local and long distance trade networks to the road and rail links to port, capital city, and customs office.

Intrinsically authoritarian, this process of standardization could only be imposed with violence and was resisted both actively and passively, resulting in a mosaic of complex outcomes. The colonial project might not have completed its immanent desire to produce self-contained national economies malleable to the designs of international capital. However, it did mark a profound historical transition which defined the historical possibilities of independence. In spite of the vibrant African political currents of the late 1950s and 1960s, African statesmen inherited political and economic kingdoms that had been structured by colonialism. This structure was irrespective of whether these kingdoms were inherited through negotiations or armed struggle.

The postcolonial trajectories of African economies leave one impressed by both the variety of change and the durability of the sinews of global capitalism in the continent. These sinews are tough but also malleable, not necessarily rigid. In the 'developmental' period from independence to the first oil price hike in 1973, national economic planning, large scale public investment, and foreign capital (in the form of multilateral loans or transnational direct investment) created economic growth, at least on paper.

Negative real interest rates prevailed through most of the 1970s, until the second oil shock of 1979, encouraging both excessive borrowing and lending. However, 1979 also marked a radical change in global economic policy, inaugurated with the 'Volcker Shock' (so called after Paul Volcker, then Chairman of the Board of Governors of the Federal Reserve) when the United States suddenly and dramatically raised interest rates. The sudden change of interest rate policy increased the cost of African debt precipitously, since a majority of debt stock was held in dollars. The majority of the newly independent states had been effectively delivered into at least twenty years of indentured labour. From that point on access to finance became a key policing mechanism directed at African populations.

Globalized Neoliberalism or Imperialism Running Riot?

Marx never used the term imperialism. But it remains a key part of any analysis of contemporary global capitalism. The sinews of political power and accumulation that are derivative of capitalism's birth as a global creature might have twisted and turned, but they continue to connect African societies to a complex, combined, and uneven global political economy which has hardly served the people of Africa favourably.

Imperialism has almost always been a concept used to evoke a critique of the global political economy: to identify the inequities of what is now called 'globalization'; to condemn the bullying tactics of Western states; to investigate the cultural arrogance and discursive authoritarianism of liberalism's marriage to 'freedom, equality, property and Bentham,' that is, capitalism. Imperialism has also been associated with political struggle as a device to identify oppressive forces working at an international level as a means to political action.

Imperialism has come to encompass different meanings to the extent that one has to clarify what one means by imperialism before using the term. Imperialism has a much longer history than its contemporary pretender, 'globalization,' and one can discern three principal 'angles' that writers take with the concept. First, imperialism relates to a process of capital export from developed capitalist economies to the colonies.

Second, it addresses itself to the economic dominance of the 'core' of the world-system in the postcolonial regions of the world: the pernicious effects of transnational corporations, unequal exchange in trade and technological dominance. In this second sense inequalities between states, and within the interstate system, create opportunities for exploitation of the periphery by the core.

Finally, in a third context, imperialism refers to the predominance of the United States and its militarized bullying of so many postcolonial states since 1945. One might dub these three approaches as 'expansive,' 'dependency,' and '*yanqui*' imperialism respectively. Each has a kernel of truth, but each approach in itself tends to reduce the complexities and contradictions of global capitalism to a single argument. What is needed is to bring these themes together—to move beyond each of these three categories—in a global political economy of capitalism to demonstrate the relevance of imperialism to Africa's contemporary global situation. The best way to do this is by looking at actual regimes of accumulation.

The three perspectives, and the political claims that they have generated, have produced much debate: is imperialism the last stage or pioneer of capitalism as Nkrumah argued? Is imperialism a product of monopoly capitalism or the need for 'peripheries' as Luxemburg argued? And most recently has the world reached a stage of post-imperialism, where capitalism has become sufficiently de-centred that it no longer has a 'home address'? The notion of post-imperialism is pre-emptive. Fred Halliday (in an essay in M. Rupert and H. Smith, ed, *Historical Materialism and Globalization,* 2002) demonstrates this by presenting a condensed 'constitution' of imperialism, which hardly seems archaic, especially with respect to Africa:

- The inexorable expansion of capitalism as a socioeconomic system on a world scale;
- The necessarily competitive, expansionist, and warlike character of developed capitalist states;
- The unequal nature of capitalist expansion, and the reproduction on a world scale of socioeconomic inequalities;
- The creation on a world scale of structures of inequality of power and wealth not only in the economic, but also social, political, legal, and cultural spheres;

The generation, through the very process of capitalist expansion, of movements of resistance, of anti-imperialism, is part of the contradictions of neoliberal globalization.

These five points serve to delineate the core of imperialism's meaning. The three earlier positions are here conflated and rearranged into corollary processes within the expansion of world capitalism. The most incisive way of using the notion of imperialism is to maintain a strong sense of historical location and to understand the contours of economic and political intervention as part of that historical process. This is the couplet that makes the notion of imperialism a useful starting point to understand Africa's global relations: structures of inequality reproduced through a capitalist system of both political and economic power. But we need also to remember that the transplanted structures of colonialism have borne their own seedlings in rapidly growing, and often rapacious, economic and political elites. The benevolent languages of liberation, development, modernization and progress are everywhere tainted by accumulation fashioned in greed and graft.

Clearly, capitalism continues its expansion and deepening penetration across and within space, but its social forms are diverse and historically-constituted, not derivative of a form of 'metropolitan' capitalism, no matter how strongly they might be influenced by the latter. For example, Marxism provides more analytical space than is generally recognized to understand processes of capitalist expansion that are not reducible to the maxim that Africa (or anywhere else) sees its future in the heartlands of capital. Imperialist dynamics play themselves out in interaction with more localized forms of accumulation and political power: the global constitution of capitalism as Gruffydd-Jones (2006) calls it; not African exceptionalism/essentialism but the complexity of social forms of accumulation in specific contexts.

In addition, there is a diversity of market processes that link societies to global flows of commodities. But, the complexity of capital's expansion needs careful treatment. The increasing attention paid to networks opens a path to insightful research on global capitalism, but it also runs the peril of downplaying what is obvious to all observers: the persistent, and historically structured concentration of power emanating from the West.

This means substantial historical continuity in the patterning of global power between North and South.

For those that doubt this, consider Marx's words in the opening quotation above and the following remarks by Lord Young, a minister in the Thatcher government and former chair of Cable and Wireless:

When you're talking about kickbacks, you're talking about something that's illegal in this country (UK)...But there are parts of the world I've been to where we all know it happens and, if you want to be in business, you have to do it.

International capital 'goes naked' in the postcolonial countries, and meets populations armed with only weak mechanisms with which to make corporations accountable. Often states fail to serve the protective needs of their populations, sometimes because of deliberate arbitrary rules shaped in elite self-aggrandizement, and sometimes because they are empty vessels long plundered and left to crumble.

But, this 'frontier' is policed by those very 'modern' states that provide the ideal type for so many World Bank institutional capacity building programmes. These rich states have embarked, in quasi private/public form, on an outreach mission to underwrite the regime of accumulation and ensure the good health of the profit margins of their own companies abroad. Western states (and other institutions) make it safer and more lucrative for international capital, notably through the 'regime of intermediacy' which regulates the flow of international finance to debt-burdened states.

The patterning of state inequalities mirrors longer histories of global economic inequality. Networks maintain themselves through the key connections they establish with large transnational firms, the latter sustaining political connections with their 'own' powerful states. A global system of states, radically unequal in their power and interrelations is intrinsic to global capitalism, not an extrinsic system with which capital has to reconcile itself. The recognition of a political economy of unequal states must necessarily be accompanied by an equally important recognition that political power and institutions also work at different levels, whether sub- or supra-national.

These different levels of power interact either to reinforce each other or to compete for citizens/subjects. The geography of security and claims to sovereignty have become extremely complex in the Democratic Republic of Congo—as a result of state collapse and the emergence of what Duffield calls 'shadow economies.' The key lesson here is that, contra the imagery of networks, 'capitalism does not just appear,' but requires political force of states and their institutions to regulate its actions: what orthodox social scientists dub security and the rule of law; what Ellen Woods would call the separation of the moments of coercion and expropriation.

In fact, imperialism rules through a chain of political linkages that bring together ruling class elites and authoritarian technocrats at the top who design the strategies and policies to be implemented by the petit bourgeois electoralists. The elite establish the national institutional parameters within which the upwardly mobile electoral petit bourgeois political class mobilizes and demobilizes the masses (Mentan 2009).

The imperialist class of the TNS establishes hegemony over the ruling class; the ruling class exercises hegemony over the petit bourgeois and the petit bourgeois maintains influence over sectors of the leadership of the mass social movements. The theoretical point is that imperialism rules via indirect hegemony. Their interests are articulated by subordinated petit bourgeois politicians via ideologies 'modified' to accommodate the demands of those below.

For example, the imperial ruling class speaks to the collaborator ruling class of free markets, easy credit, loans, reciprocal benefits in free trade and joint ventures. The ruling class speaks to the petit bourgeois of 'democracy', 'elections', 'parties', 'power sharing', economic opportunities, 'commissions' and upward mobility. The petit bourgeois electoralist bellow to the masses against 'neo-liberalism', 'globalization', the need for 'alternatives' and the corruption and venality of the 'old order'. The left electoralists mouth the rhetoric of a 'new model', of 'pressuring the elites' and of 'recapturing the party'. The social-movement leaders who are linked to electoralists tell their mass bases that 'circumstances are not ripe for a break,' 'we need to return to the bases' and 'we have to focus on sectoral reforms.' By such statements, the petit bourgeois convinces social movement leaders to refrain from independent class struggle for political power.

New Forms of Capitalist Accumulation and Expansion

The general point of the above discussion is that using imperialism as a concept does not mean reducing Africa to a passive recipient of Western intervention. New forms of accumulation emerge within Africa, products of social relations in specific places and their articulation to broader networks of trade and production. There are complexities to the interplay between state power and private economic power, an interplay that is changing its patterns in response to both external forces and popular movements.

These latter often use the language of empowerment, expressed in a right to use and have access to resources. Meanwhile, external forces are themselves hardly set in stone. In this respect, there is a complex set of relations between imperialist states, multilateral and pseudo-private agencies. Intermediary financial flows to Africa act to promote investment by 'home' companies.

These companies then become sites of contestation. New forms of accumulation are infused with new forms of inequality and differentiation. F. Cooper (1997) speaks of the 'lumpy' nature of capitalist penetration in Africa, 'places where power coalesces surrounded by those where it does not, where social relations become dense amidst others that are diffuse.' These dense nodes of accumulation are far from having socially beneficial effects. There is a broader political point that emerges here: imperialism reveals that capitalist development in Africa fails to be developmental; instead it is a story of external dominance and socially damaging and extroverted forms of accumulation.

This is why imperialism is still important, and why it provides a far more useful starting point than the blanket term 'globalization' in understanding Africa's relations with the global political economy. Embedded in critique, imperialism refuses to accept that bourgeois civilization has lived up to its own historic claims of progress and well being. Those who wish to imagine a politics of progress, development, and popular well-being would do well to (re)engage with the concept of imperialism, in order to identify and challenge both the hypocrisy of Northern idealism and self-serving discourses of benevolence.

Indeed, 'The state in Africa has become increasingly alien and harmful to the very population it rules over. It is incapable of defending the people from internal and external barbarism. Instances are that it has become part of the problem.' (Hameoso 1992). Why would this dismal situation be so after some 50 years of 'self-rule'?

The answer lies in the ...paradoxical character of the state in the continent as a whole. It is at the best of times a state split in two: a schizophrenic state, a state torn apart between… the democratic forces of the people, and… the imperialist forces of the international financial oligarchy. This split is in evidence right through all the police, the court system, the parliament and even the government itself (including the cabinet), and we might add, even the political parties. Indeed, even individual political leaders sometimes display schizophrenic tendencies when they feel impelled… to respond to the democratic demands of the people, and … feel the pressure of international capital on them which impels them to suppress those very demands (from the people) they would want to respond to but cannot (Mentan 1999).

Indeed, globalized neoliberalism has triumphed in Africa. But, the African States are enforcers or perpetrators of globalized neoliberalism, while the African people are the victims of this ideology.

In other words, the new global order under the hegemony of the neo-liberal paradigm means deregulation of national economies and undermining the African nation state. The market assumes control more and more while social policy is driven down with the argument of 'personal responsibility.' Growing impoverishment and social exclusion of ever-larger African groups are the inexorable consequences. In the course of the worldwide liberalization of markets since the seventies, tariffs and quotas to protect national economies were dismantled and borders were opened to grant boundless 'freedom of control' to transnational corporations in the name of privatization.

An increasing power shift away from the African nation state to 'global players' (transnational corporations) is in full swing. Ever more often, authorities without responsibility for the population decide upon existential questions for the whole society. Public responsibility is denied. Freedom is understood as freedom of economic concentration of power. The market itself is elevated to the organizing and regulating principle of the African state.

This book is partially predictive and partially prescriptive. Its point of departure is to examine the relationship between neoliberal globalization theory and state theory to argue that even African nation-states are the principal agents of globalization as well as the guarantors of the political and material conditions necessary for global capital accumulation. In contrast to those who see a nebulous logic of empire, a network state, or even a global state as the repositories of a new sovereignty, this book suggests that globalization, in its current form, is actually a new form of American imperialism.

However, the state in Africa has not become irrelevant with the ascendancy of global capitalism and neoliberalism. Rather, its structure and function are becoming harmonized to the interests of the globalist bloc as its loyal servant or enforcer of its policies. Hence, it is being transformed into a repressive, personalist, centralized, and clientelistic domestic neoliberal state. The current African state, as its colonial inheritance, and its instruments of repression--the military, police and bureaucracy--are therefore acting on behalf of a transnational capitalist class, rather than in its own narrow national interest.

Summary and Conclusion

Today, the world in which Africa lives is witnessing the fourth epoch in the history of capitalism. The first epoch began with the end of feudalism and the rise of mercantilism; the second was identified with the industrial revolution and the formation of the bourgeoisie and the Westphalian nation-state system; and the third came into being with corporate capitalism at the dawn of the twentieth century. Currently, at the beginning of the fourth epoch, capitalism has emerged victorious in the aftermath of two global wars and the rise and fall of international socialism.

In addition, capitalism has withstood the appeal of African and other Third World liberators who sought to establish an alternative to capitalism. The world capitalist economy is currently undergoing a transition toward a global economy. Although seemingly congruous, the definitive difference between these economies lies in their respective reach. The first three stages of capitalism operated and produced from within a nation-state serving a national economy and were financially linked to other nation-states through trade and the international market, while the current stage, thanks in large part to the technological advances of the late twentieth century, is more deeply intertwined with, and dependent on, a larger number of nations as the mobility of capital has allowed for the modes of production to cross borders.

Section Two

Early Globalization and the Commodification of the African

Preview

Until recently, Western scholarship ignored West Africa. The blind spot reflects Europe's historical view of Africa as a continent to be exploited, not examined. To Europe, Africa was a market for products and a source of raw goods. In short, it was an object of mercantilism—the economic system by which colonial powers economically exploit weaker regions. Thus, West Africa was defined in terms of economic goods—the Ivory Coast, the Gold Coast, the Slave Coast. Beneath the definitions imposed by mercantilism, however, lay a remarkable network of peoples and cultures that amazed and even frightened the West.

Nineteenth-century Europe revolutionized trade through the development of steam power that sent trains across continents and large cargo ships across the sea. Construction projects, such as the Suez Canal, were proposed to link Africa and Asia to a trade-hungry Europe. With the advent of quinine, which effectively removed the worst threat of malaria, demand for tropical goods grew. Then, in 1867, vast diamond fields were discovered in South Africa and huge resources of gold were reported. Europeans began to dream of diamonds and gold strewn across Africa. Suddenly, the interior of Africa was being pierced by iron tracks.

The political theorist Karl Marx (1967) commented on the changes that such railroads brought in their wake:

> You cannot maintain a net of railways over an immense country without introducing all those industrial processes necessary to meet the immediate and current wants of railway location, and out of which there must grow the application of machinery to those branches of industry not immediately connected with the railways. The railway system will therefore become the forerunner of modern industry. Modern industry . . . will dissolve the hereditary divisions of labour (McElroy 2005).

Back on the European continent, nations were racing to industrialize, to establish new markets for their goods and shut out their rivals. This renewed interest in colonies that could be forced to provide raw materials and cheap labour as well as buy finished goods. Inevitably, West Africa became entangled in European politics. The Franco-Prussian War of 1870 occurred at the beginning of what has been called the 'scramble for Africa.'

When Prussia defeated France, the French restored their honour by seeking conquest abroad. The astute German chancellor Otto von Bismarck encouraged such ventures because they stoked hostility between the French and English, both of whom he viewed as enemies.

The Europeans colonized with an arrogance born of nationalism and the technological age. Charles Darwin's popular theory of evolution was twisted to mean that the 'more evolved' white man had a right to preside over the 'less evolved' African. Economic factors also fuelled anti-African sentiments. For example, the British felt encumbered by indigenous barriers to commerce: that is, by the sophisticated and well-established local market network. From French Senegal down to the Niger River, a series of markets exchanged native goods for Western ones, and the markets were not necessarily under British authority. In fact, many Africans were becoming anti-British, especially when English traders used armed force. Ensuring European economic interests meant establishing political control. Eventually, they established a colonial Westphalian state system to ensure repressive control, and exploitation of African resources.

Chapter Five

Slavery and Capitalist Globalization

Overview

The legacy of slavery points to the dismantling of African manhood. On the issue of agency and structure, this legacy offers useful guidance toward recognizing the importance of both human agency and historical structures in historical processes. The European enslaving states and their roles in cross-cultural interactions acknowledge that states do not entirely control their own destinies but nevertheless deeply influence the development of these exchanges, sometimes decisively so.

Regarding the theme of the global and the local, the legacy emphasizes the reciprocal influence of global dynamics and local circumstances and agrees that analyses must take both into account to be successful. However, the theme of cross-cultural interaction is crucial to understanding the world and its development through time by probing the environment, society, and agency and historical change through the slave trade, social inequality, religious interaction, poverty, disease, racism, and urbanization.

Introduction

Globalization was the root cause of modern slavery. Slavery epitomized a most exploitative form of globalization. The slave trade may have been a type of trade, but it was not free trade. Free trade, as Adam Smith would have it, is based on voluntary exchange and mutual benefit. Moreover, goods and services that are traded must have a rightful owner and men, needless to say, cannot be owned. By definition, therefore, slave trade could never be free trade. '(B)lack slavery was essential to the carrying on of commerce, which in turn was fundamental to the making of the modern world'(James Rawley 2005: 4).

In other words, the modern world was built upon the blood, sweat, and tears of African ancestors. How? And, why? The answer is not far to seek. Capital, Karl Marx wrote, comes on the face of the earth dripping blood and dirt from head to toe. Indeed, when we look at the beginning of capitalist development, we have the impression of being in an immense concentration camp. Force was the main lever, the main economic power in the process of primitive accumulation. Capitalist development therefore required an immense leap in the wealth appropriated by the European ruling class and the number of workers brought under its command. In other words, primitive accumulation consisted in an immense accumulation of labour-power—'dead labour.' This wealth was appropriated in the form of stolen goods, 'living labour' in the form of human beings made available for exploitation. Primitive accumulation was thus realized on a scale never before matched in the course of human history. This 'living labour' was African labour.

Significantly, the tendency of the capitalist class, during the first three centuries of its existence, was to impose slavery and other forms of coerced labour as the dominant work relation, a tendency limited only by the workers' resistance and the danger of the exhaustion of the work-force. The slave trade was one of the most important business enterprises of the 17th century. The nation states of Europe stabilized themselves and developed their economy mainly at the expense of African people. During the latter half of the century; Colbert, a Frenchman, stated that, 'no commerce in the world produces as many advantages as that of the slave trade'(Williams 1970: 144).

The wealth of the New World in the form of sugar, tobacco, metals, gold, cotton, and so on, was extracted by African labour and then exported from the colonies through the capitalistic enterprise of Western Europe. Western Europe drew profits from the trade in slaves, commodities produced, service of shipping, the development of new industries based on processing raw materials, financing, and insurance. According to Eric Williams (1966: Chapter I, pp. 3–29), no other commerce required so large a capital as the slave trade which kept the wheels of metropolitan industry turning. Cities such as Liverpool, Amsterdam, and Bristol were built upon slave labour. The capital and raw materials derived from the African slave trade contributed significantly to the Commercial and Industrial Revolution.

Slavery in Africa Before European Incursions

Slavery is the social and legal designation of specific persons as property, for the purpose of providing labour and services for the owner without the right of the slave to refuse, or gain compensation. Where slavery has been a legal practice, slaves were held under the control of another person, group, organization, or state. The legal designation of slavery has become rare in modern times, as most societies now consider slavery to be illegal, and persons held as in such condition are considered by authorities to be victims of unlawful imprisonment.

A specific form, known as chattel slavery, is defined by the absolute legal ownership of a person or persons by another person or state, including the legal right to buy and sell them just as one would any common object. Historically, slaves were captured. Warfare often resulted in slavery for prisoners if no one paid ransom. It originally may have been more humane than executing those who would return to fight if they were freed, but the effect led to widespread enslavement of those of other groups; these sometimes differed in ethnicity, nationality, religion, or race, but often were the same. The dominant group in an area might take slaves with little fear of suffering a like fate, but the possibility might be present from reversals of fortune.

Slave traffic was old to Africa, with the holding of domestic slaves an integral part of the social structure. The *Krus (Klaos)* have been among the few that did not subject their own tribes to bondage, nor have they been enslaved by other tribes. They have been, throughout history, the great transporters of slaves; and while maintaining freedom for themselves; they have held other tribe members. In a great portion of the Liberian interior the system has not been extremely oppressive on the slave, and it is difficult for the stranger to distinguish a slave from a free member of the native household. They can, however, be easily enough recognized by natives; though living and working with the masters, they lack minor privileges. The Krus (Klaos) had the peculiar custom of sending the sons out with their slaves to cut palm nuts. It was imperative that the son scale the trees, even though dangerously high, to cut down the nuts; the slaves gathered them and brought them back with the tools. Behind this tradition is the idea of qualifying the sons to meet any situation' (Johnson, C.S., Bitter Canaan 1987).

European and Arab institutions of slavery compared with the African social institution of slavery were brutal and degrading and were designed to prove they were superior to Africans. European and Arab need for slave labour was 'demand driven.' By this I mean that, slave labour was essential for the achievement of their economic activities, that is, agriculture, and the mining of gold, diamonds and other minerals. Therefore, whether or not the African chiefs (headmen) cooperated with them in providing slaves for their enterprises, they would have taken them by any means possible, because this was a decision they had made prior to leaving their respective countries for Africa.

The Eastern Slave Trade

The Arab slave trade is the longest yet least discussed of the two major trades. It began in the 7th century AD as Arabs and other Asians poured into Northern and Eastern Africa under the banner of Islam, either converting or subjugating the African societies they came upon. In the beginning there was some level of mutual respect between the blacks and the more Caucasian-Semitic Arabs. Mihdja, a black man, is said to be the first Muslim killed in battle, while another, Bilal, is regarded as a 'third of the faith.' Dhu'l-Nun al-Misri, born in Upper Egypt near Sudan, is regarded as the founder of Sufism. Today Sufism's greatest stronghold is in Southern Egypt and Sudan. Islamic prosperity was based upon black as well as Arabic genius.

But as Islamic prosperity grew, so did an air of hostility towards many blacks, Muslim or otherwise. Some Arabs complained about having to work next to blacks in high positions. After the Prophet's death, even the descendants of Bilal received negative treatment. Arabic writings became laced with anti-black sentiment. The reaction of blacks at that time can be seen in the writings of a contemporary 9th century black scholar in residence at Baghdad by the name of Abu 'Uthman' Amr Ibn Bahr Al-Jahiz. Al-Jahiz, in order to confront a growing tide of anti-black sentiment in the Muslim world, published a highly controversial work at the time titled, *Kitab Fakhr As-Sudan 'Ala Al-Bidan*, 'The Book of Glory of the Blacks over the Whites.' Al-Jahiz in his work contended that even the Prophet Mohammad's father may have been of African lineage.

These new attitudes towards blacks by Arabs marked the beginning of African enslavement. Though not based solely on race, the Arab slave trade did focus heavily upon Africans whom Arabs now saw as inferior to themselves. At first these Arabs raided African villages themselves to seek humans for sale. This not being always successful, they soon enlisted the aid of fellow African Muslims or recently converted blacks. Wrapping themselves within Islam, these converts rationalized the slavery of their non Muslim brethren as the selling of 'unbelievers.' At other times the Arabs would demand tribute in the form of human bodies from Africans weary of the fight against Arabic-Islamic incursions. The Arabs took advantage of regional wars in Africa to buy captives from the victor. They also used the old divide-and-conquer technique. They worked one group against the other and took or killed the best and strongest.

The Arab slavers raided at nightfall, during dinner time. Africans who resisted or tried to run were shot and killed. Most adult men were killed as the Arabs favoured women and children for sale. The captives then endured a long and torturous march through the African countryside as the slavers searched and gathered more captives. Young men, women, and children were bound by hand and by neck throughout this journey, enduring beatings and rapes along the way. Those who fell sick or dead were left behind. Others remained bound to living captives.

After surviving the torturous ride aboard the Arab slave ships, Africans were taken to the slave markets. Here Muslim men would inspect their intended purchases. Women and young girls were degradingly probed by these men in public or private stalls to test their sexual worth. Those that did not survive their time in these markets were left out to rot. It is said that hyenas, very numerous in the region, gorged themselves on human flesh.

The Eastern slave trade dealt primarily with African women: a ratio of two women for each man. These women and young girls were used by Arabs and other Asians as concubines. Filling the harems of wealthy Arabs, they often bore them a host of children. This sexual abuse of African women would continue for nearly 1200 years.

The Eastern slave trade also dealt in the sale of castrated male slaves: *Aghas* or eunuchs. Used as guards and tutors, these slaves were central to familial peace, protection and order in many wealthy Muslim households. Eunuchs were created by completely amputating the scrotum and penis of 8-to-12-year-old African boys. Hundreds of thousands of young boys may have been subjected to this genital mutilation. Many bled to death during the gory procedure. The survival rate of this process ranged from 1 in 10 to 1 in 30. Owing to the enormous length of the Arab slave trade, from 700 to 1911AD, it is impossible to be certain of the number of Africans sold in this system. Estimates place the number somewhere around 14 million: at least 9.6 million African women and 4.4 million African men.

Globalization of African Labour Power

The Industrial Revolution in Europe represents the first face in the history of globalization of African labour. The explanation as given by Mazrui (2005) in a lecture is that 'This marriage between technology and economics resulted in previously unknown levels of productivity. Europe's prosperity whetted its appetite for new worlds to conquer. The Atlantic slave trade was accelerated, moving millions of Africans from one part of the world to another.' The first act of globalization against Africa by Europe was a unilateral act of war, announced or unannounced. Were there any African kings or queens in any of the European countries or in the US when ships set sail for Africa to capture slaves for profit? The obvious answer is: No!

Europeans had already decided to raid Africa for slaves. They didn't need the agreement of Africans on that. Hence, the concept of 'trade' is a fallacy. The African so-called slave 'trade' was a demand-driven market out of Europe and America. It was not a supply-driven market out of Africa. Africans did not seek to sell captives to the Europeans as an original act. Slavery in one form or another is therefore intrinsic to the global ideology of capitalist expansion. And in this process of capitalist globalization the African slave was controlled, dominated, exploited and animalized.

European Mercantilist Assaults on Africa

The earliest phase of capitalist globalization took the form of the destruction of African governance institutions, ripping apart the social fabric, and domination of the continent. Karl Marx (1967) referred to this epoch in capitalist development as 'primitive accumulation' or the period when the West was breaking free from feudalism but had not yet entered the era of capitalism. According to Hopkins (1973: 87):

> In the three centuries before the industrial revolution the focus of the trade moved from the Mediterranean to the Atlantic, from Venice and Genoa to Liverpool and Nantes. This momentous shift of economic power was the product of fundamental changes in the economic and technological basis of European society at the close of the Middle Ages.

The boost in trade increased the wealth of European merchants and enhanced their power. Historically, this form of domination of Africa corresponds to the era of mercantilism in Europe, a period which set the stage for the eventual collapse of European feudalism. The West used every crude method in their penetration, domination and exploitation of African society. The purpose was not to rule or govern; the purpose was unrestrained looting and plunder without parallel in Africa's history. The most horrendous form of it lasted from the fifteenth century to the early eighteenth century (Williams 1966; Hopkins,1973: note 3,pp. 78-117).

According to Marx, the history of this period is written in the annals of mankind in 'letters of wood and fire.'(Karl Marx 'Capital,' vol. 1, note 2), p. 714). It was characterized by 'the turning of Africa into a warren for the commercial hunting of black skins.'(Marx, ibid.: 751).

The effects of this period in Africa can be briefly summarized as follows:

(a) massive depletion of the African population, especially among the most relevant and productive groups;
(b) massive destruction of the entire fabric of African society -disruptions in socio-cultural relationships and, above all, the diversion of interest from productive activities to plunder and loot as a way of life; and
(c) the pillage of the resources of Africa under the guise of international trade.(Okolo 1982:68-103).

Hopkins (ibid. : note. 3:117) sums it up more succinctly that 'The chief effect of the overseas slave trade in the New World was to populate and develop the abundant land resources of the Americas and the West Indies.' He further observes:

> It remains true that the slave and sugar trades brought great wealth too the principal entrepots, such as Liverpool and Nantes, and to manyother leading cities. It is impossible to account for the economic vitality of these parts in the eighteenth century, their physical and demographic expansion, and the remarkable overflow of money into cultural activities, without stressing the causative, though not exclusive, role of the Atlantic commerce.(ibid.: 117-118 and Walter Rodney 1973: 103-162).

Slavery as an Institution of Globalization

When in 1492, Columbus, representing the Spanish monarch, discovered the New World, he set in train the long and bitter international rivalry over colonial possessions for which, after four and a half centuries, no solution has yet been found. Portugal, which had initiated the movement of international expansion, claimed the new territories on the grounds that they fell within the scope of a papal bull of 1455 authorizing her to reduce to servitude all infidel people. In order to avoid controversy Spain and Portugal sought arbitration and, as Catholic powers, turned to the pope—a natural and logical step in an age when the universal claims of the papacy were still unchallenged by individuals and governments. After carefully sifting the rival claims, the pope issued, in 1493, a series of papal bulls which established a line of demarcation between the colonial possessions of the states: the east went to Portugal and the west to Spain.

Although the announcement of the fact came much later, the European 'Scramble for Africa,' and subsequently Asia and North America, started with this act. The labour and raw materials of Africa, Asia, South America, and the West Indies financed the European Industrial Revolution. In the year 1457, the Council of Cardinals met in Holland and sanctioned, as a righteous and progressive idea, the enslavement of Africans for the purpose of their conversion to Christianity, and their exploitation in the labour market as chattel property.

This demonic scheme speedily gained the sanctimonious blessing of the pope and became a standard policy of the Roman Catholic Church and later the Protestant Churches, enduring three centuries. And thus the ghastly traffic in human misery was given the cloak of respectability and anointed with the oil of pontifical righteousness in Jesus' name. And so, the slave trade began, inaugurating an era that stands out as the most gruesome and macabre example of man's disregard for the humanity of man.

There is no way to understand the African slave trade without understanding slavery as an institution. It is almost as old as human societies. Every people has at some time or another been slaves! In fact,

Europeans enslaved other Europeans for a much longer time than they enslaved Africans. Yet this slavery did not give birth to racism, though it did lay the basis for feudalism.

Slavery was a permanent feature of the ancient world, in Egypt, Kush, Greece and Rome. The African slave period is best known because it is the most recent—and the best documented. These documents on slavery have often done more to confuse the issue than to explain the subject. Most people write about slavery in a manner that makes the victim feel guilty. There is probably more dishonesty related to the interpretation of this subject than any other known to man.

The 'Christians' of European descent have never felt at ease in an honest discussion of this subject, because every examination of the subject will prove that slavery and the slave trade were the incubator for present day racism (Montagu 1963: 2–3). Lord Bryce(Snyder 1962: 25–39), says that: 'self-conscious racial feeling hardly existed in any country until the French Revolution.' In spite of what seems to be an exaggeration, there is more than an element of truth in what Lord Bryce has said if we qualify this by making a distinction between racism, which was rampant, and self-conscious racial feeling, which was developing.

From the sixteenth century onward, Europeans ranged the earth conquering, mainly, defenceless people. They set themselves up as ruling aristocracies. In this world-wide rape of peoples and countries, they destroyed many cultures and civilizations that were old before Europe was born. Their rationales and justifications for these actions were the rankest form of racism ever conceived by the human mind. This tragedy continued during the era of colonialization in the sixteenth and seventeenth centuries and again in the era of neo-mercantilist revival called imperialism that had so many articulate defenders in the nineteenth century.

The Christian Church was the handmaiden for the development of racism. While it propagated the theory that all men were created equal in the sight of God, in practice, it found all sorts of arguments to prove that non-European peoples, especially black men, were inferior and could not be considered as men in the general sense. A search for ways to justify European domination over most of mankind led biologists to the works of Linnaeus and Buffon. Thus, the classification of races began. In deciding the distinctions between higher and lower races, the Europeans, of course, became the hierarch of races. In many ways this was a continuation of the rationales set up to justify the slave trade. We will have to look at this trade, and the periods of its development again and again in order to understand that we are now reaping the bitter harvest of human discord and social dislocation that was planted over five hundred years ago.

The African slave trade—like African history in general—is often written about and rarely ever understood. The story of the African slave trade (Davidson 1961, Chapter I, and pp 1–25) is essentially the story of the consequences between the passing of the Roman Empire in the eighth century and the partial unification of Europe, through the framework of the Catholic Church. In the fifteenth century, Europeans were engaged mainly in internal matters within their own continent. With the opening up of the New World, after the expulsion of the Moors from Spain during the latter part of the fifteenth century, the Europeans started to expand beyond their homeland, into the broader world. They were searching for new markets and materials, new manpower and new lands to exploit.

The African slave trade was created to accommodate this new expansion.

The Europeans, mainly the Portuguese who came to the West Coast of Africa in the fifteenth century, were not at first looking for slaves. The search for gold and other treasures lured them to Africa. They did not have to fight their way onto the continent. They came as guests and were treated as guests. Finally, when they grew strong enough, they turned on their hosts and decided to stay as conquerors. The basis for the future European industrial revolution had already been established. They had already created an embryo technology—principally the gun.

The Chinese had gunpowder before the rise of Europe and the African had iron. It is interesting to speculate on why they did not put the iron and gunpowder together and form a partnership to take over the world, inasmuch as they knew each other and were carrying on peaceful trade for a number of years, along the coast of East Africa. The Europeans created the gun to protect themselves from other Europeans. During the fifteenth century, they found other territories for this weapon, though they still needed it in the never-ending wars with their neighbours.

In the centuries that followed, they used this weapon and other advantages, mainly a large fleet of ships and mercenary sailors and soldiers, to take over most of the world. In so doing, they destroyed a large number of nations and civilizations that were older than Europe. In order to justify this destruction, a monster that still haunts African lives was created: racism. The slave trade and the colonial system that followed were, figuratively, the mother and father of this catastrophe.

The opening up of the New World opened up more than new territory. It opened up a new era in human relations, mostly bad. The Europeans, being 'Christians,' had to find a way to live with their consciences after the formal starting of the slave trade. The Africans made the original mistake of asking the Europeans to settle some of their family disputes. Unfortunately, the Europeans many times conquered both branches of the family.

The Europeans were no strangers to Africa, and this really wasn't their first meeting. But in order to justify the slave trade, they had to forget, or pretend to forget, all that they had previously known about Africa. They had to forget that a lot of the early culture of Europe has an African base. They also had to forget that there were periods when Africans and Europeans lived in comparative harmony and Europeans married into African royalty and saw no difference in one royal personage and another. Therefore, the Europeans had to forget that the Africans had a history and a heritage that could command respect.

In the opening up of the territory called the New World, two competing slave systems were set in motion, and each of these systems served as some form of racism. The dehumanization of the African had started in European textbooks, geographies, and travel books. In South America and the Caribbean, the plantation owners generally bought slaves in large lots and kept the lots together principally because they thought they could work them better that way—and they were right. In the United States, however, where the most vicious form of racism was manifested, the slavery system operated more like a brokerage system. A plantation owner could and would very often buy ten slaves and re-sell five of them before the end of the week. This meant the immediate breaking up of the cultural continuity, linguistic continuity, and all the other things that held the African together within Africa. This discontinuity, therefore, created a family dislocation that the African American has not recovered from right up to this day. This dislocation was also a form of racism.

The mentality, the rationales, and the various ways of justifying the slave trade had already started in Europe with Europeans attempting to justify the enslavement of other Europeans. This is a neglected aspect of history that is rarely ever taken into consideration. There was at first a concerted effort to obtain European labour to open up the vast regions of the New World. It is often forgotten that, in what became the United States, white enslavement started before African enslavement.

In an article, 'White Servitude in the United States,' *Ebony Magazine*, November, 1969, the African American historian Lerone Bennett, Jr., gives the following information about this period: 'When someone removes the cataracts of whiteness from our eyes, and when we look with unclouded vision on the bloody shadows of the American past, we will recognize for the first time that the Afro-American, who was so often second in freedom, was also second in slavery.'

In fact, white servitude was the historic proving ground for the mechanisms of control and subordination used in Afro-American slavery. The plantation pass, the fugitive slave law, the use of the overseer and the house servant and the Uncle Tom, the forced separation of parents and children on the auction block and the sexual exploitation of servant women, the whipping post, the slave chains, the branding iron; all these mechanisms were tried out and perfected first on white men and white women.

The enslavement of both 'red' men and white men in the early American colonies was a contradiction of English law. The colonies were founded with the understanding that neither chattel slavery nor villeinage would be recognized. Yet, forced labour was widely used in England. This system was transferred to the colonies and used to justify a form of slavery that was visited upon 'red' and white men (Hart 1906/1969).

It was decreed that the apprentice must serve his seven years, and take floggings as his master saw fit; the hired servant must carry out his contract for his term of service; convicts of the state, often including political offenders, were slaves of the state and sometimes sold to private owners overseas. The colonists claimed those rights over some of their white fellow countrymen. A large class of 'redemptioners' had agreed that their service should be sold for a brief term of years to pay their passage money. There was also a class of 'indentured' or 'indented' servants bought by their masters and under legal obligation to serve for a term of years and subject to the same penalties of branding, whipping and mutilation as African slaves. These forms of servitude were supposed to be limited in duration and transmitted no claim to the servant's children. In spite of this servitude, the presumption, in law, was that a white man was born free.

The English settlers had, at once, begun to enslave their Indian neighbours, soothing their consciences with the argument that it was right to make slaves of pagans. In large numbers, the Indians fled or died in captivity, leaving few of their descendants in bondage. The virgin soil of the new English settlements continued to need more labour. This led to a fierce search for white labour that subsequently led to a search for African labour.

Slavery and the Rise of Capitalist Globalization

Slavery existed in Africa before the transatlantic variant. But, it was never the dominant mode of labour mobilization on the continent at any period before European ravages. The dominant forms of labour mobilization over the broad span of African history involved kinship relations and tribute labour within relatively localized political communities. Indigenous African slavery systems tended to exist in relation and distinction to such primary means of mobilization.

Slavery was therefore defined primarily as kinlessness, marginality, lack of capacity to make social claims in return for labour or subordination in the locally normal way. Such labour relations in Africa were rather like those in the plantation production in the Americas and elsewhere at the time. That is, they represented a sort of proto-proletarianization in which physical coercion of alienated labour operated mainly through direct control of the bodies of labourers, and it was their bodies, rather than their labour-power, that were commoditized.

The horrors of the New World slave system are staggering. The slave population of the Americas reached 33,000 in 1700, nearly three million in 1800 and peaked at over six million in 1850. During this period a million and a half died during the passage to the New World, large numbers died beforehand and between a tenth and a fifth died within a year of landing. This huge and businesslike system remains one of the great tragedies of human history. Robin Blackburn (1997:5) suggests that it points us towards the 'dark side of progress' in that the inhumanity of the system developed side by side with huge steps forward in knowledge and technique, such as the exploration of the Atlantic and the development of new navigational techniques. At the heart of the system lay a huge contradiction.

The people who colonized the New World were largely those who rejected most strongly the old order in Europe. Yet just as unfree labour was dying out in Europe it began to develop on a massive new scale in the Americas. This contradiction was only resolved by the complete radicalization of New World slavery so that skin colour and slavery became inextricably linked. Apologists for the system argue that slavery had always existed. This may be true but history would become meaningless if reduced to such generalities. History must aim to uncover the historic specificity of social forms as well as their links with the past. The Atlantic slave system did indeed emerge from previous systems but in the process slavery was extended in scale and transformed in form.

Blackburn traces the emergence of the slave trade from existing patterns of slavery in Africa. The story follows the Portuguese discoveries and the origins of the Atlantic slave trade through to the emergence of Brazilian sugar from 1600. However, it was the English colonial system that really developed and eventually dominated the Atlantic trade and the system of slave plantations. The profits of slavery were central to the primitive accumulation that paved the way for English industrialization. England's unique economic position both assisted and was assisted by the development of the colonies. The capitalist transformation of agriculture helped to create a landless proletariat which was available for emigration or for wage labour in England. The transformation of the English economy helped to create a market for the new goods of the colonies. Initially, it was wage labour which worked the new plantations in Barbados and elsewhere. British emigrants would be contracted to work as indentured servants for three, five or seven years for the plantation after which they would be free to pursue other employment. In 1638 Barbados had 2,000 indentured servants and only 200 African slaves. By 1653 there were 20,000 slaves and only 8,000 indentured servants.

European indentured servants faced enormous hardships on the estates. The work was extremely hard, conditions appalling and life expectancy was short. Escaped servants were made to serve double time for their master. A repeated escape could lead to branding. Like slaves, the servant was regarded as a piece of property and was valued according to the amount of tobacco or sugar that could be expected to be produced before the indenture expired.

The plantation owners faced two problems. As the demand for the plantation exports rose rapidly, they needed more and more labour. As emigration from Britain was, by and large, voluntary it could not guarantee to meet the needs of the system. At the same time, stories drifted back of life in the colonies which tended to discourage volunteers for the indenture system. Thus it was the growing demand for secure supplies of labour which produced the shift towards African slavery. In this context, the mid-seventeenth century saw the rapid growth of the slave plantation in the English Caribbean.

This explanation of the rise of Caribbean slavery was pioneered by Eric Williams (1943) who outlined the shifts from enslavement of the local Indian populations, to the use of European convict or indentured labour to African slavery. In Williams' words, the origin of black slavery lay with economic, not racial motives: 'It had to do not with the colour of the labourer, but the cheapness of the labour.'(rev.1964:19).

Slavery and Primitive Accumulation

Africans sold into the Atlantic slave trade (or one of the northern and eastern routes leading to the core Islamic world) were human beings turned into chattel, that is subject not only to the ownership of others (this is characteristic of many forms of servitude throughout human experience) but even used as commodities and capital to be exchanged for or invested in the production of non-human goods. Critical to Eric Williams' work was the hypothesis that the profits of the 'triangular trade' between Europe, Africa and the New World had 'made an enormous contribution to Britain's industrial development.' (ibid.: 105).

However, this view has been controversial among historians, including Marxists. Firstly, slavery has tended to be seen as a backward and unproductive system which could not therefore have produced sufficient profits to assist capitalist accumulation. Secondly, the debate on the transition to capitalism has tended to focus on the internal economic and social changes that were necessary for capitalist development. This debate has tended to ignore or minimize the role of external factors.

Blackburn draws on many recent studies of the economics of New World slavery. Using a variety of quantitative techniques, economic historians have been able to show that the slave plantation could be a profitable enterprise that could compete well with other possible investments (ibid: Chapter IX). This was the case despite a variety of factors which did tend to make the plantation system resistant to innovation. The second issue, of slavery and the transition to capitalism, relates to a question raised by Marx. Marx pointed out the various ways in which capitalism reproduced the conditions for its existence. However, there remained a problem:

> The accumulation of capital pre-supposes surplus-value; surplus-value pre-supposes capitalistic production; capitalistic production pre-supposes the pre-existence of considerable masses of capital and of labour-power... The whole movement, therefore, seems to turn in a vicious circle, out of which we can only get by supposing a primitive accumulation... an accumulation not the result of the capitalist mode of production, but its starting point *(ibid.*:667).

The development of capitalism required a number of transformations such as the creation of wage-labour. Once capitalism was established it became a continuous process of reproducing and expanding investment. What Marx asks here, however, is: what was the source of the original funds for capitalist investment?

Marx himself was well aware that the history of capitalism provided a number of possible sources. 'The discovery of gold and silver in America, the extirpation, enslavement and entombment in mines of the aboriginal population, the beginning of the conquest and looting of the East Indies, the turning of Africa into a warren for the commercial hunting of black skins, signalized the rosy dawn of the era of capitalist production. These idyllic proceedings are the chief moments of primitive accumulation.' (Marx, ibid., Ch.XXXI, p.703).

Again Blackburn argues that the most recent research tends to support the 'Williams thesis'. For example, a number of historians have revised down the growth rate of the British economy during the industrial revolution. Blackburn suggests that this would strengthen the role of colonial trade in funding industrialization. Working on figures for 1770, Blackburn argues that triangular trade profits may have provided anything between 20.9% and 55% of Britain's gross fixed capital formation.

Plantation profits may have assisted economic development in a number of ways. By increasing the general prosperity of the economy they may have boosted the industrialization process. They may also have eased the credit difficulties of the new industrialists. The early industrial processes involved a lengthy turnover time. In other words a capitalist might have to wait a long time to realize the profits from an investment. In such circumstances credit was vital. The profits of slavery helped to lubricate this process. Financial bills, drawn on plantation products such as sugar or tobacco, began to circulate as a form of money. In the absence of sufficient institutional sources of credit, plantation funds helped to fill the gap.

American Slavery as Capitalist Relation of Production

The history of the United States—indeed, the history of the entire New World—has been dominated by the theme of slavery and freedom (Davis and Steven Mintz 1998). In the 320 years from 1500 to 1820, every European immigrant who arrived in the New World was matched by at least two African slaves. It was African slaves and their descendants who furnished the basic labour power that created dynamic New World economies and the first international mass markets for such consumer goods as sugar, rice, tobacco, dyestuffs, and cotton (Bushman 1998: 351–74).

Yet, from the outset, the New World was seen by many, like the biblical Promised Land, as a space for new beginnings, for possibilities that would break free from the coercive bondage to the past. Paradoxically, the debasement of millions of workers to a supposedly bestial condition of repetitive time appeared to liberate other human beings to take control of their destiny, to 'remake' themselves. This profound contradiction lay close to the core of the self-presentation of the new United States, which was 'conceived in liberty' but based on slave labour, dedicated to certain 'propositions' or principles, such as 'all men are created equal,' but no less committed to compromises that protected the autonomy and political power of men who owned human property.

The slave system in America was unique in human history. Sometimes slaves were treated cruelly; at other times with kindness. They were more often used as a sign of affluence, a way of displaying one's wealth and of enjoying luxury, rather than as the means for the systematic accumulation of wealth. Previously, slavery had existed in hierarchical societies in which the slave was at the bottom of a social ladder, the most inferior in a society of unequals. While each society normally preferred to choose its slaves from alien people, it did not limit its selection exclusively to the members of any one race. Slave inferiority did not lead necessarily to racial inferiority. In contrast to this, slavery in America was set apart by three characteristics: capitalism, individualism, and racism.

Capitalism increased the degree of dehumanization and depersonalization implicit in the institution of slavery. While it had been normal in other forms of slavery for the slave to be legally defined as a thing, a piece of property, in America he also became a form of capital. Here his life was regimented to fill the needs of a highly organized productive system sensitively attuned to the driving forces of competitive free enterprise. American masters were probably no crueller and no more sadistic than others, and, in fact, the spread of humanitarianism in the modern world may have made the opposite true. Nevertheless, their capitalistic mentality firmly fixed their eyes on minimizing expenses and maximizing profits. Besides being a piece of property, the American slave was transformed into part of the plantation machine, a part of the ever-growing investment in the master mushrooming wealth.

The development of slavery in America resulted from the working of economic forces and not from climatic or geographic conditions. When the first twenty Africans reached Virginia in 1619, the colony comprised small plantations dependent on free white labour. While some historians believe that these immigrants were held in slavery from the beginning, most think they were given the status of indentured servants. English law contained no such category as slavery, and the institution did not receive legal justification in the colony until early in the 1660s. Although the fact of slavery had undoubtedly preceded its legal definition, there was a period of forty years within which the Africans had some room for personal freedom and individual opportunity. Rumours of deplorable working conditions and of indefinite servitude were reaching England and discouraging the flow of free white labour. To counter this, a series of acts was passed that legally established the rights of white labour, but they did nothing to improve the status of the African. In fact, their passage pushed them relentlessly towards the status of slave.

The price of tobacco declined sharply in the 1660s and drove the small white farmer to the wall. Only those with enough capital to engage in large-scale operations could continue to make a profit. In order to fill the need for the huge labour supply required by large-scale agriculture, the colonial legislature passed laws giving legal justification to slavery. At the same time, Charles II granted a royal charter establishing a company to transport African slaves across the ocean and thereby increase the supply of slaves available to the colonial planter.

Until this time, the number of Africans in the colony had been very small, but thereafter their numbers grew rapidly. The African slaves provided the large, dependable, and permanent supply of labour that these plantations required. The small white planter and the free white labourer found the road to economic success had become much more difficult. To be a successful planter meant beginning with substantial capital investment. Capitalist agriculture substantially altered the social structure of the colony. On one hand, it created a small class of rich and powerful white planters. On the other, it victimized the small white planters, or white labourers, and the ever-growing mass of African slaves.

The second unique factor in American slavery was the growth of individualism. While this democratic spirit attracted many European immigrants, it only served to increase the burden of slavery for the African. Instead of being at the bottom of the social ladder, the slave in America was an inferior among equals. A society that represented itself as recognizing individual worth and providing room for the development of talent rigidly organized the entire life of the slave and gave him little opportunity to develop his skills. In America, a person's worth became identified with economic achievement. To be a success in Virginia was to be a prosperous planter, and white individualism could easily become white oppression leaving no room for black individualism. The existence of slavery in a society that maintained its belief in equality was a contradiction that men strove diligently to ignore.

Perhaps this contradiction can be partly understood by seeing the way in which individual rights had come into being in English society. Instead of springing from a belief in abstract human rights, they were an accumulation of concrete legal and political privileges that had developed since Magna Carta. Viewing it in this light, it may have been easier for the white colonists to insist on their rights while denying them to the slaves. Nevertheless, the existence of slavery in the midst of a society believing in individualism increased its dehumanizing effects.

The third characteristic that set American slavery apart was its racial basis. In America, with only a few early and insignificant exceptions, all slaves were Africans, and almost all Africans were slaves. This placed the label of inferiority on black skin and on African culture. In other societies, it had been possible for a slave who obtained his freedom to take his place in society with relative ease. In America, however, when a slave became free, he was still obviously an African. The taint of inferiority clung to him. Not only did white America become convinced of white superiority and black inferiority, but it strove to impose these racial beliefs on the Africans themselves.

Slave masters gave a great deal of attention to the education and training of the ideal slave, In general, there were five steps in moulding the character of such a slave: strict discipline, a sense of his own inferiority, belief in the master's superior power, acceptance of the master's standards, and, finally, a deep sense of his own helplessness and dependence. At every point this education was built on the belief in white superiority and black inferiority. Besides teaching the slave to despise his own history and culture, the master strove to inculcate his own value system into the African's outlook. The white man's belief in the African's inferiority paralleled African self hate.

Slavery has always been an evil institution, and being a slave has always been undesirable. However, the slave in America was systematically exploited for the accumulation of wealth. Being a slave in a democracy, he was put outside the bounds of society. Finally, because his slavery was racially defined, his plight was incurable. Although he might flee from slavery, he could not escape his race.

In the seventeenth century, while the British colonies were being established in North America and their slave system was being created, the English Crown underwent a series of severe shocks including two revolutions. Although it eventually emerged secure, the monarchy managed to survive only by making its peace with the emerging commercial and industrial forces. These same crises undermined the authority of the Church as a powerful institution in society. The nonconformist sects were the stronghold of the merchant class and spread rapidly in the American colonies. There, instead of being a check on the commercial spirit, the Church itself had become dominated by the middle class.

Equally important is the fact that in colonial America the level of religious life was very low. Most colonists, with the exception of the original founders who had fled religious persecution, did not come for religious freedom but for economic advancement. When some Virginians at the end of the seventeenth century, petitioned the government to build a college for the training of ministers, they were told to forget about the cure of souls and instead to cure tobacco. The result was that the planter class, unchallenged by any other powerful institutions, was free to shape a slave system to meet its labour needs. In any conflict that arose between personality rights and property rights, the property rights of the master were always protected.

In contrast, the South American planter would not have such a free hand in shaping his own affairs. The Renaissance and Reformation had not made the same impact on Spain and Portugal as they had on the rest of Western Europe. Consequently, secularization and commercialization had not progressed as far in eroding the traditional power and prestige of the Crown and the Church. Although both institutions readily compromised with capitalist interests and strove to develop a working alliance with them, neither the Crown nor the Church in Spain and Portugal had ever been taken over by the commercial interests.

Both Spain and Portugal had had continuous contact with slavery extending back into ancient times. Roman law as well as the Church fathers had concerned themselves with it, and these concepts had been incorporated into Spanish and Portuguese law. Also, slaves continued to exist in both countries down to modern times. Therefore, when Portugal began importing slaves from West Africa in the fifteenth century, the institution of slavery was already in existence. Before long, significant numbers of African slaves were to be found in both Portugal and Spain. When the South American planters began importing slaves, slavery already had a framework and a tradition within which the planter had to operate.

The Spanish Crown devoted a great deal of time and energy to the supervision of its overseas possessions. Instead of permitting considerable local autonomy as the British did, the Spanish Council of the Indies in Madrid assumed a stance of illiberal, paternal, bureaucratic control. From the point of view of the colonial capitalists, the cumbersome royal bureaucracy was always involved in troublesome meddling that impeded their progress. As part of the careful management of its colonies, the Crown strove to control the operation of the slave trade. Similarly, it was concerned with the treatment of the African slaves within the colonies. The Spanish Crown included the slaves as persons instead of relegating them solely to the status of property at the disposal of their owners. The Church, as a powerful institution, jealously guarded its right to be the guardian and protector of social morality. Besides being concerned with influencing individual behaviour, the Church insisted that it was a social institution with the right to interfere in matters relating to public morals.

In fact, it was through this role that the Church was able to exercise its worldly powers. While condemning slavery as an evil and warning that it endangered those who participated in it, the Church found it expedient to accept slavery as a labour system. However, it insisted that the African slaves must be Christianized. Missionaries were sent to the trading stations on the African coast where the captives were baptized and catechized. The Church feared that the purity of the faith might be undermined by the infusion of pagan influences. Then, when a slave ship reached the New World, a friar boarded the ship and examined the slaves to see that the requirements had been met. The Church also insisted that the slaves become regular communicants, and it liked to view itself as the champion of their human rights.

The degree to which the individual rights of the slave were either protected or totally suppressed provides a clearer insight into the differences between North American and South American slavery. The laws outlining the rights of slaves have been traditionally placed into four categories: term of servitude, marriage and the family, police and disciplinary powers, and, finally, property and other civil rights. In both systems the term of servitude was for life, and the child's status was inherited from its mother. Children of slave mothers were slaves, and children of free mothers were free regardless of the status of the father. Inherited lifetime slavery was the norm.

Manumission—granting freedom—was infrequent in British North America. Occasionally, masters who had fathered slave children would later give them their freedom. A few other slaves were able to purchase their own freedom although, strictly speaking, this was a legal impossibility. The slave was not able to own property according to the law, and this meant that the money with which he purchased his freedom had always belonged to his master. Obviously, he could only do this with his master's fullest cooperation.

In South America, however, manumission was much more frequent. This practice received highly favourable social sanction, and masters often celebrated national holidays, anniversaries, birthdays, and other special events by manumitting one or more of their favourite slaves. The law also defended the right of the slave to purchase his own freedom. He had the right to own property and could accumulate funds with which he might eventually achieve his dream. He also had the right to demand that his master or the courts set a fixed price for his purchase which he could then pay over a period of years. Sundays and holidays were for the slave to use as he saw fit, and, in some cases, he was also guaranteed a couple of hours every day for his own use. During this time he could sell his services and save the proceeds. The law also stated that parents of ten or more children were to be set free. Finally, slaves could be freed by the courts as the result of mistreatment by their masters.

While there was much sentiment in North America supporting marriages among slaves, and there was much animosity against masters who separated families through sale, the law was unambiguous on this point. Slaves were property, and therefore could not enter into contracts, including contracts of marriage. Jurists also noted that to prevent the sale of separate members of a family would lower the sale price, and this was to tamper with a man's property. Therefore, property rights had to be placed above marriage rights. In contrast, in South America the Church insisted that slave unions be brought within the sacrament of marriage.

The Church also strove to limit promiscuous relationships between slaves as well as between masters and slaves, and it encouraged marriage instead of informal mating. Also, the law forbade the separate sale of members of the family, husband, wife, and children under the age of ten.

The general thrust of the laws outlining police and disciplinary powers in North America was to entrust complete jurisdiction to the master. One judge had laid down the law that the master's power must be absolute in order to render slave obedience perfect, and, although the courts were empowered to discipline slaves in certain situations, the masters generally acted as judges, juries, and dispensers of punishment. In those rare cases where the law did protect the slave against extreme mistreatment, its protection was nullified by the universal proscription against any slave or black person testifying in court against any white. The court also had assumed that it was irrational for a man to destroy his own property, and, therefore, it was impossible for a master to commit premeditated murder against one of his own slaves.

However, in South America the court exercised much more jurisdiction over the slave. Crimes committed by a slave were prosecuted by the court, and, if a slave was murdered, this case was prosecuted by the court as if the victim had been a free man. The law also made a more concerted attempt to protect the slave against mistreatment by his master. A certain type of state lawyer was an official protector of the slaves; he received regular reports on slave conditions from priests as well as from special investigative officials who had been appointed by the state for this purpose. Mistreatment could lead both to the freedom of the slave and to the imprisoning of the master. The law had devised an ingenious system whereby the fine was divided equally between the judge, the informer, and the state treasury.

Finally, the slave in North America could not own property and had absolutely no civil rights. The law clearly stated that the slave could not own or inherit property, nor engage in buying and selling except at the pleasure of his master. In contrast, the slave in South America could own property, could engage in buying and selling, and was guaranteed Sundays, holidays, and other times to work for his own advancement. In short, the law implied that while the master could own a man's labour, he could not own the man as a person.

It is not easy to make a final comparison between these two slave systems. South American masters often evaded the law and could be exceedingly brutal, and North American masters were often much more lenient than the law required. Conditions moreover, were usually more severe in South America, and this fact may have worsened the actual material situation of the South American slave. Nevertheless, in North America the slave was consistently treated as a 'thing.' In South America there was some attempt to treat him as a man. This fact made a profound difference in the way in which the two systems affected the slave as an individual, and in the way in which they impinged upon the development of his personality.

Slaveryand Character Deformation

The study of American slavery, frequently consisting of a heated debate concerning the institution's merits, has, in recent years, branched into new directions. Scholars have become engaged in the comparative examination of differing slave systems such as those of North and South America. More recently, Stanley M. Elkins has begun an enquiry into the impact of a slave system in forming the individual character of the slaves within that system. In his provocative study, Slavery: A Problem in American Institutional and Intellectual Life, he has made some interesting comparisons between the American slave system and the German concentration camps and has endeavoured to account for their respective impacts on character formation through the social- psychological theories of personality formation.

In Elkins's thinking, the concentration camps were a modern example of a rigid system controlling mass behaviour. Because some of those who experienced them were social scientists trained in the skills of observation and analysis, they provide a basis for insights into the way in which a particular social system can influence mass character. While there is also much literature about American slavery written both by slaves and masters, none of it was written from the viewpoint of modern social sciences. However, Elkins postulates that a slave type must have existed as the result of the attempt to control mass behaviour, and he believes that this type probably bore a marked resemblance to the literary stereotype of 'Sambo.' Studying concentration camps and their impact on personality provides a tool for new insights into the working of slavery, but, warns Elkins, the comparison can only be used for limited purposes. Although slavery was not unlike the concentration camp in many respects, the concentration camp can be viewed as a highly perverted form of slavery, and both systems were ways of controlling mass behaviour.

The 'Sambo' of American slave literature was portrayed as being docile but irresponsible, loyal but lazy, humble but chronically given to lying and stealing. He was a child figure, often demonstrating infantile silliness and exaggeration, exasperating but lovable and, above all, utterly dependent on and attached to his master. The master explained this behaviour as the result of the slave's race or of his primitive African culture. While assuming that many slaves did approximate to the character of 'Sambo,' Elkins absolutely rejects any racial or cultural explanation. Modern African studies have not led to any evidence of a 'Sambo' type in Africa. Similarly, the literature of South America does not contain any figure comparable to him.

Apparently, 'Sambo' was not merely the result of slavery, but of the unique form of slavery that developed in North America. Unrestricted in his powers by institutions such as the Crown and the Church, the American slave master had gained total control of his slave property. In a desire to maximize the profits of his investment, he strove to develop the perfect slave. Although the slave might endeavour to conform externally while maintaining his inner integrity, eventually his performance as an ideal slave must have affected the shape of his personality. Modern existentialism has argued that how we behave determines what we are, and it is in this sense that the controlled behaviour in the concentration camp and its impact on personality formation provide an illuminating parallel to the study of American slavery.

The experienced gained in the German concentration camps during the Second World War showed that it was possible to induce widespread infantile behaviour in masses of adults. Childlike action extended beyond obedience to the guards and showed that a basic character transformation had occurred. Previous social-psychological theory stressed the ways in which an individual's personality was shaped during his earliest childhood years and emphasized the tenacity with which these early traits resisted attempt at alteration. Personality theory was not adequate to explain what occurred in the camps.

The concentration camp experience began with what has become labelled as shock procurement. As terror was one of the many tools of the system, surprise late-night arrests were the favourite technique. Camp inmates generally agreed that the train ride to the camp was the point at which they experienced the first brutal torture. Herded together into cattle cars, without adequate space, ventilation, or sanitary conditions, they had to endure the horrible crowding and the harassment of the guards. When they reached the camp, they had to stand naked in line and undergo a detailed examination by the camp physician. Then, each was given a tag and a number. These two events were calculated to strip away one's identity and to reduce the individual to an item within an impersonal system.

One's sense of personhood was further undermined by the fact that there was never any privacy. The individual had lost both his identity and his power. Everything was done to him or for him, but nothing was ever done by him. The guards had the power to dispense food, clothing, shelter, punishment, and even death. Prisoners had to request permission to use the sanitary facilities, and permission was not always forthcoming. As the inmates were not sentenced for specified periods of time, they tended to view camp life as having a limitless future.

In a relatively short time, this experience of total dependence developed characteristics of infantile behaviour in those prisoners who managed to avoid the extermination chambers. A childish humour and infantile giggling were common. Boasting and lying were widely practiced. Patterns of hero worship emerged, and the guards became the heroes. The prisoners came to accept their values including their German nationalism and anti-Semitism. Some even altered their uniforms to resemble those of the guards, and they slavishly followed orders beyond necessity. Attempts at resistance were very rare, and, when the liberating American forces arrived at the end of the war, they were surprised that there was not some attempt at mass revenge.

In comparison, the African who became an American slave underwent an experience that had some marked similarities to those of the German concentration camp. He too underwent a kind of shock procurement. Although millions of men became slaves, the event was unique to each man. Usually, he had been captured in the course of warfare that, in itself, was a humiliation. After being chained and marched to the coast, his horror must have increased when he realized that he was being sold to Europeans. It was widely believed by Africans that white men were cannibals. At the coastal station, he also had to endure the humiliation of a naked inspection by a physician. This was followed by a lengthy transoceanic trip that may well have exceeded the horrors of the train ride to the concentration camp. The crowded unsanitary conditions in the slave ships were at least as bad as those in the cattle cars, and the Africans were also beaten and harassed to keep them docile.

Moreover, the trip itself was much rougher and longer. After undergoing another inspection, the African was purchased and had to face a lifetime of bondage in an alien environment. He was stripped of identity, given a new name, and taught to envision himself and his African heritage as inferior and barbaric. The white master insisted on total obedience and created a situation of utter dependence. He supplied food, clothing, shelter, and discipline, and he was in a position to control the slave's friends and mating. The 'Sambo' of literature mirrored reality, this life of dependency created infantile characteristics in many of the slaves and taught them to reject their past while adopting the values of their masters. The American slave system, besides exploiting the African's labour, possessed and violated his person.

Three schools of mass behaviour have been suggested as explanations: Freudian psychology, the interpersonal theories of Henry Stack Sullivan, and role psychology. Freudian psychology has put total emphases on early childhood experiences and is the least suited for this purpose. It could be argued that the shock procurement and the total detachment from previous life that it achieved both in the concentration camps and in American slavery emptied the super-ego or conscience of its contents. Then, the creation of total dependence what followed could have resulted in infantile regression. This would account for the childlike behaviour of both 'Sambo' and the camp inmates. The slave master, the camp guard, each in his own way, became a father figure, and the respective victims internalized the value system of this symbolic father.

The interpersonal school of psychology states that the determining factor in influencing personality development can be found in the estimation and expectation of 'significant others.' Those responsible for the physical and emotional security of an individual are his 'significant others.' For a child these are his parents. As one matures, the number of 'significant others' in one's experience increases. This permits one to make decisions of one's own and to develop some individuality.

However, the child has already internalized the estimations and expectations of his parents, and this tends to shape his personality for the rest of his life. Still, acquiring new 'significant others' as an adult can be important in reshaping the adult personality. Both the American slaves and the camp prisoners were thrust into situations in which they had a new single 'significant other.' This was a situation similar to that of childhood, and it could have had the same impact in shaping personality. All previous 'significant others' had been made insignificant, and, in each case, the estimations and expectations of this new significant other became internalized into the personality of the victims.

Role psychology holds the most promise for explaining the impact of a social situation in determining the development of individual personality. In role psychology the individual and society can be compared with the actor and the theatre. Society provides the individual with a number of roles, and the individual's behaviour is his performance, the way in which he plays them.

Normally, each individual plays a number of roles simultaneously. While some are pervasive and extensive in scope, others are limited and transitory, the role of man or woman is extensive, but that of customer or student is transitory. Society also endows some roles with considerable clarity, while leaving others open to individual interpretation. The roles people play and the way in which they play them determine personality. Within

American slavery as well as within the German concentration camps, the number of roles available was severely limited, and both the slave master and the camp guard defined them very clearly.

Both demanded a precise and careful performance. There were those whose performance was faultless.. While the concentration camp guard guaranteed its performance through terror and torture, the slave master usually used more subtle means. Besides punishment for missed cues, masters displayed considerable fondness for slaves who played their part well. By restricting role availability and by carefully defining the performance, society could create a group personality type, and, through changing roles, society could change personality.

Although the innovative use of personality types has further illuminated the nature of the American slave system, it has tended to blur the individual experiences and contributions of millions of Africans into a vague amorphous abstraction. The technique has provided important insights into the plight of the slave as the victim of a dehumanizing system, but it tends to obscure the active participation of Africans in American life.

Further, it is a crude generalization that, in fact, included many types within it. While most slaves were plantation field hands, there were many whose lives followed different lines and for whom slavery was a very different experience. Some slaves departed sharply enough from the 'Sambo' image to become leaders in insurrections. These men were usually urban slaves possessing unusual talents, and thereby escaping much of the emasculation that the typical slave had to endure.

Emphasizing the slave as the victim of the slave system further reduces him to a passive object by insisting that the slave was effectively detached from his African heritage. Many scholars, including Elkins, believe that the attempt to discover Africanisms in America by researchers such as Melville J. Herskovits has led to trivial and insignificant results. This belief is reinforced by the example of the German concentration camps. There, people from wide variety of social and educational backgrounds reacted in highly similar ways. Apparently the individual had been detached from his prior life, and his reactions to the camp were shaped in a standardized manner. Similarly, it is argued, the slave was stripped of his heritage, so that none of his African background could influence his life in America. His personality and behaviour were shaped exclusively by the unique form of American slavery.

However, if we apply the experiences gained in the Chinese prisoner-of-war camps during the Korean War, some doubts on this point can be raised. While Americans from a wide variety of social and educational backgrounds behaved with a marked similarity to each other, thereby appearing to prove that their previous experiences were irrelevant to their reactions to the camp, there was, in contrast, a significant difference between the behaviour of the American and Turkish prisoners who had both been fighting the Korean War. The morale of the American prisoners was easily broken, and each one strove to look out for himself, even at the expense of his comrade's life. In contrast, the Turks maintained military discipline and group solidarity. This evidence would seem indicate that, while individual differences were insignificant, cultural differences did influence adjustment to the camp situation.

There are also grounds to believe that different value systems influenced the way in which contrasting cultures adjusted to slavery. While the African made the adjustment successfully, the American Indian, when he was enslaved, did not. The African's agricultural labour had contained many similarities to the work required on the plantation, but the Indian, accustomed to a migratory hunting existence, was totally unprepared for plantation slavery. He found nothing in it to sustain his values or his will to live, and he was unable to make the adjustment.

If the African's agricultural background helped his adaptation to American slavery, then we must assume that his detachment from his heritage was not complete. Perhaps, besides influencing his life as a slave, his African background may have found its way into other aspects of American society. However, it would seem that because the African came to believe in his own inferiority, there must have been very little conscious attempt to keep his culture alive. Certainly, the recent Black Power movement, that intended to revive pride in race and in the past, bears eloquent testimony to the degree to which any conscious link with the African past had been suppressed.

Nevertheless, mental and emotional habits can continue without any conscious intention, and habits of this kind are important for the formation of personality, Moreover, it is possible that the image of 'Sambo' as an exasperating child may tell as much about the mentality of the white master who perpetuated the picture as it does about the slave whom it depicted. Perhaps the picture of the childlike slave is also a reverse image of the sober, patronizing white master whose life was rooted in austerity. To such a man spontaneity and exuberance might well have seemed infantile.

The life of a slave did not give him much opportunity to create artefacts that could later be catalogued as evidence of African influence. However, he did create a unique music. While Negro spirituals were not imported directly from Africa, they were more than an attempt to copy the master's music. They represent a highly complex fusion of African and European music, of African and European religion, and of African and European emotion. Blues and jazz that emerged at a later date represent a similar creative tension. They clearly evolve from the experience of the African in America and include in them elements that can be traced directly to Africa. Jazz is now viewed throughout the world as American music. It demonstrates the fact that the African immigrant was not totally detached from his heritage and that he has made significant contributions to American culture. While American slavery did violate the person of the slave, some Africans, in the face of it all, managed to maintain some sense of individuality and manhood.

Slavery and the Rise of Racism as an Ideology of Domination

The Atlantic slave trade was different from all earlier slavery in several respects. Most important is that it was the first form of slavery that was solely motivated by commercial incentives. It was the Europeans who turned slavery into an industry. In spite of its risks, illegality, and blighted social status, slave trading was enormously profitable. In earlier times, slaves were used as domestic workers and soldiers, since there were no plantations or industrial factories where millions of slaves' labour was needed. The African slave-trade was a capitalist invention. It was the large-scale capitalist mode of production which required cheap labourers that induced the slave trade. It was the Industrial Revolution in Europe that made it necessary to traffic in human lives on a colossal scale.

In a word, The discovery of gold and silver in America, the extirpation, enslavement and entombment in mines of the aboriginal population, the beginning of the conquest and looting of the East Indies, the turning of Africa into a warren for the commercial hunting of black-skins, signalled the rosy dawn of the era of capitalist production. These idyllic proceedings are the chief moments of primitive accumulation. On their heels treads the commercial war of the European nations, with the globe for a theatre... If money according to Augier, 'comes into the world with a congenital blood-stain on one cheek', capital comes dripping from head to foot from every pore with blood and dirt(Karl Marx, Capital, Vol. 1).

The brutality and viciousness of capitalism are well known to the oppressed and exploited of this world. Billions of people throughout the world spend their lives incessantly toiling to enrich the already wealthy; while throughout history any serious attempts to build alternatives to capitalism have been met with bombings, invasions, and blockades by imperialist nation states. Although the modern day ideologues of the mass media and of institutions such as the World Bank and IMF never cease to inveigh against scattered acts of violence perpetrated against their system, they always neglect to mention that the capitalist system they lord over was called into existence and has only been able to maintain itself by the sustained application of systematic violence. It should come as no surprise that this capitalist system, that we can only hope is now reaching the era of its final demise, was just as rapacious and vicious in its youth as it is now. The 'rosy dawn' of capitalist production was inaugurated by the process of slavery and genocide in the western hemisphere, and this 'primitive accumulation of capital' resulted in the largest systematic murder of human beings ever seen.

However, the rulers of society have found that naked force is often most economically used in conjunction with ideologies of domination and control that provide a legitimizing explanation for the oppressive nature of society. Racism is such a construct and it came into being as a social relation that condoned and secured the initial genocidal processes of capitalist accumulation—the founding stones of contemporary bourgeois society.

While it is widely accepted that the embryonic capitalist class came to power in the great bourgeois revolutions of the 17th and 18th centuries, what is comparatively less well known is the crucial role that chattel slavery and the plunder of the 'New World' played in calling this class into being and providing the 'primitive accumulation of capital' necessary to launch and sustain industrialization in Europe. The accidental 'discovery' of the western hemisphere by the mass murderer Christopher Columbus in 1492 changed everything for the rival economic and political interests of the European states. The looting and pillaging of the 'New World' destabilized the European social order, as Spain raised huge armies and built armadas with the unending streams of gold and silver coming from the 'New World,' the spending of which devalued the currency reserves of its rivals. The only way Portugal, England, Holland, and France could stay ahead in the regional power games of Europe was to embark on their own colonial ventures.

In addition to the extraction of precious minerals and the looting and pillaging of indigenous societies, European merchant-adventurers realized that substantial profits could also be made through the production of cash crops on the fertile lands surrounding the Caribbean Sea. The only problem was that as the indigenous population either fled from enslavement or perished from the diseases and deprivations of the Europeans, there was no one left to raise the sugar, tobacco, cotton, indigo, and other tropical cash crops that were so profitable. A system of waged labour would not work for the simple reason that with plentiful land and easy means of subsistence surrounding them, colonists would naturally prefer small scale homesteading instead of labouring for their masters. As the planter Emanuel Downing of Massachusetts put it in 1645: 'I do not see how we can thrive until we get a stock of slaves sufficient to do all our business, for our children's children will hardly see this great continent filled with people so that our servants will still desire freedom to plant for themselves, and not stay but for very great wages.'

Capitalistic social relations have always been based on compulsion, and they require as a precondition that workers possess nothing but their capacity to labour. The would-be developers of the wealth of the 'New World' thus turned to forced labour in complete contradiction of all the theories of bourgeois economists because unfree labour was the only kind of labour applicable to the concrete situation in the Americas.

Although slavery is now, and has almost always been equated with unfree black labour, it was not always, or even predominantly so. Capitalists looked first to their own societies in order to find the population to labour in servitude on the large-scale plantations necessary for tropical cash crop production. Eric Williams, in his groundbreaking work Capitalism and Slavery, noted that in the early stages of colonialism 'white slavery was the historic base upon which Negro [sic] slavery was constructed.' Between 1607 and 1783 over a quarter million 'white' indentured servants arrived in the British colonies alone where they were set to work in the agricultural and industrial processes of the time. The shipping companies, ports, and trading routes established for the transport of the poor, 'criminal,' and *lumpen* elements of European society were to form the backbone of the future slave trade of Africans.

Slavery became an exclusively black institution owing to the dynamics of class struggle as repeated multi-ethnic rebellions of African slaves and indentured European servants led the slaveholders to seek strategies to divide and conquer. The fact that an African slave could be purchased for life with the same amount of money that it would cost to buy an indentured servant for 10 years, and that the African's skin colour would function as an instrument of social control by making it easier to track down runaway slaves in a land where all whites were free wage labourers and all black people slaves, provided further incentives for this system of racial classification.

In the colonies where there was an insufficient free white population to provide a counterbalance to potential slave insurgencies, such as on the Caribbean islands, an elaborate hierarchy of racial privilege was built up, with the lighter skinned 'mulattos' admitted to the ranks of free men where they often owned slaves themselves. The concept of a 'white race' never really existed before the economic systems of early capitalism made it a necessary social construct to aid in the repression of enslaved Africans.

Xenophobia and hostility towards those who were different than one's own immediate family, clan, or tribe were certainly evident, and discrimination based on religious status was also widespread but the development of modern 'scientific' racism with its view that there are physically distinct 'races' within humanity, with distinct attributes and characteristics is peculiar to the conquest of the Americas, the rise of slavery, and the imperialist domination of the entire world.

Racism provided a convenient way to explain the subordinate position of Africans and other victims of Euro-colonialism, while at the same time providing an apparatus upon which to structure the granting of special privileges to sectors of the working class admitted as members of the 'white race.' As David McNally (2006) has noted, one of the key components of modern racism was its utility in resolving the contradiction as to how the modern European societies in which the bourgeoisie had come to power through promising 'freedom' and 'equality' were so reliant on slave labour and murderous, yet highly profitable colonial adventures. The development of a concept like racism allowed whole sections of the world's population to be 'excommunicated' from humankind, and then be murdered or worked to death with a clear conscience for the profit of the capitalist class.

To get a sense of the scale of slavery and its economic importance, and thus an understanding of the material incentives for the creation of ideological constructs such as 'race,' a few statistics regarding the English slave trade from Eric Williams' book Capitalism and Slavery help to put things in context. The Royal African Company, a monopolistic crown corporation, transported an average of 5,000 slaves a year between 1680 and 1686. When the ability to engage in the free trade of slaves was recognized as a 'fundamental and natural right' of the Englishman, one port city alone, Bristol, shipped 160,950 slaves from 1698-1707. In 1760, 146 slave ships with a capacity for 36,000 slaves sailed from British ports, while in 1771 that number had increased to 190 ships with a capacity for 47 000 slaves. Between 1700 and 1786 over 610,000 slaves were imported to Jamaica alone, and conservative estimates for the total import of slaves into all British colonies between 1680 and 1786 are put at over two million. All told, many historians place the total number of Africans displaced by the Atlantic slave trade as being between twelve and thirty million people—a massive historical event and forced migration of unprecedented proportions.

These large numbers of slaves and the success of the slave trade as a jump starter for capitalist industrialization, came from what has been called the 'triangular trade'—an intensely profitable economic relationship that built up European industry while systematically deforming and underdeveloping the other economic regions involved. The Europeans would produce manufactured goods that would then be traded to ruling elites in the various African kingdoms. They in turn would use the firearms and trading goods of the Europeans to enrich themselves by capturing members of rival tribes, or the less fortunate of their own society, to sell them as slaves to the European merchants who would fill their now empty ships with slaves destined to work in the colonial plantations. On the plantations, the slaves would toil to produce expensive cash crops that could not be grown in Europe. These raw materials were then refined and sold at a fantastic profit in Europe.

In 1697, the tiny island of Barbados with its 166 square miles, was worth more to British capitalism than New England, New York, and Pennsylvania combined, while by 1798, the income accruing to the British from the West Indian plantations alone was four million pounds a year, as opposed to one million pounds from the whole of the rest of the world. Capitalist economists of the day recognized the super profitability of slavery by noting the ease of making 100% profit on the trade, and by noting that one African slave was as profitable as seven workers in the mainland. Even more importantly, the profits of the slave trade were ploughed back into further economic growth. Capital from the slave trade financed James Watt and the invention and production of the steam engine, while the shipping, insurance, banking, mining, and textile industries were all thoroughly integrated into the slave trade.

What an analysis of the origins of modern capitalism shows is just how far the capitalist class will go to make a profit. The development of a pernicious racist ideology, spread to justify the uprooting and enslavement of millions of people to transport them across the world to fill a land whose indigenous population was massacred or worked to death, represents the beginnings of the system that George W. Bush defends as 'our way of life.' For revolutionaries today who seek to understand and transform capitalism and the racism encoded into its very being, it is essential to understand how and why these systems of domination and exploitation came into being before we can hope to successfully overthrow them.

Racism as a Divider of the Exploited Working Class

The idea of race, both the popular and the taxonomic, can be viewed for what it is: a confused and dangerous idea which happened to fit the social requirements of a thoroughly exploitative period. 'Race' was developed as a direct response to the exploitation of other peoples, to provide both a pretext and a justification for the most unjustifiable conduct, the enslavement, murder, and degradation of millions of human beings.

Much of the social analysis that focuses on the injustices and inequalities in every society has been influenced by the ideas of Karl Marx and the Marxist tradition (Robert Tucker 1978; Heilbroner 1980; Sweezy 1981). Central to Marxism is the understanding that capitalism is an economic system with two major classes. The capitalist class owns and controls the means of production, capital, and continually tries to increase its profits. The economic class, which is the large majority of the population, is the working class. They sell their labour power, their capacity to work, in return for a wage. Profits come largely from paying employees less than the value they add to production. Marx called this exploitation. Conflict between these two classes is inherent in a capitalist system. Workers try to raise their wages and improve their working conditions. Employers try to limit wages and increase the amount of work done per hour. The employer has the upper hand because workers fear losing their jobs and not finding another one soon. This is the usual situation because generally there is significant unemployment.

Exploitation, in the Marxist sense, can only be ended by the working class overthrowing capitalism. Workers can, however, improve their economic situation by forming unions and other organizations. The more disunity among workers, the weaker is their ability to effectively challenge the employer. This insight is central to the Marxist analysis of racism, which focuses on attempts by capitalists to divide black and white workers. If white workers identify primarily as whites rather than as workers, they will not act on their common class interests with black workers. The way to end racial oppression and class exploitation is an interracial and united working class. Racism in the United States is defined as the systematic oppression of African-Americans and other people of colour and the related ideology of white supremacy and black inferiority. These two aspects of racism have shaped U.S. society from the early 1600s until the present day.

The origins of racism in the United States can be directly traced to the European conquest of the Americas, to a rapidly expanding capitalism in Western Europe and what was to become the United States seeking a cheap and growing supply of food, beverages, tobacco, and increasingly, cotton. These needs were met by a system of production in the Americas based on land seized from its inhabitants, American Indians, and the kidnapping, transporting and selling into slavery of millions of Africans. The slave trade created much of the wealth subsequently invested in textile, shipbuilding and other emerging capitalist enterprises in the north-east United States and Europe. Marxists call this the 'primitive accumulation of capital.' (Hogan 1984; James 1963).

By the late 17th century, slavery became the established labour system for the production of these agricultural commodities. African people became enslaved, not because of European aversion to blackness, but because more labour could be coerced from Africans than from either Native Americans (Indians) or European indentured servants. African societies did not have the political and military strength to resist the seizure of their people. The ideology of black inferiority developed as a rationalization or justification for slavery; it was not the cause of slavery (Geschwender 1978). By people of colour, sometimes referred to as minorities, one is actually referring to people whose origins are non-European—including American Indians, Asian Americans, African-Americans and Latinos. These various 'racial' groups, e.g., white, Latina, black are socially constructed categories that shape one's life and interactions with others but are biologically meaningless. There is only the human race, not a white race, a black race, and so on. (Miles 1989; Takaki 1993).

Plantation Economy and Slavery

A plantation economy is an economy that is based on agricultural mass production, usually of a few staple products grown on large farms called plantations. Plantation economies are usually dependent on outside forces, owing to the fact that the products being harvested en masse are cash crops to be exported. Throughout history, countries with plantation economies have usually been in South America, the Caribbean, and Africa, and usually during the historical period of colonization, although Fordlândia is a 20th century example.

Plantation economies are also historically associated with slavery, particularly in the United States. Plantation economies usually benefit the large countries to which they are exporting; they usually take the raw materials grown on the plantation and return manufactured goods, making a profit. Throughout most of history, the countries receiving the crops have usually been in Western Europe.

In *Christopher Columbus and the Afrikan Holocaust*, John Henrik Clarke asserts that the voyages of Christopher Columbus marked the starting point of world capitalism and the beginning of Europe's colonial domination of the world. Columbus set in motion an act of criminality that influences our very life today. Clarke described the period between 1400-1600 as the point in history when Europe freed itself from the lethargy of the Middle Ages. During this period, Europe witnessed the renewal of nationalism as well as the political transformation from feudalism to nation states through the centralization of power by the monarchs. The African slave trade played an important role in the stabilization of Europe's economy, its transition to capitalism, the development of the nation state, and the establishment of their imperial empires. The opening of the Atlantic led to the development of Europe's commercial empire and industrial revolution.

While Ghana was the headquarters of the African slave trade, tropical America was the real centre of the trade. 36 of the 42 slave fortresses were located in Ghana. Aside from Ghana, slaves were shipped from eight coastal regions in Africa including Senegambia, Sierra Leone, Ivory Coast and the Liberia region, Gold Coast, Bight of Benin, Bight of Biafra, central Africa, and south-east Africa (from the Cape of Good Hope to the Cape of Delgado, including Madagascar). The slave trade had the greatest impact upon central and western African. According to James Rawley, West Africa supplied three-fifths of the slaves for export between 1701-1810. Half of the slaves were exported to South America, 42% to the Caribbean Islands, 7% to British North America, and 2% to Central America.

The continuing demand for African slave labour arose from the development of plantation agriculture, the long-term rise in prices and consumption of sugar, and the demand for miners. Not only were the Africans skilled labourers, they were also experts in tropical agriculture. Consequently, they were well-suited for plantation agriculture. The high immunity of Africans to malaria and yellow fever compared with Europeans and the indigenous peoples made them more suitable for tropical labour. While white and red labour were used initially, Africans were the final solution to the acute labour problem in the New World.

The economic systems that dominated the African slave trade reflected the transitions in Europe's economic systems. Initially, mercantilist views characterized the conduct of the slave trade. The primary purpose of mercantilism, an economic system that developed during the transition of Europe from feudalism to nation-states, was to unify and increase the power and monetary wealth of a nation through strict government regulation of the national economy. Therefore, 16th century organization of the trade was entrusted to a company that was given the sole right by a particular nation to trade slaves and to erect and maintain forts.

However, these monopolistic companies had two major opponents: the planter in the colonies, who complained of insufficient quantity and poor quality of high priced slaves, and the merchants at home. The failure of monopolies to deliver enough slaves led to free trade in the 18th century. While it is easy to analyse the various economic systems utilized in the African slave trade, it is far more difficult to determine a precise estimate of how profitable the trade was.

The slave trade was one of the most important business enterprises of the 17th century. The nation states of Europe stabilized themselves and developed their economies mainly at the expense of African people. During the latter half of the century, Colbert, a Frenchman, stated that, 'no commerce in the world produces as many advantages as that of the slave trade' (Williams, *From Columbus to Cast*ro, 144). The wealth of the New World in the form of sugar, tobacco, metals, gold, cotton, and so on was extracted by African labour and then exported from the colonies through the capitalistic enterprise of Western Europe. Western Europe drew profits from the trade in slaves, commodities produced, service of shipping, the development of new industries based on processing raw materials, financing, and insurance.

According to Eric Williams, no other commerce required so large a capital as the slave trade, which kept the wheels of metropolitan industry turning. Cities such as Liverpool, Amsterdam, and Bristol were built upon slave labour. The capital and raw materials derived from the African slave trade contributed significantly to the Commercial and Industrial Revolutions. According to James Rawley, the 'black slavery was essential to the carrying on of commerce, which in turn was fundamental to the making of the modern world' (2005:4). In other words, the modern world was built upon the blood, sweat, and tears of Africans.

Effects of the Trans-atlantic Slave Trade on Africa

The changes in African life during the slave trade era form an important element in the economic and technological development of Africa. Although the Atlantic slave trade had a negative effect on both the economy and technology, it is important to understand that slavery was not a new concept to Africa. In fact, internal slavery existed in Africa for many years. Slaves included war captives, the kidnapped, adulterers, and other criminals and outcasts. However, the number of persons held in slavery in Africa, was very small, since no economic or social system had developed for exploiting them (Manning p.97).

The new system—the Atlantic slave trade—became quite different from early African slavery. The influence of the Atlantic slave trade brought radical changes to the economy of Africa. At the time of the Atlantic slave trade, Africa was an area that had far-flung interests based on agriculture, industry, and commerce (Curtin p.54). Complex stratified societies based on settled village agriculture were developed throughout the continent. 'Essentially agricultural, the peoples of Africa displayed a remarkable degree of specialization within this ancient economic pursuit,' (Franklin p. 18).

In addition to agriculture, craftwork was a significant area of economic activity. Even less complex communities included people with various skills. Furthermore, the use of metals played an important role. Iron was developed very early in the economy of Africa; Africa exported iron for many years, and blacksmiths and other ironworkers were found in many parts of the continent. Africans also worked in silver, gold, copper, and bronze. Lastly, the internal slave trade played a role in the economy. Slaves represented a small part of the total value of African exports (Klein p.56). The tendency of communities to specialize in a particular phase of economic activity made it necessary for them to maintain commercial contact with other communities and countries in order to secure the things that they did not produce.

Some villages, for example, specialized in fishing, others concentrated on metallurgy, while others made weapons, utensils, and so on. Traders travelled from place to place to barter and to purchase. Upon returning they were laden with goods that they then sold within their own community. As the Atlantic route expanded, accounting for nearly two thirds of all Africans leaving the continent, it created systems for the gruesome work of collecting and exporting slaves and brought the expansion of a system of slavery in Africa itself. The rising prices for slaves, steadily driven by increasing American demand, powerfully influenced local African developments where slave trade was well established. For example, in some cases such as the kingdom of the Kongo to the south of the Zaire or Congo River, slave trade was quickly organized from a region that had only limited slavery and became a steady exporter of slaves (Klein p. 58). Large-scale warfare, in which obtaining slaves for the Atlantic trade was a major theme, became more common.

The effects of slave raids and slave trade soon led to civil wars, kidnappings, and disruptions, which brought about the decline of the existing kingdoms on the one hand and the rise of new but smaller ones on the other. Entire trading networks became intimately tied up to the supply of slaves to the Atlantic economy. Certain regions found the slave trade so attractive that they gave up their interests in gold mining and trading goods, and turned to the profitable business of capturing and exporting slaves. Agriculture also suffered as a result of the expansion of the slave trade. Various viable agricultural lands in the interior of many of the exporting regions in Africa were abandoned for the sake of a more profitable business.

As a result of slavery, the concept of a family, an important aspect of African life, changed. The most damaging effect of this transformation involved children. Because most of the captive slaves taken were male, women had to take on new tasks to sustain the economy, thus devoting less time to their families. The men who remained began to take on second and third wives, mostly to produce more children, a ready source for the slave market. As greed and insatiability for money grew, many women often had their children kidnapped and enslaved. Raising children became a business. As the result of the damaging changes brought to Africa by the Atlantic slave trade, the overall development of the economy and technology suffered.

Without slave exports, Africa would have had fewer imported goods because many slaves were exchanged for various forms of money. In fact, the export of slaves was very profitable and it did bring wealth to the African sellers. However, very little of this wealth was invested in expanding African production and improving the economical and technological developments (Klein p.67). As mentioned above, as the prices for slaves grew, entire trading networks became tied to the supply of slaves. As a result, Africa did little to increase its economical and technological development beyond the slave trade.

By the end of the nineteenth century nearly five or six million persons were held in slavery on the African continent (Manning p.63). Although internal slavery existed on the continent prior to the Atlantic slave trade, African slavery had little if any effect on the economy. As explained throughout this paper, the expansion of the Atlantic slave trade brought radical changes to the economy of Africa. These changes played a major role in the development of the economy and technology of the continent.

Effects of Slavery on the African Diaspora

Slavery has had a role in the economic development of the United States. Slaves helped build the roads upon which they were transported. The cotton, tobacco, and sugar cane harvested by slaves became important exports for the USA and the Caribbean countries. Slavery in the United States had important political implications. During the westward expansion of slavery during the early and mid-1800's, many northerners feared that the South would gain control of Congress if the western territories entered the Union as slave states. Attempts by the North to exclude slavery from these territories angered the South and helped bring on the American Civil War in 1861.

There is a pragmatic tendency to consider the effects of slavery in purely monetary terms, and even then the context is often dropped. There is a broad array of effects arising from the adoption of slavery. In terms of the economics of slavery, slaves provide a cheap source of labour. The reason that slave labour was cheap was because there was much agricultural work to be done, and to hire non-slave workers would have been more expensive. As European managers came to understand the vulnerability of workers in the tropics, they gave more attention to the diets of their slave labourers to reduce the death rate from scurvy, malaria, typhoid, yellow fever and other diseases..

Still in many ways slavery was first and foremost financially based in nature; if agricultural machines had been invented and could have been had at less cost than the equivalent number of slaves per work area, than slavery would have quickly become a thing of the past in the Americas because of the bottom-line economics of the situation. In the end, slavery was abolished not only because it was morally repugnant but because European growers no longer needed cheap slave labour.

The basis of slavery is a slave master and the serf. While the treatment of slaves varied, it's evident that in those cases where slaves were treated better, slaves were accorded more 'humanitarian' lifestyles, in the sense that they were more likely to be productive, trained and efficacious, perhaps taking pride in their work. The alternative 'harsh' treatment had the opposite reaction, reducing morale, lowering productivity, requiring higher levels of supervision, but importantly also removing all incentive for 'slave' workers to find a more productive way of accomplishing the task.

Toil is the source of inspiration if you are free to realize the benefits. By implication, slavery was undermining innovation in a second way. For these reasons, America did benefit from slavery in the short term by solving a short term shortage of plantation labour, but in the long term it only undermined the productivity incentive, and thus a nation's capacity to produce wealth. A look at US economic growth during the periods of slavery and after will demonstrate as much.

A further effect of slavery was relatively to denigrate the value of manual labour itself. Hard work became something people did if they were forced to do it, rather than for self-improvement. It created an idle slave-owning aristocracy who, while asset rich, were income poor. Although they didn't pay their slaves a wage, they were still responsible for feeding, housing, providing simple medical care, and (in some cases) education for all of the slaves' lives, from birth to death. Even if a slave was too old, young or crippled to work, he still had to be supported by someone. If a slave wasn't treated reasonably, he would only do the minimum work necessary. Slavery caused fear, suspicion and hatred between slave masters and serfs. Often these feelings escalated into uprisings resulting in the destruction of property, murder, rape, incarceration or desertion. These conflicts also increased the cost of business and judicial intervention.

Slave Response to Slavery as Capitalist Exploitation

Undoubtedly, the slave's most common response to his condition was one of submission. There was no hope of his returning to Africa, and there was no realistic expectation that the situation would be significantly altered. The hopelessness of his plight created a deep sense of apathy. However, even this acceptance of his master's values may have reflected African influences. It was common for a defeated tribe in West Africa to adopt the gods of its victors within the framework of its own religion. This attitude would have facilitated the African's adjustment to slavery in an alien culture.

The majority of slaves worked in the fields on large plantations. The majority of them were herded into large work gangs, supervised by overseers, and carefully directed in the accomplishment of whatever task was necessary for that day. Others were regularly assigned to a specific task without constant supervision and were held responsible for its completion. In this way it was possible for them to develop some sense of initiative. House slave were usually better off than field hands, but, because they lived in such proximity to their masters, they were much quicker to adopt the master's values and tended to be more obsequious.

Another significant group of slaves, both on the plantation and in the city, developed their talents and became skilled craftsmen: barbers, blacksmiths, carpenters, and a wide variety of other trades. Masters who could not fully utilize the skills of such a craftsman rented their property to their neighbours. In some cases, master permitted the slave to be responsible for hiring himself out and allowed him to keep some of the profits. The variety of experiences permitted within slavery allowed significant variations in the types of slaves who emerged.

Even apparently submissive slaves developed techniques of passive resistance. The laziness, stealing, lying, and faked illnesses, which were usually attributed to the slave's childlike behaviour, may have been deliberate ways of opposing the system. Masters complained that many of their slaves were chronic shirkers. When slaves dragged their feet while working, it was seen as evidence of their inferiority. When white union workers behave similarly, it is labelled a slowdown.

Other slaves appear to have indulged in deliberate mischief, trampling down crops, breaking tools, and abusing livestock. A southern physician, Dr. Cartwright, concluded that this behaviour was symptomatic of a mental disease peculiar to Africans (Coombs 2008). He labelled the disease Dysaethesia Aethiopica and insisted that masters were wrong in thinking that it was merely rascality. He also concluded that the slave's chronic tendency to run away was in reality the symptom of yet another African disease, Drapetomania, which he believed would eventually be medically cured. Finally, some slaves engaged in active resistance. Most of the slave insurrections in America were very small, and most were unsuccessful. The three best known insurrections were those led by Gabriel Prosser, Denmark Vesey, and Nat Turner.

The masters consistently refused to see examples of passive or active resistance as signs of manhood. Lying and stealing were never interpreted as passive resistance, but were always attributed to an inferior savage heritage, as was slave violence. Prosser, Vesey, and Turner, instead of being numbered among the world's heroes fighting for the freedom of their people, were usually represented as something closer to savages, criminals, or psychopaths. Modern historical scholarship has been influenced by the interpretation of slave behaviour, which stressed the impact of the system on the slave, rather than his response to it. Consequently, it has failed to give proper recognition to African contributions to American life.

American abolitionists, Black and white, were fighting against a form of racism that had begun to crystallize itself in the embryo of the colonies' educational systems, filtering down from the attitude prevailing in the churches. During the period of the founding fathers, the African Americans heard promises about democracy, but the American promises really weren't made to them. That was the basis of their dilemma during the formative period of this country, and it is the basis of their dilemma right now. America was born in racism, and it has evolved in racism.

Finally, in the early years of the nineteenth century, the system of chattel slavery gave way to the colonial system, after the British abolished slavery—at least on paper—in 1807. This was not the end of racism as it affected Africans and other people of colour throughout the world; it was only a radical change in how it would be manifested. The Europeans would now change the system of capturing Africans and other people of colour and enslaving them thousands of miles from their homes. They would now enslave them on the spot, within their own countries, and use those countries as markets for the new goods coming out of the developing European industrial revolution, as well as use the homes of the colonialized and their labours to produce the grist for new European mills. So the industrial rise of the West has as its base a form of racism. Racism helped to lay the base of the present economic system we now call capitalism.

Theoretical racism, in the main, is of nineteenth century origin in America and in Europe. And yet the nineteenth century was a century of the greatest resistance against racism. It was during that century when Africans the world over began to search for a definition of themselves.

The concept of African redemption is of nineteenth century origin. The theoretical basis of the Black Power concept started in 1829, with the publication of David Walker's *Appeal.* The great Black ministers of the nineteenth century, such as Henry Highland Garnet, Samuel Ringgold Ward, and Prince Hall, who founded the black Masons, were all using Christianity in a struggle against racism.

The high-water mark of the Africans' reaction to European racism came in the middle of the nineteenth century in the presence of great Black intellects such as: Martin R. Delany and Edward Wilmot Blyden. Delany wrote a number of outstanding papers on the subject; the best of these papers were brought together in his book, *Origin of Races and Color* published in 1880. During this period, the great defenders of the Africans' history, culture and right of self-determination, were Black Americans and 'West Indians.' Singularly, the most outstanding was Edward Wilmot Blyden. Edward Wilmot Blyden, who was born in what is now the Virgins Islands, was the intellectual bridge between Africa, the Caribbean Islands and the United States during the second half of the nineteenth century. Some of his nineteenth century plans and programmes for the redemption of Africa were realized in the twentieth century.

Many of our modern day African American youth, who have mouthed the phrase 'Black and beautiful,' do not know that Edward Wilmot Blyden said the same thing, and much better, over fifty years before they were born. Dr. Blyden went back to Africa, physically and spiritually, and started to reclaim his heritage in the eighteen-fifties. He became, in many ways, more African than some African-born Africans, and he became the defender of the history and culture of that continent and its people.

Dr. Blyden did not originate the formalized Pan-African idea. This started among a few 'West Indian' and African American intellectuals in the early years of the twentieth century as a reaction against the enslavement of, and discrimination against, Africans in the New World and their reputed backwardness on the continent of Africa. This group came to view the problems of the African people as a whole, and their solutions aimed at bringing prestige and dignity to the entire people. They came to reject any white-dominated society as unfit for African people's habitation and thought in terms of establishing societies and nations in which Blacks would have unfettered opportunities for demonstrating their talents. Unquestionable, they were influenced by those British and American 'humanitarians' who wished to 'regenerate' Africa and under whose auspices free Blacks from Britain and North America and founded the colonies of Sierra Leone (1787) and Liberia (1822).

The early Pan-African nationalists optimistically regarded Sierra Leone and Liberia as a new kind of society which could combine the best in western and African cultures. They believed that sustained New World African 'repatriation' would result in the establishment of major progressive African nations through whose agency the African people would make a distinctive contribution to world civilization. Such were the views of Paul Cuffee, Daniel Coker, Hilary Teage, Elijah Johnson, Lott Cary and John B. Russwurm, all of whom played prominent roles in the early history of Liberia or Sierra Leone or both, and all of whom but Cuffee died in the service of the new societies for which they held such high hopes.

With the death of the above leaders, the next Pan-African figure to emerge was Edward Wilmot Blyden who, because of his intellectual brilliance, his single-mindedness of purpose, and a long life, became easily the greatest of the Pan-African figures of the nineteenth century. Blyden became a convert to Pan-Africanism in 1850 at the age of eighteen, while on a visit to the United States from his native St. Thomas. The young West Indian had come to the United States to seek entrance into a theological college. Not only were his applications turned down because of his race, but he had the traumatic and humiliating experience of witnessing the recently passed Fugitive Slave Law unscrupulously brought in to operation against the free Blacks of New York; he himself 'feared being seized for a slave.'

From his American and other experiences as well as from his readings, Blyden became convinced the Black people would never be treated as the equal of whites in the New World. In the meantime, he had learned of Liberia and had become greatly excited by the possibilities for development of the former colony of the American Colonization Society which in 1847 had achieved full sovereign status as a Republic. Accordingly, Blyden emigrated to Liberia, arriving there in late January, 1851. The remainder of Blyden's long life, apart from visits to Europe and America, was spent doing 'race work' in English-speaking Africa.

Unquestionably, it is primarily as a man of letters and ideas, rather than as a man of action, that Blyden made his greatest impact. He began writing at the age of eighteen, at first for the colonization journals of America. His writings, apart from condemning slavery and advocating the emigration of free African Americans to Liberia, were concerned with proving that the Black Race had a history and culture of which it could be proud. Thus, at the outset of his career, he realized that an indispensable prerequisite to Pan-African action was the creation of pride and self-esteem among his people.

I wish to note here that Edward Wilmot Blyden articulated a vision of African development that profoundly disagreed with conventional views. His often controversial positions were discussed in the numerous books and pamphlets that he published, including *A Voice from Bleeding Africa* (1856), *Liberia's Offering* (1862), *the Negro in Ancient History* (1869), *The West African University* (1872), *From West Africa to Palestine* (1873), *Christianity, Islam and the Negro Race* (1887), *the Jewish Question* (1898), *West Africa before Europe* (1905), and *Africa Life and Customs* (1908).

Near the end of the nineteenth century, the great intellectual giant, W.E.B. DuBois took up this fight and ably carried it to the middle of the twentieth century. He is the father of the present struggle against racism and for African redemption. Men like Marcus Garvey, though they differed with W.E.B. DuBois, would draw in part on his intellectual conclusions on this subject.

There is now an international struggle on the part of people of African descent against racism and for a more honest look at their history. On university campuses and in international conferences they are demanding that their history be looked at from a Black perspective or from an Afrocentric point of view. This has taken the struggle against racism to the world's campuses, where the theoretical basis of racism started. This has helped to create new battle lines and a lot of fear and frustration on the part of white scholars. They still do not recognize that removing the racism that they created is the healthiest thing that present day Black scholars can contribute to the world; that in the cry for Black power and Black history, Black people are saying a very powerful, complex, yet simple thing: 'I am a man.'

The struggle against racism all along has been a struggle to regain the essential manhood lost after the European expansion into the broader world and their attempts to justify the slave trade. This struggle has brought us to where we are now, standing on the 'Black and Beautiful' plateau. From this position, Black people will walk into another stage, much higher and more meaningful for mankind. After reclaiming their own humanity, I think they will make a contribution toward the reclamation of the humanity of man. First they will have to realize that in the kind of world we live in, being Black and beautiful means very little unless one is also Black and powerful. There is no way to succeed in the struggle against racism without power. That was a part of the new reality and the new mission for liberation.

Summary and Conclusion

Globalization is best conceived as a process of inexorable worldwide integration that applies to all spheres of life. Historically, it is a process that encompasses the internationalization of trade, manufacturing, and business enterprises. As it relates to Africa, the transatlantic slave trade, the so-called 'legitimate trade,' and the activities of the Royally Chartered Companies from various European countries were part of the early markers of globalization and the precursors of current foreign direct investment that compel race, racism, and gender to affect social conditions and economic development initiatives in Africa in a myriad of ways.

With historical hindsight, the idea that Africans belong to an inferior race has been pervasive in European and American thought. The concept of 'race'—the socially constructed categorization of humans based on external appearance, stereotypes, and myths about physical, mental and psychological capacity; cultural difference; and the capacity to be civilized or uncivilized—has been deployed to support a hierarchy in which Europeans are categorized as superior and Africans the most debased. From the earliest Christian exegesis to Shakespeare and his heirs in Western literature and on to theories of scientific racism, black has been predominantly characterized as evil, while white has been seen as good and pure. Consequently, social discrimination, economic exclusion, and racial segregation have marginalized peoples of African descent from global political, social, and economic systems.

Moving from the margins to the centre in these systems has proved to be challenging and, in some cases, elusive. This elusive move of Africans to the centre, meanwhile, takes African marginalization as a timeless reality generated by characteristics that are argued to be essential to Africans. The presumption of an intrinsic and immutable African racial inferiority has generated a self-fulfilling prophecy in Africa's marginality. This has led to a conflation of presumed racial inferiority, economic impoverishment, and lack of political power. This 'reality' is so disheartening that African educational systems are mired in the reproduction of colonial ideological 'Otherizing' of Africans. That explains why many Africans embrace a marginalized social, political, and economic characterization as emerging out of something deep in their nature.

Evidence of the depth of social privations in the African continent has engendered the debate on the continent's future defined as being between Afro-pessimistic and Afro-optimistic perspectives. The Afro-pessimists, observing that anomie, disillusionment, and alienation have become pervasive among the impoverished majority (a condition made even more difficult by the flamboyant gestures of the *noveaux riches*), see no hope for positive, autonomous development. In particular, they see the problems faced by the continent as driven by domestic stimuli, including the failure of leadership exemplified by a kleptocratic 'politics of the belly,' (Bayart, op.cit.) through which criminalized states sponsor 'economies of plunder.'

The Afro-optimists do not dispute that the age of globalization has also coincided with the rending of the social fabric in the African continent, but they are hopeful that an African renaissance will emerge out of the detritus of the continent's historical experiences. For them, the sources of Africa's marginalization are external, derived from the exploitation of the age of exploration and colonization. Even independence and postcolonial relations have brought new kinds of economic dependency and the persistence of colonization in other forms.

Yet, while the imposition of changes that have benefited external forces has rendered African communities weaker in many respects, it has also made them stronger in others, because a few people have become extremely wealthy, and new forms of communal organization for self-help have been instituted to provide services that the state is no longer willing or able to offer. It is out of the stronger elements of African resilience that its renaissance is expected to spring. Pervasive and enduring social inequalities will only be defeated with dogged and relentless planning and an optimistic belief in African agency-THE AFRICAN STATE, not THE STATE IN AFRICA.

Chapter Six

Colonial Globalisation or the Extension of European Westphalian State to Africa

Overview

The Westphalian System is used as a shorthand by academics to describe the system of states which the world is made up of today. The Westphalian system had its limits. For one, the principle of sovereignty it relied on also produced the basis for rivalry, not community of states; exclusion, not integration was legalized. In the aftermath of the 11 March 2004 Madrid attacks, Lewis 'Atiyyatullah, who claims to represent the terrorist network al-Qaeda, declared that 'the international system built-up by the West since the Treaty of Westphalia [*sic*] will collapse; and a new international system will rise under the leadership of a mighty Islamic state.' It has also been claimed that globalization is bringing an evolution of the international system past the sovereign Westphalian state.

However, European nationalists and some American paleoconservatives such as Pat Buchanan (2002 and 2006) hold a favourable view of the Westphalian state. Supporters of the Westphalian state oppose socialism and some forms of capitalism for undermining the nation state. A major theme of Buchanan's political career, for example, has been attacking globalization, critical theory, neo-conservatism, and other philosophies he considers detrimental to today's Western nations. During the 1980s and early 1990s, the emerging literature on globalization focused primarily on the apparent erosion of interdependence sovereignty and Westphalian sovereignty. Much of this literature was primarily concerned to criticize realist models of international politics in which the Westphalian notion of the state as a unitary actor are taken as axiomatic (Camilleri and Falk 1992).

THE STATE IN AFRICA originated from the class forces of the European metropoles. This alien state in Africa continues its colonial function of integrating the continent more firmly into the orbit of capitalist globalization or imperialism. The decisive factor in its social orientation is an orientation that explains the state's primary function of subordinating Africa's resources to the profit impulse of multinational capital. The contradictions of global capitalism that radiate with peculiar intensity in Africa promise an uncertain future for the postcolonial capitalist state, as it becomes increasingly difficult for the dominant classes to maintain their grip on the institutions of the state.

Introduction

Studies on colonialism as politics and the politics of colonialism have tended to focus on two main issues: the nature of the colonial state and African resistance. Discussion and debate on the colonial state have centred on its specificities and construction, how to classify African colonial states and administrations, the dynamics of colonial power and civil society, and the demise or reconstitution of the colonial state into the postcolonial state. Crawford Young has argued quite forcefully that the African colonial state derives its peculiarity from the fact that it enjoyed only some of the crucial attributes of the modern state (territory, population, sovereignty, power, law, and the state as nation, an international actor, and an idea) and could not exercise some of its imperatives (hegemony, autonomy, security, legitimacy, revenue, and accumulation).

This is because the colonial state in Africa was created in the late nineteenth century, long after both the modern metropolitan state and the generic colonial state had been formed, which allowed for no experimentation. Also, as a conquest state imposed by force, its hegemony was excessively coercive, so that it enjoyed little legitimacy. Moreover, its territoriality was ambiguous, its sovereignty and institutions of rule were extraverted and resided in the imperial metropole, and its revenue base was weak. Charged with the onerous tasks of consolidating colonial rule, linking the colony to the metropole, and establishing or promoting colonial capitalism, the result was that the colonial state was both interventionist and fragile, authoritarian and weak, and exercised domination without hegemony, all of which ensured its eventual downfall.

All colonial states, irrespective of their ideologies and administrative systems, justified themselves in the names of civilization and pacification. Economic motivations of colonialism were assiduously downplayed. Moreover, all colonial powers used African intermediaries in their administrative systems because they lacked personnel and local knowledge and in order to minimize African resistance and administrative costs. They also used chartered companies in some of their colonies in the early years.

Genesis of Euro-africa

Long before Western European colonization, ancient Africa had full knowledge of, and contact with, much of the world around the Mediterranean and the Middle East. Romans and Greeks, the people of the Iberian Peninsula, and the Arabs, traded with much of Africa. Africa also had growing trade with the orient. The advent of Christianity and later of Islam also meant that Africa evolved cultural relationships with much of the Middle East. Historians tell us that the process of colonization was slow and long drawn out. This was mainly due to two factors. First, European capacity to travel far and wide only grew slowly. Secondly, Europe was not conscious of the true wealth potential of Africa. Western European colonization of Africa raised consciousness of the immense wealth of the continent.

The main effects of this colonization by Western European powers in Africa were:

1) The breaking of pre-existing patterns of economic and social life, through the introduction of new labour regimes (systems of recruiting and organizing labour);
2) All colonial labour regimes involved an intensification of labour compared with pre-colonial modes of organizing labour in production;
3) Compulsory means were employed to obtain the supply of labour for plantations, mines and settler estates; and,
4) Colonial legislation and administration concerning money taxation, property titles in land and the commercialization of agriculture linked to the international economy, radically altered the nature of rural social relations, and caused the formation of new social classes among the indigenous African populations.

Understanding the Meaning of Colonialism

Colonialism is a practice of domination, which involves the subjugation of one people to another. One of the difficulties in defining colonialism is that it is difficult to distinguish it from imperialism. Frequently the two concepts are treated as synonyms. Like colonialism, imperialism also involves political and economic control over a dependent territory. Turning to the etymology of the two terms, however, provides some suggestion about how they differ. The term colony comes from the Latin word *colonus*, meaning farmer. This root reminds us that the practice of colonialism usually involved the transfer of population to a new territory, where the new arrivals lived as permanent settlers while maintaining political allegiance to their country of origin. Imperialism, on the other hand, comes from the Latin term *imperium*, meaning to command. Thus, the term imperialism draws attention to the way that one country exercises power over another, whether through settlement, sovereignty, or indirect mechanisms of control.

Colonialism is therefore not a modern phenomenon. World history is full of examples of one society gradually expanding by incorporating adjacent territory and settling its people on newly conquered territory. The ancient Greeks set up colonies as did the Romans, the Moors, and the Ottomans, to name just a few of the most notorious examples.

Colonialism, then, is not restricted to a specific time or place. Nevertheless, in the sixteenth century, colonialism changed decisively because of technological developments in navigation that began to connect more remote parts of the world.

Fast sailing ships made it possible to reach distant ports while sustaining closer ties between the centre and colonies. Thus, the modern European colonial project emerged when it became possible to move large numbers of people across the ocean and to maintain political sovereignty in spite of geographical dispersion. This entry uses the term colonialism to describe the process of European settlement and political control over the rest of the world, including Americas, Australia, and parts of Africa and Asia.

Historically, Europe's early contacts were limited to stop-overs on coastal areas and villages mainly in west Africa. These early contacts were fairly informal, what Basil Davidson (1973) terms a period of 'mutual discovery'. Encounters were few and far between. Staging points, where the crew could pack water and provisions became regular ports of call, and the Europeans, led by the Portuguese, started to erect permanent settlement structures and fortifications.

This began early in the 15th century. Very soon the Portuguese sailed around the Cape on their way to India and 'discovered' eastern Africa, where eventually they established staging posts such as Fort Jesus in today's Kenya. The British reached Benin in the mid-sixteenth century. It was from such points that the exploration of the interior of Africa began. This was to lead to one of the major destabilizing processes that Europe was ever to undertake in Africa—the slave trade.

The Slave Trade: an Overview

Early trading contacts took a wrong twist, as the European desire to exploit African wealth began to grow. Towards the end of the sixteenth century the Portuguese began raiding invasions of the Angolan kingdoms. This heralded the beginning of the slave trade. They began by shipping Africans to Brazil; this continued until the second half of the 19th century.

From 1593 to 1700, 1-3 million Africans were uprooted and transported to the new world, mainly the northern part of mainland South America. From 1701 to 1810 the slave trade grew by leaps and bounds and another six million people were taken. Between 1811 and 1870 another 1.9 million Africans followed, some of them now to southern USA and the Caribbean.

The British, French, Spanish, Portuguese, Germans and Dutch were all involved in this process. The effect of this on African society is not difficult to imagine; it was disastrous. Many of the young, able bodied men were taken and those that resisted capture were killed. Africans were employed to hunt Africans. Slaves were transported to the new world to produce tropical crops such as sugar for European consumption. Normal production in Africa suffered enormously. African population in those years was not large, and to have it depleted by some ten million was disastrous. In the Congo the population was halved. This inhuman trade brought a great deal of wealth to Europe, especially Britain and France, fuelling their industrial revolution, but bringing poverty and destruction to Africa.

Colonial Invasion and Partition of Africa

The abolition of the slave trade, the growth of European imperialism, and improved capacity for effective conquest led to yet another stage in the African-European contact. At the beginning of the 19th Century, the search for markets and raw materials was paramount in the development of the manufacturing industry. Companies such as the Royal Niger Company, the British East Africa Company, the British South Africa Company, and others, mainly French, Dutch and German, mushroomed.

These companies, with the assistance of the gunboat, pushed the interest of European capital into the heart of Africa. The number of settlers and missionaries grew. The colonial economic structure tended primarily to serve the interests of a limited number of settlers, officials and the private foreign-owned exporting and importing firms. The more the Europeans penetrated into Africa the more they realized the wealth that Africa had to offer, both in terms of minerals and the production of tropical crops. This led to rivalry and conflict among European powers, and a hasty and haphazard process of closure. The period led up to the Scramble for Africa.

The British, French, Germans, Belgian, Italians, Portuguese and Spanish all wanted a piece of the African cake and at the Berlin conference of 1884-5 defined the broad limits for expansion for each of the interested parties. There was no part of Africa in which the Europeans had no interest nor for which they had no design. An effective agreement had in fact long preceded this conference. The French had established their 'priority of interest' in North Africa as early as 1830 by invading Algeria. Britain did the same in lower Egypt and the Red Sea as a major passage to India.

But all was not smooth. Africans mounted stiff resistance everywhere. Europe had the upper hand only because of the superiority of their weapons. It took France twenty years to subdue west Africa. The British fought nine major battles against the Africans in today's South Africa between 1779 and 1877. In 1878 they were in fact defeated by the Zulu nation at Isandhlwana.

Similarly the Portuguese, the Germans, the Dutch and the Italians fought many wars against the indigenous people they were attempting to subjugate. It is true to say that there was no total peace anywhere in the colonies and uprising flared from time to time. If the years 1880-1900 were broadly those of conquest and the 'establishment of presence', the decades 1900-1920 may be defined as the period of pacification during which installation of colonial rule was made complete.

Colonialism or Extension of Imperial State to Africa

Imperial states established the political conduits through which African societies engaged the global political economy. In many ways, this engagement can be seen as a process of simplification, reducing complex social forms to basic national templates: the zoning of agricultural production; the reduction of varied cultures of ownership and norms of trade to 'chieftaincies' and the regulations of marketing boards; and the redirecting of local and long distance trade networks to the road and rail links to port, capital city, and customs office. Intrinsically authoritarian, this process of standardization could only be effected with violence and was resisted both actively and passively, resulting in a mosaic of complex outcomes.

The colonial project might not have completed its immanent desire to produce self-contained national economies malleable to the designs of international capital, but it did mark a profound historical transition which defined the historical possibilities of independence. In spite of the vibrant African political currents of the late 1950s and 1960s, statesmen inherited political and economic kingdoms that had been structured by colonialism, whether these kingdoms were inherited through negotiations or armed struggle.

The difficulty of defining colonialism stems from the fact that the term is often used as a synonym for imperialism. Both colonialism and imperialism were forms of conquest that were expected to benefit Europe economically and strategically. The term colonialism is frequently used to describe the settlement of places such as North America, Australia, New Zealand, Algeria, and Brazil that were controlled by a large population of permanent European residents.

The term imperialism often describes cases in which a foreign government administers a territory without significant settlement; typical examples include the scramble for Africa in the late nineteenth century and the American domination of the Philippines and Puerto Rico. The distinction between the two, however, is not entirely consistent in the literature. Some scholars distinguish between colonies for settlement and colonies for economic exploitation. Others use the term colonialism to describe dependencies that are directly governed by a foreign nation and contrast this with imperialism, which involves indirect forms of domination.

The confusion about the meaning of the term imperialism reflects the way that the concept has changed over time. Although the English word imperialism was not commonly used before the nineteenth century, Elizabethans already described the United Kingdom as 'the British Empire.' As Britain began to acquire overseas dependencies, the concept of empire was employed more frequently. Thus, the traditional understanding of imperialism was a system of military domination and sovereignty over territories. The day to day work of government might be exercised indirectly through local assemblies or indigenous rulers who paid tribute but sovereignty rested with the British.

The shift away from this traditional understanding of empire was influenced by the Leninist analysis of imperialism as a system oriented towards economic exploitation. According to Lenin, imperialism was the necessary and inevitable result of the logic of accumulation in late capitalism. Thus, for Lenin and subsequent Marxists, imperialism described a historical stage of capitalism rather than a trans-historical practice of political and military domination. The lasting impact of the Marxist approach is apparent in contemporary debates about American imperialism, a term which usually means American economic hegemony, regardless of whether such power is exercised directly or indirectly (Young, 2001). Given the difficulty of consistently distinguishing between the two terms, this study will use colonialism as a broad concept that refers to the project of European political domination from the sixteenth to the twentieth centuries that ended with the national liberation movements of the 1950s in Africa.

'Legitimacy?' of Colonial Imperialism

Since the Crusades and the conquest of the Americas, political theorists have struggled with the difficulty of reconciling ideas about justice and natural law with the practice of European sovereignty over non-Western peoples. In the nineteenth century, the tension between liberal thought and colonial practice became particularly acute, as dominion of Europe over the rest of the world reached its zenith.

Ironically, in the same period when most political philosophers began to defend the principles of universalism and equality, the same individuals still defended the legitimacy of colonialism and imperialism. One way of reconciling those apparently opposed principles was the argument known as the 'civilizing mission,' which suggested that a temporary period of political dependence or tutelage was necessary in order for 'uncivilized' societies to advance to the point where they were capable of sustaining liberal institutions and self-government.

The 'legitimacy' of colonialism thus became a topic of debate among French, German, and British philosophers in the eighteenth and nineteenth centuries. Enlightenment thinkers such as Kant, Smith and Diderot were critical of the barbarity of colonialism and challenged the idea that Europeans had the obligation to 'civilize' the rest of the world. At first it might seem relatively obvious that Enlightenment thinkers would develop a critique of colonialism.

The system of colonial domination, which involved some combination of slavery, quasi-feudal forced labour, or expropriation of property, is antithetical to the basic Enlightenment principle that each individual is capable of reason and self-government. The rise of anti-colonial political theory, however, required more than a universalistic ethic that recognized the shared humanity of all people. As suggested above, the universalism and humanism of Thomism proved to be a relatively weak basis for criticizing colonialism. Given the tension between the abstract universalism of natural law and the actual cultural practices of indigenous peoples, it was easy to interpret native difference as evidence for the violation of natural law. This in turn became a justification for exploitation.

Diderot was one of the most forceful critics of European colonization. In his *Histoire des deux Indes*, he challenged the view that indigenous people benefit from European civilization and argued that the European colonists are the uncivilized ones. He claimed that culture ('national character') helps to inculcate morality and reinforces norms of respect, but these norms tend to dissipate when the individual is far from his country of origin. Colonial empires, he believed, frequently become the sites of extreme brutality because when the colonists were far away from legal institutions and informal sanctions, the habits of restraint fell away, exposing natural man's full instinct for violence (Muthu 2003).

In Book VIII of *Histoire des deux Indes*, Diderot also refutes the dominant justifications for European colonialism. Although he grants that it is legitimate to colonize an area that is not actually inhabited, he insists that foreign traders and explorers have no right of access to fully inhabited lands. This is important because the right to commerce (understood to encompass not only trade but also missionary work and exploration) was used as a justification for colonization by Spanish thinkers in the sixteenth and seventeenth century. Emblematic of this approach was Victoria's conclusion that an indigenous people could not exclude peaceful traders and missionaries without violating the Law of Nations. If the native peoples resisted these incursions, the Spanish could legitimately wage war and conquer their territory. Diderot specifically challenged this view, noting that the European traders have proven themselves 'dangerous as guests.' (Muthu 2003: 75).

Before enlightenment thinkers could articulate a compelling critique of colonialism, they had to recognize the importance of culture and the possibility of cultural pluralism. The claim that all individuals are equally worthy of dignity and respect was a necessary but not sufficient basis for anti-imperialist thought. They also had to recognize that the tendency to develop diverse institutions, narratives, and aesthetic practices was an essential human capacity. The French term *moeurs* or what today would be called culture captures the idea that the humanity of human beings is expressed in the distinctive practices that they adopt as solutions to the challenges of existence. The work of enlightenment anti-imperialists such as Diderot and Kant reflects their struggle with the tension between universalistic concepts such as human rights and the realities of cultural pluralism. The paradox of enlightenment anti-imperialism is that human dignity is understood to be rooted in the universal human capacity for reason.

Yet when people engage in cultural practices that are unfamiliar or disturbing to the European observer, they appear irrational and thus undeserving of recognition and respect. Diderot's solution was to identify particularity as the universal human trait. In other words, he emphasized that human beings all share similar desires to create workable rules of conduct that allow particular ways of life to flourish without themselves creating harsh injustices and cruelties. (Muthu 2003: 77) There are infinite varieties of solutions to the challenges posed by human existence. Societies all need to find a way to balance individual egoism and sociability and to overcome the adversities that stem from the physical environment. From this perspective, culture itself, rather than rationality, is the universal human capacity.

Unlike many other eighteenth and nineteenth century political philosophers, Diderot did not assume that non-Western societies were necessarily primitive (e.g. lacking political and social organization) nor did he assume that more complex forms of social organization were necessarily superior. One of the key issues that distinguished critics from proponents of colonialism and imperialism was their view of the relationship between culture, history and progress. Most of the influential philosophers writing in France and England in the eighteenth and nineteenth centuries had assimilated some version of the developmental approach to history that was associated with the Scottish Enlightenment.

While the Scots quite consciously took their lead from Montesquieu, they went on to develop a unique and profoundly influential eighteenth-century historical narrative known as the four-stages thesis. In that story, all societies were imagined as naturally moving from hunting, to herding, to farming, to commerce, a developmental process that simultaneously tracked a cultural arc from 'savagery,' through 'barbarism,' to 'civilization.' This meant that for the Scots, 'civilization' was not just a marker of material improvement, but also a normative judgment about the moral progress of society. The Scottish Enlightenment thinkers were central to the creation of an historical imaginary that described a civilizing process, one marked most significantly by increasing refinement in modes of social interaction, which they saw as tied to the advent of commercial society. This, in turn, produced a historical narrative, which celebrated the emergence of a shared Western civilization based on the emergence of wealth and commerce. (Kohn and O'Neill 2006).

The language of civilization, savagery, and barbarism is pervasive in writers as diverse as Edmund Burke, Karl Marx, and John Stuart Mill. It would therefore be incorrect to conclude that a developmental theory of history is somehow particular to the liberal tradition; nevertheless, given that figures of the Scottish Enlightenment such as Ferguson and Smith were among its leading expositors, it is strongly associated with liberalism. Smith himself opposed imperialism for economic reasons. He felt that relations of dependence between metropole and periphery distorted self-regulating market mechanisms and worried that the cost of military domination would be burdensome for taxpayers. (Pitts 2005).

The idea that civilization is the culmination of a process of historical development, however, proved useful in justifying imperialism. According to Uday Mehta, liberal imperialism was the product of the interaction between universalism and developmental history (1999). A core doctrine of liberalism holds that all individuals share a capacity for reason and self-government. The theory of development history, however, modifies this universalism with the notion that these capacities only emerge at a certain stage of civilization. For example, according to John Stuart Mill (hereafter Mill), savages do not have the capacity for self-government because of their excessive love of freedom. Serfs, slaves, and peasants in barbarous societies, on the other hand, may be so schooled in obedience that their capacity for rationality is stifled. Only in commercial society are the material and cultural conditions ideal for individuals to realize and exercise their potential.

The consequence of this logic is that civilized societies like Great Britain are acting in the interest of less-developed peoples by governing them. Imperialism, from this perspective, is not primarily a form of political domination and economic exploitation but rather a paternalistic practice of government that exports 'civilization' (e.g. modernization) in order to foster the improvement and native peoples. Despotic government (and Mill doesn't hesitate to use this term) is a means to the end of improvement and ultimately self-government.

Of course, Mill, a life-long employee of the British East India Company, recognized that despotic government by a foreign people could lead to injustice and economic exploitation. These abuses, in turn, if unchecked, could undermine the legitimacy and efficacy of the imperial project. In *Considerations on Representative Government* (1861), Mill identified four reasons why foreign peoples were not suited to governing dependencies. First, metropolitan politicians were unlikely to have the knowledge of local conditions that was necessary for effectively solving problems of public policy. Second, given cultural, linguistic, and often religious difference, European colonists were unlikely to sympathize with the native peoples and more likely to act tyrannically. Third, even if the Englishmen abroad really tried to act fairly to native peoples, their natural tendency to sympathize with those similar to themselves (other foreign colonists or merchants) would likely lead to distorted judgment in cases of disputes. Finally, British colonists and merchants went abroad primarily to acquire wealth with no long term investment and little effort, which meant that their economic activity was likely to exploit rather than develop the country. These arguments also echoed points made in Edmund Burke's voluminous writings assailing the misgovernment in India, most notably Burke's famous Speech on Fox's East India Bill (1783).

For Mill, parliamentary oversight was no solution. First of all, it would politicize decisions, making imperial policy a result of the factional struggles of party politics rather than technocratic expertise. Furthermore, given that members of the House of Commons were accountable to their domestic electors, it would guarantee that imperial policy would be aimed exclusively at maximizing British self-interest rather than promoting good government and economic development in the dependencies.

Mill's solution to the problem of imperial misgovernment was to eschew parliamentary oversight in favour of a specialized administrative corps. Members of this specialized body would have the training to acquire relevant knowledge of local conditions. Paid by the government, they would not personally benefit from economic exploitation and could fairly arbitrate conflicts between colonists and indigenous people. Mill, however, was not able to explain how to ensure good government in a situation in which those wielding political power were not accountable to the population. In this sense, Mill's writing is emblematic of the failure of liberal imperial thought.

Nineteenth century liberal thinkers held a range of views on the legitimacy of foreign domination and differed about what tactics should be used to achieve that goal. Alexis de Tocqueville, for example, made a case for colonialism that did not rely on the idea of a 'civilizing mission.' Tocqueville recognized that colonialism probably did not bring good government to the native peoples, but this was irrelevant since his justification rested entirely on the benefit to France. Tocqueville insisted that French colonies in Algeria would increase France's stature vis-à-vis rivals like England; they would provide an outlet for excess population that was a cause of disorder in France; and imperial endeavours would incite a feeling of patriotism that would counterbalance the modern centrifugal forces of materialism and class conflict.

Tocqueville was actively engaged in advancing the project of French colonization of Algeria. Tocqueville's first analysis of French colonialism was published during his 1837 electoral campaign for a seat in the Chamber of Deputies. As a member of the Chamber of Deputies, Tocqueville argued in favour of expanding the French presence in Algeria. He travelled to Algeria in 1841 composing an 'Essay on Algeria' that served as the basis for two parliamentary reports on the topic. (Tocqueville 2001).

Unlike the more naïve proponents of the 'civilizing mission,' Tocqueville recognized that the brutal military occupation did little to introduce good government or advance civilization. In an apparent reversal of the four-stages theory of the Scottish Enlightenment, he acknowledged that 'we are now fighting far more barbarously than the Arabs themselves' and 'it is on their side that one meets with civilization.' (Tocqueville 2001: 70). This realization, however, was not the basis of a critique of French brutality. Instead, Tocqueville defended controversial tactics such as destroying crops, confiscating land, and seizing unarmed civilians. His texts, however, provide little in the way of philosophical justification and dismiss the entire just war tradition with a curt statement that 'I believe that the right of war authorizes us to ravage the country.' (Tocqueville 2001: 70). Tocqueville's writing on Algeria, the French national interest is paramount and moral considerations are explicitly subordinate to political goals.

Tocqueville's analysis of Algeria reflects little anxiety about its legitimacy and much concern about the pragmatics of effective colonial governance. The stability of the regime, he felt, depended on the ability of the colonial administration to provide good government to the French settlers. Tocqueville emphasized that the excessive centralization of decision-making in Paris combined with the arbitrary practices of the local military leadership meant that French colonists had no security of property, let alone the political and civil rights that they were accustomed to France.

Tocqueville was untroubled by the use of martial law against indigenous peoples, but felt that it was counterproductive when applied to the French. For Tocqueville, the success of the French endeavour in Algeria depended entirely on attracting large numbers of permanent French settlers. Given that it was proving impossible to win the allegiance of the indigenous people, France could not hold Algeria without creating a stable community of colonists. The natives were to be ruled through military domination and the French were to be enticed to settle through the promise of economic gain in an environment that reproduced, as much as possible, the cultural and political life of France.

After a brief period of optimism about 'amalgamation' of the races in his Second Letter on Algeria' (Tocqueville 2001: 25), Tocqueville understood the colonial world in terms of the permanent opposition of settler and native, an opposition structured to ensure the economic benefit of the former. The most influential contemporary proponent of this view is Immanuel Wallenstein, who is known for world-system theory. According to this theory, the world-system involves a relatively stable set of relations between core and peripheral states as functional in internal division of labour that is structured to benefit the core states. (Wallenstein 1974-1989).

The Imperial or Colonial State in Africa

The state under European colonial capitalism was not a neutral organization. The state structures (army, police, government departments, Parliament) were not a neutral governing body, ruling in the interests of all. When workers went on strike they were met by police dogs and rubber bullets, as well as media hostility and the threat of dismissal. But the bosses who exploited African workers and threw people out of work or off the land and into more misery never faced punishment. Who has ever heard of the bosses being assaulted and arrested by the police during a strike? Unthinkable!

The state was there to protect the interests of this minority, the ruling class, if not by persuasion then by force. Laws were made not to protect the populace but to protect those who owned the property and had the power. The colonial state was built in a way that allowed the European minority to rule the African majority: it was a very centralized, bureaucratic, hierarchical (top-down) structure of rule over a territory that concentrated power in the hands of the few at the top. There was absolutely no way that ordinary people could participate in the running of this apparatus.

These features -authoritarianism, violence, centralization, bureaucracy, hierarchy, territory, class rule- are the defining characteristics of all states. The colonial state was imposed on Africans for this purpose. The general understanding of the state in Africa today is based on the definition enshrined in the Treaty of Westphalia (1648).On the basis of this definition the state has been the most important and most characteristic of all modern institutions. Most of the institutions, political, civil and bureaucratic, of the existing community of states are legacies of a period of global colonization.

Although the global colonial state apparatus had the backing of different imperial states the pattern of governance, by and large, and the character of the institutions, as well as the objectives of the imperial states was common. Whether it was the Subcontinent of South Asia which was made to celebrate, in 1897, the Golden Jubilee of the reign of Empress Victoria, or whether it was the Philippines passing from one Imperial sovereign to another in 1898, there ran a uniform thread of similar institutions serving imperial interests. The objectives of the Raj or of the Colonial State were also the same all over the world, irrespective of the imperial state: Britain, France, Germany, Holland, Spain, Italy or the latter-day, USA.

The first objective of the colonial system was to expropriate and export the raw produce of the colony to use of the manufactures in the imperial State. It thus ensured the industrialization of the imperial country and the provision of jobs and infrastructures to its own citizens and cities. The colony was depleted of its own wealth. The second objective of the colonial state was to hold the colony as a captive market for its manufacturers. In one viscous circle of economic activity of international trade the colony was both a supplier of raw produce and a purchaser of Imperial manufacturers. It thus lost on birth bargains as raw produce was undervalued and the import of manufactures was over-taxed, and they were sold at monopolistic rates.

To service these two objectives the Imperial State did, no doubt, provide for a certain infrastructure in the colony. But this, too, was designed mainly to enable expropriation of the raw produce and the free movement of imperial manufacturers. A mere infrastructure of roads and railways could not, alone, win to the imperial state the abundance of the colony. A civil and military apparatus to subdue and tax was required.

A greater premium was therefore put on the empowerment of those institutions that served the objectives of the Imperial state. Along with a highly developed state structure of revenue collection, the Imperial state established a sophisticated bureaucratic apparatus for the maintenance of law and order. The maintenance of law and order, in fact, became the third objective of the colonial system. The establishment of peace, and its maintenance, so as to obtain the other objectives, also impelled the imperial administration to ensure that planters and feudal landlords became strong, while its competitor, the native bourgeoisie, and remain weak, dependent and impoverished. This was the goal pursued by the imperial civil bureaucratic structure. The military complemented this task by ensuring prolonged periods of 'pax imperia.'

Generally, there is a predominance of Eurocentric analysis of the nature of the state in Africa. Max Weber provides the bench mark for most contemporary analysis of the state by attributing to the state the following properties: a) its unchallenged control of the territory within the defined boundaries under its control: b) its monopolization of the legitimate use of force within its borders: and 3) its reliance upon impersonal rules in the governance of its citizens and subjects (Harberson & Rothchild 2000:7).

This is the thinking European colonialists had when they established their vassal states in Africa. The definition also includes a state capacity to extract resources for its own support as an important requirement for statehood within the empire. The colonial state in Africa was an all-powerful, absolute, and arbitrary occupying force. It imposed taxes, redistributed land, instituted forced labour, decided where everyone could live, who should produce what and how.

Establishment of the Imperial State in Africa

According to *The Economist* print edition of Dec. 23rd, 1999, Europeans were slow to seize Africa, ruthless in doing so, harsh when they had done it. Indeed, they were doers only of harm. In fact, European colonists devastated Africa like nothing else in the continent's history. Africa was the nearest of all the targets of European empire-builders in 1884. Yet, save for its far south, it was the last to be grabbed. Its coast had been known to Europeans for centuries and was dotted with their trading posts. But until around 1860 the interior was protected. Fevers killed off intruding white men, roads were few and cataracts blocked access by river. Then, setting off from their enclaves along the shores, European explorers began to walk old Arab trade routes. They searched for the truth of ancient stories about the 'dark continent' and the sources of its mighty rivers.

By 1862 they had reached the source of the Nile. A little later, they traced the route of the Niger. They confirmed the reality of Africa's fabled riches—ivory, gold, diamonds, emeralds, copper. Entrepreneurs also saw that, instead of buying crops like cotton or palm oil from its villagers, they could set up plantations and use cheap local labour to work them. Africa was becoming too valuable to be left to the Africans. The European grab for Africa was neither inevitable nor consistent. Britain at first opposed a carve-up, but ended with the richest parts: today's South Africa, Ghana and Nigeria. Belgium's King Leopold II was one of Europe's least powerful rulers. But once he had carved out the Congo basin as a personal fief, other countries were quick to stake claims. Otto von Bismarck, Chancellor of the strong new Germany, put in a bid for huge chunks of East and West Africa.

Europeans, quick to fight each other at home, were loath to do so for slices of a continent that they barely knew. Besides, it would set a bad example to the natives. So in 1884 the powers met in Berlin to share Africa out. In some areas, ignorant of people and geography alike, they made frontiers simply by drawing straight lines on the map.

The Africa they seized was technologically in the Iron Age, and politically divided into several thousand units, some based on language and culture, others on conquest, paying tribute to their conquerors. Much of the continent was in turmoil, as slaving gangs sent out by some of its own rulers spread war and sent communities fleeing.

Some Africans resisted the takeover, but the Europeans, no slouches at savage violence, most often swept their spear-wielding armies aside with the Maxim gun and repeater rifle, and brutally crushed local resistance. Much of Africa gave in without a fight, its kings signing away their sovereignty with a thumb-print. Many allied with the intruders, maybe believing that these would not stay long and would give help against some local rival. Some tried to play one set of Europeans off against another. Others were overawed by technology: the kingdoms of northern Nigeria surrendered to forces, led by a handful of white men, far smaller than their own.

By 1914 Europeans ruled all of Africa, bar Liberia, the state founded by America for its ex-slaves, and Abyssinia (Ethiopia), an ancient kingdom which had fought off the Italians in 1896. Posing as parents to Africans, Europeans counted them, taxed them and ordered their communities into tribes—or, where true tribes did not exist, invented them. Meanwhile, the best land was taken for plantations, and the minerals dug out and shipped off to be processed in Europe (a division of labour—and, inversely, of profits—which, except in South Africa, largely continues today). The storehouse was steadily exploited, but Africans saw little of its wealth.

In sum, the European occupation of Africa was short-lived—barely a generation in some areas. After the second world war (in which many Africans died fighting for the Allies), America wanted an end to European imperialism, and African leaders, often socialist and aided by the Soviet Union, wanted self-rule. In Algeria, Kenya and Rhodesia, white settlers tried to keep power by force, but in time lost support from 'home.' White South Africans—far more numerous and longer in place—held out into the 1990s, but, facing unrest and outside pressure, had to give up.

Perhaps the Africans' worst loss was not of land or power but self-respect.

It is too soon to draw up a balance-sheet of colonialism. Perhaps the Africans' worst loss was not of land or power but self-respect, as the newcomers taught them that their ways, cultures and gods were inferior and should be abandoned. The alien religion put in their place often caught on; but the Europeans kept their version of politics, which arguably was indeed superior, for use at home, merely chucking Africa a few tattered pretences at it as they lowered the flag. Africa was left both psychologically and politically impoverished. Much of it still is so.

To implement the colonial capitalist economic policy in Africa required the creation of certain socio-political structures to ensure the reorganization of indigenous economies for capitalist accumulation. This compelled the installation the extension- gradual and sometimes violent- of the colonial state into the African hinterland. The concept 'colonial state' is employed here to denote its characteristic difference from the state as it emerged in the context of European capitalism. The colonial state in Africa was imposed from above and supervised a captive population and economy, which together were 'protected' for European metropolitan capitalism. The colonial state was largely responsible to the metropolitan state.

The latter provided unusual limits to its operation. Colonial capitalism was a 'bastard' form of capitalism as the state's presence was over-arching and also denied indigenous capitalist entrepreneurs from any substantial participation in the economy. It did this within African territories through legislation which undercut local and favoured European capital and allowed the latter considerable freedom of operation. The colonial state underwrote the process of European capital accumulation by encouraging labour recruitment (many times forcefully) and the payment of low wages and by restricting labour unionisation. Agricultural producers were denied direct access to markets except through European merchant houses which manipulated prices.

Control of the colonial economy affected the process of class formation as the colonial state encouraged differential participation in the economy by various regions and communities among the colonized population. Trade had existed between African communities and Europeans before colonization. In this pattern of trade, relatively equal partners had exchanged their goods without the need for domination. Colonization introduced the domination of one partner. European capital seized control of trade and resources from the hands of local traders and reduced them to producers, wage earners or both. This debasement ensured a constant production of commodities for export which did not depend upon the goodwill of indigenous rulers.

Types of Colonial Rule

European colonialism in Africa involved efforts to remake African societies in accordance with prevailing European cultural paradigms and to have Africans fulfil metropolitan needs. Colonialism was also about Africans' responses to European efforts to tinker with their societies, their economies, and their polities. Some Africans embraced the opportunities provided by colonialism; some resisted them; and most probably ignored them as long as they could until they were drawn inexorably into economies and communities shaped by wider colonial and international economies.

Once claims were made and borders were drawn for territories in Africa, European nations had to come up with a plan for how to govern their newly acquired colonies. There are four main ways in which European nations ruled African colonies. Keep in mind that each of these four divisions is a broad category that historians use to talk about types of colonial rule. Within each category, details of individual and local situations varied from place to place.

In the early days of colonialism, European nations allowed the establishment of private companies that were granted large territories to administrate in Africa. These companies were formed by businessmen who were interested in exploiting the natural resources of the territories they were allowed to govern. These companies could set up their own systems of taxation and labour recruitment. For their part, the European powers that provided ***charters*** for these companies did so because the companies took responsibility for all of the expenses related to establishing and administering the colonies. This was a good deal for the European countries. They had the political benefit of having additional colonies in Africa, but not the expense.

The British East Africa Company, established in 1888, colonized Kenya on behalf of Britain. It made treaties that claimed to offer protection to various peoples of East Africa in exchange for recognition of the company's sovereignty by African rulers. It governed Kenya until 1893. The British South Africa Company, another example of company rule, was formed in 1887. It lasted longer than the British East African Company. The B.S.A.C., under the control of John Cecil Rhodes, using force and coercion colonized three territories in south-central Africa: Nyasaland (Malawi), Northern Rhodesia (Zambia), and Southern Rhodesia (Zimbabwe).

The Company governed these colonies until 1923. These companies were eventually unsuccessful in that they were unable to generate consistent profits for their *shareholders*. Governing a colony was expensive, and the companies faced opposition from Africans and missionaries over the harsh nature of company rule. By 1924, all Company rule was replaced by various forms of European colonial governance.

The French, Belgians, Germans, and Portuguese are considered to have used 'direct rule' in governing their African colonies. They had centralized administrations, usually in urban centres that stressed policies of ***assimilation***. This means that the colonialists had the intention of 'civilizing' African societies so they would be more like Europe. As part of this strategy, colonialists did not try to negotiate governance with indigenous African rulers and governments. Indigenous authorities had a subordinate place in these administrations. Direct rule also used the strategy of ***'divide and rule'*** by implementing policies that intentionally weakened indigenous power networks and institutions. Primarily, the British used 'indirect rule' to govern their colonies. This system of governance used indigenous African rulers within the colonial administration, although they often maintained an inferior role. Overall, these colonial strategies of state control assumed that all Africans were organized as 'tribes' with chiefs.

However, this was not always the case. Africa had diverse types of government ranging from highly centralized states to 'stateless societies.' As a result, indirect rule increased divisions between ethnic groups and gave power to certain 'big men' who had never had it before in precolonial history. Consequences of these significant changes in social organization and identity are still being felt today. In addition, settler rule was practiced in Kenya, a British colony in East Africa, and in Algeria, a French colony in North Africa.

Practice and Legacy of the Imperial State in Africa

There is a general *consensus* among Africanist historians that colonialism is morally wrong. It is not difficult to understand this conclusion. Colonialism, after all, is a political system in which an external nation takes complete control of a territory in another area of the world. Moreover, the colonized people do not invite the colonial power, nor do they have any say in how they are governed. Colonialism is by definition and practice un-democratic.

In spite of the universal recognition that colonialism is morally *reprehensible*, there are differing opinions on the social, economic, and political consequences of colonialism. Since colonialism was practiced differently throughout Africa, the consequences of colonial rule will differ from colony to colony. In this section, we will look briefly at some of the general outcomes of colonialism in Africa.

a. Political Practice and Legacy

You learned in the last activity that there were four different forms of colonial rule practiced in Africa: Company, Direct, Indirect, and Settler. The practice of governing was somewhat different depending on the form of colonialism. In spite of these differences, all colonial governments shared certain *attributes.*

1. Colonial political systems were un-democratic

No matter what form colonial rule took, all colonial systems were un-democratic. Colonial governments did not allow popular participation. Decisions and policies were made with little or no input from the African peoples. Even in the case where decisions or policies may have benefited some people, they were still un-democratic since there were no mechanisms for the people to officially express their opinions.

2. Law and Order ('Peace') was a primary objective of colonial governments

As you learned above, colonial rule was most often imposed without consent from the African people. Understandably, people were not happy with being governed without any representation, and colonial governments faced the potential of civil disobedience or outright resistance to their rule. Consequently, the maintenance of 'peace' and law and order was a top priority of colonial governments. As a result, in most African colonies, more money was spent on developing and maintaining a police force and an army then was spent on education, housing, and health-care combined!

3. Colonial governments lacked capacity

Most colonial governments were not rich. The European colonial powers were not willing to fund the governing of their colonies in Africa fully. Each colony was responsible for raising most of the revenue (money) needed to fund the operations of colonial rule. Different colonies attempted to raise revenues. But no matter how rich in resources a colony was, the government lacked the income and revenue necessary to develop a government system able to go beyond maintaining law and order. This meant that colonial governments were not able to provide basic infrastructure, such as roads and communication networks, nor were they able to provide basic social services such as education, health care, and housing.

4. Colonial governments practiced 'divide and rule'

Given the lack of capacity and the strong emphasis on law and order, all forms of colonial rule engaged in 'divide and rule,' by implementing policies that intentionally weakened indigenous power networks and institutions. Post-colonial ethnic conflicts in many parts of Africa have their roots in colonial policy of separating language, religious, and ethnic groups, and these policies often created or exacerbated group differences.

b. Economic Practice and Legacy

Two primary factors or agenda influenced colonial economic practice. First, from early in the 19th century, Europeans believed that Africa was rich in natural resources, and one of reasons for colonialism was the desire to gain control of Africa's rich natural resources. Secondly, as indicated above, European colonial powers did not want to spend their own money to establish and maintain their colonies in Africa.

Rather, they insisted that each colony (if at all possible) supply the revenues necessary to govern the colony. Each individual colonial government in Africa developed economic policies and practices that fit these two agendas. Each had to meet these two goals of generating wealth for the imperial state in Europe while simultaneously generating revenues for the local colonial rule had a lasting impact on economic practice in Africa.

Just as there were a variety of types of colonial rule, there were also different types of colonial economies in Africa. However in spite of differences, there were some similarities between all types of colonial economic practice.

1. Emphasis on exploitation of raw materials for export

Colonial regimes concentrated on finding and exploiting the most profitable natural resources in each colony. In mineral-rich colonies, the emphasis was placed on mining. In other territories, the colonial power identified agricultural products suitable for export to Europe. In either case, the emphasis was on developing the resources for export, not for local use or consumption. Profits from the export of mineral and agricultural goods were also sent to Europe. Profits that could have been used to promote social and economic development in the colonies were not available. The small taxes levied on exports went to support colonial rule.

2. High demand for labour.

Mining of minerals and the production of crops for export necessitated a ready supply of inexpensive labour. Consequently, colonial governments exerted considerable effort 'recruiting' labour for these endeavours. At times colonial governments resorted to policies of forced labour in order to provide adequate labour for mines and plantations. At other times, their tactics were not as harsh, but in almost all situations, Africans laboured in poor working conditions, for long hours, with inadequate pay. To improve the pay and working conditions of the labours would have lessened profits. The demand for labour also resulted in large-scale movements of people from areas that were not involved in colonial production to areas, including new urban areas, where colonial production occurred.

c. Social Practice and Legacy

In most African colonies, given the lack of revenue, very little was done officially to promote social change or social development. However, the colonial experience had a dramatic impact on African societies. Once again, it is important to remember that the colonial impact on Africa was not uniform across the continent. However, some social consequences were experienced in most African colonies.

1. Movement of People

Colonial economic and political practices resulted in the massive movements of people in most African colonies. In some locales, migrations were primarily from one rural area to another. In other places, the migration was from rural areas to urban areas. In either case, these movements resulted in dislocation of peoples that impacted society and culture. Social and cultural beliefs and practices were challenged by these migrations. Long-held practices had to be adapted (and at times were completed abandoned) to fit the new circumstances. In U.S. history, rural to urban migration in the early 20th century had a similar impact on American society and culture.

2. Colonialism intruded into the social organization of households and families

Families were often split up by migration. For example, men recruited to work in mines and on plantations often had to leave their families behind. As a result, women and adolescents were forced to take on new roles and to cope in absence of their husbands and fathers. Even when families remained unaffected by migration, they underwent considerable stress and change as the result of the colonial experience. Prior to colonialism, the ***extended family*** structure was the norm in most African societies. But by the end of colonial era, ***the nuclear family*** was becoming the norm in many African countries. It led to the d*islocation of Families.*

3. Urbanization

A number of pre-colonial African societies had towns and small cities. However, even in these societies, most people were engaged in agriculture in rural villages or homesteads. During colonialism, urbanization occurred fairly rapidly in many African colonies. Urban living resulted in changes in economic activities and occupation, and in changes in the way people lived. These changes often challenged existing values, beliefs, and social practices.

4. Religious changes

There was a significant change in religious belief and practice as a result of colonialism. At the beginning of the colonial era, less than five per cent of the people in Africa identified themselves as Christian. Today, nearly fifty per cent of the people in Africa identify themselves as Christians. Colonial rule provided an environment in which Christianity, in many forms, spread in many parts of Africa.

While Islam was widespread in Africa prior to the coming of colonialism, it also benefited from colonialism. British and French colonial officials actively discouraged Christian mission work in Moslem areas. Peace and order established by colonial rule provided an environment in which Islam could consolidate its hold in certain African colonies. However, in spite of these significant changes, many Africans continued to hold to and practice traditional religions.

5. Education

Throughout human history, all societies have practiced a form of 'public' education. Education is the method by which families and societies transfer beliefs, values, and skills between generations. Throughout human history, education has mainly been informal. That is, values and knowledge were learned in informal settings in the home, church, and through work and play. It is has only been in the past 200 years that public education has become more formalized, taking place in schools with an added emphasis on ***literacy*** and ***numeracy***-reading, writing, and mathematics.

Koranic Schools were widespread in the Islamic areas of Africa prior to the coming of colonial rule. Koranic schools focused on learning to read the Koran, the holy book of Islam. The Koran was written in Arabic. Consequently, students learned to read Arabic, and not their local language, at the Koranic schools. However, schools that emphasized literacy and numeracy in African languages were not common. Proponents of colonialism claimed that it was necessary to enlighten and civilize African peoples and societies. Given this concern, you would think that colonial governments would have made a major effort to introduce schools throughout Africa. The truth is that most colonial governments did little to support schools. Most formal schooling African colonies was a result of the work of missionaries.

Missionaries felt that education and schools were essential to their mission. Their primary concern was the conversion of people to Christianity. Missionaries believed that the ability of African peoples to read the Bible in their own language was important to the conversion process. However, most mission societies were not wealthy, and they could not support the number of schools that they really wanted. Consequently, with limited government support, most African children did not go to school during the colonial era. In fact at the end of colonial rule, no colony could boast that more than half of their children finished elementary school, and far fewer attended secondary school.

Effects of Rule by Colonial State in Africa

Colonial rule and law served as a vehicle for colonial hegemony and domination. The rule of law was therefore strictly connected to the construction of the imperial state in Africa. And that law was also inseparable from issues of family, oligarchy, as well as racial and social inequality. 'For a while', writes Basil Davidson (1973), 'colonial rule built a few roads and railways and opened a few mines and plantations (though for its own convenience and enrichment), dropping here and there a few crumbs of educational and social enlightenment. Its central effect was one of dismantlement. Within its new frontiers, it took apart, it did not put together.' According to official records, the building of a railway between 1921 and 1932 in the Belgian Congo meant the forced recruitment of 127,250 men. By the time the railway was completed, 20,000 men had died. Not only this. The ramifications on the socio-economic structure of the society of uprooting a mass of people in this way, and its ability to produce, could not be assessed.

Colonization brought in plantation agriculture, which brought with it the settlers. This meant that not only did Africans lose the right to their land, but were also forcibly recruited to work for the European settlers. This was the case all over the continent—Kenya, Mozambique, South Africa, Namibia, Angola, Zimbabwe. In areas that were not conducive to western settlement, new cash crops were introduced, mainly destined for

European markets and consumption. Rubber, cocoa, coffee, tea, sugar, tropical fruits, palm oil and cotton ate up a growing proportion of arable land.

In Algeria, for instance, the French turned the fertile coastal uplands to growing vines for the production of wine for export. Before the coming of the French the people grew cereals, raised mutton for home consumption and were self-sufficient. When European settlement was at its zenith fewer than one thousand European landowners possessed about one-seventh of all arable land in Algeria.

In South Africa, the white settlers, making up less than 15% of the population, owned 88% of the land. The African had been pushed to the marginal, non-productive land. Colonial authorities gave concessions to the metropolitan countries to open up mines. Once more African labour was exploited to extract African wealth for the benefit of the metropolitan rich.

In 1900, the whole vast area of French Equatorial Guinea (now Chad, Gabon, Central Africa and Congo) was divided among forty concession companies who enjoyed a thirty-year charter. The companies were to enjoy the benefit of all the product of their concession, whatever it may be. This is what one writer called the 'economy pillage', which made companies 'parasites' on African life and labour, to say nothing of its effect on the ecology.

The colonial authorities extracted 15% tax from the companies. The poll tax required of the people was paid in rubber and ivory. In the Congo, King Leopold, who had the entire country as a PRIVATE property, handed out to European concession companies the sole rights not only to land and labour within a given region (often very large), but also to the fruits of the forest and the soil. This opened the area to wilful despoliation of the land and its people. The Scramble for Africa meant the balkanization of the continent, or the amalgamation of peoples who have little common history. The Economic Commission for Africa (ECA 2008) in its 'sustainable development for Africa report' wrote:

'Few other regions in the world show such a multitude of fairly small states both as far as production and population go. The only similar region of some importance is Central America.' Balkanization has impeded industrial development. Colonization has led the African economy to be very closely aligned to that of the metropolitan countries. It has also created small elite which in its attitudes and consumption patterns is similar to that of the metropolitan countries.

Unable to produce its own goods and services, Africa relies heavily on imports from the west. This in turn means that it has got to go on producing more and more raw materials for European industry in order to earn the foreign exchange it so desperately needs to maintain the kind of life that it has inherited from the colonial masters. What Africa produces today from its mines, plantations and cash crops is far in excess of what is needed to feed Africa. Then why is Africa starving? The simple answer is that Africa has no control over its resources; the beneficiaries are not Africans but Americans and Europeans who are relentlessly milking Africa dry.

The legal complexities, worked out by the same Europeans, mean it is all clear and above board. Today we have 'legitimate' national governments. They make the rules under which 'foreign capital' operates within their respective boundaries. But is this true? Consequences of attempts for outright nationalization have been catastrophic. Zambia, for example, has been brought down to its knees.

African mineral wealth is staggering. Copper, diamonds, gold, tin, bauxite, iron, uranium and coal is being mined at breathtaking speed, perhaps in the fear that soon the tables might turn and Africa will put a stop to it. Africa today exports cotton, coffee, tea, fruits, cut flowers, cocoa, rubber, even fresh vegetables in winter, while it starves. The price of the primary commodities is fixed by the west and Africa has to produce more and more to maintain the necessary level of imported processed goods and machinery from the west. The price of the industrial product is always up, and does not obey market rules; while agricultural and mineral products from Africa fetch less and less.

The Sahel was and is suffering from drought and starvation. Yet in 1983-4 five Sahelian countries produced 154 million tons of cotton fibre compared to 22.7 million in 1961-2. They also set another record. In 1984 they imported 1.77 million tons of cereals compared to 200,000 tons a year in the early 1960s. As Timberlake (1985) put it: 'The fact that cotton can be grown but grain cannot has more to do with government and aid agency policy than with rainfall.'

In Kenya a peasant desperate for more land to grow food crops cannot cut or uproot coffee or tea plants. The Sudan, a country that is currently facing one of the worst famines in its recent history, has massive acreage under cotton, and has recently invested with multinationals in one of the biggest irrigated sugar cane growing and processing schemes.

All these examples show the legacy of colonization, which left Africa neatly tied to the economy of the west and dependent on it. Africa receives aid from the west. Yet aid has failed to produce any tangible result. The reason is that most aid money goes to finance aid personnel, and the rest to buy western goods and services. It rarely produces anything lasting. Timberlake states that more than half of the $7-8 billion spent yearly by donors goes to finance the more than 80,000 expatriates and personnel working in public agencies under official aid programmes. They create employment at home, and employment opportunity abroad. The loser is Africa.

What then are the modern consequences of the Scramble for Africa? We have seen that colonization has had a cancerous effect on Africa, destroying its natural development, and weakening Africa by tying it closely to European interest. Trade has failed to produce equality as earlier prophets of the free market suggested it would; on the contrary it has helped and is helping to widen the gap between the rich and the poor.

Africa is working for Europe and not for its own people. Despite drought and devastation Africa is still producing and exporting to Europe an ever increasing quantity of agricultural and mineral products.

Yet its gains are shrinking. The exhaustion of mineral wealth will result in even more famine and devastation, with Africa having nothing to show for it after decades of exploitation. As the Bible puts it: 'For unto everyone that hath shall be given, and he shall have abundance; but from him that has not shall be taken away even that which he has.' (Matthew XXV, 29). This is the consequence for Africa, the victim of western imperial avarice and greed.

Summary and Conclusion

The contemporary state system in Africa today is a reflection of, and affected in a number of ways by, its European colonial origins. The new nation-state that emerged out of the process of decolonization in the post-Second World War period was euphemistically called the 'developmental state'. It exhibited many features of the imperial state in its political formation. The European parliamentary/presidential models, for example, were adopted by all African nation-states. These states had two basic characteristics—in terms of its political and economic agenda, and in terms of its 'infrastructural capacity'.

a. State reflects colonial partition

To begin with, the territorial definition of the state reflects the administrative boundaries of the colonial partition. A handful of African states have historical continuity with a precolonial epoch, but most originated as units of colonial administration. The imperial powers paid little heed to African cultural or political units in dividing up the continent. As a consequence, African state boundaries frequently divide ethno-linguistic groups. Also, African states have, with few exceptions, extensive internal diversity-ethnic, racial, linguistic, and religious.

b. Institutionalizing alien rule

A second major legacy of the colonial state was organized as a structure of institutionalizing alien rule; its vocation was domination of a subjugated population. A command mentality, a paternalistic mode of rule, a hegemonic relationship with the populace: these attributes of the colonial state are deeply ingrained in the daily routines of administration. Legally and practically, the colonial state considered the indigenous populace as subjects, not citizens. The African leadership that succeeded to power has, to varying degrees, endeavoured to eradicate this heritage. The inertia of the colonial state tradition is powerful, however, and continues to colour state-society relationships.

c. The process of yielding power

A third crucial effect of the colonial state lay in the process by which it yielded power to African successor regimes. One by one, in the three decades following World War II, colonial powers became persuaded that nationalism was an irresistible force. In a handful of cases, this conclusion was forced upon the colonizer by prolonged armed struggle (Algeria, 1954 to 1962; Guinea-Bissau, 1961 to 1974; Mozambique, 1964 to 1975; Angola, 1961 to 1975; Zimbabwe, 1973 to 1979). In most instances the withdrawing power recognized the need for accommodation with nationalist forces by negotiation. Once this conclusion was reached, the colonial power retained considerable means to influence the terms and method of decolonization.

The formula for decolonization generally called for creating political institutions closely modelled on the colonizing power's constitutional structure. The formal institutions of constitutional democracy-elected parliaments, competitive parties, and politically recruited cabinet-were hastily grafted onto the authoritarian bureaucratic colonial state. Yet in the home countries this process was a long and gradual one, before constitutional democracy was institutionalized. African states were asked to make an instantaneous transition from colonial subjugation to representative democracy. Enormous difficulties arose, and in most the initial constitutional structures failed to survive.

Some differences in this process are worth noting. Limited African participation, through appointive membership on consultative legislative councils, had existed before World War II in West African territories under British rule, and in coastal Senegal, then a French colony. Except for territories with settler populations, British colonial power tolerated earlier and more extensive associational activity, including political parties, than did other colonial powers. It is no accident that popular commitment to democratic values and insistence on a competitive party system appear most strongly rooted in Nigeria, where African political participation and expression began early.

The French, in keeping with the centralist ideology of the French state, permitted modest but very visible African representation in the French National Assembly in Paris long before an African voice was tolerated in Africa itself. A Senegalese leader, Blaise Diagne, entered the French Parliament in 1913 and served as junior minister in four French cabinets. Not until 1956 were territorial assemblies with significant power created in French-ruled tropical Africa. The Belgians prohibited African political activity until urban elections in 1957 and parties were not tolerated until 1959, the year before independence.

In conclusion, the COLONIAL STATE inherited by African countries at independence had the following attributes:

a) Export economies over-reliant on primary sector (minerals, coffee, cocoa, tea, vegetable oil, sisal, cotton, groundnuts, etc. All of them were monocrop economies;
b) Raw material exports were biased towards Europe, not local or regional markets; manufacturing was never part of the colonial deal and this condemned the colonies to disadvantages of unequal exchanges in international trade;
c) Colonial investments paid little or no attention to local imperatives in such a way that transport infrastructures only revolved around moving goods from the point of extraction to a port for onward transmission to Europe;
d) Underdevelopment of human resources was rampant. The case of Guinea Bissau is instructive here. After 300 years of colonial rule, Portugal left Guinea with 14 graduates, an illiteracy rate of 97%, only 265 miles of paved road and a single factory, of course a beer factory for Portuguese troops;
e) Export of surplus. All profits generated in African colonies were never reinvested in the continent. They were exported to the European metropoles leading invariably to the undercapitalization of African economies; and,
f) Imposition of imperial currencies. Imperial currencies as the franc, pound sterling, etc., were used as conduits for piping away financial resources from Africa to Europe.

Chapter Seven

Decolonizing Imperial State in Africa, 1945-60: *Plus ça change, plus c'est la même chose*

Overview

There is certainly no shortage of probable causes that have helped or hindered African development. However, rather than providing the potential for economic development, structural characteristics of the colonial globalizing system both created and perpetuated underdevelopment in Africa. The colonial global system under the hegemony of European civilization was born of centuries of genocide, subjugation and exploitation, and continues to promulgate these symptoms systematically within the framework of the current international order.

The impact of this European colonialism taps into both the internal and external causes of underdevelopment in Africa today. Internally, the political and economic structures of the colonial state were conditioned to meet the repressive as well as exploitative needs of the respective imperial states, leaving the former African territories unable to develop after the fall of the colonial empires. Externally, colonialism helped create the structural dependencies that the inherited states in Africa faced after the fall of formal colonial ties. Overall, virtually all components of underdevelopment in social and economic life in Africa date from the colonial period.

Historically, colonialism in Africa has been characterized as a land scramble by the European states, who hoped to increase their power, wealth, and prestige. The last wave of colonialism was codified with the Conference of Berlin in 1884-85, which set up 'effective occupation' of the areas under European control. Colonial administrative boundaries were established without regard for the divisions in African society or geography that existed before colonial occupation. Through these acts, Europeans decided how they could best break down traditional social and economic networks for more efficient social control and resource extraction.

The economic dimension of this dominance was a crucial component. Once the European governments had decided who 'owned' which territories, they proceeded to extract resources. To facilitate this extraction, the Conference 'established the rules by which Africa would participate in the world economy.' Under these 'rules,' Africa was forced 'to produce raw materials and agricultural goods to meet the needs of Europe's industries and consumers.' As a result, traditional agricultural economies were forced to specialize in 'cash crops meant for export.' This transformation was only possible through dependence upon foreign distribution and consumption. The colonial system thus brought power and economic benefit to the Europeans at the expense of their colonies.

Such economic dominance and exploitation did not readily dissipate with the end of colonialism. Rather the era of neocolonialism—political independence without economic independence—began. The transition from formal colonialism into neocolonialism marked a move from direct to indirect European control exercised mostly through economic relations. Furthermore, this continuation of economic dependence was the intended result of neocolonialism. While the colonial states continued to benefit, the states in Africa became more dependent on the Europeans because there was no economic integration among the former colonies or any provision for making the economy self-sustained and geared to its own local goals. As a result, Africa was denied development of trade links and the patterns of dependence fostered by colonial rule continued. Thus patterns of formal economic domination were simply replaced by structural constraints upon the states in Africa. Being unprepared to compete in the global market, the integration of these new states into the world economy merely deepened their colonial dependency.

Introduction

Decolonization was among the most significant phenomena of the twentieth century. Indeed, it helped shape the history of the past century, and in one way or another, either directly or indirectly, affected the lives of nearly everyone, all across the globe. In its shape and duration, decolonization varied from place to place. Furthermore, it has been evaluated in many different ways. But in each case, the importance of decolonization is beyond question.

The Second World War evidently marked a final watershed as it set in motion the process of 'decolonization,' i.e., the undoing of the world's empires and the setting free of the colonies and the creation of independent countries. After 1945, as a result of this process, there appeared the so-called Third World, aka the 'South' or the under-developed or less-developed world. The process of decolonization was far from being a stable and rational undertaking, and it resulted in much tension, conflict and disunity. By the time the dismantling of the colonies was over in the 1970s, Britain wound up 'losing' it all (India, Africa, Burma, Ceylon, Malaysia, etc.), as did also the Dutch, French and Portuguese (and US). Even as the colonial empires disappeared, the after-effects (the legacies of colonialism) remained. Here are some general points to consider:

- Many democratic constitutions that did not last long
- most of the new countries also faced difficult modernization issues (both economic and cultural), i.e., how to catch up with the more advanced economies of the world
- a wide range of situations (economic, resources, education, cultural, etc.) prevailed in the new countries
- nationalists who fought to achieve independence against the colonial regimes were now firmly militant, and once in power, it was usually difficult to reign in those militaristic tendencies
- the widespread appeal of radical political alternatives to the peoples who were struggling after the colonial period
- internal divisions in the new countries were often artificial yet they ended up causing significant problems. One major source of problems was borders.
- With regard to the world political stage, when considering the decolonization process also keep in mind:
- the impact of the Cold War on the process, as both sides in the Cold War tried to lure the new countries onto their side of the conflict, i.e., either pro-communist or pro-democracy
- by the 1950s, there was an attempt made at creating various regional organizations in the world, organizations that were independent of the Eastern or Western blocs. Much of this came under what became known as the Non-Aligned Movement
    - 1955, Bandung (actually the 2nd such conference)
    - 1945, Arab League
    - 1963, Organization of African Unity (OAU)
    - 1973, Organization of Petroleum Exporting Countries (OPEC)

A Brief Theoretical Overview

Today, people in Africa still erroneously think of decolonization in terms of conquering power over the juridical-political boundaries of a state, that is, by achieving control over a single nation- state (Grosfoguel 1996). As evidence has shown, the old national liberation and socialist strategies of taking power at the level of a nation-state are not sufficient because global coloniality is not reducible to the presence or absence of a colonial administration (Grosfoguel 2002) or to the political/economic structures of power.

One of the most powerful and deceptive myths of the 20th century was the notion that the elimination of colonial administrations amounted to the decolonization of the world. This led to the myth of a postcolonial world in general, and Africa in particular. The heterogeneous and multiple global structures put in place over a period of 450 years did not evaporate with the juridical-political decolonization of, say Africa, over the past 50 years. Africa continues to live under the same colonial power matrix. With juridical- political decolonization Africa moved from a period of global colonialism to the current period of global coloniality.

Although colonial administrations have been almost entirely eradicated and the majority of the African periphery is politically organized into independent states, non-European, especially African people are still living under crude European/Euro- American exploitation and domination. The old colonial hierarchies of European versus African remain in place and are entangled with the international division of labour and accumulation of capital at a world-scale (Quijano 2000; Grosfoguel 2002).

Herein lies the relevance of the distinction between colonialism and coloniality. Coloniality, or what Kwame Nkrumah calls neo-colonialism, allows Africans to understand the continuity of colonial forms of domination after the end of colonial administrations, produced by colonial cultures and structures in the modern/colonial capitalist world-system. Coloniality of power refers to a crucial structuring process in the modern/ colonial world-system that articulates peripheral locations in the international division of labour with the global racial/ethnic hierarchy and the inscription of Third World immigrants in the racial/ethnic hierarchy of metropolitan global cities.

Peripheral nation-states and non-European people live today under the regime of global coloniality imposed by the United States through the International Monetary Fund (IMF), the World Bank (WB), the Pentagon and NATO. Peripheral zones like Africa thus remain in a colonial situation even though they are no longer under colonial administration. The juridical reconsolidation of colonial borders, reinsulation of the nation-states from popular pressure mobilized against colonialism, concentration and monarchization of power, and construction of informal patrimonial networks to bridge the gap between the neo-colonial state and society accounted for this disengagement of the state from the expectations of the masses.

Historical Perspective

The legacy of the European colonial state has played a critical role in shaping the fate of a troubled African continent. The high number of European nations competing for power on the continent and the necessity to achieve effective occupation swiftly and make African colonies self-financing drove colonial states toward policies of 'ruthless extractive action'. The persistent, virulent racism that distanced colonial rulers from their African subjects was especially central to imperial state history in Africa.

Colonialism is the practice of creating settlements in lands geographically distant from the parent land. Historically, this involved killing or subjugating the indigenous population. With the spread of Hellenic and Roman culture and technology by the Roman Empire, the Renaissance and the Enlightenment of the fifteenth and sixteenth centuries and the Industrial Revolution of the eighteenth and nineteenth centuries, most of the world has at some point been colonized by a European country. The most notable colonial powers were Rome, Greece, Britain, France, Spain, Portugal, the Netherlands, and Denmark.

The ascension of the colonial ideology was based on the belief that colonies were an essential attribute of any great nation. Whether the reason was economic, political, or diplomatic the quest for overseas possessions was of paramount concern for European nations. Thus more explorations took place, and these events took on a new meaning. In the decade preceding the Berlin Conference in which fourteen western nations attended the three-month session was(is) considered to be the crux of European colonialism. Europeans needed to satisfy the material necessities of Europe; therefore, the dream of an African empire developed as an avenue for the extraction of capital, and as a boost to national prestige.

The hallmark of the 19th century was that it completed the process of creating a world economy based on the nation-states of advanced capital and their colonies. The hallmark of the 20th century was that it witnessed the dissolution of that system of colonial empires and a mortal contest between socialism and capitalism over how this new post-colonial world was to be organized economically, socially, politically, ideologically, aesthetically. 'Globalization' is the loose term designating the system that emerged at the end of that contest, with the demise of the then Union of Soviet Socialist Republics (USSR).

The beginning of the colonial era can be dated from the end of the 15th century. Until the beginning of the 19th century, however, most of Asia and (especially) Africa had remained outside colonial sovereignty. Then the pace quickened. In the first 75 years of the 19th century, colonial powers added an average of 210,000 square kilometres of non-European territory to their possessions annually. Between the mid-1870s and the First World War (1914-18), then, the average annual conquest jumped to 620,000 s q km. By the latter date (1914), 85 per cent of the globe's surface comprised colonial powers, their colonies and former colonies.

The 20th century thus begins at the point where the colonial division of the world was already complete. This accelerated pace of colonization was partly facilitated by the technologies that we associate with the Second Industrial Revolution in the latter decades of the 19th century: mass-produced steel, industrial chemistry, the internal-combustion engine, electric power and oil as sources of energy, the spread of the railways and the telegraph as standard forms of long-distance travel and communication, and so on. Two features of that unprecedented industrial transformation were to have lasting consequences. The scales of investment in these new types of industry required concentrations of capital so stupendous that the way was paved for a new kind of separation between finance capital and industrial capital, and for periods when the former has been dominant over the latter. Second, these new types of industry spread over much of Western Europe, the United States and even Japan, so that some of these other countries - the U.S., Germany, Italy and Belgium, for example - also now entered into much more intensified inter-colonial rivalry.

With the world already divided among major colonial powers, new wars could only be wars for the re-division of the world. The competition now was not just for unoccupied territory but for export markets, sources of raw materials and the investment opportunities already cornered by the established colonial powers. Numerous local wars of colonial expansion and inter-colonial rivalry at the dawn of the 20th century thus gained a new kind of ferocious edge, leading inexorably to a general conflagration. Never in history had there been a war involving so many countries, and fought over such vast global stakes, that it could be regarded as a 'World War.' The 20th century had the distinction of being the one that more or less began with precisely such a war.

But that very period, 1870-1914, which had witnessed such new forms and scales of industrialization across the core capitalist countries, as well as such an accelerated pace of colonization in Asia and Africa, also witnessed the rise of the first mass parties of the working class in Europe and the first anti-colonial movements of the modern type in the colonized continents. The First World War, and the consequent breakdown of the European system, then had momentous consequences, within Europe and on the global scale.

That breakdown helped pave the way for a successful revolution in Russia, in territorial terms the largest country straddling the Euro-Asian land mass. It also led to great revolutionary upheavals in several European countries, such as Italy, Germany, Austria, Hungary and Spain. Communist parties were at the same time founded in many countries outside Europe, notably in India, China and other countries of East and South-East Asia.

That same breakdown of the European system also opened up the space in which the growing anti-colonial movements started becoming mass movements. And, when the system broke down again two decades later, leading to the Second World War (1939-45), the next 30 years (1945-75) witnessed the dissolution of colonial empires across Asia and Africa and the rise of socialist regimes in a dozen countries, from East Asia to East and Central Europe to Latin America.

Colonialism created a very exploitative, insensitive and oppressive state. In fact, the colonial state combined the functions of the legislature, executive and judiciary in itself, used violence without qualms, and dedicated itself to furthering the selfish interests of the metropolitan bourgeoisie at the expense of Africans. Political independence did not generally mean the dismantling of these undemocratic and repressive structures and institutions that the colonial state had put in place. The culture of misrule that followed political independence all over the continent subverted the ideals of the nationalist struggles. Claude Ake is quite clear on this point: 'The character of the colonial state did not change significantly at independence since with few exceptions; the colonial state was inherited rather than transformed. Like the colonizers before them most of the nationalist leaders regarded the state as the instrument of their will. They privatized, and exploited it for economic gain and used it oppressively to absolutize their power. Even after independence, the state in Africa has not become a reassuring presence but remains a formidable threat to everybody except the few who control it.'[1]

For instance, the borders established by the Berlin Conference in 1885 to keep competing European powers out were relegitimized through the Organization of African Unity Charter in 1963 to keep potentially 'secessionist' regions in. However, in both cases the heavily juridical foundation of the borders constituted a de facto recognition that African states could not, and would not, fully control their territories, consolidating the 'bifurcated' colonial state. As written in 1963, the Charter (article III, para. 3) established 'Respect for the sovereignty and territorial integrity of each State and for its inalienable right to independent existence'. A 1964 resolution on border problems was more specific, pledging member states 'to respect the frontiers existing on their achievement of national independence' (Jackson and Rosberg,1982: 22).

Today, the inherited legacies of devastating colonial domination and exploitation continue to have far-reaching implications for contemporary power balances, politics, and policies. Political independence in Africa did not witness the dawn of democracy and political responsibility. Even in those countries where independence came through a revolution, constraints arising from dependence, underdevelopment, and cold war politics made it virtually impossible to build true democratic structures, cultures, and processes. Angola is one such country where political independence from a brutal Portuguese regime encouraged Western support for the late Jonas Savimbi's rebel movement that continues to destabilize the economy, his death notwithstanding.

In a country like Zimbabwe, a compromised independence negotiation with the British mediated the ability of the post-colonial government to redistribute land and promote transparent governance. Today, ordinary Zimbabweans are paying for this costly miscalculation. Thus, in virtually all African social formations, the distortions and disarticulations of the colonial experience and the constraints of neo-colonial underdevelopment and dependence ensured that the opportunity to initiate a national project was compromised. In fact, Africa simply moved from one crisis to another even as efforts were made to address the numerous contradictions and conflicts that followed the post-colonial alignment and realignment of social, economic and political forces and interests.

The state inherited at independence was a violent, undemocratic (though mainly dressed in multi-party robes), and privatized structure that was barely constituted to serve as the basis of governance or efficient delivery of services. Under colonialism, public policy was not a public process. Democratic values were ignored or suppressed. Primordial loyalties were politicized and used to manipulate individuals and communities. It was insensitive to local values and needs and it imposed taxes, levies, fees, and laws at will and without consultation. Its primary concern was with maximizing profits and the general extraction of surplus to satisfy the interests of the metropolitan state and dominant classes. It relied on extreme force and used its military power to visit violence on African communities without hesitation. Communities that refused to pay taxes, contribute forced labour or acknowledge the 'legitimacy' of the colonial state were attacked or razed and their leaders killed or forced into exile. Colonial globalization produced changes in territoriality and the functions of borders, but it did not eliminated them.

Africans were made to see themselves as subjects rather than citizens and indigenous values were bastardized or wiped out. The economic, political, and social programmes of the colonial state were informed by a pathological fixation on satisfying the greed of European merchants and consumers. This state structure was not dismantled at political independence. Rather, it was simply 'whitewashed' or 'Africanized' and handed over to a carefully nurtured political elite that was extremely hungry for raw power. Leading members of the new African elite that had been carefully identified, educated or nurtured in the ways of European interests were domesticated and incorporated into the colonial political machines as political apprentices after World War II. As Claude Ake has correctly noted, 'the state-building project in Africa….only succeeded in creating a state which is mainly a coercive force unable to transform power into authority, and domination into hegemony.'[2]

To cope with this anomaly, hegemonic networks have been grown into a dense web of state-society linkages, which, like a spider's web, is fragile, yet flexible; complex, yet nearly invisible. At the most basic level, the individual strands of the web act as *conduits*, along which political support flows up, and material resources flow down. To maintain his strand of the web, each 'big man' or regime crony must gain access to the pool of state resources; to maintain the web as a whole, the 'big men' must sustain the pool of state resources, by constantly resupplying it from the global economy. According to Bayart (1993: 235), 'the social struggles which make up the quest for hegemony and the production of the State bear the hallmarks of the rush for spoils in which all actors - rich and poor— participate in the world of networks'.

At political independence therefore, the new elite inherited a state with limited legitimacy and without hegemony. This condition complicated the nature of political engagements. Of course, since only a handful of elites were involved in the contestations for power, the various governments they formed reflected and represented those narrow interests. Thus, right from Election Day the legitimacy of the government was compromised. In trying to exercised control, the elites have had to rely on force, manipulation, and violence. With time, politics degenerated into warfare. This was a war in which everything was deployed and no prisoners were taken. Pluralism and tolerance were thrown overboard with democracy, and intolerance and bestiality, at best, insensitivity to the plight of the disadvantaged became the order of the day. The foundation for instability, bad governance, corruption, violence, waste and the recycling of underdevelopment became firmly established. The rest of the story should be nothing new to any of us.[3]

The dominant class at political independence was a pathetic parody of what a dominant class really is. This reality complicated the continent's chances of engaging the forces of neocolonialism and the contradictions of underdevelopment. Thus, right from the 1960s, the possibility of building new structures of accommodation, pluralism and good governance were mediated, even subverted by the nature of Africa's political elite. The new elite, including the nationalists, settled into an unequal, exploitative, and subservient relationship with foreign capital at the expense of the workers and peasants. Aside from the fact that it was small in size, it was also a very pretentious, underdeveloped, dependent, corrupt, and highly fragmented class. It lacked confidence in itself. It was reliant on foreign tastes, markets, and its world-view was externally determined. It had only a tenuous relationship to production and its accumulative base depended on its lucrative but unproductive relationship with foreign capital. Its economic strategy was largely determined by its ability to divert public resources away from development and basic needs into private interests and foreign bank vaults. With its tenuous accumulative base, the African bourgeois class turned to the state as its instrument of accumulation.

Thus, rather than building a productive base in industry and agriculture, the bourgeois class began to extend the powers of the state to build up its own capital base. This required the abridgement of popular rights, the diversion of public resources to serve private ends, the construction of extensive security networks, and increasing intolerance for the opposition. It also required the development of vicious strategies of primitive accumulation and political containment that saw the working classes and peasants as the main victims. With time, the media, students, trade unions, peasant associations, minorities, and professional groups became victims of the emergence of the 'big man' syndrome.

Those who captured the state, its instruments of force and resources, simply personalized it, wiped out all features of sensitivity, and imaginary and real enemies were found and immediately eliminated or forced into distant exile. Local 'axes of evil' were found as necessary and were subjected to the most brutal and merciless power of the state. However, each act of brutality and repression bred new cells of opposition to the state, its institutions and agents. Within two decades of political independence therefore, the continent was littered with military coups and counter-coups, civil and inter-state wars, ethnic violence, agitations for autonomy by minorities, alienation of the public from the state and its custodians, and the withdrawal of support for public policies.

Good governance was thrown over-board and leaders busied themselves with the construction of dubious ideologies, personality cults and looting their respective treasuries. As political decay, uncertainty, violence, and disillusionment replaced the euphoria of *Uhuru*, even fractions of the power elite began to construct parallel structures of power and opportunities. This was evidenced in the use of foreign schools for the wards, reliance on foreign hospitals for medical attention, use of foreign banks, airlines and advisers; the use of private security in place of public police, the reliance of private water bore-holes and private electricity generators in place of publicly provided alternatives, and investments abroad rather than in the local economy.

The state was hardly the sort of force that was capable of opening up the political space, mobilizing the people, and building a true foundation for democratic politics and constitutional rule. Indeed, for most Africans, the state became 'largely regarded as a hostile force to be evaded, cheated, defeated and appropriated as circumstances permit.' Hence, rather than perceive it as a force to organize society, support individual and collective initiatives for accumulation and survival, most Africans 'have turned away from the state to seek safety and fulfilment in their community, ethnic group or nation. The demands which they make on these social formations have turned them into informal polities, in competition with the state.'[4]

The truth is that the state is largely perceived as enemy and its custodians seen as crooks and unreliable characters. Loyalty is given to the ethnic or community group in the first instance because the state has failed woefully to inspire confidence, patriotism or commitment. Those that have tried to shift loyalties away from the ethnic group to the nation-state have been forced to 'return to base' as their hopes for a democratic, transparent, and supportive state evaporates in the face of criminal corruption, waste, violence, and at best illiberal political conduct. Worse still, its custodians have become obstacles to the attainment of the basic reasons why people agree to live together in plural communities. The 'big man' in Africa has always been and remains a danger to society. This is a really dangerous, undemocratic character whose track record shows nothing but corruption, waste, violence, human rights abuses, misplaced priorities, and a pathological commitment to the recycling of mediocrity.

Crucible of the Colonial State and Counter-currents

Between 1945 and 1960, dozens of colonial territories in Africa achieved autonomy or outright independence from their European colonial rulers. There was no one process of decolonization. In some areas, it was peaceful, and orderly. In many others, independence was achieved only after a protracted war. A few newly independent countries acquired stable governments almost immediately; others were ruled by dictators or military juntas for decades, or endured long civil wars. Some European governments welcomed a new relationship with their former colonies; others contested decolonization militarily. The process of decolonization coincided with the new Cold War between the Soviet Union and the United States, and with the early development of the new United Nations.

Decolonization was often affected by superpower competition, and had a definite impact on the evolution of that competition. It also significantly changed the pattern of international relations in a more general sense. The creation of so many new countries, some of which occupied strategic locations, others of which possessed significant natural resources, and most of which were desperately poor, altered the composition of the United Nations and political complexity of every region of the globe.

In the mid to late 19th century, the European powers colonized much of Africa and Southeast Asia. During the decades of imperialism, the industrializing powers of Europe viewed the African and Asian continents as reservoirs of raw materials, labour, and territory for future settlement. In most cases, however, significant development and European settlement in these colonies was sporadic. However, the colonies were exploited, sometimes brutally, for natural and labour resources, and sometimes even for military conscripts. In addition, the introduction of colonial rule drew arbitrary natural boundaries where none had existed before, dividing ethnic and linguistic groups and natural features, and laying the foundation for the creation of numerous states lacking geographic, linguistic, ethnic, or political affinity.

While the United States generally supported the concept of national self-determination, it also had strong ties to its European allies, who had imperial claims on their former colonies. The Cold War only served to complicate the U.S. position, as U.S. support for decolonization was offset by American concern over communist expansion and Soviet strategic ambitions in Europe. Several of the NATO allies asserted that their colonial possessions provided them with economic and military strength that would otherwise be lost to the alliance. Nearly all of the United States' European allies believed that after their recovery from World War II their colonies would finally provide the combination of raw materials and protected markets for finished goods that would cement the colonies to Europe. Whether or not this was the case, the alternative of allowing the colonies to slip away, perhaps into the United States' economic sphere or that of another power, was unappealing to every European government interested in postwar stability. Although the U.S. Government did not force the issue, it encouraged the European imperial powers to negotiate an early withdrawal from their overseas colonies.

However, as the Cold War competition with the Soviet Union came to dominate U.S. foreign policy concerns in the late 1940s and 1950s, the Truman and Eisenhower Administrations grew increasingly concerned that as the European powers lost their colonies or granted them independence, Soviet-supported communist parties might achieve power in the new states. This might serve to shift the international balance of power in favour of the Soviet Union and remove access to economic resources from U.S. allies. Events such as the Indonesian struggle for independence from the Netherlands (1945-50), the Vietnamese war against

France (1945-54), and the nationalist and professed socialist takeovers of Egypt (1952) and Iran (1951) served to reinforce such fears, even if new governments did not directly link themselves to the Soviet Union.

Thus, the United States used aid packages, technical assistance and sometimes even military intervention to encourage newly independent nations in the Third World to adopt governments that aligned with the West. The Soviet Union deployed similar tactics in an effort to encourage new nations to join the communist bloc, and attempted to convince newly decolonized countries that communism was an intrinsically non-imperialist economic and political ideology. Many of the new nations resisted the pressure to be drawn into the Cold War, joined in the 'nonaligned movement,' which formed after the **Bandung Conference** of 1955, and focused on internal development.

The newly independent nations that emerged in the 1950s and the 1960s became an important factor in changing the balance of power within the United Nations. In 1946, there were 35 member states in the United Nations; as the newly independent nations of the 'third world' joined the organization, by 1970 membership had swelled to 127. These new member states had a few characteristics in common; they were non-white, with developing economies, facing internal problems that were the result of their colonial past, which sometimes put them at odds with European countries and made them suspicious of European-style governmental structures, political ideas, and economic institutions. These countries also became vocal advocates of continuing decolonization, with the result that the UN Assembly was often ahead of the Security Council on issues of self-governance and decolonization. The new nations pushed the UN toward accepting resolutions for independence for colonial states and creating a special committee on colonialism, demonstrating that even though some nations continued to struggle for independence, in the eyes of the international community, the colonial era was ending.

European colonialism led to the subjugation of Africa during the twentieth century. Using religious conversion as an excuse, Catholic expansionism engulfed the land and consumed the resources of the native population. Draining indigenous assets for European benefit, colonization in Africa eventually led to civil unrest and a push for independence after the American and French revolutions. A later facet of the same colonialism, called imperialism, occurred in Africa during the late nineteenth century. Earlier, European greed had ruined Africa by a filthy exploitation of African people as a cheap means of slave labour. During the Scramble for Africa, European imperialistic powers carved up Africa and its resources into political partitions at the Berlin Conference of 1884-85. By 1905,

African soil was completely controlled by European might, mainly Britain, France, Portugal, Germany, and Italy. As a result of colonialism and imperialism, Africa suffered long term effects, such as the loss of important natural resources like gold and rubber, economic devastation, cultural confusion, geopolitical division, and political subjugation. However, European domination also brought better roads, railways, harbours, hospitals, education, and modern agricultural methods.[5]

What caused decolonization efforts in Africa? Revolutionary thought originated as Africa watched the successful revolutions of the United States and France. If the United States could be free, why not Africa? Secondly, international powers forgot colonial conquests as the limelight centred on Napoleon Bonaparte, whose empire was creeping onto their very doorstep. Thirdly, interracial relationships of Europeans with natives led to social divisions in Africa-some Europeans enjoyed high status as landowners, while Africans had fewer privileges and lower social standing. At the social median were Africans demoted to the bottom of the social ladder and stuck with the lowest jobs and fewest opportunities. As racially based discriminations grew, pent up tension simmered and nationalistic hatred bubbled in this colonial mélange. In the end, colonial racism coupled with revolutionary ideas and international disregard helped ignite the African wars for independence. Thus Ghana gained its independence in 1957 and once the unstoppable impetus of independence was underway, most other African colonies threw off European control throughout the 1960's.[6]

Indeed, a combination of three circumstances and three different trends of Allied promises, better education, and the forces of nationalism led to African emancipation. African desire for independence was based on witnessing the successful revolution and subsequent self rule of its neighbour nation, India, led by the exemplary pacifist Mahatma Gandhi. Secondly, African decolonization occurred with the international confrontation of the Cold War. Because the Soviet Union was attempting to promulgate its Communist ideology, major European powers feared that their desperate colonies would turn to Communism as a radical means of obtaining independence. Racism was the third circumstance which affected the decolonization of Africa. Unlike Latin America, Africa did not have the racial mixture in the colonies, since Europeans had not settled and intermixed with the natives elaborately. Instead, the racial prejudice was rooted in European belief of the inferiority of Africans based on cultural differences, lack of political involvement and lower education.[7]

African decolonization was merely a fulfilling of promises. Desirous of discarding the economic burden of maintaining huge empires, Allied powers promised independence to Africa after World War II. In a second differing aspect, the better education of a few people played a huge part in informing and activating the multitudes. Lending a voice to the people of Africa, the support of intellectuals and well educated individuals united the masses by a surge of nationalism. This desire for change, for national awakening, for throwing off the colonial rule, became the final element which enabled Africans to push for independence through intellectual appeal, political campaign and bloody uprisings. In 1957, Ghana became the first African nation to become independent. Further African decolonization occurred with the independence of Guinea, Nigeria, Sierra Leone, Tanzania, Congo, Uganda, Kenya, Zambia, Morocco, Tunisia, Algeria, Malawi, Gambia, Botswana, Swaziland, Cameroon, Chad, the Central African Republic, Côte d'Ivoire, Gabon, Madagascar, Mali, Senegal, and Niger.[8] By the end of the 1970s, almost no African soil remained constricted by colonial rule.[9]

The results of decolonization continued to affect Africa long after colonialism was gone. Because the mother countries had exercised full political control during colonization, political instability ensued after the colonial governing influence was gone. Although democracy in government was attempted, racial and ethnic inequality in Africa was too deep seated to permit egalitarianism. Secondly, the partitions established during colonization led to border disputes in the newly decolonized states. During the violence, aggression, and civil war which further split the new states, French West and Equatorial Africa was divided into the separate countries of Senegal, Côte d'Ivoire, etc.

Of course, the border wars coupled with colonial exploitation of natural resources led to the third result of decolonization-economic disaster. Under colonialism, the colonies had been totally dependent on the mother countries to buy their raw materials such as cash crops or minerals. When the mother country's support for the narrow cash crop based economy was gone, the entire economy threatened to crash. Stripped of its natural resources and without a stable government, Africa needed to diversify and industrialize its economy, but lacked the means. Only by borrowing huge amounts of money were the new countries able to stay afloat. In this fourth result of decolonization, debt led to African susceptibility and dependence on its lenders. In a condition known as neocolonialism, the countries or bankers which loaned money to Africa used those loans as a means of exerting economic or political control over Africa.

In the aftermath of decolonization, Africa displayed the same four results found in Latin America. Political instability occurred with the introductions of Marxist and capitalist influence, along with continuing friction from racial inequalities. Inciting civil war, black nationalist groups participated in violent attacks against white settlers, trying to end 'white minority rule' in the government. Further violence occurred with disagreements over the partitions made during the colonization. Despite widespread acceptance of these partitions, border disputes such as those between Chad and Libya, Ethiopia and Somalia, and Nigeria and Cameroon are nursed even today.[10] In another result of colonialism followed by decolonization, the African economy was drained of natural resources with no opportunity to diversify from its colonial export of cash crops. Suffering through famine and drought, Africa struggled to industrialize its poverty stricken work force without sufficient funds.

In an attempt to influence the Third World to adopt the ideology of either capitalism or Communism, the United States and the Soviet Union loaned food and money to Africa. In this fourth circumstance of post decolonization, debt was a result of the poor economic set up of colonialism. To feed, educate, and modernize its masses, Africa borrowed huge sums of money from various nations, bankers and companies. In return, the lenders tried to exert political power over Africa, even though technically not in charge. Sadly, the borrowed money did not fix the devastated economy. Since the massive loans in both Africa and Latin America have been squandered by mismanagement and corruption of dictators, social issues such as education, healthcare, and political stability were ignored.[11]

In sum, three main phenomena led to decolonization—colonial desire for independence based on the successful emancipation of other nations, European distraction with international affairs, and native resentment against racial discrimination. Three additional aspects, including the Allied promises of independence after World War II, better educational opportunities, and a wave of nationalism.

Indeed, the advent, spread, and triumph of nationalist organizations across twentieth-century Africa hastened the liquidation of European colonial regimes. Africans articulated demands for decolonization within the boundaries of individual colonial units where nationalists opposed self-determination for ethnic groups within an existing state, but militantly demanded its broader application to eliminate European colonial rule. The retention of the colonial territorial legacy in postcolonial Africa legitimized inherited frontiers and institutions as a critical way to define and distinguish one national state from another. Territorial integrity and present boundaries form a symmetrical linkage which accords international juridical recognition—a critical measure of stability and continuity—to empirically weak postcolonial states in Africa. Finally, the results of decolonization including political instability, border disputes, economic ruin, and massive debt continue to plague both Africa to this present day.

Legacy of the Colonial State in Africa

Modern African nation-states are creations of the European colonial bourgeoisie and the political elites that serve their interests. These political elites, acting through the instruments of power that states provide, create the conditions needed for capitalist production and exchange. The function of the state is to maintain a social order. It does this not only by providing for the common defence, but also by its laws and social and economic policies. A crucial function of the bourgeois state is the protection of private property and enforcement of contracts.

But capitalist society is divided by classes with different and even conflicting interests. Within it the interests of the capitalist class are dominant in so far as other classes are dependent on it. For example, the interests of wage labour within such a society lie in the wages and benefits they receive and the conditions under which they work. But their very employment depends on capital being able to realize a profit from its use of wage labour. Thus in maintaining the social order, the state invariably promotes the interests of capital because it is only if capital can profit that labour will be employed at all. In capitalism, as in all divided societies, the function of the state leads it to promote the interests of the dominant class within civil society. It is thus that the political elite serves the economically dominant class of capitalists.

In line with this logic, the conception of the state used in this book is both an entity that acts, in the last instance, on behalf of the ruling class (which, in the case of Africa, is the metropolitan bourgeoisie) and as a set of institutions that constitutes an arena for class struggles. Thus, the state in Africa continues its colonial function of integrating the continent more firmly into the orbit of capitalist imperialism. That is to say, the state in Africa originated from the class forces of the European metropoles and it remains the decisive factor in its social orientation, an orientation that explains its primary function of subordinating Africa's resources to the profit impulse of multinational capital.

The contradictions of global capitalism that radiate with peculiar intensity in Africa promise an uncertain future for the postcolonial capitalist state, as it becomes increasingly difficult for the dominant classes to maintain their grip on the institutions of the state. For example, the eruption of unabashed imperial globalization is a profound historical vindication of the Marxist analysis of contemporary capitalism. During the post-war boom, apologists of the profit system dismissed Lenin's 1916 masterwork, *Imperialism: the Highest Stage of Capitalism*, as outdated and irrelevant, pointing to the supposedly progressive and 'democratic' tendencies of modern capitalism. They mistook the restraints on the great powers imposed by the standoff between the United States and the Soviet Union, the pressure of working class struggles at home and the eruption of anti-colonial upheavals in the 'Third World' for proof that imperialism was a thing of the past.

Today, Lenin's (1939:89) summing up of the basic features of monopoly capitalism, and his insistence that it necessarily entails 'reaction all down the line,' read like a precise distillation of contemporary World Bank/ IMF, American politics and Washington's foreign policy. Imperialist capitalism, Lenin said, is 'annexationist, predatory, plunderous.' It wages war 'for the division of the world, for the partition and repartition of colonies, [for] 'spheres of influence' of finance capital.' 'Capitalism,' he continued, 'has grown into a world system of colonial oppression and of the financial strangulation of the overwhelming majority of the people of the world by a handful of 'advanced' countries.'

He added: 'To the numerous 'old' motives of colonial policy, finance capital has added the struggle for the sources of raw materials, for the export of capital, for 'spheres of influence,' i.e., for spheres for profitable deals, concessions, monopolist profits and so on; in fine, for economic territory in general.' In fact, this social layer is parasitic to the core. It has contempt for democratic methods and institutions, and employs Mafia-type methods to achieve its ends. Now they are projecting these methods onto the global arena to steal what they cannot grab by conventional means.

Studies on colonialism as politics and the politics of colonialism have tended to focus on two main issues: the nature of the colonial state and African resistance. Discussion and debate on the colonial state have centred on its specificities and construction, how to classify African colonial states and administrations, the dynamics of colonial power and civil society, and the demise or reconstitution of the colonial state into the postcolonial state. Crawford Young (1994) has argued quite forcefully that the African colonial state derives its peculiarity from the fact that it enjoyed only some of the crucial attributes of the modern state (territory, population, sovereignty, power, law, and the state as nation, an international actor, and an idea) and could not exercise some of its imperatives (hegemony, autonomy, security, legitimacy, revenue, and accumulation).

This is because the colonial state in Africa was created in the late nineteenth century, long after both the modern metropolitan state and the generic colonial state had been formed, which allowed for no experimentation. Also, as a conquest state imposed by force, its hegemony was excessively coercive, so that it enjoyed little legitimacy. Moreover, its territoriality was ambiguous, its sovereignty and institutions of rule were extraverted and resided in the imperial metropole, and its revenue base was weak. Charged with the onerous tasks of consolidating colonial rule, linking the colony to the metropole, and establishing or promoting colonial capitalism, the result was that the colonial state was both interventionist and fragile, authoritarian and weak, and exercised domination without hegemony, all of which ensured its eventual downfall.

All colonial states, irrespective of their ideologies and administrative systems, justified themselves in the names of civilization and pacification. Economic motivations of colonialism were assiduously downplayed. Moreover, all colonial powers used African intermediaries in their administrative systems because they lacked personnel and local knowledge and in order to minimize African resistance and administrative costs. They also used chartered companies in some of their colonies in the early years.

In imperialist historiography, colonial power was portrayed as unassailable because it was for Africa's good. For the opposite reason it was decried in nationalist historiography, which stressed its oppressiveness and incapacity to withstand the full might of nationalist struggle. Dependency writers tended to disregard the importance of politics because they believed that neither the colonial state nor African resistance could stop the ineluctable juggernaut of the world capitalist system, while Marxists subsumed colonial politics to either local class struggles (waged by the numerically small working classes, and only reluctantly and later were struggles by the much larger peasantries considered) or anti-imperialist struggles mediated by communist parties in the imperial metropoles themselves or the Soviet Union.

Many of the early studies failed to examine the ways that colonial power was specifically deployed, engaged, contested, deflected, or appropriated. When Peter Ekeh published his influential essay 'Colonialism and the Two Publics in Africa' (1975), colonial civil society began to attract serious scholarly attention. He argued that colonialism created two publics that he called the primordial and civic publics, whose dialectical relationships accounted for the political problems of postcolonial Africa.

The first public is associated with primordial groupings, sentiments, and activities; the second is associated with the colonial administration and is amoral, lacking the generalized moral imperatives operative in the private realm and in the primordial public. The two publics emerged because colonizing ideologies of legitimation denigrated African societies and cultures and glorified European colonial rule, while African bourgeois ideologies of legitimation accepted colonial ideas and principles to justify the leadership of the elites in the fight against colonialism and the inheritance of the postcolonial state.

Both ideologies envisaged and sought to separate the indigenous and colonial publics, in which different conceptions of citizenship, morality, and material expectations prevailed. Thus colonial civil society was characterized by the bifurcation of the public realm, which accounts for the centrality of ethnicity in African politics and the disjunction between the state and society that has bedevilled postcolonial Africa.

The configuration of colonial rule in Africa led first to the institutionalization of two systems of power under a single authority: one urban, based on civil power and rights, excluding the colonized on the basis of race, the other rural, where tradition and culture incorporated the colonized into the rule of custom. Second, colonial rule in Africa led to the privileging of state-ordained and state-enforced traditions that had least historical depth and were monarchical, authoritarian, and patriarchal, so that customary power and law became an integral part of a decentralized despotism. Finally, with custom becoming the language of force, colonial rule led to rationalizing the appropriation and management of land and the mobilization of labour under the colonial rubric.

This bifurcated state power, civil and customary, first crystallized in equatorial Africa—as 'indirect rule' in British colonies and 'association' in French colonies—and later spread to older colonies to the north and south, including South Africa, where apartheid represented the last attempt at reorganizing the state structure to incorporate the 'native' population in a world of enforced tradition. The challenges confronting African countries in the struggles for independence and after were to democratize the state and particularly customary power, deracialize civil society, and restructure unequal external relations of dependency.

African Nation States

The creation of nations in Africa, a product of belligerent European colonial regimes, has been one of the most destructive legacies left on the African continent by the powers of Europe. Much of the political turmoil we witness today stems from the imposition of nations where there was no popular, financial or physical infrastructure. The boundaries imposed on Africa were artificial, bearing no resemblance to the sociocultural groupings of the populations. Because African colonies were established to enrich the occupying European powers, the economies and governments of most African states were externally oriented. African nations forced to supply Europe with cheap labour and raw materials became more closely connected to Britain, France, Germany and Portugal than to one another. While we can hold recent leaders of African nations responsible for some postcolonial problems, we should acknowledge that they inherited a structure of militarized nations bent on subjecting the masses while extracting a profit.

Africanist historians are also well aware that colonialists, to expedite their occupation and administration of Africans, relied on notions of tribes as separate, not fluid or interdependent groupings. The colonial regimes defined and empowered some (like the Tutsi) and dispossessed others (the Hutu). Tribalism in Africa is not primordial; like ethnicity and nationalism globally, it is an expression and function of power relations and competition for resources. Many news reports date the tensions in Rwanda to 1959, but the conflict has historical roots more complicated than Africa's post-colonial inability to govern itself.

A combination of three circumstances and three different trends of Allied promises, better education, and the forces of nationalism led to African emancipation from the imperial state. African desire for independence was based on witnessing the successful revolution and subsequent self rule of its neighbour nation, India, led by the exemplary pacifist Mahatma Gandhi. Secondly, African decolonization occurred with the international confrontation of the Cold War. Because the Soviet Union was attempting to promulgate its Communist ideology, major European powers feared that their desperate colonies would turn to Communism as a radical means of obtaining independence. Racism was the third circumstance which affected the decolonization of Africa. Africa did not have the racial mixture in the colonies, since Europeans had not settled and intermixed with the natives. Instead, the racial prejudice was rooted in European belief of the inferiority of Africans based on cultural differences, lack of political involvement and lower education.

African decolonization was merely a fulfilling of promises. Desirous of discarding the economic burden of maintaining huge empires, Allied powers promised independence to Africa after World War II. In a second differing aspect, the better education of a few people played a huge part in informing and activating the multitudes. Lending a voice to the people of Africa, the support of intellectuals and well educated individuals united the masses by a surge of nationalism. This desire for change, for national awakening, for throwing off the colonial rule, became the final element which enabled Africans to push for independence through intellectual appeal, political campaign and bloody uprisings. In 1957, Ghana became the first African nation to become independent. Further African decolonization occurred with the independence of Guinea, Nigeria, Sierra Leone, Tanzania, Congo, Uganda, Kenya, Zambia, Morocco, Tunisia, Algeria, Malawi, Gambia, Botswana, Swaziland, Cameroon, Chad, the Central African Republic, Côte d'Ivoire, Gabon, Madagascar, Mali, Senegal, and Niger. By the end of the 1970s, almost no African soil remained constricted by colonial rule.

The results of decolonization continued to affect Africa long after colonialism was gone. Because the mother countries had exercised full political control during colonization, political instability ensued after the colonial governing influence was gone. Although democracy in government was attempted, racial inequality in Africa was too deep seated to permit egalitarianism. Secondly, the partitions established during colonization led to border disputes in the newly decolonized states.

Of course, the border wars coupled with colonial exploitation of natural resources led to the third result of decolonization-economic disaster. Under colonialism, the colonies had been totally dependent on the mother countries to buy their raw materials such as cash crops or minerals. When the mother country's support for the narrow cash crop based economy was gone, the entire economy threatened to crash. Stripped of its natural resources and without a stable government, Africa needed to diversify and industrialize its economy, but lacked the means. Only by borrowing huge amounts of money were the new countries able to stay afloat. In this fourth result of decolonization, debt led to African susceptibility and dependence on its lenders. In a condition known as neocolonialism, the countries or bankers which loaned money to Africa used those loans as a means of exerting economic or political control over African states.

In the aftermath of decolonization, Africa displayed the four results. Political instability occurred with the introductions of Marxist and capitalist influence, along with continuing friction from racial inequalities. Inciting civil war, Black Nationalist groups participated in violent attacks against white settlers, trying to end 'white minority rule' in the government. Further violence occurred with disagreements over the partitions made during the colonization. Despite widespread acceptance of these partitions, border disputes such as those between Chad and Libya, Ethiopia and Somalia, and Nigeria and Cameroon are nursed even today. In another result of colonialism followed by decolonization, the African economy was drained of natural resources with no opportunity to diversify from its colonial export of cash crops. Suffering through famine and drought, Africa struggled to industrialize its poverty stricken work force without sufficient funds.

In an attempt to influence the Third World to adopt the ideology of either capitalism or Communism, the United States and the Soviet Union loaned food and money to Africa. In this fourth circumstance of post decolonization, debt was a result of the poor economic set up of colonialism. To feed, educate, and modernize its masses, Africa borrowed huge sums of money from various nations, bankers and companies. In return, the lenders tried to exert political power over Africa, even though technically not in charge. Sadly, the borrowed money did not fix the devastated economy. Since the massive loans in Africa were squandered by mismanagement and corruption of dictators, social issues such as education, healthcare, and political stability were ignored.

In essence, the Berlin Conference was very important in African history because of the way it sought to minimize competition among the European colonial powers in their haste to acquire mineral rich lands in Africa. Debate about the perceived positive and negative aspects of colonialism has occurred for centuries, amongst both colonizer and colonized, and continues to the present day.

Political Impact

The Africa of a century ago consisted of a large number of autonomous empires and communities. Some of these societies were large and powerful; others were smaller and weaker. When the Europeans finished drawing their lines of partition, these states had been condensed into about 50 pieces of territory all of which came under European colonial rule. The systematic, indiscriminate partition (scramble) drawn without any well defined, regional criteria in full cognizance of the ethno cultural, geographical and ecological realities of Africa brought different ethnic groups (tribes) having different historical traditions, cultures and speaking different languages under one or more colonial power. This situation disrupted the political development of these social groups; furthermore, ethnic groups were cleaved into fragments.

These lines of partition also run-across pre- existing nations, ethnicities, states, kingdoms and empires. The Ewes for instance are divided by the boundary between Ghana and Togo while A*kan* are found in the Ivory Coast and in Ghana. The *Senufo* now live in Mali, the Ivory Coast and in Burkina Faso. This explains the border disputes between Burkina Faso and Mali, etc. These lines also brought about the uneven sizes and unequal distribution of natural resources and economic potentialities of these states. Some of the states emerged from the partition as giants e.g. Nigeria with an approximated area of 357,000 square miles, whiles others came out as midgets e.g. Gambia with an approximated area of 4000 square miles. Some states have few boarders e.g. Gambia with one boarder whiles others had many boarders e.g. Mali with seven boarders. This makes it difficult to check the problems of security and smuggling. Even though the partition has negative impacts it also contributed to the appearance of independent African states of today. The partition of Africa by imperial colonial powers boundaries, in place of the innumerable lineage and clan groups, city states, kingdoms and empires without any fixed boundaries. It is significant that the boundaries of these states have been maintained ever since independence.

Colonialism caused the loss of sovereignty which is the loss of the right of a society to control its own destiny, to play in its own development, to conduct its own diplomacy and internal relations, to decide which outside nations to associate with or to emulate and above all to manage or even mismanage its own affairs, derive pride and pleasure from its success and derive lessons, frustration and experience from its failures. Many African nationalists and critics of colonialism see the independence gained from the withdrawing colonial powers as only partial liberation. Some call it 'false independence.' Full or real freedom, they believe, will come with economic independence.

African nations are said to be currently in a phase of neo-colonialism - a new form of imperial rule stage managed by the colonial powers to give the colonized the illusion of freedom. At the 1961 All-African People's Conference held in Cairo neo-colonialism was defined as 'the survival of the colonial system in spite of the formal recognition of political independence in emerging countries which become the victims of an indirect and subtle form of domination by political, economic, social, military or technical means.' The implication is that western powers still control African nations whose rulers are either willing puppets or involuntary subordinate of these powers.

The other type of subjugation that emerged in Africa which was, in effect, an economic extension of colonialism was settlerism. It has been established by a number of historians and political theorists that white settlers in Africa, or in other areas for that matter, took land for themselves, and in the process exacted political control over its indigenous inhabitants. Settler communities ignored and opposed all pleas for African education, promotion of Africans to responsible jobs, or the exercise of political rights such as the freedom to express political ideas or form political organizations.

Colonialism Bred Political Crisis

In disrupting pre-colonial political systems that worked for Africans and imposing alien models, colonialism laid the seeds of political crisis, say its critics. By redrawing of the map of Africa, throwing diverse people together without consideration for established borders, ethnic conflicts were created that are destabilizing the continent. The new nation-states were artificial and many were too small to be viable. Less than a third of the countries in Africa have populations of more than 10 million. Nigeria, the major exception to this, was imbued with ingredients for its self-destruction. Western multi-party democracy imposed by colonial powers polarized African societies. One of the most important social impact colonialism had on West Africa is the introduction of new bureaucracy of civil servants and a new judiciary system. These institutions especially the judicial system have not undergone any fundamental changes in any of the independent states.

Socio-cultural Impact

Urbanization: Not only did pre-existing towns expand, but completely new urban centres emerged following the establishment of the colonial system e.g. Abidjan in Ivory Coast, Takoradi in Ghana, Port Harcourt and Enugu in Nigeria. All these new urban centres were created either as ports or harbours, mining centres, administration centre, etc. The population of Accra jumped from 17,892 in 1901 to 135,926 in 1948. There is no doubt the quality of life for West Africa's population was improved through the provision of piped water, hospitality, better housing and sanitary facilities.

Christianity, Islam and expansion of western education during the colonial period

Christianity gained far more converts and penetrated further. Islam also gained a lot of grounds . The spread of western education was mainly due to the action of the Christian missionaries. by 1930s there were very few areas in West Africa where elementary education wasn't common. By 1940 universities also became common in almost all the colonies except in the Portuguese and Belgium colonies. Every modern West African state is thankful to its colonial master for introducing western education. Only reactionary aristocrats in northern Nigeria would today thank the British for keeping out western education in their region. It is clear to most northerners that they were placed at a disadvantage to the south by the educational gap between the two regions.

Provision of lingua franca for each colony

Almost all the colonies adopted a colonial language for communication which broke the ethnic language barrier between tribes. It, in many respects, distorted and abrogated the essence of African cultural norms and institutions. The systematic approach that the European invaders utilized to usurp land in Africa has contributed greatly to the disunity and dysfunction of indigenous Africans; coups take place in Africa not because Africans cannot govern themselves, but because African leaders have inherited a colonial legacy that tends to pit African against African, or brother against brother. This schism can be traced directly to the different types of colonial masters that held sway on the continent. Each colonial power pursued a cultural policy that it believed would give it efficacious results, and a policy that was in tune with his philosophy of colonial administration.

Economic Impact

The prime legacy of colonialism was the integration of colonies into the international capitalist economy. It enables African elites to consume products of western civilization without having to go through the difficult and long-term process of building the productive base of their societies. It is far easier to shop in the global market than try to build industries yourself.

One important economic benefit was the provision of infrastructure of roads, railways, harbours and ports, the telegraph and telephone. The basic infrastructure of every modern African state was completed during its colonial period. Some states have not improved upon the colonial infrastructures even after impendence. Development of the primary sector of Africa's economy happened during the colonial period. It was during this period that the mineral potential of many African states were discovered and modern scientific mining introduced. Above all, it was during this period that the productions of such cash crops like cotton, peanuts, palm, cocoa etc. became the main feature of the political economy of many African states.

The transportation and communication infrastructure that was provided was not only inadequate but was also very unevenly distributed in nearly all the colonies. The roads and railways were built in areas with the potential for cash crops and with mineral deposits. They were actually meant to facilitate the exploitation of African resources but not to promote the accessibility and the development of all the regions in the economy.

Colonialism saddled most colonies with monocrop economies

During the colonial period, each colony was made to produce a single cash crop or two and no attempts were made to diversify the agricultural economy. The habit of producing these single cash crops appears to have become so ingrained that it has not been changed to any appreciable degree since independence. Africans were encouraged to produce what they don't consume and to consume what they don't produce. It is lamentable that the legacy has not changed materially in most of the African states. To this day they have to rely on the importation of edible oil, rice, maize and other food stuff to survive.

Africa's poor states gained little or nothing from colonialism. But its elites bloomed as a result of it. They were given a ladder to climb the global pyramid. West African wealthy states e.g. Nigeria who today lives on the upper layers of the pyramid, certainly owe their fortune to colonialism. Without opportunities created by the linking of Africa to the western world, it is unlikely that indigenous ruling classes would have catapulted themselves from pre-capitalist levels of wealth to modern bourgeoisie affluence. So the answer to the often posed question, 'did Africans benefit from colonialism' is, the elites definitely gained while the poor majority did not.

The results of colonization including political instability, border disputes, economic ruin, and massive debt, a dysfunctional underdeveloped tributary economy in the hands of a bifurcated state continue to plague Africa to this present day. The current state in Africa is a colonial creation, and thus did not emerge from the needs of Africans. European colonial authorities turned over to the local African elite the state institutions at their disposal. Unfortunately, those who inherited the colonial state were inexperienced or not in touch with the people they represented and thus never bothered to reconstruct the inherited imperial state.

Summary and Conclusion

The colonial state left what are today's main features of the state (puppet or neo-colonial) in African societies. A distinction is necessary here. A puppet state is defined in the sense of a state which claims popular legitimacy but which is significantly dependent on an external power. In some cases, the process of decolonization was managed by the decolonizing power to create a neo-colony that is a nominally independent state whose economy and politics permit continued foreign domination. Neo-colonies are not normally considered puppet states.

Plus ça Change, Plus C'est la Même Chose

By and large, the following features are eloquent testimonies of both puppet and neo-colonial state systems left behind by withdrawing colonialists in Africa:

- a large section of African population engaged in rural economic activities;
- a large section of their productive system engaged in producing
- cash crops, extracting raw materials and manufacturing products to meet the demand in industrialized countries;
- the productive system is 'fractured': with a modern sector engaged in high level technology production, generally not for local consumption, and a traditional sector engaged in labour-intensive low-technology production. This situation reflects into extremely polarized distribution of income, creating large pockets of poverty as the outcome of low wages, unemployment and underemployment.
- modernization processes are sustained only through heavy external financing which generate a vicious circle economic growth-foreign indebtedness.

- their system of production is dependent upon flows of capital, technology and demand from former colonial powers.
- regionally, African countries are connected to the Western European economies.

This existential situation derives from the main effects of colonization by Western European powers (Todaro 2000):

1. The BREAKING of pre-existing patterns of economic and social life, through the introduction of new labour regimes (systems of recruiting and organizing labour)
2. All colonial labour regimes involved an INTENSIFICATION OF LABOUR compared with pre-colonial modes of organizing labour in production.
3. Compulsory means were employed to obtain the supply of labour for plantations, mines and settler estates.
4. Colonial legislation and administration concerning MONEY TAXATION, PROPERTY TITLES in land and the COMMERCIALIZATION OF AGRICULTURE linked to the INTERNATIONAL ECONOMY, radically altered the NATURE OF RURAL SOCIAL RELATIONS, and caused the formation of NEW SOCIAL CLASSES among the indigenous population.
5. The above features survived the end of colonization (direct foreign rule), and have continued to develop in politically independent less developed societies.

The combined effects of the activities of the repressive and exploitative colonial state apparatus shaped what can be considered the common characteristics of African societies at the beginning of the XXI century:

a. Low levels of standard of living, characterized by low incomes, inequality, poor health, and inadequate education.
b. Low levels of productivity.
c. High rates of population growth and dependency burdens.
d. High and rising levels of unemployment and underemployment.
e. Substantial dependence on agricultural production and primary-product exports.
f. Prevalence of imperfect markets and limited information.
g. Dominance, dependence and vulnerability in international relations.

Indeed, decolonization in Africa involved more than a transfer of political power from Europeans colonizers to nationalists. Rather, it was a 'multilayered process' of social, economic and cultural transformation which took place on a wide geographic scale, unfolded with varying speeds, and peaked around 1960. Key for the transition from colonial to postcolonial times was the formation and transformation of elites, conceptualized as social groups who command over certain resources (political support, economic power, symbolic resources such as communication or knowledge).

These groups had not yet found the attention they deserved. And that explains why the organizers of decolonization examined their trajectories on three distinct levels: by looking at colonial state institutions, indigenous elites, metropolitan elites, and the international context which often brought third-party interventions (such as the Commonwealth, France-Afrique, Francophonie, UNO, IMF, World Bank, WTO, etc.) to ease the implementation of their 'theory of collaboration' as a point of departure. This examination led to identifying four major allies of the colonial powers in Africa—royalty and aristocracies, trading minorities, ethnic minorities, and the civil service—and showed how World War II opened up opportunities for new nationalist elites.

The post-colonial state could not act in the interests of the people it purports to serve and from whom it is expected to draw its 'legitimacy.' The question that occupies the minds of all Africans is: WHY? There are two trends that tend to marginalize or question the role of THE STAE IN AFRICA in the postcolonial era. The first of these is the inherent anti-statism that is informed by neoliberal, managerialist, and communitarian agendas, each of which in their way has influenced approaches to development and poverty alleviation in Africa.

The second stems from a complex assortment of radical and critical ideas associated with the anti-colonial struggle that challenge the global ascendancy of capitalism, liberal democracy, Western culture and neoliberal welfare theories. The post-colonial state has been cornered into being a partial omnipotent institution enforcing the will of TNCs and does not act as a social guardian. It is a 'predator' or a vehicle for primitive accumulation for politically powerful groups including national as well as foreign state actors (TNCs), comprising financiers, politicians and bureaucrats.

References

1. Claude Ake. (1994), *Democratization of Dispowerment in Africa.* Port Harcourt: CASS Occasional Monograph No. 1, p. 7. .
2. Ibid, pp 6-7.
3. Claude Ake. (2001). The Feasibility of Democracy in Africa, op. cit. and Claude Ake, Democracy and Development in Africa. Ibadan: Spectrum Books for African Centre for Democratic Governance.
4. Claude Ake, Democratization of Dispowerment, op. cit, p. 7
5. Pink Monkey.com.(2004). '*Decolonization.*' *World History.* 28 May,, retrieved June 20,2004. <http://www.pinkmonkey.com/studyguides/subjects/euro_his/chap6/e0606301.htm>
6. NA.(2004). '*Latin America in the 19th Century.*' *World History.* 28 May. 2004. < http://www.hcc.hawaii.edu/distance/hist/latinam.htm> accessed 08/02/09.
7. NA.(2004). '*French and British Colonial Styles.*' *World History.* 28 May. 2004. < http://www.bbc.co.uk/worldservice/africa/features/storyofafrica/14chapter2.shtml> accessed 06/25/09.
8. Ostara Publications.(2004). '*The Collapse of Colonialism.*' *World History.* 28 May. 2004. < *http://www.white-history.com/hwr65.htm*> accessed 06/23/09.
9. Encyclopedia.com. (2004). '*Africa.*' *World History.* 28 May. 2004. <http://www.encyclopedia.com/html/section/Africa_OutlineofHistory.asp> accessed 09/29/06.
10. Encyclopedia.com. (2004). '*Post Independence.*' *World History.* 28 May. 2004. <http://www.bbc.co.uk/worldservice/africa/features/storyofafrica/14chapter10.shtml> accessed 10/18/08.
11. NA.(2004). ' *Economic Challenges.*' *World History.* 28 May. 2004. < http://www.hcc.hawaii.edu/distance/hist/neocol.htm> accessed 12/28/05.

Chapter Eight

African Developmentalist/ Nationalist State?

Overview

Africa is a vast and exotic continent of about 900 million people in 54 independent countries. It has a total area of over 30 million square kilometres. Africa is rich in mineral and natural resources. It possesses 99 percent of the world's chrome resources, 85 percent of its platinum, 70 percent of its tantalite, 68 percent of its cobalt, and 54 percent of its gold, among others. It has significant oil and gas reserves. Nigeria and Libya are two of the leading oil producing countries in the world. Further, Africa is the home to timber, diamonds, and bauxite deposits. Revenues from their extraction should provide funds for badly needed development, but instead have fuelled state corruption, environmental degradation, poverty, and violence. Rather than being a blessing, Africa's natural resources have largely been a curse.

Africa's vast mineral wealth and strategic significance have encouraged foreign powers to intervene in African affairs. During the Cold War era, 1945-1990, there was increasing superpower intervention in Africa. The United States and the Soviet Union were major players on the African scene. The 19th-Century scramble for Africa saw the great powers rush to control land so they could exploit natural resources. The key question for many is: will the exploitation of Africa's rich resources benefit anyone other than the continent's elites?

Oil is perhaps the most important lure, with competition between foreign states and companies to secure resources so intense it attracts more than 50 per cent of all foreign direct investment. In 2006, annual Foreign Direct Investment (FDI) raised to a historic high of $38.8 billion, exceeding record levels of 2005—a growth of 78 per cent from 2004. According to the UN World Investment Report, FDI cash was concentrated in a few industries, notably oil, gas and mining. And six oil-producing countries—Algeria, Chad, Egypt, Equatorial Guinea, Nigeria, and Sudan—hogged around 48 per cent of it.

European firms represent roughly two-thirds of the total FDI in Africa. More than half of European investment originates from the UK and France, going mainly to countries with which they have historic ties. French oil companies such as Total, locked out of the Middle East through France's opposition to the Iraq war, have made large investments in Francophone countries such as Cameroon, Chad, and Gabon. The US is interested in the region as a cheap and reliable alternative to the increasingly volatile Persian Gulf. West Africa already supplies about 12 per cent of US crude oil imports, and America's National Intelligence Council predicts that this share will rise to 25 per cent by 2015.

As is often the case with oil, military involvement follows behind trade. In February 2007 the US set up an Africa command (Africom). It has established bases in and signed access agreements with Senegal, Mali, Ghana, Gabon, and Namibia. Despite its own big backyard, as it were, China is generally resource-poor and Africa offers the natural resources vital to fuel its rapidly growing economy.

China looks to the Democratic Republic of Congo (DRC) and Zambia for copper and cobalt, to South Africa for iron ore and platinum, and to Gabon, Cameroon and the Republic of the Congo (Congo-Brazzaville) for timber. For oil, it has been wooing Nigeria, Angola, Sudan, and Equatorial Guinea. China is now the second largest consumer of crude oil after the US, and was responsible for 40 per cent of the global increase in demand between 2001 and 2005. Indeed, it imports 25 per cent of its crude oil from Africa.

Beijing has charmed African rulers with a triple whammy of arms sales, cancelled debt, and soft loans. Last year, President Hu Jintao and Prime Minister Wen Jiabao visited 10 African countries, including Uganda, and this increasingly intimate relationship was consummated at the China-Africa summit in October 2006, when Beijing rolled out the red carpet to almost 50 African heads of state and ministers.

The global demand for natural resources will bring benefits to Africa—increased FDI and, as exports grow, improving balance of trade figures—but one of the main concerns is that the scramble for Africa is fuelling corruption, environmental degradation, and internal dissent. The windfall gains from resource extraction cause more problems in Africa. It reduces a state's incentive to impose a free and just taxation system, and encourages corruption and acquisition of weaponry and thus develops wars. In the form of neo-colonisation, Africa is being fragmented into many pieces at the will of super power countries and concentrating more on the exploitation of Africa's rich resources than providing them the development aid. The question is: Why has Africa remained stuck in neo-colonialism, pre-industrial age of history, despite its rich natural resources, when neighbours once more impoverished and backward than Africa have either graduated, or are dramatically in the process of graduating, into the age of science and industry?

Defining Neocolonialism

In 1965 Kwame Nkrumah, President of Ghana, published a book titled *Neo-Colonialism: The Last Stage of Imperialism* which claimed that, despite official decolonization, old colonial powers were still dominating the 'third world' through less formal means:

> In place of colonialism as the main instrument of imperialism we have today neocolonialism. The essence of neocolonialism is that the State which is subject to it is, in theory, independent and has all the outward trappings of international sovereignty. In reality its economic system and thus its political policy is directed from outside. ... in an extreme case the troops of the. imperial power may garrison the territory of the neo-colonial State and control the government of it. More often, however, neo-colonialist control is exercised through economic or monetary means. The neo-colonial State may be obliged to take the manufactured products of the imperialist power to the exclusion of competing products from elsewhere. Control over government policy in the neo-colonial State may be secured by payments towards the cost of running the State, by the provision of civil servants in positions where they can dictate policy, and by monetary control over foreign exchange through the imposition of a banking system controlled by the imperial power. ... The result of new-colonialism is that foreign capital is used for the exploitation rather than for the development of the less developed parts of the world. Investment under neo-colonialism increases rather than decreases the gap between the rich and the poor countries of the world.

Neocolonialism basically refers to the maintenance of colonial or imperial forms following the recognition of independence. Closely related to neocolonialism is vestigial colonialism and imperialism, forms which may also be perpetuated through socio-economic control of ethnic minority groups by dominant societies within nations.

Neo-colonialist theory was a development in Marxist thinking that emerged during the 1950s and 1960s. The main stimulus to this development was the continued backwardness of those postcolonial nations, mainly in Africa and Asia, which had gained formal independence after 1945. Its target was modernization theory, which attempted to rationalize and justify this backwardness on the grounds that the underdeveloped nations were at an original historic stage or point similar to that which the developed nations had long since passed. Modernization theory has evolved in three waves. The first wave appeared in the 1950s and 1960s. One made the attempt to explain the diffusion of Western styles of living, technological innovations and individualist types of communication (highly selective, addressing only particular persons) as the superiority of secular, materialist, Western, individualist culture and of individual motivation and achievement (Lerner, 1958), Schramm, 1964).

This first wave of theory produced three variants (McQuail 2000: 84):

1. Economic development: mass media promote the global diffusion of many technical and social innovations that are essential to modernization (Rogers 1962).
2. Literacy and cultural development: mass media can teach literacy and other essential skills and techniques. They encourage a 'state of mind' favourable to modernity, e.g. the imagination of an alternative way of life beyond the traditional way.
3. National identity development: mass media could support national identities in new nations (colonies) and support attention to democratic policies (elections).

Most of these theories have been discredited because of their pro-Western bias.

The second wave of modernization theory is a part of the critical theory that was popular in the 1970s and 1980s. It does not support but criticize the influence of Western modernization. This is held to be a case of Western cultural and economic imperialism or dominance (Schiller, 1976). One of the theories concerned is *media dependency theory*. Peripheral (developing) countries are assumed to be dependent on mass media in the core (the Western world). The third wave of modernization theory rising in the 1990s is the theory of late-, high- or post modernity. It tries to be more neutral, being not in favour or against Western modernization. Rather it attempts to unearth the contradictions in the modernization process and to explain the consequences of modernity for individuals in contemporary society (Giddens 1991a, 1991b). Giddens showed that modern society is characterized by time-space distantiation and disembedding mechanisms.

Traditional society is based on direct interaction between people living close to each other. Modern societies stretch further and further across space and time using mass media and interactive media. Disembedding mechanisms such as money, symbolic means, English as the *lingua franca* and the Internet help to lift out and activities in an abstract or online form that were once embedded in particular material goods and in places. Benjamin Barber tried to explain the clash of Western and non-Western cultures of the world in his *Jihad versus McWorld: How the Planet is both Falling Apart and Coming Together* (1996).

This theme of the combination of unification and fragmentation in society and in media use also is present in the work of Meyrowitz (1993)—See Medium Theory- and van Dijk (1993, 1991/1999). Van Dijk tries to explain the rise of the new media such as computer networks and mobile telephony as important tools for modern life. They enable scale reduction and scale extension, a unitary and a fragmented world and, finally, a world that is both social and individualized (network individualism). In sum, according to modernization theory, just as the developed nations had progressed, so too would the undeveloped regions—if, of course, they followed the economic, social, political, and even cultural prescriptions laid down for them by their former political overlords in the West.

In response, early theorists of neo-colonialism such as Paul Baran pointed out that, unlike the developed metropolitan states, the underdeveloped nations lacked a virile bourgeoisie capable of spearheading the tasks of political and economic development. Caught between a dominant metropolitan bourgeoisie and a rising international labour movement, the bourgeois classes in ex-colonial states were paralyzed and ultimately threw their lot in with reaction, ensuring continued underdevelopment and stagnation.

As Baran commented, '... whatever differences and antagonisms existed between large and small landowners, between monopolistic and competitive business, between liberal bourgeois elements and reactionary feudal overlords, between domestic and foreign interests, were largely submerged on all important occasions by the overriding common interest in staving off socialism.' This resulted in a situation in which 'the possibility of solving the economic and political deadlock prevailing in the underdeveloped countries on the lines of a progressive capitalism all but [disappeared].'[1]

The prominent neo-colonialist theorist Andre Gunder Frank also disputed the contention, central to modernization theory, that the developed nations had ever been in a state of underdevelopment; they may at one stage have been undeveloped, but that was an entirely different state. For Frank, underdevelopment was an inescapable consequence of capitalism. As he put it, it represented the 'historical product of past and continued economic and other relations between the satellite underdeveloped and the now developed metropolitan countries . . . [and was] an essential part of the development of capitalism.'[2]

The emergent strands of neo-colonial theory were articulated clearly at the Third All-African Peoples' Conference in Cairo in 1961. There neo-colonialism was identified as the 'survival of the colonial system in spite of formal recognition of political independence in the emerging countries, which became the victims of an independent and subtle form of domination by political, military, or technical [forces].'[3] Eight aspects of neo-colonialism were identified. These included 'puppet governments represented by stooges and based on . . . big bourgeois compradors or corrupt civil or military functionaries'; a 'regrouping of states before or after independence by an imperial power in federation or communities linked to that imperial power'; 'Balkanisation . . . [or] a deliberate creation of artificial entities'; the 'economic entrenchment of the colonial power before independence and its continuation after independence'; incorporation 'into colonial economic blocs' and 'economic infiltration' by former colonial powers in the post-independence period 'through capitalist institutions, loans, and monetary aids.'[4]

The Cairo conference yielded the most detailed and thorough analysis of neo-colonialism and provided the framework of Kwame Nkrumah's classic text on the subject. It can be observed through its findings, and from the work of Baran and Frank, that central to the theory of neo-colonialism was the proposition that the economic domination of the colonies by the metropolitan states had markedly deformed their economic, political, and social structures. This deformity included, in particular, an underindustrialized and primitive economy and the consequent formation of a class system headed by weak bourgeois elements incapable of leading programmes of national economic or political development. Unable to free themselves from the shackles fixed by colonialism, these bourgeois classes chose ultimately to collaborate with the colonial powers, ensuring continued economic underdevelopment and persisting incorporation within these exploitative structures even after formal political independence had been achieved.

But if the theory of neo-colonialism began to flower only from the 1950s onward, its origins can be seen to stretch back much further. Both Trotsky's theory of the 'permanent revolution,' first formulated in 1906, and based on his 'law of combined and uneven development,'[5] and Mao's 1926 'Analysis of the Classes in Chinese Society,' which identified the landlords and comprador bourgeoisie as 'appendages of imperialism,'[6] were informed by concepts developed more fully by later theorists of neo-colonialism. Preceding even these two, however, was Kwame Nkrumah, and thus it is to Nkrumah, the founder of African Marxism, that our attention must now turn.

The story of James Connolly is well known, and he has been the subject of several biographies.[7] Born in Edinburgh of Irish parents in 1868, Connolly moved to Ireland in 1896, and upon his arrival he set up the Irish Socialist Republican Party. In the first public statement that he issued on its behalf, Connolly made it clear that he saw the Irish question as economic as well as political in its essential nature:

> The struggle for Irish freedom has two aspects. It is national and it is social. The national ideal can never be realised until Ireland stands before the world as a nation free and independent. It is social and economic because no matter what the form of government may be, as long as one class owns as private property the land and instruments of labour from which mankind derive their substance, that class will always have it in their power to plunder and enslave the remainder of their fellow creatures.[8]

Connolly later noted that,

> the subjection of Ireland, which is represented today as a mere political question, is instead an economic, a social question. It is only political that it may be economic. In other words, the political machinery is only held by a dominant nation in order that the social power may be held by a dominant class. The subjection of Ireland is based upon the economic dependence of the oppressed upon the oppressor. The army, navy, and police are but the instruments upon which this class enforces its domination, and the political subjection of Ireland to England means nothing more than that the possessing class were astute enough to placc the control of these instruments of domination beyond the reach of the Irish people.[9]

Connolly believed that it had been the British bourgeoisie that had introduced capitalism into Ireland, breaking up finally the last remnants of the old Gaelic communal system, and that it continued to profit in the present day from exploitation of Irish resources and from the labour power of Irish workers. He believed that the capitalist economic system was the real basis of British power and control in Ireland. The implication of this argument was that mere political independence would change little, and that only through socialism could true Irish freedom be achieved. This was made brilliantly clear in one of Connolly's most famous articles, written shortly after his arrival in Ireland:

> If you could remove the English army tomorrow and hoist the green flag over Dublin Castle, unless you set about the organisation of the socialist republic, your efforts would be in vain. England would still rule you through her capitalists, through her financiers, through her usurers, through the whole array of commercial and individualist institutions she has planted in this country. England would rule you to your ruin . . . ; nationalism without socialism . . . is only national recreancy.[10]

If we return to our earlier analysis of neo-colonialism and its constituent parts, we will observe that continued economic domination by former colonial powers over their former African colonies was, above all other factors, the material reality that called forth the development of neo-colonial theory. The significance of Connolly's writings here is that he was already grappling with this problem long before Ireland had achieved even the least measure of political independence.

Connolly's analysis, however, went much deeper than a recognition that British capitalism would continue to dominate the economy of an independent Irish capitalist state. Central to the theory of neo-colonialism was the connection between this economic dominance and the disfigurement of social, economic, and political structures within the ex-colonies. Connolly showed in his writings that he too was aware of this connection, and made it the subject of close examination. In particular, Connolly argued that British economic control in Ireland had hamstrung the development of the native Irish bourgeoisie. He depicted this class as weak and slavishly attached to the British ruling class, and concluded that it would be unable to promote industrial or political development in Ireland. This was very much the central theme of Connolly's *Labour in Irish History*, published in 1910, but based on articles that he had been writing since his arrival in Ireland. In this work, after tracing the central role played by the poorest classes in the long struggle for Irish independence, contrasting this with the opportunism of the élites, who had consistently betrayed this struggle, Connolly pointed out that the Irish bourgeoisie had a 'thousand economic links' binding them to English capitalism, and that 'only the working class remain as the incorruptible inheritors of the fight for freedom in Ireland.'[11]

Throughout most of Ireland, with the exception of the Northeast, the Irish bourgeoisie was represented by the Irish parliamentary party, which was reunified in 1900. This party had as its aim Home Rule, a limited degree of political autonomy falling short of independence and retaining Ireland for the empire. Connolly therefore saw as one of his main political objectives the exposure of the class nature of this party and the limitations of its project. In *Erin's Hope*, Connolly's first major work, published in 1897, he dismissed the claims of the Home Rulers that the establishment of a limited form of independence would facilitate Irish economic development. British capitalism had been perfecting its industrial development for a century and a half; Connolly pointed out, and it had established markets for its goods all over the globe. Connolly also noted the challenge that British capitalism was facing from even more efficient and vibrant bourgeois powers in the US and Europe.

'Remember all this,' he concluded,

> and tell me how poor Ireland, exhausted and drained of her life-blood at every pore, with a population almost wholly agricultural and unused to mechanical pursuits, is to establish new factories and where she is to find the customers to keep them going. She cannot create new markets. This world is only limited after all, and the nations of Europe are pushing their way into its remote corners so rapidly that in a few years, at most, the entire world will have been exhausted as a market for their wares.[12]

Much of James Connolly's work was innovative and represented an important contribution to Marxist thought as a whole. Marxism at this point in its development had not begun to deal with the specific problems that preoccupied Connolly. Most Marxists considered that only after substantial capitalist development had taken place in the colonies in the post-independence period would the conditions for socialism be created. The proposition that the native bourgeois classes within the colonies were so dominated by metropolitan capitalism that they would be unable to play the progressive historic role in promoting industrial and political development laid down for them by Marxist theory lay unexplored. The idea that the colonies would remain underindustrialized exporters of raw materials (in Ireland's case, of agricultural produce) as a result of this subjection was not examined.

Irish Marxism emerges from this study as having anticipated many of the key tenets of the theory of neo-colonialism. Owing to the nature of the political terrain in which they were active, Irish Marxists were forced to engage with the national issue as well as social questions and with the connections between the two. James Connolly was central to this development. An innovative Marxist theoretician, Connolly argued that the two questions were interrelated. The British bourgeoisie exerted both economic and political sovereignty in Ireland. Any form of political self-government that left untouched these economic relations would not weaken overall British power in Ireland. The state that emerged was, for Connolly, a client state of British imperialism in which the economic and political interests of the British ruling class were served, maintained, and saved from effective challenge. It was a state that, as he made clear in 1926, acted as the best instrument that Britain ever had for maintaining its control over Ireland.

The value of the theory of neo-colonialism was that it connected the continued incorporation of the ex-colonies into economic relationships beneficial to the metropolitan states with the economic, social, and political structures that prevailed within them. The continued economic domination of the metropolitan states explained the consistent weakness of the native bourgeois classes and their inability and unwillingness to break free from the cycle of exploitation and underdevelopment.

Transnational Capital and Neocolonial States in Africa

Under the political-military canopy of U.S. capitalist expansion and domination, national capitals began a new period of internationalization and external integration in the post-WWII period. Escalating international economic activity unfolded within the institutional framework of the nation-state system and the cross-border regulation of 'international regimes,' in particular, the Bretton Woods system. As multinational corporations extended their reach around the world they sought to evade the central bank controls associated with the Bretton Woods system by depositing their capital in foreign currency markets. Economic internationalization thus brought the massive spread of dollars and other core country currencies around the world. Eurodollar deposits ballooned from just $3 billion in 1960 to $75 billion in 1970—prompting the Nixon administration to abandon the gold standard in 1971 - and then climbed to over $1 trillion in 1984.

The collapse of the Bretton Woods system of fixed currency exchange and national economic regulation via capital controls was the first step in the liberation of embryonic transnational capital from the institutional constraints of the nation-state system. It signalled the beginning of the transition to the globalization epoch and also the waning of US supremacy. Liquid capital became accumulated in offshore capital markets established by nascent transnational banks seeking to evade the regulatory powers of national states. In the 1970s the transnational banks began to recycle this liquid capital through massive loans to Third World governments.

Newly liberated global financial markets began to determine currency values, to destabilize national finances, and to undermine the national macro-economic management of the earlier Keynesian regime of capitalism. By the early 1990s some $1 trillion in various currencies was being traded daily, all beyond the control of national governments. The dramatic loss of currency control by governments meant that state managers could no longer regulate the value of their national currency. The power to influence state economic policymaking passed from these state managers to currency traders, portfolio investors, and transnational bankers - precisely, the representatives of transnational finance capital - by virtue of their ability to move funds around the world. Offshore capital markets grew from $315 billion in 1973 to over $2 trillion in 1982, and by the end of the 1970s, trade in currencies was more than 11 times greater than the value of world commodity trade. And because this global movement of liquidity created unpredictable conditions of profitability, transnational corporations reduced their risks by diversifying their operations around the world, thus accelerating the entire globalization process and the political pressures for a TNS apparatus.

What was taking place structurally were long-term movements in the world capitalist system - the rise of the global economy and the emergence of transnational finance capital as the hegemonic fraction of capital on a world scale, as money capital became the regulator of new global circuits of production rather than investment capital. As Stephen Gill has argued, the international economic turmoil that began in the early 1970s was not, in fact, reflective of the breakdown of world capitalism, as some believed at the time. Rather, it was precisely the rough bumps of the emergence of transnational capital, concentrated in transnational financial capital.

Transnational capital needed an entirely new global political and economic environment, one in which it would no longer be hampered by nation-states or democracy. The Keynesian welfare and developmentalist states had to be dismantled and national controls over the free movement of globally-mobile capital lifted. The new production relations of flexible accumulation had to be imposed around the world. Public sectors and non-market community spheres had to be opened up to profit making and privatized (what Marx termed the 'alienation of the state').

As transnational corporate and political elites emerged on the world scene in the 1980s as the agent of these changes they made explicit claims to building and managing a global economy through restructured multilateral and national institutions. This transnational bourgeoisie became politically organized. The formation in the mid-1970s of the Trilateral Commission, which brought together transnationalized fractions of the business, political, and intellectual elite in North America, Europe, and Japan, was one marker in its politicization. Others were: the creation of the Group of 7 forum at the governmental level, which began institutionalizing collective management of the global economy by corporate and political elites from core nation-states; the creation of the OECD, formed as a supranational institution by the 24 largest industrialized countries to observe and coordinate their national economies; and the creation of the World Economic Forum, which brought together the top representatives of transnational corporations and global political elites.

Studies on building a global economy and transnational management structures flowed out of think tanks, university centres, and policy planning institutes in core countries. This increasingly organized global elite articulated a coherent programme of global economic and political restructuring centred on market liberalization—the so-called 'Washington consensus'—and set out to convert the world into a single unified field for global capitalism. It pushed for greater uniformity and standardization in the codes and rules of the global market—a process similar to the construction of national markets in the 19th century but now replicated in the new global space. The G-7 in 1982 designated the IMF and the World Bank as the central authorities for exercising the collective power of the capitalist national states over international financial negotiations. At the Cancun Summit in Mexico in 1982, the core capitalist states, led by the United States, launched the era of global neo-liberalism as part of this process and began imposing structural adjustment programmes on the Third World and the then-Second World, as I discuss in the next section. Transnational elites promoted international economic integration processes, including the NAFTA, the EU, and the APEC, among others. They created new sets of institutions and forums, such as the WTO, the Multilateral Agreement on Investment (MAI), and so on. In this process, the existing supranational institutions, such as the Bretton Woods and the UN institutions were not bypassed but instrumentalized and transformed.

For instance, during the 1980s, the composition of loans to the former Third World changed dramatically. In 1981, 42 percent of net loans came from commercial banks and 37 percent from multilateral agencies. By 1988, private banks supplied only 6 percent and the multilaterals 88 percent of net loans. In effect, the Bretton Woods institutions loaned public funds to national states to repay the private banks, and then utilized the resultant financial power centralized in their hands to acquire control over economic management and political authority that comes with it. For its part, the World Bank shifted in the 1980s from project loans to policy loans aimed at restructuring local economies and integrating them into the global economy. The reformed Bretton Woods institutions took the reins in organizing global economic restructuring, especially through neo-liberal programmes.

Similarly, the UN conference system helped achieve consensus on reshaping the world political and economic order, while UN agencies such as the United Nations Development Programme (UNDP) and the UN Conference on Trade and Development (UNCTAD) began to promote the transnational elite agenda of economic liberalization. The UNDP's frequently cited annual *Human Development Report*, for instance, while highly critical of global inequalities, is explicit in calling for more globalization and liberalization as the remedy. Speaking before the World Economic

Forum in 1998, UN Secretary General Kofi Annan explained how the UN seeks to establish the international security and regulatory environment, and the social, political and ideological conditions, for global markets to flourish:

> [The UN agencies] help countries to join the international trading system and enact business-friendly legislation. Markets do not function in a vacuum. Rather, they arise from a framework of rules and laws, and they respond to signals set by Governments and other institutions. Without rules governing property, rights and contracts; without confidence based on the rule of law; without an overall sense of direction and a fair degree of equity and transparency, there could be no well-functioning markets, domestic or global. The UN system provides such a global framework - an agreed set of standards and objectives that enjoy worldwide acceptance. A strong United Nations is good for business.

The Uruguay Round of world trade negotiations that began in 1986 in Punte del Este, Uruguay under the auspices of the GATT, established a sweeping new set of world trade rules to regulate the new global economy based on: 1) freedom of investment and capital movements; 2) the liberalization of services, including banks; 3) intellectual property rights; 4) a free movement of goods. The free movement of goods ('free trade') meant largely freedom of intra-firm trade, which accounts for up to two-thirds of world trade and which itself is a commercial expression of globalization production. On the conclusion of the Uruguay Round the GATT created the WTO, in 1995, to supervise this new 'free trade' regime. Although its powers are far from absolute, the WTO is perhaps the archetypical transnational institution of the new era. The WTO assumes unprecedented powers to enforce the GATT 'free trade' provisions. It has independent jurisdiction, its rules and rulings are binding on all members, and has the power to sanction, to overrule state and local powers, and to override national regulatory powers. The theoretical import here is that the WTO is the first supranational institution with a coercive capacity not embedded in any particular nation-state but rather directly in the transnational corporate and political elite community.

The proposed MAI would extend this capacity. Negotiations over the MAI grew out of the Uruguay Round and have been sponsored by the OECD. The proposed agreement amounts to a 'charter of rights' for transnational capital. It would give transnational corporations near-absolute freedom from national state legal and political restrictions on cross-border investment and bind national as well as local governments right down to the municipal level to its provisions. The MAI is, in the words of Joseph Roberts, 'an agreement among the world's largest corporate investors to achieve a common and user friendly global legal system of the sort cartels sought for individual industries. The GATT liberalizations, the creation of the WTO and the MAI negotiations were backed by a powerful and well-organized lobby of transnational corporations (TNCs).

The TNCs have increasingly come to operate openly as organized political as well as economic entities, a throwback to the old chartered trading companies of the mercantile era that were vested by imperial powers with sovereign authority over colonial domains. Historically, newly strengthened ruling classes can quickly constrict state autonomy as they make more intensive use of the state in times of major capitalist restructuring. But the TNS appears to represent capital and nothing else; the fusion of the state and capital would seem to be unprecedented under globalization, suggesting the need to rethink the meaning of state autonomy and review existing theories of the state.

The GATT's global rules have generated tensions with national blocs in their competition with transnational blocs and the policies they promote (e.g., over farm policies) and evince the national/transnational class tensions discussed earlier. As the ups and downs in farm policy in the 1980s made clear, national blocs from core countries such as the United States and the EU member states were able to use their more powerful national states to advance their interests intentionally. This confused many observers, who saw it as a sign that nation-state and North-South competition rather than globalization remained at the core of world political dynamics.

As the 1990s progressed the transnational bloc was able to impose its agenda of agricultural commodity liberalization, which makes global sourcing possible. (In turn, the collapse of agricultural sectors in the former Third World accelerated the proletarianization process bound up with globalization.) By the late 1990s the TNS as an institution attempting to impose its authority on a fluid and spatially open process of capital accumulation was assuming some powers and historic functions that the nation states had lost in organizing collective action to facilitate and reproduce this process in the global economy.

The creation of a capitalist superstructure which carries out at the transnational level functions indispensable for the reproduction of capital, especially those that national states are unable to perform, is not to say that a TNS has fully become consolidated as a fully functioning political, administrative, and regulatory structure. There is no clear chain of command and division of labour within the TNS apparatus, or anything resembling, at this time, the type of internal coherence of national states, given the embryonic stage of this process. Nonetheless, the TNS has developed mechanisms to assume a growing number of functions traditionally associated with the national state.

What are some of these functions and how did the TNS begin to assume them? One is compensation for market failure. Here we have IMF bailouts of Mexico, Southeast Asia, Brazil, etc. Another is money creation. The creation of EU currency showed that this can be transnational. A third is legal guarantees of property rights and market contracts. The WTO would suggest that this may be supranationally enforced. Yet another is the provision of public goods (social and physical infrastructure). The social policies, investment decisions and resource mobilization determining infrastructure are increasingly set supranationally and then execution is carried out through national states. In a similar vein, fiscal intervention, credit creation, tax redistribution, and even control over capital and labour allocations are increasingly activities designed in the supranational policy arena for execution by national states. And although police surveillance and military power has remained largely at the nation-state level, the TNS has increasingly developed military mechanisms.

For example, the United Nations has assumed an expanded role in global policing. It was involved in 'preventative diplomacy' or 'peacekeeping' in 28 conflicts in 1994, compared with 5 in 1988, involving 73,393 military personnel, compared with 9,570 in 1988. Despite this expanded TNS activity, there are numerous functions that the TNS has not been able to assume, such as reigning in on speculation and excesses that so characterize the frenzied 'casino capitalism' of the global economy. Identifying the functions of the TNS does not imply functional analysis so long as the conditions under which these functions are unfulfilled are specified and problematized.

In sum, it is out of this process that a TNS apparatus began to emerge, not as something planned as such, but as the political consequences of the social practice and class action of the transnational capitalist class in this historic juncture, and as an apparatus that is not replacing but emerging out of the pre-globalization infrastructure of world capitalism. We can get a glimpse in this way how the TNS exerts a determining influence on class formation around the world. The relationship between capitalist development and the state is mutually determining rather than unidirectional. The recursive influence of the TNS on global class formation is precisely what we would expect from an historical materialist theoretical understanding of the state as an element of political mediation between social forces and productive structures that serves to reproduce or transform class and group relations. But this snapshot of the rise of a TNS is not complete. We need to examine as well the transformation of the national state since this is an integral part of the rise of a TNS.

Neocolonial Context

The transition from formal colonialism to one of constitutional independence did not end the poor's struggle but instead enabled the British colonial rule to 'reassess the local arrangements for supervising the colonial economy' (Campbell 1987: 86). This reassessment provided for more colonial domination. 'The dilemma of Jamaica today arises from the island's neocolonial status. Freed from British dominion in 1962, Jamaica became an uncharted economic entity, with the responsibilities but not the means for true independence' (Nicholas, 1996: 18). In essence, the term neocolonialism refers to the point when a nation shows the external sign of political independence yet remains economically dependent.

As Kwame Nkrumah explains, 'the economic system and thus the political policy [in neo-colonies] is directed from the outside...Neocolonialism is the worst form of imperialism. For those who practice it, it means power without responsibility and for those who suffer from it, it means exploitation without redress' (quoted in Nicholas 1996: 18). This section will explore the framework behind current neocolonialism in Africa, some examples of neocolonial activity and their effects, and the complicated situation created as a result.

Separatism and irredentism were the principal factors that made the introduction of slave trade in Africa relatively easy in the 16th century with the consequent vast human tragedy. They also paved the way to colonization in the 19th and 20th centuries after the abolition of slavery. The coming under the same imperial neocolonial control of hitherto warring nationalities or ethnic groups did give the promise of integration into larger political entities. And indeed virtually all of the present 54 member states of ECA are the product of some form of integration or the other.

The French colonial administration, unlike its British counterpart, did establish a higher level political organization. Its 13 territories were grouped into two federations -the French West Africa—Afrique Occidental Française (AOF) and French Equitorial African Federation—Afrique Equitorial Française (AEF). The former, whose capital was Dakar, was made up of eight territories—Mauritania, Senegal, French Soudan (now Mali); French Guinea, Dahomey (now Benin), Niger, Cote d'Ivoire, and Upper Volta (now Burkina Faso). French Equitorial African Federation was made up of Central Africa, Chad, Congo, Gabon, and Cameroun. Brazzaville was its capital. The trusteeship territories of Togo and

Cameroun administered by France had separate status. Each federated units had its own currency and although the organic unions were much more administrative than economic unions, each did have tremendous potential for economic development after independence if they had not been disbanded.

After World War II, each territorial assembly elected five of its members to its federal *Grands Conseils.* However, as the demand for self-government intensified, France reversed its policy. It aborted and dismantled the regional political integration process. In 1956, without any consultation with the African political leadership, the French colonial authority launched the process of balkanization and in 1958 formally abolished both the AOF and AEF as political organizations. The result was that independence was granted to the 14 territories (including Togo) separately. Each became a sovereign state and member of the United Nations. Sovereignty for these states in Africa was political only; none of the new states was viable in an economic sense. Creating viable nation states out of these nominally independent units became the difficult and challenging tasks of the founding fathers.

Had independence been granted to the two federations only, the history of post-colonial West and Central Africa would have been different. What preoccupied the new nations was the need to minimize the restrictions and constraints that fragmentation and balkanization had imposed through vigorous and relentless promotion of economic cooperation and integration. In fact, some of the initiatives predated independence. For example, the *Union douaniere de* I' *Afrique de* I' *Quest (West African Customs Union)* consisting of Cote d'Ivoire, Senegal, Dahomey, Mauritania, Niger, Mali, and Upper Volta was established in June 1959. The *Conseil de* l'*Entente* whose members were Cote d'Ivoire, Upper Volta, Niger and Dahomey was established also in 1959. Indeed, Senegal and French Soudan were so opposed to the French-induced balkanization that they attempted to create the federation of Mali which initially included Upper Volta and Dahomey. But once France granted independence to each territory, the federation collapsed.

While the British colonial administrations did not go as far as their French in linking their territories into federal unions, they did not entirely neglect the possibilities of economic cooperation. In British West Africa, they established a common currency and common services. Common research institutes were also established for the four colonies—Nigeria, Gold Coast, Sierra Leone and Gambia—for their main export commodities -cocoa, oil palm, timber and groundnut. In addition, an airways company-the West African Airways Company- was established for the four.

In East Africa, a customs union was established for Kenya and Uganda as far back as 1917. It was extended to Tanganyika in 1927. The union provided for free trade among the countries as well as a common external tariff, a common currency and common income tax regime. Common services for railways, posts and telecommunications and research were also established. This development was encouraged by the fact that Kenya, because of its semi-temperate climate, attracted settlers from the United Kingdom who invested in industry and agriculture and needed a larger market to exploit.

After independence, the evolutionary process of regional cooperation and integration in Africa virtually became a movement to the extent that within fifteen years after independence over 20 intergovernmental multi-sectoral economic cooperation organizations had been established and over 120 single sectoral multi-national and bilateral organizations, meant to promote technical and economic cooperation, had been set up. Not surprisingly, therefore, many of the economic and technical cooperation entities or schemes, which had been launched with lot of fanfare in the 1960s, had become moribund by the beginning of the 1970s. However, the African governments in their relentless pursuit of economic cooperation and integration continued to set up new institutions. Indeed, the 1960s could be regarded as Africa's integration decade.

The ECA, on its part, took a number of initiatives during the decade to broaden the scope of sub-regional cooperation. It particularly encouraged economic cooperation and integration that would cut across the colonial, francophone-anglophone divide. To this end, it sponsored several intergovernmental meetings of all the then 14 independent West African countries in 1966. These meeting were held successively in Niamey, Accra, Dakar and Monrovia to consider the draft Articles of Association for West African Economic Cooperation prepared by the ECA Secretariat.

All these efforts ended in failure. Thus in spite of independence, West Africa remained divided into francophone and anglophone enclaves. The limited attempts to break the barrier were concentrated at the bilateral level, e.g. Senegal-Gambia, Nigeria-Niger and Ghana-Guinea-Mali experiments. They were not successful either. Yet, as far back as 1945 at the fifth Pan-African Congress held in Manchester, the establishment of a West African Union as a means of combating the exploitation of the economic resources of West African territories and for ensuring the participation of the indigenous people of the sub-region was high on the agenda.

It was not until May 1975 when the Economic Community of West African States (ECOW AS) encompassing all the sixteen West African countries -9 francophone, 5 anglophone and 2 lusophone was established that a break-through was achieved in overcoming the language divide. But this was the result of a strong determination on the part of the two countries – Nigeria and Togo – that took the initiative in sponsoring the establishment of ECOWAS.

Mechanisms for Control of Neocolonial States

Client States

The United States has established what are called **client states** throughout the world. A client state is a government that is dominated by another (imperialist) government; it is controlled by a foreign state. It is dependent on the economic or military support of a more powerful country. Other names for client states include satellite state, puppet government and vassal state. The degree to which the imperialist government controls the client state obviously varies quite a bit. In some cases the client state is completely controlled by the imperialist state, in others it has a considerable degree of independence. The fact that Poland and Romania didn't always go along with absolutely everything Moscow wanted doesn't change the fact that they were Soviet client states, the same is true of American client states. There are also a variety of different ways that can be used to insure that client states are obedient.

As with imperialism in general, the use of client states is not something the American Empire invented. The system of client states most familiar to the majority of Americans was the system used by the Soviet Empire to maintain control over Eastern Europe and a few other countries. This is not a new phenomenon. Nazi Germany set up several client states during World War Two and the Roman Empire relied extensively on client states. Napoleon also set up client states in Europe; he set one up in Spain when he invaded the country, deposed the king, and made his brother the new king.

The United States has done the same thing around the world. The United States uses many different means to maintain control of its client states and dominate the globe. This includes military force, proxy militaries, enforcer states, CIA terrorism, foreign aid, coups, sanctions and subverting elections.

Military Intervention

The military has been the backbone of empires ever since they were first formed many millennia ago. It is the spear of imperialism. If an imperialist state's military is strong enough it can simply force its will upon any weaker country. This is true of the American Empire as well as past empires. After the Second World War the United States declared itself the 'global policeman' willing to use military force anywhere in the globe should its interests require it. After the defeat in Vietnam the empire altered so as to rely less on the US military. As a result of that defeat military planners had to deal with what they called the 'Vietnam syndrome.' Unrest in the homeland would rise quite rapidly in any lengthy military intervention, especially if it resulted in the loss of significant amounts of American lives.

In response, military strategy has been altered. When US military intervention is used they send in an overwhelming amount of force to insure that they rapidly and decisively defeat their enemy with few casualties on the American side. In addition the US relies extensively on air power because doing so minimizes US casualties and allows the US to attack an enemy for long periods of time without suffering significant losses. This insures that a large anti-war movement cannot develop and interfere with the operations of the empire. If the military cannot rapidly and decisively defeat their opponent with few casualties then some other mechanism of control is usually used.

Proxy Forces

Often when military force is needed the United States will use proxy forces instead of its own military. This involves supporting and funding armed groups that attack whatever enemy the empire has targeted.

These proxies can be rebel armies, terrorist networks, paid mercenaries, other nation-states or any other armed organization. In addition to funding such groups the US often provides other forms of assistance such as sending military advisors to help plan strategy, CIA assistance, attacks on enemy targets and sharing intelligence. Examples of the use of proxy forces by the empire include the use of the contras against Nicaragua, the Islamic Fundamentalists during the 80s and late 70s against the Soviet's Afghan puppet government, UNITA against Angola and Iraq against Iran (during the Iran-Iraq war). Proxy forces are often used in situations where combat will be long and bloody or greatly stress the resources of the empire.

Because of the 'Vietnam syndrome' the US military cannot be used in these situations so proxy forces are used instead. Sometimes proxy forces are combined with the US military. One common strategy is to use the US air force to pulverize the target country while a proxy army takes over the ground. Using only the air force makes large casualties much less likely, thereby avoiding the 'Vietnam syndrome.' This was used during the war with Yugoslavia when the US used the Kosovo Liberation Army as a proxy ground force while simultaneously bombing Yugoslavia.

Another example of this was during the war in Afghanistan with the Taliban. The US air force bombed the Taliban while a proxy army, the Northern Alliance, did the bulk of the ground fighting. Once the Taliban's back had been broken the US army helped clean up the remaining Taliban forces. In other cases proxy forces are used to assist full-fledged military intervention as was done in Vietnam, the Iraq war and elsewhere.

Neocolonial States

Neocolonialism in Africa, whose most eloquent exponents have been Frantz Fanon and Amilcar Cabral, is assured by the bifurcated state. Here, it commonly refers to the type of state and society that succeeded formal colonialism and that has been characterized, in the first instance, by the transfer of the state apparatus to an indigenous conservative petty bourgeoisie, and, thereafter, by the dual process of indigenous capitalist class formation and compradorization.

The US sometimes uses one client state to control other client states. It acts as a regional enforcer to keep the other countries in line. Often this means acting as a proxy force to beat on disobedient countries. Sometimes these client states will have their own client states and practice neocolonialism in them. In addition to non-US 'first-world' countries, there is a semi-periphery of states that exists between the periphery and the core that is subordinated to the core and part of the 'Third World' but also acts as enforcer states and exploits other 'third world' countries.

The semi-periphery is the better off section of the 'third world,' they are economically more dominant and regionally more powerful as compared to other 'Third World' countries. They act so as to keep other periphery countries in line and to maintain the empire. Enforcer states include Britain, France, South Africa, Iran under the Shah, Australia and Israel.

Foreign Intelligence Agencies

The Central Intelligence Agency (CIA) is a key component in the American Empire. Generally, the CIA attempts to put into power and keep in power groups who will go along with US neocolonial policies and overthrow those who will not. In addition to gathering information the CIA also conducts various covert activities designed to defend and expand the empire. This includes assassinations, inciting unrest, torture, raising private armies, *coups d'état*, rigging elections and assorted other terrorist activities.

The CIA has assassinated and attempted to assassinate numerous government officials and opponents of the empire. Often this is done through a proxy; they hire someone to do it for them. The agency has attempted to assassinate Fidel Castro over two dozen times. While Allende was in office in Chile they carried out assassinations of government officials, including General Rene Schneider, in the hopes of getting anti-Allende people who would carry out a coup into higher positions in the military. One of the worst terrorist attacks in Middle Eastern history was a car bomb detonated in Lebanon by CIA proxies. The CIA is the largest terrorist organization on the planet.

Foreign Aid

Foreign aid is essentially a bribe to keep the countries receiving it in line. If they get too far out of line foreign aid is reduced or cut off entirely. In addition foreign aid can also be given to help a country do something that helps US imperial interests, such as attacking one of America's enemies or suppressing rebellions by groups that threaten corporate profits. That aid can help them achieve whatever goal they had, which can help the empire. This money is frequently used to buy weapons from US arms manufacturers and therefore, in addition to making other countries dependant on the US, subsidizes US arms corporations. Military aid can also help the US control other countries and implement neocolonialism by establishing links with other countries' militaries. If you can get the military on your side they may overthrow the government for you. That's why the US sometimes sells weapons and military aid to countries which are otherwise hostile (such as Iran or Chile under Allende).

Coups D'état

A coup is the overthrow of the government by people in a position of authority, usually by military officers. The United States has supported, instigated and directly organized many coups against governments with policies it did not like. The CIA has often played a key role in these coups. Guatemala is a well documented example of this. In 1951 Jacobo Arbenz was elected president of Guatemala by a landslide in a free election. He said his goal was, 'to convert Guatemala from a dependant nation with a semi-colonial economy to an economically independent country; second, to transform our nation from a backward nation with a predominantly feudal economy to a modern capitalist country; and third, to accomplish this transformation in a manner that brings the greatest possible elevation of the living standard of the great masses of the people.' (quoted on Keen/Wasserman, p. 439) This goal conflicted with the US-based United

Fruit Company, which dominated Guatemala's economy. The various social reforms Arbenz implemented, especially his agrarian reform, threatened their profits. In addition, Guatemala could potentially threaten to serve as a good example towards those seeking independence. As one state department official noted, 'Guatemala has become an increasing threat to the stability of Honduras and El Salvador. Its agrarian reform is a powerful propaganda weapon; its broad social programme of aiding the workers and peasants in a victorious struggle against the upper classes and large foreign enterprises has a strong appeal to the populations of Central American neighbours where similar conditions prevail.' (Chomsky, 1995: 25-91).

So the CIA decided to overthrow this capitalist democracy. The CIA hired 300 mercenaries and flew in unmarked planes to overthrow the government with the help of reactionary sections of the Guatemalan military. Arbenz was forced out of power and a military dictatorship initially led by Castillo Armas was installed. The dictatorship immediately launched a reign of terror against opponents of the regime, killing around 100,000 people over the next 40 years. Arbenz's reforms were undone and neocolonial policies favouring the oligarchy and foreign companies (like the United Fruit Company) implemented.

Sanctions

Placing embargos and sanctions on disobedient countries can be an effective means of punishing them for their disobedience. Sanctions can often ruin, or at least hurt, the economy of whichever country they are directed at. This can prove very effective in neutralizing the threat of a good example; if their economy is ruined they will not be providing a very good example of independent development to anyone. This has been used effectively against Cuba to harm their economy so that they provide less of a good example (although it's probably not as harmful as many of Castro's supporters make it out to be). Sanctions were also placed on Nicaragua during the period of Sandinista rule for similar reasons.

When Allende was in power the US placed sanctions on Chile to 'make the economy scream' (in Nixon's words), which played a significant role in undermining Allende's rule. Usually sanctions are used in combination with some other mechanism of control. A country under sanctions for a long enough period of time will see its economy weaken and thus be much easier to attack either with the US military, proxy forces or through CIA terrorism and coups. The conquest of Iraq in 2003 by the US military was made much easier by the preceding 12 years of sanctions and semi-regular bombing.

A closer look would reveal a much more robust sanctions policy, one which is both formal and informal. Any sanctions policy requires a normative framework for its implementation. Since the 1990s, the framework has been that of 'good governance'— the 'liberal imperialism' to which our authors refer—which comprises of both economic and political criteria of proper international behaviour and which constitute the basis of lending by the IFIs (the IMF and the World Bank) to indebted peripheral states. The majority of peripheral states, outside 'emerging markets', have depended almost exclusively on the IFIs for credit, given that they have been shut out of private capital markets ever since the onset of the debt crisis of the early 1980s.

What is more, private capital today tends to follow the credit ratings of the IFIs and a handful of credit-rating agencies for their own lending decisions, such that the global management of good governance becomes highly centralized. And, given that the IFIs are dominated by the imperialist states, they are subject to their geopolitical interests, while simultaneously the same states employ the IFIs as a 'multilateral' cover for their aggression against indebted peripheral states; that is, imperialist states need not necessarily impose 'formal' sanctions of their own against transgressors. But even beyond the IFIs, imperialist states, together with their corporate media allies, can punish a target state informally by increasing the level of economic and political 'risk' associated with it; this is done by propagating a discourse of 'roguery', whereby capital responds spontaneously by fleeing.

In this context, good governance has come to include not only economic conditionalities but also the political conditionalities of multi-party elections, respect for the rule of law, and respect for human rights. In theory, these conditionalities apply to all transgressors; in practice, they are selectively demanded of certain states whose 'roguery' threatens world order, and suspended for others that demonstrate commitment either to macroeconomic reforms or to the geo-strategic plans of the transatlantic alliance that weakened their military and infrastructure.

Subverting Elections

Another means of controlling other countries is through subverted elections. Basically, if the US can insure that the section of the elite who will implement the policies the US wants wins the elections then it will help the US maintain control over that country. This involves funding pro-US groups, spreading propaganda denouncing whichever group(s) the US is opposed to and sometimes using violence against those groups. In the past the CIA has spearheaded these efforts but today the National Endowment for Democracy has taken over that role.

In addition the US sometimes threatens to cut off aid or use force against the country if the voters vote the wrong way, effectively putting a gun to their head. Subverting elections only works if the military & state bureaucracy already has some degree of loyalty to the empire, otherwise they can overthrow the US-backed candidate should s/he win the election. Subverting elections is preferable to the empire than overthrowing an elected government because it is less risky but such an overthrow will be attempted if the elections go the wrong way. This was done to Italy in the 1948 elections. The very first National Security Council Memorandum was about planning for this. The CIA feared the victory of leftists in the election instead of those Washington favoured (mostly leftover brown shirt thugs from Mussolini's days) and so spent millions of dollars on propaganda and payoffs to ensure Washington's candidates won. Just in case it didn't work, they also organized a secret paramilitary army with hidden stockpiles of weapons and explosives that would overthrow the government, with the help of the US military, if the wrong people won the election. Washington's candidates won, they successfully subverted the election, and the use of their secret army proved unnecessary.

Global Pillars of Neocolonialism

The IMF, World Bank and WTO are central pillars in the global economy and have been called the 'architects of the world economy.' The IMF and World Bank were originally established at the Bretton Woods Conference in 1944. They were mainly funded by the United States to re-build the shattered world economy after it broke down during the Great Depression of the 1930s and World War II. Two significant institutions that implement neocolonialism are the International Monetary Fund (IMF) and the World Bank (WB). Both institutions use the large third world debt as a means of control to make periphery countries implement policies favourable to foreign capital. Third-world governments in the decades after world war two who borrowed from the World Bank and private investors created this debt. This money was meant for 'development' to build up the country's infrastructure and as a bribe to keep them on the American side in the cold war.

In many cases these countries at the time were under US-backed dictatorships that were completely unresponsive to their own population, grabbing World Bank loans to their countries for their own personal fortune. There are no records of where 80% of the money loaned to Argentina during its military dictatorship went. In most cases the individuals who took out these loans are no longer in power and have run off with their fortunes but the people living in these countries, who had little or no say in taking out the loans, are now expected to pay off the debt. When Richard Nixon ended the gold standard and devalued the dollar this further increased the debt since most of the loans were taken out in US dollars. The standard justification for charging interest on loans is that the lender takes a risk and the interest is payment for that risk.

There are many problems with this reasoning, the most obvious being that it doesn't apply to real life. Whenever investors lose large amounts of money the state steps in to rescue them; there is no significant risk. This happened with the third world debt in the late 70s and 80s when it became obvious that these periphery countries would not be able to pay off their debts and that some very bad investments had been made. The World Bank stepped in and bought up the portion of the debt owed to private interests. This debt is so large that it will never be paid off; it is simply a means of controlling the periphery.

The IMF and World Bank will only extend loans if countries agree to accept 'structural adjustment programmes' (SAPs). SAPs are not democratically decided upon by the people of the debtor countries. They are forced down the throats of the people of the former colonial world. To pay off the loans, the IMF and World Bank demand governments raise money by selling off public assets and companies (privatization) and cutting state expenditure on social services like healthcare, education, childcare, and pensions. SAPs require countries deregulate and open up their economy to 'free trade' by cutting subsidies to local industries and slashing trade barriers and tariffs. Countries must open up their economies to foreign business (usually multinationals from Western countries), remove restrictions on foreign investments, and allow corporations access to the workers and natural resources of the country at bargain basement prices. The vast majority of the profits made by the multinationals is taken out of the country and brought home (repatriated) to the West. SAPs encourage export-oriented growth (selling cheap raw materials or commodities on the world market, like cash crops, garments, or computer chips) to generate hard currency. All in all, the IMF and World Bank SAPs turn countries into loan repayment machines, generating easy profits for the world's richest corporations and banks.

IMF policies also both directly and indirectly impact workers in the US and other advanced capitalist countries. Because they are partially funded with public money, the IMF and World Bank redistribute wealth from working people in the US (through their taxes), and funnel it to programmes which benefit the multinational corporations based in the US. This redistribution of wealth upwards to the richest Americans is similar to that which accompanies any public subsidization of corporations.

Big corporations, though serviced by US government money, are accountable to no 'national interest' but only to their own shareholders. The effects of IMF/World Bank programmes are to lower wages and working conditions worldwide, which exerts a downward pressure on workers' living standards in the industrialized countries as well.

When periphery countries are unable to make the payments on their debt they turn to the IMF for help. The IMF offers loans so that they can make their payments. In exchange the periphery must implement what are called Structural Adjustment Programmes (SAPs), which essentially means handing over their economic policy to the control of the IMF. Both the IMF and World Bank are controlled by 'first world' governments, with the US in the dominant role, and so not surprisingly the policies they implement favour those countries.

SAPs mean cutting education, healthcare and other social services, privatization of state assets (which often includes things like water), making it easier for foreign companies to take over the economy and orienting the victim's economy towards exports (usually to 'first world' countries), rather than domestic needs. In many cases countries must charge user fees for things like going to school or basic healthcare. Officially these SAPs are supposed to help the economy and get the government out of debt, but they never do that in practice. Virtually every country where it is implemented eventually goes into a depression. Argentina, which for a time was the IMF's star pupil, has plunged into a deep depression as a result. Many other countries have had their economies ruined by these policies - Indonesia, Russia, Thailand and many more.

Debt has only grown. Joseph Stiglitz, winner of the 2001 Nobel Prize in economics and former chief economist for the world bank, said, 'a student who turned in the IMF's answer to the test question 'What should be the fiscal stance of Thailand, facing an economic downturn?' would have gotten an F. ... Not only was the IMF not restoring economic confidence in East Asia, it was undermining the region's social fabric. ... All the IMF did was make East Asia's recessions deeper, longer, and harder. Indeed, Thailand, which followed the IMF's prescriptions the most closely, has performed worse than Malaysia and South Korea, which followed more independent courses.' (Stiglitz, 'What I Learned at the World Economic Crisis') These policies may ruin the economies of countries on the periphery, but they enrich the owners of 'first world' multi-national corporations and, to a lesser extent, 'third world' elites. What is called **'free trade'** is also a form of neocolonialism. Imperialist nations implement so-called 'free trade' policies so as to open up the economies of periphery countries to exploitation by companies from the core countries.

Multinational corporations can then invest and sell their products in periphery countries, enabling them to run less developed periphery companies out of business and dominate their economy. Those industries from powerful nations that can't compete with weaker nations' industries are protected by the state so as to ensure that they can out-compete 'third world' industries. For example, when the US steel industry faced troubles in 2002 the Bush administration (a big proponent of free trade) implemented tariffs so as to protect US industries. Free trade prevents periphery countries from doing the same thing to protect their industries. The only areas of the economy that are liberalized are those in which the dominant countries can out compete their opponents, in other areas state protection reigns.

American industries which are the most competitive internationally are also highly subsidized—biotechnology, pharmaceuticals, agribusiness, high-tech industry, etc. These subsidized industries are then able to out-compete unsubsidized competitors in the periphery. For historical reasons in the US this subsidy is done largely through the military. The state pays for research & development and if the results of that research (such as the internet) prove profitable the private sector takes it over and reaps the profit.

The public pays the cost, a small group of capitalists reap the benefits. Free trade means state protection and subsidies for the rich & powerful but market discipline for everyone else. As Thomas Friedman, a pro-capitalist pro-interventionist columnist for the *New York Times* of March 28, 1999, put it, 'The hidden hand of the market will never work without a hidden fist — McDonald's cannot flourish without McDonnell Douglas, the builder of the F-15. And the hidden fist that keeps the world safe for Silicon Valley's technologies is called the United States Army, Air Force, Navy and Marine Corps.'

Far from spelling the end of states, Ellen Meiksins Wood has argued that the globalization of capitalism requires a system of multiple states under the hegemony of an imperial state that maintains 'a delicate and contradictory balance between suppressing competition and maintaining conditions in competing economies that generate markets and profit.' (Wood 2003) Such a system of multiple states requires a global policeman with sufficient military force to prevent the emergence of competing forces globally or regionally that could lead to interimperialist rivalries. In the words of the Bush administration's National Security Strategy of 2002, it requires 'full spectrum dominance.' The implication of this view of the so-called neo-conservatives then is that military dominance by the U.S. is not just an expression of unilateralist nationalism, it is also functional for the system of globalized states that global capital requires. Thus is the logic of capital confounded with the logic of state power (at least for the hegemonic imperial state).(Harvey 1994).

Whatever the ultimate outcome of the globalization of capital, so far it has not been able to dispense with states. Indeed the existence of multiple states has been functional in many ways. Even William I. Robinson (2003: 274), who is otherwise a critic of state-centric theories in this era of globalization, admits that 'National boundaries ... are mechanisms functional for the supply of labour on a global scale and for the reproduction of the system. Here we see how the continued existence of the nation-state serves numerous interests of a transnational capitalist class.' So far Wood is right to assert that 'the more universal [i.e. global] capitalism has become, the more it has needed an equally universal system of reliable local states' (Wood op.cit:152) as it has also needed a dominant imperial state. But that does not mean, as she claims, that 'the 'globalized' world is more than ever a world of nation states.' (Wood ibid:154). Rather, it means it is a world of globalized states, i.e. states serving the interests of global capital rather than their nations.

The role of the compliant state explains why in the late 1990s the underdeveloped world owed a total of $2.5 trillion in international debt to big banks and the IMF and World Bank. 'Developing' nations paid the West nine times more in debt repayment than they received in 'aid' from Western countries. For example, after the devastating floods in Mozambique - destroying the homes of more than a million people - Western countries coughed up a bare $40 million in 'aid.' But Mozambique pays more than $70 million dollars a year in debt repayments to Western banks! While diseases like cholera and malaria are spreading rapidly after the floods, only 1.1% of the GDP is spent on health care-down 75% after nearly a decade of IMF imposed austerity programmes.

Mozambique is far from the only country in this destructive situation:

- Between 1982 and 1990, according to Timothy Gorringe (1999: 66-67), $927 billion was loaned to underdeveloped countries; but in the same time, these debtor countries paid $1345 billion to international banks in debt service.
- Debtor countries began the 1990s 61% more in debt than they were in 1982. Sub-Saharan Africa's debt increased by 113% in this period (Gorringe, ibid.).
- According to the World Bank, poverty in Africa increased by 50% between 1994 and 2000. Why? One reason is that virtually every nation in sub-Saharan Africa entered into a structural adjustment programme in the 1980s.

Yet for the entire decade, GNP in the region fell by 2.2% per year, and per-capita income declined to pre-independence levels. All of Sub-Saharan Africa spends $10 billion a year in debt service to banks, more than is spent on health and education *combined* for the entire region. In confirmation, Martin Cook and Bill Hopwood in their *Global Warning: Socialism and the Environment*, London: Militant Publications, 1996, p.91- 92), state, for example, Zimbabwe between 1990 and 1993 cut its spending on primary health and basic education by 33% under the auspices of an IMF imposed SAP.

With the inherited state in Africa as accomplice, the main thrust of 'neo-liberalism' has been to open up markets in the 'under-developed' countries. Then, the multinational corporations can sell their products at a cheaper rate than can local businesses and take over their economies. Neo-liberal cuts are engineered to destroy all subsidies for the production of domestic goods, aid for domestic farmers, and programmes to foster domestic small businesses. Neo-liberalism (free trade) has been an absolute disaster for the peoples of the poorer countries. Under the guise of free trade, corporations have robbed the wealth of these countries and stored it in the vaults of the major banks of the West. This economic super-domination of these countries is merely a less overt version of the directly racist colonialism of the past. It is against this background that we can begin to understand the wave of wars and ethnic violence that has swept Africa in the past period as the problems of unemployment, inequality and poverty have tremendously increased.

Summary and Conclusion

Africa's worst socio—economic problems are better considered as deep-rooted manifestations of a peripheral capitalism manipulated at will by imperialist powers, accompanied by the rise of complicit local ruling elites. Three sets of closely-related problems can be identified, associated with what Fanon described as 'false decolonization.'First, colonialism's artificial borders, racism and ideological control, ethnic divide-and-rule strategies, land acquisition, labour control, suppression of competition from indigenous sources, military conflict (independence struggles), and replacement by African nationalism together guaranteed a future of distorted economics and failed states. Second, for women, pre-colonial patrilineal systems evolved into colonial forms of inequality (e.g., minority status and legal guardianship), which often persisted and evolved as post-colonial forms of structured oppression (e.g., market-related bride price). Third, political continuities from past to present include unreformed state structures, international political and cultural relations with colonial powers, and especially class alliances involving compradorism (local sellouts working in league with international oppressors).The economic structure of Africa's neocolonial societies was relatively homogenous, suffering from international commodity price fluctuations, an overdose of foreign debt and 'dependency.' That structure resulted in uneven formal working-class organization across the continent, resulting periodically in strikes in especially the mining and railway industries. But the forces of law and order were invariably stronger and treacherous. Racism often flared worst just prior to independence, as settlers held on to privileges with sophisticated state repressive capacity, much of which carried over after majority rule was won. So the post-colonial state was quickly harnessed for neocolonial duty. This allowed, in turn, Africa to continue expanding exports notwithstanding terribly unfair terms of trade (the difference between prices paid for exports in relation to prices paid for imports).

The peak of demand for Africa's raw materials, before synthetic substitutes were invented, was during World War II. From the mid-1970s, terms of trade worsened dramatically, in part because of export-oriented policies, which most African countries were compelled to adopt once they experienced debt crisis. The prices of primary commodities (other than fuels) have risen and fallen according to a deeper rhythm. Exporters of primary commodities, for example, have fared particularly badly when financiers have been most powerful. The cycle began with falling commodity prices (1973), rising foreign debt (1970s), dramatic increases in interest rates (1979), a desperate intensification of exports, which lowered prices yet further (1980s), and in some cases outright bankruptcy.

This process impoverished nearly the entire non-industrialized Third World, with occasional, erratic exceptions in oil-producing regions. For Africa, the trend to declining terms of trade was especially devastating because of the continent's extraordinary dependence on a few export commodities. Export-led growth strategies, pursued since the 1970s by virtually all Third World countries, meant that Africa's market share also shrunk drastically.

Meanwhile, willing bankers promoted corruption and capital flight-in the DRC, for example, Mobutu Sese Seko was thought to be illegitimately worth U.S. $5 billion by the time of his 1996 overthrow. The cost of imported oil rose dramatically in 1973 and 1979 and markets for raw materials stagnated and declined, requiring a short-term substitute for foreign-currency revenues in the form of loans. During the first part of the 1980s, the World Bank and IMF took over as creditors to ensure that African countries repaid Northern commercial bank loans in exchange for power over virtually all aspects of public policy in African countries. This resulted, uniformly, in austere macroeconomic policies that emphasized liberalization, export orientation, and an end to social subsidies.

But incoming funds continued to decline and by 1984 net financial resource transfers to the Third World were negative for the first time, as countries spent more on interest payments than they gained in new loans. By the end of the decade, the net South-North transfer had reached $50 billion a year, which reflected the success of financiers in shifting the repayment burden to not only Northern taxpayers but also to Third World citizens. Developing countries found that by 2000 they still had more than $2 trillion in foreign debt to repay (up from $1.3 trillion during the early 1980s when the debt crisis broke out and $1.4 trillion in 1990). Each year during the late 1990s, African countries paid $162 billion more than they received in new loans, up from $60 billion in 1990. There was little hope of balancing accounts by attracting inflows of foreign direct investment.

Another crucial issue was the militarization of the continent associated, initially, with colonial resistance to change and then to neocolonial power plays that inexorably resulted from partial transitions. Thanks in part to Cold War machinations and lubrication provided by arms dealers, many African countries witnessed extraordinary social, civil, and regional conflicts ranging from genocide to attempted coups. In sum, debt, trade, investment, wars, and more recent scourges like HIV/AIDS-exacerbated by the refusal of pharmaceutical corporations to sell medicines at affordable prices-all compel Africans to fight for peace and justice locally, by invoking continental and international anti-capitalist themes.

References

1. Paul Baran,(1970). 'On the Political Economy of Backwardness,' In R. Rhodes (ed.), *Imperialism and Underdevelopment: A Reader* (New York, p. 289.
2. Andre Gunder Frank, 'Development of Underdevelopment,' ibid., p.5.
3. Michael Barratt Brown (1974). *Economics of Imperialism.* London: Harmondsworth, Penguin: p. 256.
4. James O'Connor. (1970). 'The Meaning of Economic Imperialism,' in Rhodes, *Imperialism and Underdevelopment,* 117. For a discussion on the political economy of underdevelopment in the present, see Samir Amin, 'Imperialism and Globalization,' *Monthly Review* 53:2 (June 2001).
5. Leon Trotsky, *Permanent Revolution & Results and Prospects* (New York, 1969), passim.
6. Mao Tse Tung. (1967). 'Analysis of the Classes in Chinese Society,' in *Selected Works.* Peking: Foreign Languages Press: Pp 1:13.
7. For example, Desmond Greaves .(1986). *Life and Times of James Connolly.* London; Samuel Levenson, *James Connolly: A Biography* (London, 1977); Kieran Allen,

Politics of James Connolly (London, 1990); Donal Nevin, *James Connolly: A Full Life* (Dublin, 2005).

8. Greaves, *Connolly*, 75.
9. *Workers' Republic*, 2 Sept. 1899.
10. *Shan Van Vocht*, 8 Jan. 1897.
11. James Connolly .(1933). *Labour in Irish History.* ITGWU ed.: Dublin, p. 3.
12. James Connolly, (1923).*The Irish Revolution.* Erin's Hope: Dublin, p. 8.

Section Three

New World (Dis)Order Assaults Capitalist Neo-colonial State System in Africa

Preview

The African continent is littered with failed states. Most of these states are economic backwaters, social apologies and political ruins. This landscape runs from the Casablanca to the Cape Town and from The Horn of Africa in the East to the Island of No Return in the West Atlantic. Most of these states true to type were the creatures of imperial convenience. As a quid pro quo, the inherited colonial states were meant to serve a purpose after which their ontological legitimacy or ***raison d'être*** would then expire. At this expiration; the states, naturally not designed for African self-propulsion were condemned to tether on the brink, and finally implode upon the inglorious weight of their inherent contradictions.

Colonialism designed and inspired these problems. But the decadence was then driven along by a horde of African native pirates well trained in the fine art of piracy. This set of political actors was rogue personalities weaned on selfishness. They were brilliant students of patrimonial kleptocracy and political perversity. In about four decades they completely outclassed colonial perfidy and bested them in thievery. They did an inglorious job of mismanaging Africa, so much so that the state in Africa today has lost its authority and the laughing stock of the world.

Any appraisal of state failure in Africa reveals its peculiar ability of spawning a chain reaction, which forcefully compels its cognizance. It shocks the mind back to a rethink of its shallow assumptions, in a way that success cannot. The failure of one construct can have such concentric effect for all other endeavours in its environment as to forcefully warrant its imprisonment of our attention.

In this situation, state failure then rises to be appraised to serve as a critique of the present, and a launching pad for future success. Here, then, state failure becomes a catalyst to success. It is only in this light that one can look backwards on the battlefields of African history, littered with the fractured and fragmented pieces of African dreams. This section occupies itself with the appreciation of this history of state failures, to explore the lessons that are imperative if Africa can ever escape this present predicament and bequeath a worthy future to its posterity. (Franklyne Ogbunwezeh, http://globalpolitician.com/articleshow.asp?ID=493&cid=6 - *3/27/2005)*

Chapter Nine

From Welfare/Developmentalist to Neo-liberal Nation State in Africa

Overview

Since independence in the 1960s, there have been external and internal pressures on THE STATE IN AFRICA to downsize, become more streamlined and allow the market to operate as openly as possible. The two policies adapted that have had the most profound effect were privatization of state owned companies and pressure to lower taxes, both of which has greatly reduced the state's ability to provide a viable welfare state as before. The 1970s were marked by unprecedented growth of giant corporations operating in dozens of African countries. With the increased economic power came increased influence on state policy.

The economic elites utilized this influence to pressure states to privatize state owned companies because it was argued that it would 'level the playing field' and allow for competition and innovation. THE STATE IN AFRICA caved in and many social services disintegrated with it. Moreover, the lowering of taxes has greatly diminished the ability of dispossessed African countries to provide a robust welfare state. Economic studies have indicated that putting more money into citizen's pockets stimulates consumption and economic growth. Again the welfare state is sacrificed for the good of economic growth. The state of social welfare in Africa has continued to erode as economic and political elite deems its existence as obstacle to capitalist 'economic growth and prosperity.'

Introduction

There is no region of this world that has not experienced wars, but while many parts of the world have moved towards greater political and economic stability and co-operation, Africa, particularly sub-Saharan Africa, remains a cauldron of instability and economic deprivation. Globalism, which in simple terms means a worldwide network of interdependence, is a phenomenon, which emerged at the end of the Cold War and the advent of the information revolution.

While economic interdependence and liberalization has been acclaimed as the only hope for prosperity for the world, it has also been blamed as source of conflict in many parts of the world. This thesis examines the nexus between globalization and contemporary African conflicts with case studies of conflict scenarios in four African countries namely, the Democratic Republic of Congo, Sierra Leone, Nigeria and Guinea to ascertain the extent to which globalization played a role in sustaining these conflicts. Our observation here is that contemporary African conflicts have both national and international underpinnings, and include political, social and economic parameters. On the socio-political side, the conflicts are directly related to the circumstances surrounding the acquisition of independence, the multiethnic composition of the states, and the more often cited causes generally subsumed under the generic label governance. It also shows that the increased liberalization and expansion of international trade, which occurred in the aftermath of the Cold War, has exacerbated the level and intensity of the conflicts.

A Short Theoretical Overview

As the transnational ruling bloc emerged in the 1980s and 1990s it carried out a 'passive revolution' in the Gramscian sense, involving modifications made from above in global social and economic structure through the agency of TNS apparatuses. Alongside the process of creating a supranational apparatus, this ruling bloc set about to penetrate and restructure national states. As capital became liberated from the nation-state, and along with it, the types of rigidities associated with Fordist-Keynesian accumulation and their drag on profits, the social structures of accumulation negotiated between capital, labour, and diverse subaltern classes began to disintegrate. In the United States and other core countries this spelled the end of the Fordist era. In the second world, it spelled the rise of transnationalized fractions among aspiring elites who began to liaison with the global bourgeoisie and articulate a project for full (re)integration into world capitalism. In the Third World, the nationalist bourgeoisie, petty-bourgeois, and revolutionary regimes became displaced by transnationalized fractions of local elites as multi-class developmentalist projects unravelled.

In the aggressive pursuit of its project the transnational capitalist class has conducted prolonged ideological campaigns aimed at legitimating the dismantling of welfare and developmental states and at disseminating the global capitalist ideology of consumerism and individualism. It has forged opportune alliances, in some cases with forces of the Right and the Far Right, and the subaltern classes organized into right-wing populism. The was the case with the conservative forces in the U.S. Republican party identified with Ronald Reagan in the early 1980s, behind whose right-wing populist rhetoric were powerful representatives of transnational capital. In other cases, it has entered into coalitions with left-of-centre and progressive, and even leftist, forces that have provided legitimacy for austerity and economic restructuring, or that have been able to exercise a social control function that the transnational capitalist class and its local agents could never have achieved. This may be the case, for instance, with the African National Congress in South Africa, with socialists and communists in Europe, and former revolutionary movements in Central America.

If the accumulation of money capital outside of the nation-state system was one important aspect in the process of economic globalization, it was also a key mechanism in the incorporation of countries, especially peripheral ones, into the transnationalization process, and more generally, in the transformation of welfare and developmentalist into neo-liberal states. The debt crisis of the 1980s imposed the power and authority of global capitalism within the very structure and functioning of Third World national states. Debt led to the reinsertion of countries and regions around the world into a reorganized global economy. The massive infusion of recycled liquid capital into the Third World in the 1970s, linked to the concentration of economic power in transnational finance capital, had profound effects on existing groups and class constellations in the periphery.

The need to earn foreign exchange to pay back the debt (the structural power of transnational capital over debtor states along with the direct pressures of core national states enforced payback) forced nations to restructure their economies in favour of exports in accordance with the changing structure of world market demand. Over an extended period, debt contraction and subsequent reservicing had the consequence of strengthening those sectors with external linkage, redistribution quotas of accumulated political and economic power towards new fractions linked to transnational capital. At a certain point in this process the debtor nation is unable to maintain fiscal solvency and turns to the supranational economic institutions for assistance which is made conditional on the adoption of a structural adjustment or 'neo-liberal' programme.

The neo-liberal programme was designed in the 1970s and 1980s by the international financial agencies and the think tanks of the newly organized transnational bourgeoisie. This programme calls for the elimination of state intervention in the economy and the regulation of individual nation-states over the activities of capital in their territories. It seeks to achieve the conditions in each country and region of the world for the mobility, free operation, and expansion of capital. The adjustment programmes become the major mechanism of adjusting local economies to the global economy. Between 1978 and 1992 more than 70 countries undertook 566 stabilization and structural adjustment programmes imposed by the IMF and the World Bank. What took place through these programmes was a massive restructuring of the productive apparatus in these countries, and the reintegration into the global capitalism of vast zones of the former Third World, under the tutelage of the emergent TNS.

Specifically, these programmes pursue macroeconomic stability as an essential requisite for the activity of transnational capital. This model seeks to harmonize a wide range of fiscal, monetary, industrial, and commercial policies among multiple nations, as a requirement for fully mobile transnational capital to function simultaneously, and often instantaneously, among numerous national borders. In the neo-liberal model, stabilization, or the package of fiscal, monetary, exchange and related measures intended to achieve macroeconomic stability is followed by 'structural adjustment': a) liberalization of trade and finances, which opens the economy to the world market; b) deregulation, which removes the state from economic decision making (but not from activities that service capital); c) privatization of formerly public spheres that could hamper capital accumulation if criteria of public interest over private profit is left operative.

This model thus generates the overall conditions for the profitable ('efficient') renewal of capital accumulation through new globalized circuits, and along with it, for social reproduction in the age of globalization. Neo-liberalism is in this way the 'grease' by which global capitalism tears down all non-market structures. By prying open and making accessible to transnational capital every layer of the social fabric, neo-liberalism helps dissolve the boundaries between the national and the global.

Here we see the nuts and bolts of the transnationalization of the state. Economic restructuring begets political restructuring as power is redistributed in society, and also within the state apparatus itself, towards emergent transnational nuclei of local dominant groups. The adjustment process facilitates a simultaneous contraction in overall demand and a transfer of income and resources from workers and small-scale producers to large producers and bureaucratic personnel tied to transnational capital. Restructuring results in a transfer of state resources from programmes supporting working class reproduction to those state agencies connected to the globalization, in which the technical criteria of 'efficiency' replaces all social criteria that might contravene the logic of cross-border capital accumulation. It similarly effects a transfer of power from programme-oriented ministries (social services, education, labour, etc.) to Central Banks, treasuries and finance and economic ministries, and the foreign ministry. As resources are transferred from the domestic to the external sector, and from these to the world market, transnational pools in each nation are strengthened. These transnationalized fractions became incorporated into the transnational bourgeoisie and set about to capture local states. In fact, it is not uncommon for Central Bank presidents to be appointed by the IMF or the WB.

The movement towards Central Bank independence has the purpose of insulating the commanding heights of national state policy making from any public control or accountability, and also, and insulating these organs of the state that tie each national economy to the global economy from other organs of the national state that could come under public pressure. A WB report was explicit on this matter. Reforming the state, the report asserted, begins 'with a few critical enclaves [that] typically include the ministry of finance, the central bank, and the tax collection agency...[restructuring these organs] can mostly be achieved through executive order...[and should] establish effective macroeconomic management by an insulated technocratic elite.'

Local technocratic elites come to operate through the networks of the TNS that bypass the formal channels of government and other social institutions subject to popular influence. Power passes upwards to supranational structures, including financial networks, as this supranational political integration proceeds. There is a loss of any democratic control by popular classes over policymaking and resource allocation. Decision-making and regulatory mechanisms emanating from supranational agencies and from local contingents of the transnational bourgeoisie are superimposed on national-states, which themselves become absorbed into the emergent TNS apparatus. However, while the TNS does impose neo-liberal adjustment programmes, the supranational integration of national state apparatuses does not necessarily come from the outside, and is as much the result of strategies pursued by local dominant groups in the process of transnationalization as it is of external imposition that is generally emphasized in the literature (reflecting the national-global dualism). When state managers adjust national economies to the global economy they are doing so not necessarily because they are compelled to by some 'external' (extra-national/global) force. This national-global duality is a mystification.

Structural adjustment programmes thus help undermine the multi-class political coalitions and social projects that developed in the pre-globalization period, such as the populist projects and the 'developmental states' in the Third World (although the core countries, save Great Britain, have not generally adopted IMF programmes, the same adjustment pressures emanating from the global economy undermine the Keynesian welfare projects there). New transnational blocs come to replace these multi-class coalitions. For this purpose, WB and IMF structural adjustment programmes emphasize 'policy dialogue' and 'institution building' as a way of organizing coalitions in governments sympathetic and attuned to the restructuring programme. Labour and popular classes are expunged by the new dominant bloc from the political coalitions and social projects of the pre-globalization period.In the 1980s the TNS charted a new model of development. The World Bank in 1980 redefined development, no longer as national economic growth, but as successful 'participation in the world market.' At the core of the new development model was a wholesale shift from production for domestic markets to production for the world market, signalling the subordination of local circuits of accumulation to new global ones. Later in that decade, the definition was extended to include a policy of broad liberalization.

The new development model is based on each country's rearticulation to world markets through the introduction of new economic activities linked to global accumulation, the contraction of domestic markets, the cheapening of labour through casualization and social austerity to make it 'competitive,' and the opening up of each country's public sectors, protected industries, and natural resources to commercial exploitation. Through this process the neo-liberal states institutionalize locally the new global class relation discussed earlier. The neo-liberal national states of the late twentieth century reflect the new historic correlation of social forces that emerged following the breakup of the capitalist state structures that were shaped by particular class struggles in the period from the 1890s into the 1970s.

Hence, far from the 'end of the nation-state,' as a slew of recent studies has proclaimed, we are witness to its transformation into neo-liberal states. These neo-liberal states as component elements of a TNS provided essential services for capital. National governments serve as transmission belts and filtering devices for the imposition of the transnational agenda. In addition, they perform three essential functions: 1) adopt fiscal and monetary policies which assure macro-economic stability; 2) provide the basic infrastructure necessary for global economic activity (air and sea ports, communications networks, educational systems, etc.), and; 3) provide social order, that is, stability, which requires sustaining instruments of direct coercion and ideological apparatuses. When the transnational elite speaks of 'governance' it is referring to these functions and the capacity to fulfil them. This is made explicit in the WB's *World Development Report* for 1997, *The State in a Changing World,* which points out that the aegis of the national state is central to globalization. In the WB's words, 'globalization begins at home.'

But the functions of the neo-liberal state are contradictory. As globalization proceeds, internal social cohesion declines along with national economic integration. The neo-liberal state retains essential powers to facilitate globalization but it loses the ability to harmonize conflicting social interests within a country, to realize the historic function of sustaining the internal unity of nationally-conceived social formation, and to achieve legitimacy. The result is a dramatic intensification of legitimacy crises, a contradiction internal to the system of global capitalism.

Neolibaralism as Ideology of State Reconquest

Neoliberalism has become one of the most pervasive, if not, dangerous ideologies of the 21st century. Its pervasiveness is evident not only by its unparalleled influence on the global economy, but also by its power to redefine the very nature of politics itself. Free market fundamentalism rather than democratic idealism is now the driving force of economics and politics in most of the world, and it is a market ideology driven not just by profits but by an ability to reproduce itself with such success that, to paraphrase Fred Jameson, it is easier to imagine the end of the world than the end of neoliberal capitalism.

Wedded to the belief that the market should be the organizing principle for all political, social, and economic decisions, neoliberalism wages an incessant attack on democracy, public goods, the welfare state, and non-commoditized values.

Under neoliberalism everything either is for sale or is plundered for profit. Public lands are looted by logging companies and corporate ranchers; politicians willingly hand the public's airwaves over to powerful broadcasters and large corporate interests without a dime going into the public trust; Halliburton gives war profiteering a new meaning as it is granted corporate contracts without any competitive bidding and then bilks the U.S. government for millions; the environment is polluted and despoiled in the name of profit-making just as the government passes legislation to make it easier for corporations to do so; public services are gutted in order to lower the taxes of major corporations; schools more closely resemble either malls or jails, and teachers are forced to get revenue for their school by hawking everything from hamburgers to pizza parties. As markets are touted as the driving force of everyday life, big government is disparaged as either incompetent or threatening to individual freedom, suggesting that power should reside in markets and corporations rather than in governments (except for their support for corporate interests and national security) and citizens.

Under neoliberalism, the state now makes a grim alignment with corporate capital and transnational corporations. Gone are the days when the state 'assumed responsibility for a range of social needs.'[1] Instead, agencies of government now pursues a wide range of "deregulations,' privatizations, and abdications of responsibility to the market and private philanthropy.'[2] Deregulation, in turn, promotes 'widespread, systematic disinvestment in the nation's basic productive capacity.'[3] Flexible production encourages wage slavery and disposable populations at home. And the search for ever greater profits leads to outsourcing which accentuates the flight of capital and jobs abroad. Neoliberalism has now become the prevailing logic in the United States, and according to Stanley Aronowitz .'..the neoliberal economic doctrine proclaiming the superiority of free markets over public ownership, or even public regulation of private economic activities, has become the conventional wisdom, not only among conservatives but among social progressives.'[4]

The ideology and power of neoliberalism also cuts across national boundaries. Throughout the globe, the forces of neoliberalism are on the march, dismantling the historically guaranteed social provisions provided by the welfare state, defining profit-making as the essence of democracy, and equating freedom with the unrestricted ability of markets to 'govern economic relations free of government regulation.'[5] Transnational in scope, neoliberalism now imposes its economic regime and market values on developing and weaker nations through structural adjustment policies enforced by powerful financial institutions such as the World Bank, the International Monetary Fund (IMF), and the World Trade Organization (WTO). Secure in its dystopian vision that there are no alternatives, as England's former Prime Minister Margaret Thatcher once put it, neoliberalism obviates issues of contingency, struggle, and social agency by celebrating the inevitability of economic laws in which the ethical ideal of intervening in the world gives way to the idea that we 'have no choice but to adapt both our hopes and our abilities to the new global market.'[6] Coupled with a new culture of fear, market freedoms seem securely grounded in a defence of national security, capital, and property rights. When coupled with a media driven culture of fear and the everyday reality of insecurity, public space becomes increasingly militarized as state governments invest more in prison construction than in education. Prison guards and security personnel in public schools are two of the fastest growing professions.

In its capacity to dehistoricize and depoliticize society, as well as in its aggressive attempts to destroy all of the public spheres necessary for the defence of a genuine democracy, neoliberalism reproduces the conditions for unleashing the most brutalizing forces of capitalism. Social Darwinism has been resurrected from the ashes of the 19th century sweatshops and can now be seen in full bloom in most reality TV programmes and in the unfettered self-interests that now drives popular culture. As narcissism is replaced by unadulterated materialism, public concerns collapse into utterly private considerations and where public space does exist it is mainly used as a confessional for private woes, a cut throat game of winner take all, or a advertisement for consumerism.

Neoliberal policies dominate the discourse of politics and use the breathless rhetoric of the global victory of free-market rationality to cut public expenditures and undermine those non-commodified public spheres that serve as the repository for critical education, language, and public intervention. Spewed forth by the mass media, right-wing intellectuals, religious fanatics, and politicians, neoliberal ideology, with its ongoing emphasis on deregulation and privatization, has found its material expression in an all-out attack on democratic values and on the very notion of the public sphere.

Within the discourse of neoliberalism, the notion of the public good is devalued and, where possible, eliminated as part of a wider rationale for a handful of private interests to control as much of social life as possible in order to maximize their personal profit. Public services such as health care, child care, public assistance, education, and transportation are now subject to the rules of the market. Construing the public good as a private good and the needs of the corporate and private sector as the only source of investment, neoliberal ideology produces, legitimates, and exacerbates the existence of persistent poverty, inadequate health care, racial apartheid in the inner cities, and the growing inequalities between the rich and the poor.[7]

As Stanley Aronowitz points out, the Bush administration has made neoliberal ideology the cornerstone of its programme and has been in the forefront in actively supporting and implementing the following policies:

[D]eregulation of business at all levels of enterprises and trade; tax reduction for wealthy individuals and corporations; the revival of the near-dormant nuclear energy industry; limitations and abrogation of labour's right to organize and bargain collectively; a land policy favouring commercial and industrial development at the expense of conservation and other pro environment policies; elimination of income support to the chronically unemployed; reduced federal aid to education and health; privatization of the main federal pension programmes, Social Security; limitation on the right of aggrieved individuals to sue employers and corporations who provide services; in addition, as social programmes are reduced, [Republicans] are joined by the Democrats in favouring increases in the repressive functions of the state, expressed in the dubious drug wars in the name of fighting crime, more funds for surveillance of ordinary citizens, and the expansion of the federal and local police forces.[8]

Central to both neoliberal ideology and its implementation by the Bush administration is the ongoing attempts by free-market fundamentalists and right wing politicians to view government as the enemy of freedom (except when it aids big business) and discount it as a guardian of the public interest. The call to eliminate big government is neoliberalism's great unifying idea and has broad popular appeal in the United States because it is a principle deeply embedded in the country's history and tangled up with its notion of political freedom. And yet, the right wing appropriation of this tradition is racked with contradictions in terms of neoliberal policies.

The advocates of neoliberalism have attacked what they call big government when it has provided essential services such as crucial safety nets for the less fortunate, but they have no qualms about using the government to bailout the airline industry after the economic nosedive that followed the 2000 election of George W. Bush and the events of 9/11. Nor are there any expressions of outrage from the cheerleaders of neoliberalism when the state engages in promoting various forms of corporate welfare by providing billions of dollars in direct and indirect subsidies to multinational corporations. In short, government bears no obligation for both the poor and dispossessed or for the collective future of young people.

As the laws of the market take precedence over the laws of the state as guardians of the public good, the government increasingly offers little help in mediating the interface between the advance of capital and its rapacious commercial interests. Neither does it aid non-commodified interests and non-market spheres that create the political, economic, and social spaces and discursive conditions vital for critical citizenship and democratic public life. Within the discourse of neoliberalism, it becomes difficult for the average citizen to speak about political or social transformation, or to even challenge, outside of a grudging nod toward rampant corruption, the ruthless downsizing, the ongoing liquidation of job security, or the elimination of benefits for people now hired on part-time.

The liberal democratic vocabulary of rights, entitlements, social provisions, community, social responsibility, living wage, job security, equality, and justice seem oddly out of place in a country where the promise of democracy has been replaced by casino capitalism, a winner-take-all philosophy, suited to lotto players and day traders alike. As corporate culture extends even deeper into the basic institutions of civil and political society, buttressed daily by a culture industry largely in the hands of concentrated capital, it is reinforced even further by the pervasive fear and insecurity of the public that the future holds nothing beyond a watered down version of the present.

As the prevailing discourse of neoliberalism seizes the public imagination, there is no vocabulary for progressive social change, democratically inspired visions, or critical notions of social agency to expand the meaning and purpose of democratic public life. Against the reality of low wage jobs, the erosion of social provisions for a growing number of people and the expanding war against young people of colour at home and empire-building abroad, the market-driven juggernaut of neoliberalism continues to mobilize desires in the interest of producing market identities and market relationships that ultimately sever the link between education and social change while reducing agency to the obligations of consumerism.

As neoliberal ideology and corporate culture extend even deeper into the basic institutions of civil and political society, there is a simultaneous diminishing of non-commodified public spheres—those institutions such as public schools, independent bookstores, churches, non-commercial public broadcasting stations, libraries, trade unions and various voluntary institutions engaged in dialogue, education, and learning—that address the relationship of the individual to public life and foster social responsibility and provide a robust vehicle for public participation and democratic citizenship. In the vacuum left by diminishing democracy, religious zealotry, cultural chauvinism, xenophobia, and racism have become the dominant tropes of neoconservatives and other extremist groups eager to take advantage of the growing insecurity, fear, and anxiety that result from increased joblessness, the war on terror, and the unravelling of communities.

As a result of the consolidated corporate attack on public life, the maintenance of democratic public spheres from which to launch a moral vision or to engage in a viable struggle over politics loses all credibility—not to mention monetary support. As the alleged objectivity of neoliberal ideology remains largely unchallenged within dominant public spheres, individual critique and collective political struggles become more difficult.[9] It gets worse. Dominated by extremists, the Bush administration is driven by an arrogance of power and inflated sense of moral righteousness mediated largely by a false sense of certitude and never ending posture of triumphalism. As George Soros points out this rigid ideology and inflexible sense of mission allows the Bush administration to believe that 'because we are stronger than others, we must know better and we must have right on our side. This is where religious fundamentalism comes together with market fundamentalism to form the ideology of American supremacy.'[10]

As public space is increasingly commodified and the state becomes more closely aligned with capital, politics is defined largely by its policing functions rather than an agency for peace and social reform. As the state abandons its social investments in health, education, and the public welfare, it increasingly takes on the functions of an enhanced police or security state, the signs of which are most visible in the increasing use of the state apparatus to spy on and arrests its subjects, the incarceration of individuals deemed disposable (primarily people of colour), and the ongoing criminalization of social policies. Examples of the latter include anti-begging ordinances and anti-loitering that fine or punish homeless people for sitting or lying down too long in public places.[11]

An even more despicable example of the barbaric nature of neoliberalism with its emphasis on profits over people and its willingness to punish rather than serve the poor and disenfranchised can be seen in the growing tendency of many hospitals across the country to have patients arrested and jailed if they cannot pay their medical bills. The policy, right out of the pages of George Orwell's 1984, represents a return to debtors prisons, which is now chillingly called 'body attachment,' and is ' basically a warrant for... the patient's arrest.'[12]

Neoliberalism is not simply an economic policy designed to cut government spending, pursue free trade policies, and free market forces from government regulations; it is also a political philosophy and ideology that affects every dimension of social life. Neoliberalism has heralded a radical economic, political, and experiential shift that now largely defines the citizen as a consumer, disbands the social contract in the interests of privatized considerations, and separates capital from the context of place.

Under such circumstances, neoliberalism portends the death of politics as we know it, strips the social of its democratic values, and reconstructs agency in terms that are utterly privatized and provides the conditions for an emerging form of proto-fascism that must be resisted at all costs. Neoliberalism not only enshrines unbridled individualism, it also destroys any vestige of democratic society by undercutting its 'moral, material, and regulatory moorings,'[13] and in doing so it offers no language for understanding how the future might be grasped outside of the narrow logic of the market. But there is even more at stake here than the obliteration of public concerns, the death of the social, the emergence of a market-based fundamentalism that undercuts the ability of people to understand how to translate the privately experienced misery into collective action, and the elimination of the gains of the welfare state.

There is also the growing threat of displacing 'political sovereignty with the sovereignty of the market, as if the latter has a mind and morality of its own.'[14] As democracy becomes a burden under the reign of neoliberalism, civic discourse disappears and the reign of unfettered social Darwinism with its survival-of-the-slickest philosophy emerges as the template for a new form of proto-fascism. None of this will happen in the face of sufficient resistance, nor is the increasing move toward proto-fascism inevitable, but the conditions exist for democracy to lose all semblance of meaning in the United States.

Educators, parents, activists, workers, and others can address this challenge by building local and global alliances and engaging in struggles that acknowledge and transcend national boundaries, but also engage in modes of politics that connect with people's everyday lives. Democratic struggles cannot under emphasize the special responsibility of intellectuals to shatter the conventional wisdom and myths of neoliberalism with its stunted definition of freedom and its depoliticized and dehistoricized definition of its own alleged universality.

As the late Pierre Bourdieu argued, any viable politics that challenges neoliberalism must refigure the role of the state in limiting the excesses of capital and providing important social provisions.[15] At the same time, social movements must address the crucial issue of education as it develops throughout the cultural sphere because the 'power of the dominant order is not just economic, but intellectual–lying in the realm of beliefs,' and it is precisely within the domain of ideas that a sense of utopian possibility can be restored to the public realm.[16] This restoration is what the Washington Consensus denied.

Trojan Horses of Africa's Reconquest: IMF and World Bank

Africa has experienced its best economic performance in many years. In 2004 Africa grew at 5.1 percent, up from 3.7 percent in 2003. Between 1990 and 2003, Africa's economies grew at an average of 2.6 percent annually. This improved growth has had a mixed bag of consequences, increasing opportunities to meet key Millennium Development Goals (MDGs) targets and improving human well-being, which can have positive spin-offs for the environment as options increase. However, Sub Sahara Africa (SSA) must grow on average at 7 percent per year to reduce income poverty by half by 2015. Only six African countries, mostly in North Africa, are likely to meet the Millennium Development Goals (MDGs) of halving the number of people living on less than a dollar a day. The MDGs remain underfinanced—by more than US$40,000 million overall.

There is considerable variation between the economic achievements of countries in the region – with prices of oil and metals, low cotton and cocoa prices, dollar depreciation and euro appreciation, the locust plague in the Sahel region, rainfall, corruption, and political conflict and instability being important contributing factors. Solid growth was expected to continue between 2005 and 2007 at an average rate of 4.7 percent as the effect of new oil fields in Central Africa wears off. The high level of vulnerability to external shocks (such as prices and the loss of preferential treatment), environmental factors such as weather conditions, and conflict make these key areas for policy focus and collaborative initiatives. This close relationship to the environment is indicative of the need for better environmental monitoring and, in particular, risk and disaster warning systems to support greater preparedness and more effective responses.

The reforms clearly incorporate much of the agenda originally laid out in the now somewhat discredited Washington Consensus.[17] The main thrust of the Washington Consensus is a set of actions which, if taken at an early stage of transition, should facilitate a smooth evolution into the world economy. It consists of elements of macroeconomic reform (liberalization, stabilization and fiscal austerity) stressing the importance of bringing down inflation and establishing economic growth. In addition it incorporates a number of elements of microeconomic reform (e.g. privatization, promoting FDI), as well as structural/administrative reforms (e.g. property rights, replacement of quantitative restrictions. Specifically:

1. *Fiscal Discipline*: Limits to budget deficits.
2. *Public Expenditure Priorities*: Redirect expenditure toward building human capital and infrastructure.
3. *Tax Reform*: Broaden tax base and cut marginal tax rates.
4. *Financial Liberalization*: Abolish interest rate controls
5. *Exchange Rates*: Introduce unified and competitive exchange rates
6. *Trade Liberalization*: Replace quantitative restrictions by tariffs and then reduce the tariffs over time.
7. *Foreign Direct Investment*: Encourage increased international capital inflows.
8. *Privatization*: Privatize state enterprises
9. *Deregulation*: Regulate only safety, environment, and financial sectors (i.e., prudential supervision)
10. *Property Rights*: Introduce secure enforcement at low cost.

While progress of reform design and implementation varies considerably by categories, the September 2003 Coalition Provisional Authority (CPA) reforms have little to say about numbers 1 and 2, no doubt due to the great uncertainty surrounding oil revenues and the external debt situation, and foreign assistance. Surprisingly, number 10, property rights, a key element of the neoliberal reforms has received less attention than one might have expected. Perhaps the intent of the CPA is to simply differ many of the specific legalities to an elected Iraqi government.

This interpretation is lent credibility by the fact that very little has also been implemented or even discussed in the important areas of the augmented Washington Consensus - a set of complementary measures aimed at strengthening supporting institutions: (1) Corporate governance, (2) Anti-corruption, (3) Flexible labour markets, (4) World Trade Organization (WTO) agreements, (5) Financial codes and standards, (6) Prudent capital account opening, (7) Non-intermediate exchange rate regimes, (8) Independent central banks/inflation targeting, (9) Social safety nets, and (10) Targeted poverty reduction. Of these only some initial, albeit limited, progress has occurred in (5) and (8). Iraq has applied for permission to become an observer, and ultimately a member of the WTO.**18** Yet, when they began to intervene on that continent in the late 1970s and early 1980s, their stated goal was to 'accelerate development,' according to a World Bank document, familiarly known as the 'Berg Report,' published in 1981. But as the following editorial will show, the actual record is just disastrous.

The main pretext for their intervention was to 'help solve' the debt crisis that hit African countries in the late 1970s, following the combination of internal and external shocks, notably sharp fluctuations in commodity prices and skyrocketing interest rates. The remedy they proposed, known as stabilization and structural adjustment programmes (SAPs), achieved the opposite, and contributed to worsening the external debt and exacerbating the overall economic and social crisis.

In 1980, at the onset of their intervention, the ratios of debt to gross domestic product (GDP) and exports of goods and services were respectively 23.4% and 65.2%. Ten years later, in 1990, they had deteriorated to respectively 63.0% and 210.0%! In 2000, the debt to GDP ratio stood at 71.0% while the ratio of debt to exports of goods and services had 'improved' somewhat, at 80.2%, according to the World Bank's Global Development Finance.

The deterioration in debt ratios is reflected in the inability of many African countries to service their external debt. As a result, accumulated arrears on principal and interests have become a growing share of outstanding debt. In 1999, those arrears accounted for 30% of the continent's debt, compared with 15% in the 1990s and 5.0% for all developing countries. To compound the crisis, African countries are getting very little, in terms of new loans, except to pay back old debts. As a result, since 1988, the part of accumulated arrears in 'new' debt is estimated at more than 65%.

Between 1980 and 2000, Sub-Saharan African countries had paid more than $240 billion as debt service, that is, about four times the amount of their debt in 1980. Yet, despite this financial haemorrhage, SSA still owes almost four times what its owed more than twenty years ago! One of the most striking illustrations of this apparent paradox is the case of the Nigerian debt. In 1978, the country had borrowed $5 billion. By 2000, it had reimbursed $16 billion, but still owed $31 billion, according to President Obasanjo.

The Nigerian case is a good example of the structural nature of Africa's debt crisis and of the power imbalance that characterizes world economic and financial relationships. It is this general context that allowed the IMF and World Bank to increase their influence in African countries. One good illustration of this has been the rapid rise in the share of the World Bank and its affiliate, the International Development Association (IDA), in SSA's debt. The combined share of both, which was barely 5.1% of SSA's total debt in 1980, had jumped to 25.0% in 1990 and to more than 37% in 2000, according to the World Bank. In other words, the World Bank group has become the principal 'creditor' of many Sub-Saharan countries, which explains the enormous sway it holds over these countries' policies.

One way they exercise this influence is through the imposition of stiff conditionalities on African countries in exchange for loans and credits. Financial liberalization, aimed at attracting more foreign investments to compensate for shortfalls in export revenues, instead fostered more instability, due to the volatility of exchange rates resulting from speculative short-term capital flows. This, combined with higher interest rates, 'crowded' out both public and private investments. For instance, investments as a percentage of gross domestic production (GDP) fell from an annual average of 23% between 1975 and 1979 to an average of 18% between 1980 and 1984 and 16% between 1985 and 1989. They recovered somewhat in the 1990s, but averaged only 18.2% between 1990 and 1997, according to UNCTAD. These statistics are consistent with those given by the World Bank, which show that the annual investment ratio averaged 18.6% and 17.2% in 1981-1990 and 1991-2000, respectively.

These low investment ratios resulted in a contraction of output. Real GDP growth, which averaged 3.5 % in the 1970s, fell to 1.7%, between 1981 and 1990, according to the World Bank. However, this masks the sharp declines recorded in the 1980s, dubbed 'the lost decade' for Africa.

This is better illustrated by the negative growth rates of both GDP and consumption per capita. They fell respectively by 1.2% and 0.9% a year between 1981 and 1990. It is estimated that in 1981-1989, the cumulative loss of per capita income for the continent as a whole was equivalent to more than 21% of real GDP.

In a report released in September 2001, UNCTAD indicated that the average income per capita in SSA was 10% lower in 2000 than its 1980 level. In monetary terms, average income per capita fell from $522 in 1981 to $323 in 1997, a loss of nearly $200. The same report said that rural areas experienced an even greater decline in income. These statistics were confirmed by the World Bank, which says that income per capita in Sub Saharan Africa contracted by a cumulative 13% between 1981 and 2001.

The 2004 edition of the World Development Indicators says that SSA is the only region in the world where poverty has continued to rise since the early 1980s, that is at the onset of IFIs' intervention. According to that document, in 1981, an estimated 160 million people lived on less than $1 a day. In 2001, the number had risen to 314 million, almost double its 1981 level. This means that approximately 50% of Africa's population lives in poverty. When the threshold is $2 a day, the numbers rise from 288 million to 518 million, during the same period.

The Cost of Trade Liberalization to the State in Africa

According to the IMF and World Bank, one of the sources of Africa's crisis is its inward-looking trade system, characterized by the protection of domestic markets, subsidies, overvalued exchange rates and other 'market distortions' that made African exports less 'competitive' in world markets. In place of this system, they propose an open and liberal trading system in which tariff and non tariff barriers are kept to a minimum or even eliminated. Such a system, combined with an export-led growth strategy, would put Africa on a solid path to economic recovery, according to both institutions.

The costs associated with trade liberalization have largely offset any potential 'benefits' African countries were supposed to derive from that liberalization. First of all, trade liberalization has translated into substantial fiscal losses, since many countries depend on import taxation as their main source of fiscal revenues. Therefore, the elimination of, or reduction in, import tariffs has led to lower government revenues. But one of the most negative impacts of trade liberalization has been the collapse of many domestic industries, unable to sustain competition from powerful and subsidized competitors from industrialized countries. In fact, Africa's industrial sector has been among the biggest victims of structural adjustment.

From Senegal to Zambia, from Mali to Tanzania, from Côte d'Ivoire to Uganda, entire sectors of the domestic industry have been wiped out, with devastating consequences. Not only has the industrial sector contribution to domestic product continued to fall, but also the industrial workforce has continued to shrink dramatically. In Senegal, more than one third of industrial workers lost their jobs in the 1980s. The trend was accentuated in the 1990s, following sweeping trade liberalization policies and privatization imposed by the IMF and the World Bank, especially after the 50% devaluation of the CFA Franc, in 1994. In Ghana, the industrial workforce declined from 78,700 in 1987 to 28,000 in 1993. In Zambia, in the textile sector alone, more than 75% of workers lost their jobs in less than a decade, as a result of the complete dismantling of that sector by the Chiluba presidency. In other countries, such as Côte d'Ivoire, Burkina Faso, Mali, Togo, Zambia, Tanzania, etc. similar trends can be observed.

In several annual and special reports, the International Labour Organization (ILO) has documented the devastating impact of SAPs on employment and wages. The African Union seems to have come to grips with that devastation. It organized a special Summit on Employment and Poverty, in the capital of Burkina Faso, September 9 and 10, 2004. It was revealed during that Summit that only 25% of the African workforce is employed in the formal sector. The rest, 75%, is either in the subsistence agriculture or in the informal sector. In light of this reality, the Summit issued a Plan of Action aimed at exploring strategies to foster job creation. But such a Plan will only be credible if African countries are ready to move away from IMF and World Bank recipes, which were harshly criticized during the Summit.

UNCTAD has reported that more than 70% of Africa's exports are still composed of primary products, more than 62% of which are non processed products. This helps justify the need for more liberalization and deregulation to make African exports more 'competitive.' The second objective is to help justify the need for more liberalization and deregulation to make African economies more 'competitive' and 'attractive' to foreign direct investments. This also explains the push for more privatization. In the name of 'comparative advantage,' the export-led growth strategy forces African countries to compete fiercely for market shares, leading them to flood the same markets with more of their commodities. As a result, trade liberalization has accentuated the volatility of African commodities, whose prices experienced twice the volatility of East Asian commodity prices and nearly four times the volatility that industrial countries experienced in the 1970s, 1980s and 1990s. This has contributed to worsening Africa's terms of trade.

According to UNCTAD, if Africa's terms of trade had remained at their 1980 level:

- Africa's share in world trade would have been twice its current level
- the investment ratio would have been raised by 6.0% per annum in non-oil exporting countries
- it would have added to annual growth 1.4% per annum
- it would have raised GDP per capita by at least 50% to $478 in 1997 compared with the actual figure of $323 during that year.

The Costs of Financial Liberalization

One of the main objectives of financial liberalization is to make African countries 'attractive' to foreign direct investments. But as the experience of development shows, foreign direct investments follow development, not the other way around. In addition, despite all 'the right financial policies,' foreign investments continue to elude Africa, with less than 2% of flows to developing countries, despite having among the highest rates of return on investments in the world. And these flows are concentrated in a few oil-producing and mineral-rich countries, according to UNCTAD and the World Bank.

In reality, financial liberalization has yielded little gains. For most African countries, it has been associated with huge costs. First, it entails higher levels of foreign exchange reserves to protect domestic currencies against attacks resulting from speculative short-term capital outflows. Second, financial liberalization has increased the likelihood of capital flight, in part as a result of a greater volatility of domestic currencies. The high costs of trade and financial liberalization further weakened African economies and opened the way to the privatization of the continent.

The Privatization of the State in Africa

The starting point for any adequate explanation of the state must be the general discussions of the state in the writings of Marx and Engels. At the risk of considerable over-simplification, what they said may be reducible to a small number of general propositions:

1. The state is a product of class society, of a condition *in* which society has become entangled in irreconcilable contradictions. If any kind of orderly life is to continue in a society rent with internal divisions, the members of that society must lose their power to control the communal affairs of their society to specialised agencies and persons The state is thus not an everlasting and inevitable product of human social relations; rather, it is a product of particular forms of society, whose manner of formation divides their members against each other.

2. The very existence of the state, in this general sense, is therefore an indication of alienated social relations. Certain forms of human social relations, organized around antagonistic divisions, make impossible for all members of society to run their own society communally.
3. The existence of the state involves a particular form of the division of labour, through which some members of society specialize in directing the rest of Society. The state is thus separated from the rest of society.
4. The means of coercion are no longer the direct property of the whole of society, but are specialized into the hands of the members of the state. Thus the state is a... *public power* which no longer directly coincides with the population organizing itself as an armed force. This special public power is necessary because a self-acting armed organization of the population has become impossible since the split into classes ... This public power exists in every state; it consists not merely of armed men, but also of material adjuncts prisons, and institutions of coercion of all kinds, of which gentile society knew nothing.
5. The state apparatus, the product of Class divisions in society, anything but neutral between classes. It is a crucial element in class rule.
6. The fullest development of the state, whether in terms of the relative growth in its personnel, the relative separation of its organization and principles from those of class society, or by any other measure occurs with the development of capitalism the most completely alienated form of class society.
7. The destruction of capitalism and the construction of communism requires the smashing up of the existing state apparatus, its replacement by the armed power of the working class, and the beginning of the process of the withering away of the state altogether. A fully developed communist society, its production organized according to the famous principle 'From each according to his ability, to each according to his need!' will have no need of a state organization. It will be a self-governing community, for whose members public and private interests will coincide.

Ralph Miliband (1969) is probably the best-known of all the proponents of this thesis, according to which the modern state is the 'instrument' of the capitalist class. In sum, the state is an apparatus of violence, first and foremost, which enforces onto society a 'communal interest' or 'national interest' which is not the direct product of that society's members and which maintains the basis of the class divisions. At this high level of generality, these core propositions about the state – and thus about the need to overthrow the state and destroy it as a condition of the realization of human emancipation through communism – form part of the ABC of Marxism both as a theory of human history and as a theory of human emancipation.

Privatization of the state, like financial liberalization, is seen by the IMF and World Bank as an instrument to promote private sector development, which has been elevated to the status of 'engine of growth.' The privatization of State-owned enterprises (SOEs), including water and power utilities, has been one of the core conditionalities imposed by the two institutions, even in the context of 'poverty reduction.'

Most of the foreign direct investments registered by African countries in the 1990s came as a response to privatization of SOEs. No sector was spared, even those considered as 'strategic' in the 1980s, such as telecommunications, energy, water and the extractive industries. In 1994, the World Bank published a report assessing the process of privatization in SSA. After complaining about the slow pace of privatization throughout the region, it issued a warning to African governments to accelerate the dismantling of their public sector, accused of being 'at the heart of Africa's economic crisis.' The process of privatization peaked in the late 1990s and ever since has levelled off, despite more deregulation, liberalization and all kinds of incentives offered to would be investors.

To date, it is estimated that more than 40,000 SOEs have been sold off in Africa. However, the 'gains' from privatization, projected by the World Bank and the IMF, have been elusive. In fact, many privatization schemes have failed and contributed to worsening economic and social conditions. Almost everywhere, privatization has been associated with massive job losses and higher prices of goods and services that put them out of reach of most citizens.

Building a 'Gated' Neoliberal State in Africa

The concept of 'good governance' was promoted by the IMF and World Bank to explain the failure of SAPs. It tends to convey the idea that SAPs have failed, in large part, because 'African States' are 'corrupt,' 'wasteful' and 'rent-seeking' and because of the 'poor implementation' of policies. In other words, SAPs were basically 'sound,' it is the combination of 'rampant corruption' and lack of qualified personnel that led to the failure of these policies. Thus, 'good governance' means nothing else than the need to build a neoliberal State, subservient to the IFIs, able to effectively implement, 'sound policies' and to protect the interests of foreign investors.

Indeed, one of the main goals of the IMF and World Bank has been to discredit State-led development strategies in favour of market-led strategies. This is why one of the main targets of these institutions has been the role of the so-called 'African State' in economic and social development. To discredit that role, a two-track strategy was adopted. The first track was to attack the credibility of the Neocolonial State as an agent of development. To achieve that goal, an abundant literature has been published by the two institutions, highlighting the 'corrupt,' 'predatory,' 'wasteful' and 'rent-seeking' nature of the African State. To justify these epithets, the IFIs pointed to the 'mismanagement' of the public sector, accused of being an obstacle to economic growth and development. These attacks helped make the case for the sweeping restructure of the public sector, which, in many cases, led to its dismantling in favour of the private sector.

The second track in weakening the role of the State in development was to deprive it of financial resources. Trade and financial liberalization achieved in part that goal. As already indicated, trade liberalization not only led to a greater loss of fiscal revenues, following lower tariff barriers, but it also led to huge trade losses. This was compounded by financial liberalization which entailed further fiscal losses resulting from tax holidays and low income tax rates. To make up for these losses, the African State had to resort to more and more multilateral and bilateral loans and credits, which further alienated its sovereignty.

As a result, many Neocolonial States have been 'gated' and stripped of all but a handful of their economic and social functions. Cuts in spending mostly fell on social sectors. State retrenchment primarily aimed at eliminating subsidies for the poor, removing social protection, and abandoning its role in fighting for social justice through income redistribution and other social transfers to the most disadvantaged segments of society. This explains, among other things, the degradation of many basic social services and the explosion of poverty in Africa, since 1981, as the World Bank itself has acknowledged.

While dismantling or weakening the economic and social roles of the State, the IMF and World Bank have sought to build or strengthen the functions most useful to the implementation of neoliberal policies and the promotion of private sector development. This explains the insistence on 'capacity building' or on 'institution building,' heard over the last few years. However, the institutions that the IMF and World Bank talk about are not for development, but for markets. In other words, they propose building institutions supportive of neoliberal policies and in the service of the private sector, especially foreign investors.

Thus, the 'institution building' agenda promoted by the IMF and the World Bank has nothing to do with promoting democracy and protecting human rights. In fact, the neoliberal conception of governance undermines both since it deprives representative institutions of their role in formulating public policies following open and democratic debates. They are reduced to implementing what the IMF and World Bank and their G 8 masters decide for African countries and their people.

From Structural Adjustment to 'Poverty Reduction'?

The sign at the entrance to the World Bank's headquarters in Washington, DC reads:

'Our dream is a world free of poverty'

The IMF and World Bank claim that neo-liberal reforms, while a bitter pill to swallow, in the end lay the basis for major economic growth and therefore higher living standards. But the evidence proves the opposite. The IMF and World Bank loans have created a huge debt trap. This overwhelming debt has led to the poorest countries in the world allocating enormous portions of their national incomes towards paying interest. The sick logic of capitalism means that money is actually flowing from the world's poorest countries to the richest. The debt is one of the most important weapons with which the big capitalist powers dominate poor countries. The IMF and World Bank use the debt as leverage to pry open new markets and gain access to cheap labour and raw materials. In order to get new credit (to be able to keep up debt repayments) and not default on their loans, former colonial countries must accept the dictates of the IMF and World Bank.

After producing poverty and deprivation on a massive scale in Africa and elsewhere, the IFIs' focus on 'poverty reduction' since 1999 could not be more suspect. But to make this shift a bit more credible, the IMF's Enhanced Structural Adjustment Facility (ESAF) was renamed 'Poverty Reduction and Growth Facility' (PRGF) and the World Bank has set up a 'Poverty Reduction Support Credit' (PRSC).

There is no doubt that the shift in the rhetoric of the IFIs amounts to an admission of failure of past policies, which put too much emphasis on correcting macroeconomic imbalances and 'market distortions' at the expense of economic growth and social progress. The disastrous record of SAPs and the continued deterioration in the economic and social situation of countries subjected to IMF and World Bank programmes put into question the credibility and even the legitimacy of these institutions. Their crisis of legitimacy was exacerbated by stepped up attacks by the

Global Justice Movement and growing criticism from mainstream economists, especially from Joseph E. Stiglitz, former World Bank Chief Economist.

The Nature of Poverty Reduction Strategy Papers (PRPs)

The PRSPs are supposed to provide more freedom to developing countries in formulating their policies. This is what the Bank and the Fund call 'national ownership.' Representatives from the government, the private sector, civil society organizations - and even the poor - are supposed to 'participate' in drafting the PRSP of each country to decide on how to use the proceeds released by 'debt relief' to achieve 'poverty reduction.'

In reality, the macroeconomic framework that underpins the PRSPs is the same as that which underpinned the now discredited SAPs. That framework is nonnegotiable and includes fiscal austerity, trade and financial liberalization, privatization, deregulation and State retrenchment, etc. In essence, despite the disastrous outcome of their past policies, the IMF and the World Bank still believe that those policies are in the 'interests of the poor.' In particular, they think that trade liberalization and openness are the best—if not the only—road to growth, which they see as a 'prerequisite' for poverty reduction. Hence the export-led growth strategy advocated by the two institutions, but which has been a big failure in African and other developing countries.

A survey of 27 African PRSPs by UNCTAD in 2002 has demonstrated that all of them, without exception, contain the policies outlined above. Policies which are at odds with both the wishes and the interests of the poor, observes the document. It is this straight jacket that ties up developing countries' hands and prevents them from achieving any substantial gain in poverty 'reduction.' Most of the time, countries have failed to implement these conditions, leading to the suspension of their programmes.

In fact, the IFIs' conception of poverty views it as an isolated aspect of overall economic and social development that should be dealt with by short-term measures. Hence, the emphasis in the PRSPs on more spending for primary education and health, among others. Thus, PRSPs contain some short-term measures aimed at mitigating the negative impact of macroeconomic policies and structural reforms on the most vulnerable groups, notably the poor. However, the tools the World Bank and the IMF have proposed to achieve this goal are the same as those already tested in the past and that have aggravated poverty and deprivation in much of Africa.

In reality, PRSPs are SAPs with more conditionalities and less resources. As already indicated, a new 'generation' of conditionalities have been added to old conditionalities, with the concept of 'good governance,' analysed above. UNCTAD (2002) has revealed that between 1999 and 2000, 13 African countries had signed programmes containing an average of 114 conditionalities, 75% of which are governance-related conditionalities. One can imagine the enormous human and financial resources needed to deal with such a number of conditionalities. For this reason, the degree of compliance with IMF and World Bank-sponsored programmes has significantly declined since the mid-1990s. For instance, the rate of compliance was estimated at about 28% of the 41 agreements signed between 1993 and 1997, according to UNCTAD.

With the PRSPs, the IMF and the World Bank pursue three objectives. First, mislead world public opinion, especially in Northern countries, in making believe that they are really serious about 'reducing poverty.' And the World Bank alone counts on a huge and sophisticated propaganda machine to achieve this. With the more than 300 staff of its External Relations Department—Propaganda Department, one should say—the Bank has all the means it needs to 'explain' effectively its policies. It has achieved some success, since some big Northern NGOs, once very critical of SAPs, see the PRSPs as a 'positive shift' in the IFIs' policies.

The second objective of the PRSPs is to enlist a broad support within each country to help rehabilitate discredited and failed policies. This is what 'national ownership' and 'participation' of civil society organizations are supposed to achieve. While insisting on the 'participation' of civil society organizations, their most vocal critics, the IMF and World Bank tend to sideline representative institutions, like National Assemblies. This is another illustration of these institutions' contempt for the democratic process in Africa. Finally, with PRSPs, the IMF and the World Bank seek to shift the blame to African countries and citizens for the inevitable failure of these 'new' policies.

Summary and Conclusion

The IMF and World Bank have utterly failed in 'reducing poverty' and 'promoting development.' In fact, they are instruments of domination and control in the hands of powerful states whose long-standing objective is to perpetuate the plunder of the resources of the Global South, especially Africa. In other words, the fundamental role of the Bank and Fund in Africa and in the rest of the developing world is to promote and protect the interests of global capitalism.

This is why they have never been interested in 'reducing' poverty, much less in fostering 'development.' As institutions, their ultimate objective is to make themselves 'indispensable' in order to strengthen and expand their power and influence. They will never relinquish easily that power and influence. This explains why they have perfected the art of duplicity, deception and manipulation. In the face of accumulated failures and erosion of their credibility and legitimacy, they have often changed their rhetoric, but never their fundamental goals and policies.

This is why they cannot be trusted to bring about 'development' in Africa. If the experience of the last quarter of a century has taught Africa one fundamental lesson it is that the road to genuine recovery and development begins with a total break with the failed and discredited policies imposed by the IMF and the World Bank. In fairness to both institutions, we must recognize, however, the complicity of African leaders in the disastrous outcome of neoliberal policies. Many governments and senior civil servants have bought into the agenda promoted by the IMF and World Bank. Therefore, they bear a great responsibility in the current state of the continent. Thus, to put an end to the influence of these institutions, African social movements and progressive forces must explore strategies aimed at promoting a new kind of leadership able and willing to challenge these institutions in favour of genuine alternative development policies.

References

1. George Steinmetz. (2003). 'The State of Emergency and the Revival of American Imperialism; Toward an Authoritarian Post-Fordism,' *Public Culture* 15:2 (Spring 2003), p. 337.
2. George Steinmetz, Ibid., 'The State of Emergency and the Revival of American Imperialism; Toward an Authoritarian Post-Fordism,' p. 337.
3. Barry Bluestone and Bennett Harrison (1982). *The Deindustrialization of America: Plant Closings, Community Abandonment and the Dismantling of Basic Industry.* New York: Basic Books, p. 6
4. Stanley Aronowitz.(2003). *How Class Works.* New Haven: Yale University Press, p. 101.
5. Stanley Aronowitz, Ibid. *How Class Works*, p. 21.
6. Stanley Aronowitz. (1998). 'Introduction,' in Paulo Freire,_*Pedagogy of Freedom.* Lanham: Rowman and Littlefield, p. 7
7. Doug, Henwood. (2003). *After the New Economy.* New York: The New Press, Kevin Phillips, *Wealth and Democracy: A Political History of the American Rich.* New York: Broadway (2003); Paul Krugman, *The Great Unraveling: Losing Our Way in the New Century.* New York: W.W. Norton (2003).
8. Stanley Aronowitz, *How Class Works, ibid.*, p. 102.

9. Of course, there is widespread resistance to neoliberalism and its institutional enforcers such as the WTO and IMF among many intellectuals, students, and global justice movements, but this resistance rarely gets aired in the dominant media and if it does it is often dismissed as irrelevant or tainted by Marxist ideology.
10. George Soros, '*The US is Now in the Hands of a Group of Extremists,*' *The Guardian/UK* (January 26, 2004).
11. Paul Tolme. (2003). 'Criminalizing the Homeless,' In *These Times*_(April 14, 2003), pp 6-7.
12. Staff or Democracy Now, '*Uncharitable Care: How Hospitals are Gouging and Even Arresting the Uninsured,*' *CommonDreams* (January 8, 2004).
13. John and Jean Comaroff. (2000). 'Millennial Capitalism: First Thoughts on a Second Coming,' *Public Culture*_12:2, p. 332.
14. Comaroff, Ibid. (2000), p. 332.
15. Pierre Bourdieu. (1998). *Acts of Resistance: Against the Tyranny of the Market.* New York: The New Press.
16. Pierre Bourdieu and Gunter Grass. (2003). 'The 'Progressive' Restoration: A Franco-German Dialogue,' *New Left Review*_14 (march-April, 2003), p. 66.
17. Comprehensive surveys and critiques of the Washington Consensus can be found in Kaushik Basu, 'Globalization and the Politics of International Finance: The Stiglitz Verdict,' *Journal of Economic Literature* (September 2003): 885-99 and Dani Rodrik, 'Understanding Policy Reform,' *Journal of Economic Literature* (March 1996).
18. Naomi, Koppel. (2004). 'Iraq Takes First Steps Toward WTO Membership, but may have Acted too Early,' *Associated Press*, January 26, 2004.

Chapter Ten

Neo-liberal Assault on the State in Africa: Roots of State Weakness, Failure and Collapse

Overview

The 'State in Africa' has indisputably featured as one of 'crisis,' 'weakness,' 'underdevelopment,' 'disintegration,' 'decline,' 'failure,' 'fall,' 'collapse,' 'quasi –statehood,' and even 'statelessness.' These are the hallmarks of the conventional discourse on the state in Africa, which is anti-- statist and Afro pessimistic. When it was said to exist, efforts were made to dismantle or demonize the state in Africa, which in theory and practice, continues to be seen as the main 'problem' or the principal obstacle to growth, development and liberty on the continent, particularly within the context of globalization.

The reconstruction of the African society, torn and convulsed by the rampaging forces of globalization, cannot go without the reconstruction of the state whose foundations must lie on democracy, constitutionalism, and respect for human rights that are prerequisites for sustainable peace and the trumpeted African renaissance. Why? Africa's economic failed/collapsed states, backwardness and corruption have discouraged the influx of private capital from abroad. Internally, the class basis has been too weak for either a capitalist or real socialist development project. Under these circumstances, the state has become primarily a site for political opportunists to pursue spoils and lock themselves into power as warlords rather than engaging any developmental goals with all the risks of being unsaddled from power in the process. In fact, using the state and its resources has constituted a vital form of consolidating power for Africa's rulers. However, donor-sponsored reforms have threatened to curtail the opportunities of African leaders to maintain their regimes in power. Donor reforms introduced under structural adjustment programmes have sought to reduce the size and scope of government as well as to cut state spending and thereby curb the possibilities of state patronage. Reforms have also attempted to contain corruption and improve state governance.

In Uganda, for example, the relationship between donors and the government has reproduced patronage government. The donors initially hailed Uganda as a major case of economic success in Africa. They provided Uganda with large amounts of financial assistance to support the implementation of reforms. High levels of foreign aid provided the Museveni government with public resources to sustain the patronage basis of the regime. Moreover, in a context where wide discretionary authority was conferred on governing elites in the implementation of reforms, public resources were used in unaccountable and non-transparent ways to help the government maintain its political dominance. The donors began to realize belatedly that they had been propping up a corrupt warlord government in Uganda.

Externally sponsored reconstruction of battered African economies has met with limited achievements. This is partly due to three flawed assumptions on which economic development efforts are predicated. The first is that Western state institutions can be transferred to Africa. The poor record of past external efforts to construct and reshape African political and economic institutions casts doubts on the overly ambitious objectives of failed state reconstruction.

The second flawed assumption is the mistaken belief in a shared understanding by donors and African leaders of failure and reconstruction. Donors typically misread the nature of African politics. For local elites, reconstruction is the continuation of war and competition for resources and power by new means. Thus their strategies are often inimical to the building of strong public institutions or empowering the civil society through decentralization.

The third flawed assumption is that donors are capable of rebuilding African states. As experience has proven, their ambitious goals are inconsistent with their financial, military, and symbolic means. Encouraging indigenous state formation efforts and constructive bargaining between social forces and governments might prove a more fruitful approach for donors to the problem of Africa's failed/collapsed states than pouring aid into the outstretched hands of patronage networks and warlord sharks.

Introduction

Famines, genocides, tyrannies, and civil wars punctuate the world's post–Cold War narrative, a grim rondelet of disasters with the familiar refrains of starving children, chaotic refugee camps, harried aid workers, pleas for assistance, and endings indistinguishable from beginnings. These 'complex humanitarian emergencies' are no less intense and disturbing in the September 11th aftermath, in which a new form has been added via pre-emptive war. The major industrial powers of the world respond to these emergencies as if the human tumult were completely unexpected and the task itself an act of sheer altruism.

Non-profit aid groups mobilize their memberships with vivid portrayals of deprivation, United Nations officials organize yet another underfunded mission, and television networks run through a hasty media life cycle from discovery and horror to peace-keeping soldiers cuddling rescued babies. The refrain now includes Somalia, Eritrea, Rwanda, Sudan, Congo, Bosnia, Afghanistan, Cambodia, Bangladesh, and Iraq, a ledger of suffering colossal in scale and inexplicability. In fact, Africa was characterized by *The Economist* (May 13, 2000) as 'the hopeless continent.' If one sees the film 'Darwin's Nightmare,' one cannot help but despair at the massive environmental, social and economic problems facing the populations residing in and around Lake Victoria. Yet Africa received only 3 percent of the world's Foreign Direct Investment (FDI) in the early part of the new millennium.

Of course, such suffering is not inexplicable, and a growing intellectual enterprise is grappling with this enormous, and enormously complex, phenomenon. Often written by former aid workers, this literature chips away at the self-seducing pretexts of the humanitarian industry—the fabricated sense of urgency, the manipulation of images, the neglect of underlying causes. While far from offering an exhaustive account (the scale and costs of humanitarianism, after all, run to the hundreds of billions of dollars in dozens of countries), these authors shift perceptions of the 'whats' and 'whys' of these emergencies. At the same time, an intersecting academic and policy discourse on the legal and moral grounds of military intervention for humanitarian reasons is also taking shape, spurred in part by America's post–9/11 pursuits, a discourse that is far less satisfying precisely because it has the scent of a classroom (or courtroom) and not the killing fields.

Humanitarian Intervention, edited by J. L. Holzgrefe and Robert O. Keohane, explores this set of quandaries with the precision one expects of leading scholars of international law and politics searching for the ethical bases and conditions of intervention. The book includes nine essays by, among others, Tom J. Farer, Fernando R. Tesón, Thomas M. Franck, and Michael Ignatieff, as well as an introduction by Keohane. The chapters explore and also seek to mitigate the tensions between norms of international law—which generally protects state sovereignty from outside intrusions, according to the rule engraved by the Treaty of Westphalia in 1648—and a set of broader, vaguer obligations to humans who are in distress.

The emphasis on human security over the sanctity of states as the reference point for international action has gained favour in the post–Cold War period, but even before the fall of the Berlin Wall, emerging global norms supported action to protect human rights and to save lives. The embryonic value that animates much of the discussion nowadays is 'sovereignty as responsibility,' first articulated by Francis M. Deng in 1993 and quickly adopted by the UN Secretary General, which holds that sovereignty not only protects a state from unwarranted outside interference but also obligates the state to respect the basic rights and interests of its members. But the when, why, and how of intervention—especially military intervention—remain troublesome, because it is states that have armies and therefore tend to be careful about trampling the system that protects their prerogatives as well as those of the bad boys in Serbia, Liberia, Somalia, Iraq, and so on.

The famines in Africa today reveal the dissonance of reigning attitudes. In Malawi, for example, 30 percent of the population was starving when a June 2003 report, issued by a major British think tank, cited the ravaging effects of HIV/AIDS, which hits women hardest and sharply reduces agricultural production. Poverty, of course, is a root of the famine, too, and the report dutifully cites market-based solutions. A July 2003 report from the Food and Agriculture Organization (FAO), another Rome-based UN agency, notes that food consumption in African households hit by AIDS has dropped by 40 percent. 'Lighter ploughs and tools that can be used by older children, women, and the elderly' are needed, says FAO's director-general.

These are among the more enlightened actors, and still they seem to concentrate on market economics and technical fixes. True, HIV/AIDS is a new wrinkle in an old story (although disease has always been one of the four horsemen of disasters), and a startling one in its cumulative impact: we are facing the social dissolution of Africa. But even the causes of the epidemic are in part attributable to weakened states, with their inability to educate, to communicate, and to maintain the credibility, order, and authority that can cope with crises—or to compete with the humanitarian agencies that send out contradictory messages. The notion that a country like Malawi, in which one in three were starving and where young men and women have been dying in staggering numbers, can solve its problems by magically producing market-driven exports—a 'solution' that hasn't worked for Africa in pre-HIV days—speaks to the power of the market idea, not to the dying and their families. Malawi has since been declared free from hunger, thanks to a bumper crop of corn made possible by free distribution of seeds.

That Africa and other troubled regions are poorer today, with less control over their own destiny than when they were liberated from colonialism, has much to do with the global economic order and not very much to do with the 'new humanitarianism.' Still, as Duffield argues, there is a troubling connection. 'Complex emergencies arise on the borders of liberal peace where it encounters political systems whose norms differ violently from its own.' Taming these borderlands is an international security decision, and sometimes requires military intervention; at the very least, such decisions (in Washington, London, Brussels, the IMF, etc.) see economic and political development, market reform, relief, and security as bundled together to achieve the goals of the 'liberal peace'—marketization, in short, supported by 'good governance.'

Consider the problem of cattle rustling in the Horn of Africa. Tens of thousands of pastoralists are in a chronic war with bandits and each other in this semiarid region where land and water resources have tenuously supported their nomadic way of life for centuries. Beginning with British colonialism, the pastoralists have faced a gradual closure of the common resources long available to them, most recently as a result of large-scale privatization of land and water. Traditional authority systems are undermined, and conflict has become intense due to social dislocations, land tenure transformation, and the ample supply of small weapons made available during the Cold War and from various armies in the region.

These 'borderlands,' still rich in natural resources desired by the West (including wildlife tourism), are thus 'disciplined' by marketization and proxy security forces, while humanitarian agencies are called in to deal with localized famine that the donors and their NGO agents dutifully attribute to bad weather and outmoded forms of husbandry. Meanwhile, displaced pastoralists fill the cities with new shantytowns and raise an alarming level of street crime. 'Good governance' in this case is the fulfilment of privatization, delivery of aid to the beleaguered herders, and clamping down on the crime in the cities—but it is governance that cannot address proximate causes of the problems.

The Weak/Failed/Collapsed-state Cancer in Africa

It has been said that when economics turns serious, it becomes political. The Washington Consensus, a term coined in 1990 by John Williamson of the Institute for International Economics to summarize the synchronized ideology of Washington-based establishment economists, reverberated around the world for a quarter of a century. This ideology was sold around hotly as the true gospel of reform indispensable for achieving growth in a globalized market economy.

Initially applied to Latin America and eventually to all developing economies, the term has come to be synonymous with globalized neo-liberalism or market fundamentalism to describe universal policy prescriptions based on free-market principles and monetary discipline within narrow ideological limits. It promotes for all economies macroeconomic control, trade openness, pro-market microeconomic measures, privatization and deregulation in support of a dogmatic ideological faith in the market's ability to solve all socio-economic problems more efficiently, and to assert a blanket denial of an obvious contradiction between market efficiency and poverty eradication.

According to this ideology, financial-capital growth is to be served at the expense of human-capital growth. Sound money, undiluted by inflation, is to be achieved by keeping wages low through structural unemployment. Pockets of poverty in the periphery are the necessary price for prosperous centres. Such dogmas grant unemployment and poverty, conditions of economic disaster, undeserved conceptual respectability. State intervention has come to focus mainly on reducing the market power of labour in favour of capital in a blatantly predatory market mechanism.

The set of policy reforms prescribed by the Washington Consensus is composed of 10 propositions: 1) Fiscal discipline; 2) redirection of public-expenditure priorities toward fields offering high economic returns; 3) tax reform to lower marginal rates and broaden the tax base; 4) interest-rate liberalization; 5) competitive exchange rates; 6) trade liberalization; 7) liberalization of foreign direct investment (FDI) inflows; 8) privatization; 9) deregulation and 10) secure private-property rights.

These propositions add up to a wholesale reduction of the central role of government in the economy and its primary obligation to protect the weak from the strong, both foreign and domestic. Unemployment and poverty then are viewed as temporary, transitional fallouts from wholesome natural market selection, as unavoidable effects of economic evolution that in the long run will make the economy stronger. Neo-liberal economists argue that unemployment and poverty, deadly economic plagues in the short term, can lead to macroeconomic benefits in the long term, just as some historians perversely argue that even the Black Death (1348) had long-range beneficial effects on European society.

The resultant labour shortage in the short term pushed up wages in the mid-14th century, and the sudden rise in mortality led to an oversupply of goods, causing prices to drop. These two trends caused the standard of living to rise for those still living. Yet the short-term shortage of labour caused by the Black Death forced landlords to stop freeing their serfs, and to extract more forced labour from them. In reaction, peasants in many areas used their increased market power to demand fairer treatment or lighter burdens. Frustrated, guilds revolted in the cities and peasants rebelled in the countryside. The Jacquerie in 1358, the Peasants' Revolt in England in 1381, the Catalonian Rebellion in 1395, and many revolts in Germany, all served to show how seriously the mortality had disrupted traditional economic and social relations.

Neo-liberalism in the past quarter-century created conditions that manifested themselves in violent political protests all over the globe, the extremist form being terrorism. But at least the bubonic plaque was released by nature and not by human ideological fixation. And neo-liberalism keeps workers unemployed but alive with subsistence unemployment aid, maintaining an ever-ready pool of surplus labour to prevent wages from rising from any labour shortage, eliminating even the cruelly derived long-term benefits of the Black Death.

The Washington Consensus has since been characterized as a 'bashing of the state' (*Annual Report of the United Nations*, 1998) and a 'new imperialism' (Alam,1999). But the real harm of the Washington Consensus has yet to be properly recognized: that it is a prescription for generating failed/collapsed/weak states around the world, particularly among developing African economies. Why? Even in the developed economies, neo-liberalism generates a dangerous but generally unacknowledged weak/failed/collapsed-state syndrome.

In fact, success in *statism* is measured by a state's ability to deliver political goods. Security, both external and internal, is a primary political good the provision of which is the state's primary function. It provides a framework through which all other political goods are delivered. The events of September 11, 2001, revealed that even the most powerful state cannot guarantee its citizen protection from terrorism, a fact since openly acknowledged by the Bush administration. The modus operandi of the 'war on terrorism' and the Department of Homeland Security is based on the acceptance of spectacular terrorist attacks continuing in the future and their likelihood of repeated success. The aim is not to eradicate terrorism by removing its root cause, but only to make it more difficult to implement. It is a war lost before it begins.

Neo-imperialism therefore detaches economic security from legitimate state functions. Freedom from want is not considered a state responsibility by neo-liberalism. Financial security is merely a market risk that should be faced by each individual market participant. Another political good provided by the state is the enforcement of law as expressed in a system of codes and procedures that equitably regulate the affairs and interactions of the population. The state is responsible for setting and maintaining standards for equity and acceptable conducts both domestically and in its foreign relations. Neo-liberalism relieves the state from such responsibility and assigns it to the market. In the case of Africa, the disempowered state was either weakened/collapsed or failed since it could not perform its functions again. The state became a docile servant of transnational capital.

State Functions in Africa: 1960-1990

Given the historical and geographic variability of state functions, it might seem bold to declare that there are ten basic ones. Based on our reading of history, our engagement with international relations, and our first hand experience with the challenge of state building in one of its most difficult contexts in Africa, we have concluded that states in the world today must perform the following key functions to succeed:

1) Rule of Law

The most crucial function of the state is law making (i.e. establishing the rules by which society operates). Laws define both the powers and the limits of the state and the people within that state.

2) A Monopoly on the Legitimate Means of Violence

State controlled use of violence (military/police activity), encompasses three distinctive elements. Complete authority over the means of destruction and the use of force. The legitimacy needed to subordinate violence to the decision making process (voting/elections/laws). And in extreme cases, the use of force, according to the rules of law, against those citizens of the state who challenge its legitimacy.

3) Administrative Control

The state must establish a bureaucratic system of checks and balances. It has to be a system that is managed by governmental professionals who are accountable to the citizenry. Each division of the government performs specialized functions, has continuity over time, and is overseen at a higher level.

4) Sound Management of Public Finances

Create a budget and stick to it! A proper budget brings both the rights and duties of citizenship into balance. Each entitlement must have a line of expenditure and each expenditure must be matched by a source of revenue. The key elements are wealth creation and involvement of the citizenry in taxation and redistribution.

5) Investment in Human Capital

Among the many investments are the creation, development, and growth of institutions of Higher Education and the availability of a national healthcare infrastructure. Health and education produces a mentally and physically vital citizenry, which is in turn crucial to a successful state.

6) Creation of Citizenship Rights Through Social Policy

Empower citizens through equal opportunity. When the state uses social policy as an instrument for the establishment of equal opportunities, the social fabric created can lead to a sense of national unity and a shared belief in common destiny. Key social policy starts with the right to vote, and extends into regulating labour practices and establishing fiscal welfare programmes.

7) Provision of Infrastructure Services

The state must provide everyday necessities such as adequate transportation, power, water, communications, and pipelines to establish its overall ability to produce less mundane functions such as security, administration, investment in human capital, and the necessary conditions for a strong market economy.

8) Formation of a Market

The state must support the creation and expansion of an open economic market through three major measures: setting and enforcing rules for commercial activity, supporting the operation and continued development of private enterprise, and intervening at times of market failure.

9) Management of Public Assets

Every state has three areas of natural resources to oversee: the management and allocation of rights to land and water, the sustainable use of natural capital, including extractive industries (i.e. mining and drilling), the management, and protection of the environment, including forests, and the licensing of industrial commercial activities.

10) Effective Public Borrowing

Put simply, do not take on bad debt or take on too much debt. Beware of the sovereign guaranty from international lenders. Maintain public disclosure and monitoring of the fulfilment of debt obligations.

The performance of these essential functions produces a clustering effect. When the state performs all these functions simultaneously, the synergy creates a virtuous circle in which decisions in the different domains reinforce enfranchisement and opportunity for the citizenry. This supports the legitimacy of the decision makers and their decisions, builds trust in the overall system, and thereby produces a 'sovereignty dividend.' Conversely, when one or several of the functions are not performed effectively, a vicious circle begins: Various centres of power vie for control, multiple decision-making processes confuse priorities, citizens lose trust in the government, institutions lose their legitimacy, and the populace is disenfranchised. In the most extreme cases AS IN Somalia, Sierra Leone, Democratic Republic of Congo, etc., violence results. This negative cycle creates a 'sovereignty gap' to be filled easily by neocolonial vassalage as African leaders seek foreign sponsorship frantically.

This converse is very real in Africa today. The reason is very simple. A substantial appropriation of the state and use of politics by private actors such as profit-seeking transnational capitalist networks to effect sweeping appropriation and a near wholesale intertwining of state resources and politics is commonplace. This existential situation in Africa is characterized by the negotiable status of informal groups, entities and institutions situated between state and private sectors-foreign or domestic. Both tend to result in an expanded state sphere marked by ambiguity of status and responsibility. Hence, the rampant collapse of states!

Failing, fragile or failed states have become part of the international relations and development lexicon in Africa since the early-1990s. These states are often associated with poor or unstable governance, persistent extreme poverty, and potential international security threats. Yet insufficient research has been done to understand and clarify the dimensions of state failure or fragility and their implications. Regional instability, armed conflict, ethnic/tribal/religious clashes, indebtedness, hunger, poverty, (re-emerging) diseases, environmental degradation, underdevelopment are resurgent in the continent. These are just a few references produced to 'comprehend' the current state of affairs in Africa. They have been discursively presented and thus perceived as 'natural' and 'internal' problems or even 'inherent' characteristics of the continent.

These 'natural' problems, according to the dominant paradigm, have nothing to do with contemporary structures of domination in the emergent neoliberal (dis)order – let alone the historical experiences of colonial subordination. Then, the discourses and policy justifications of the Western governments easily reach the conclusion that an external intervention, whether on military terms or not, is necessary to cure these 'abnormal polities'. The IMF/WB neoliberal intervention in the 1980s and the US military interventions in the 1990s were to a large extent legitimized with reference to this rationale.

The recently popular notion of 'failed state', as a categorical representation of post-Cold War Southern polities, has been produced in accordance with this particular way of thinking. It is much more of a general category utilized by many academicians and Western policy makers to attribute all those 'internal characteristics' to a broader problem of 'state failure'. That is, for many, the African states have been failing one by one, from Somalia to Rwanda to Sudan, because of the 'internally driven natural conditions'. Why?

State Failure in Africa: Blaming the Victim?

Neo-liberal ideology is implemented through a venue of integrated global markets, free flow of capital and credit, wholesale deregulation and mandatory structural pro-market conditionalities imposed on weak and poor economies. It strips states of their sovereign authority to intervene in markets on behalf of national interests, causing state authority to collapse in all area except the protection of foreign and domestic private property. Failed states depend on globalized market fundamentals to finance their state functions and inevitably fall into collapsed-state status for lack of funds. In a sense, whereas the age of imperialism used Christian values as a pretext for empire, the age of neo-imperialism uses neo-liberalism as its missionary calling. The relationship of the neo-conservatives to the neo-liberals today is similar to the relationship of the Emperor and the Church in history. Missionaries are the velvet gloves of the ruthless hands of imperialists.

'In his famous work, Thomas Hobbes described a 'state of nature' without order where 'continual fear and danger of violent death' rendered life 'solitary, poor, nasty, brutish and short.' These words have contemporary resonance in African countries such as Sudan, Somalia, Liberia and the Democratic Republic of Congo where the central authority of the state collapsed, law and order is a far cry and territory is controlled by competing fiefdoms and gangs.'[1]

Regional instability, armed conflict, ethnic/tribal/religious clashes, indebtedness, hunger, poverty, (re-emerging) diseases, environmental degradation, underdevelopment are just a few references produced to 'comprehend' the current state of affairs in Africa. They have been discursively presented and thus perceived as 'natural' and 'internal' problems or even 'inherent' characteristics of the continent. Thus, Susan Rice and Stewart Patrick of the Brookings Institution recently devised a 'Weak States Threat Matrix' (Rice, 2006) aimed at establishing clear and transparent criteria for identifying weak states. The matrix defines weak states as economically poor states that suffer from significant gaps in three fundamental government functions: security, performance and legitimacy.

The matrix utilizes four overarching criteria which are themselves based on multiple, diverse and methodologically rigorous indexes and data sets to determine inclusions in the weak state category:

- World Bank data on national per capita gross income to assess whether states are poor;

- the Uppsala Conflict Database to assess security based on whether at least 25 conflict related deaths occurred since 1990;
- the UN Human Development Index (HDI) list of countries with 'low human development' based on achievements in three basic dimensions of human development - life expectancy, adult literacy and school enrolment, and per capita GDP - as a proxy for government performance in meeting basic human needs; and
- the World Bank Institute's Governance Matters IV database rating of governance quality to identify states in its bottom two quintiles as exhibiting a 'legitimacy gap' between the assertion made by sovereign states of the right to govern and the reality of governance quality. This database is compiled by World Bank staff from several hundred individual variables measuring perceptions of governance, drawn from 37 data sets compiled by 31 different organizations (Kauffman, et al 2005).

In the *Journal of Turkish Weekly*, of April 29, 2008**,** Caglar Dolek, reminds us that these 'natural' problems, according to the dominant paradigm, have nothing to do with contemporary structures of domination in the emergent neoliberal (dis)order–let alone the historical experiences of colonial subordination. Then, the discourses and policy justifications of the Western governments easily reach the conclusion that an external intervention, whether on military terms or not, is necessary to cure these 'abnormal polities'. The IMF/WB neoliberal intervention in the 1980s and the US military interventions in the 1990s were to a large extent legitimized with reference to this rationale.

Faultlines in Explaining State Failure in Africa

In seeking to explain 'tribalism' and 'state failure' in Africa, academics often point towards the misalignment of the nation and the state: either the post-colonial state has failed to make the nation, or nations have descended into 'tribalism' in the process of carving out a state. What is common in these two presumptions, is that all African nations or states have the power to make their counterpart; by extension, the 'failure 'of such processes is rarely problematized beyond domestic politics and historical references to the impact of colonialism. This essay will first discuss primordialist and constructivist perspectives on state—and nation—building, before highlighting the role which external factors have in defining the relationship between states and nations in contemporary Africa.

The 'failure' of African states and the demise of territorial nationalism should come as no great surprise if one subscribes to 'primordialist' or 'ethno-symbolist' theories. For thinkers such as Anthony Smith and John Armstrong, nations have their roots in a cultural basis of 'cohesive power, historic primacy, symbols, myths, memories and values' which have persisted through time (Smith, 1991:52). When colonial administrations drew African borders which suited their own purposes—and which often divided, subsumed or assumed indigenous identities—they left a devastating legacy. Post-colonial states such as Burundi, Rwanda, Nigeria and Kenya spanned a mosaic of ethnic groups which provided little cultural basis for a united nation; simultaneously, ethnic groups spanned the post-colonial states.

Nationalist leaders therefore had great difficulty maintaining the discursive energies mobilised during the struggle for independence because their territorial nationalism was inauthentic; it was not underpinned by a culturally-united ethnic community, but by a myriad of ethnic communities. In this context, efforts at 'nation building' were vulnerable to cooptation by ethnic groups as they competed to access state patronage.

Leaders struggled to define homogenous, 'legible' identities through centrally planned administrative policies—in Tanzania, for example, Julius Nyerere attempted to move all rural inhabitants into villages as he sought to create a 'modern state'. However, such policies proved futile and often damaging (Scott 1998). For thinkers such as Smith and Armstrong, whilst a culturally-underpinned nation might build a successful state, a state faces great difficulties if it is not underpinned by an authentic nation. President of Mozambique, Samora Michael, summed up a popular conclusion when he declared that 'for the nation [and, one might presume by extension, the state] to live the tribe must die' (in Mamdani 1996).

Constructivist thinkers reject the notion that successful contemporary nations are defined by persistent 'ethnic cores'. Instead, they assert that both ethnicity and nationality are, in large part, imagined. Thinkers such as Lonsdale and Ranger insist that efforts to explain contemporary political events with reference to the misalignment of 'ancient tribal identities' with modern states are ill conceived. There is nothing inevitable about ethnic competition. Indeed, drawing on the case of Kenya, Lonsdale (1994) has shown that far from being historically-rooted entities which have always existed, 'tribes'—and dynamics of ethnic competition—were largely a *response* to the new institutions and rules imposed by the colonial powers. Identities—ethnic and national—have been imagined. For Bayart, 'the ways in which Africans have adopted the territorial frameworks handed down by the colonising powers is one of the salient characteristics of the continent's recent history. The imported state was immediately taken over by autochthonous peoples' because it represented the obvious (and often only) means by which to access colonial power structures (2005: 31). The 'formation' and mobilization of ethnic identities thus represented a strategy of predation by which to gain access to the state's resources (Mentan 2009).

Primordialist and constructivist theorists agree that African post-colonial states have failed to 'make' nations. Primordialists contend that this is because it represents an impossible task without culturally united ethnic cores (nations can make states, but states cannot make nations). In contrast, constructivists dismiss the notion of 'identity-related divinities' and assert that ethnic communities in contemporary Africa were formed in large part as a *response* to the legacy of colonialism. However, these identities have frequently been mobilized in their competitive form; political tribalism. For constructivists then, states can make nations, and nations can make states, but the leaders of post-colonial states have often manipulated nations and nations have often sought to exploit the resources available in post-colonial states.

The constructivist critique is a convincing one, yet by focusing on the question at hand, we risk missing important external dynamics which contribute to relations between states and nations. Reigning international imperatives demand that a state system of some form exists (Jackson 1990). The work of the international financial institutions, international organizations and international NGOs presumes a state framework. Meanwhile growing international connectedness and systemic pressures—such as the need to engage in international diplomacy and economic negotiations, sovereignty claims, UN membership and bureaucratic requirements—compel some form of state-based identification. These 'external' factors demand that states (no matter how weak they might be) are sustained.

Yet simultaneously, these same institutions may subvert states' efforts at nation-building. For example, the Ogoni movement in Nigeria—led by Ken Saro-Wiwa's MOSOP—successfully appealed to 'formidably encompassing agents of surveillance' such as Human Rights Watch and Amnesty International in its efforts to challenge the Nigerian state (cf. Ferguson, 2006: 111). Watts (2003: 20) writes that 'MOSOP's claims were territorial as a basis for an Ogoni state, and as a way of securing 'their oil'.' The emergence of a global civil society means that processes of nation-building are no longer necessarily reserved within the national (or even nationalist) domain. A more recent—and similarly illuminating case—saw international observers and the mass media playing an important role in the Luo ethnic group's contestation of the 2007 elections in Kenya.

The postcolonial struggle to 'make' nations in Africa is frequently examined with relation to questions of 'state failure' and ethnic tensions. This essay has considered the formative relationship between states and nations by considering primordialist and constructivist perspectives. It has argued that the constructivist analysis is convincing: there is nothing inevitable about post-colonial states' failure to 'make' nations. However, by remaining within the confines of this debate, we are liable to miss the importance of external factors which are often instrumental in shaping the contradictory relationship between states and nations in contemporary Africa. The current debate is thus largely blind to processes through which African states seek to reorganize themselves in response to external interventions, and instead perpetuates analyses which view African societies in terms of their 'lacks, absences, failings and problems' (Ferguson, 2006).

Neoliberalism, Myth of 'Failed States' and Foreign Intervention

The recently popular notion of 'failed state', as a categorical representation of post-Cold War Southern polities, has been produced in accordance with this particular way of thinking. It is much more of a general category utilized by many academicians and Western policy makers to attribute all those 'internal characteristics' to a broader problem of 'state failure'. That is, for many, the African states have been failing one by one, from Somalia to Rwanda to Sudan, because of the 'internally driven natural conditions'. The discussion here is of a critical one. It mainly develops an argument that the 'failed state' is about nothing, but a mere myth constructed on the basis of the atomistic social ontology which isolates the object from the wider social and historical contexts and presents it as the atomistic agents within global capitalism.

When one looks at the vocabulary produced to define the notion of 'state failure', it can easily be understood that there is neither a single term to refer to such phenomenon nor a single definition for the concept in question. Especially since early 1990s, there has emerged a vast literature on the issue producing different categories of polities about the Southern countries. These include 'weak state', 'failed state', 'rouge state', 'collapsed state', 'collapsing state', 'disintegrating state', 'captured state', 'quasi-state'…etc. Although each of these concepts refers to different situations, they all depart from the Weberian conception of an ideal state. That is to say, the definitions about the failed states are made with reference to 'successful counterparts' existing in the West. Within this general categorization, the states like Haiti, Somalia, the former Yugoslavia, Lebanon, Sudan, Liberia, Afghanistan, Cambodia, Ethiopia, Zaire, Sierra Leone and the like have been declared as failed states.

Within the vast scholarly literature, dominated by Weberian methodology, the commonly held definition is produced by Zartman who argues that the state failure occurs when .'.. the basic functions of the state are no longer performed' in a proper way.[2] Zartman further argues that the failed states are 'No longer functioning, with neither traditional nor charismatic nor institutional sources of legitimacy, it has lost the right to rule.' Ignatieff similarly provides another Weberian account of the notion, and argues that the state failure indicates the loss of state ability to sustain its monopoly over the legitimate use of force.[3] He mentions Sri Lanka and Colombia as the examples proving such failure.

On the other hand, the writers like Fukuyama create a linkage between state failure and regional and international stability. In this perception, the failed state is presented as the one which is responsible for the humanitarian crisis, waves of immigration, regional conflicts…etc.[4] From the viewpoint of Fukuyama, failed states are the source of most dangerous problems challenging the international order today such as poverty, terrorism and drug trafficking.

As another scholarly analysis of the issue in question, Gros provides a taxonomy of five types of 'failed states' which is constructed on the condition of the fulfilment of Weberian criteria of statehood by the Southern countries. In his taxonomy, then, Gros develops the notions of 'anarchic states' (Somalia and Liberia), 'phantom' or 'mirage' states (Zaire, the Democratic Republic of Congo), 'anaemic states' (Haiti), 'captured states' (Rwanda) and the 'aborted states' (Angola, Mozambique).[5]

What is more, there have been developed even more radial approaches to the 'state failure' by utilizing the terminology of psychoanalysis. Largely found with the thesis of 'New Barbarism', these approaches defend the view that the 'state failure' occurs as a result of the internal cultural/ racial characteristics embedded in the African countries. As opposed to the ideal Western ones, the failed states represent the 'abnormal' or 'deficient' polities that are irrational, violent and even barbaric. This simply means that the 'state failure' occurs due to the existence of a 'serious illness' or 'mental or physical disorder' that should be cured by the intervention of a doctor, i.e. the Western countries. In other words, those 'failed states' are in a serious condition of mass trauma which should be treated through a whole-scale intervention. This kind of intervention, for Pupavac, perceives the .'.. recipient populations as irrational and emotionally immature and therefore implicitly incapable of determining their lives without outside professional intervention.'[6]

This 'New Barbarism' thesis simply concludes that there is no need for complex analysis for the evaluation of the African crisis or Africa as a 'failed continent' because the continent is already brutish, irrational, uncivilized and backward. *That is, Africa is underdeveloped because it is already underdeveloped and because it is African.* This commonly held scholarly position manifests itself in a similar fashion in the discourses utilized by the policy makers of the West for which the African continent demonstrates the most severe and extreme cases of state failure.

According to the official views from the US administration, the state failure results from the enduring collapse of the central authority, which is caused by such problems as revolutionary wars, ethnic wars, regime changes…etc.[7] Therefore, as already known, 'to cure the abnormal behaviours of the failed states' has become a primary objective of the UN Security Strategy within the last two decades because they have been presented as the 'new threat' to the international peace and security with their contributions to the problems like international terrorism, illegal immigration, humanitarian crisis, drug trafficking, regional conflicts, etc.

'Failed States' as Atomistic Mythical Construct

What is at stake here is the constitution of a novel category of statehood for the developing countries in order to construct the 'legitimate' grounds of intervention on any terms into the 'failed states'. Keeping in mind this vital point, the discussion from now on follows a path not towards the critique of the most ultimate aim of 'intervention'. The more critical attention is paid to the particular rationale and substantial fallacy behind the constitution of such categorical representations. As discussed above, almost all the perceptions tend to make a descriptive account of 'state failure' giving no reference to the historical and social conditions through which these polities have happened to 'fail'. That is, as Bilgin and Morton argues: .'..no reference is made to the process through which these states have become 'weak' while others have gained 'strength'. In other words, the question 'who's failed 'the failed state'?' is never asked.'[8]

The main reason of the absence of such a question is because of the very ontological constitution of failed state or mythical representation of the 'failure' itself. That is, to refer to the Barthesian notion of 'myth', the state failure is presented as natural, universal and ahistorical phenomenon that suddenly emerged with the end of the Cold War. To develop this critique, it is essential to have a deeper look at the notion of myth. Roland Barthes, an influential French philosopher, argues that bourgeoisie ideology constantly creates a process in which what is historical is presented as if it were universal and ahistorical. He, therefore, claims that bourgeois ideology decontextualizes the object from its historical and social conditions.[9] These ideological products, for Barthes, are the mere 'myths' which appear as if they were produced outside the given context. 'The myth', then, takes a purely cultural and historical object and transforms it into a universal value. [10]

In his philosophy, however, the myths are not simply illusions in our minds. That is to say, the myths are not only ideological products of bourgeoisie culture, but also they are concrete things. Here, the most fundamental premise of Barthes arises: While the myth avoids the social and historical conditions of the construction of the subject, there is awareness among the people about these historical conditions. At this point, for him, bourgeoisie ideology creates the mythology that prevents us from seeing those historical conditions. That is to say, although we are generally aware of the historical background of the mythical aspect of that ideological product, we tend to think that it is natural.[11] This is the exact ideological function of the myth.

Barthes further developed his theory in order to demystify the myth. To this aim, he relied on the Saussurian analysis of the linguistic signs, but further developed such an analysis, and constructed the theory of the semiology. Therefore, semiology is the model for the demystification of the ideological products of the bourgeoisie society. It is beyond this study to analyse this rather complex theory of semiology in which Barthes used schematic figures to deconstruct the myth. Yet, the most important thing that concerns us here is the aim of semiology: to demystify the myth with reference to the historical and social conditions in which it was constructed.

With reference to the discussion here, it is of paramount significance to realize the mythical representation of the very notion of 'failed state'. Within the framework of Barthesian arguments, the scholarly analysis as well as policy justifications mostly rely on a 'state failure' decontextualized from the wider social, historical and international contexts. Then, the 'failure' itself becomes as a fault of those underdeveloped polities (the victims) either due to intrinsic cultural features, or due to corrupted political elites… etc. Among the others, the thesis on 'New Barbarism', briefly touched upon above, provides most explicit manifestation of the mythical representation of postcolonial African 'subject'.

Moreover, within the context of African 'failed states, there is no reference to the colonial experiences of subordination through which a neo-colonial dependent state structure has been inherited. Nor is any critical attention paid towards the 'perpetuation' of the conditions of underdevelopment in the continent especially with the introduction of neoliberal policies to those already weakened African states. It has become an undeniable fact that the introduction of neoliberal structural adjustment programmes, legitimized in the name of resolving development impasse in Africa, has become main obstacle before the development objectives of the African countries. Therefore, the 'African crisis' of 1970s and 1980s have been transformed into 'African tragedy' meaning that the problems in the continent have already exceed the point of being temporal crisis.

Therefore, behind all these mythical representation of 'failed state' lies the particular social ontology which isolates the object from its social and historical conditions through which it has come into being. This is the atomistic social ontology which treats the failed states as atomistic agents constituted equally within international relations. That is to say, the juridical or political equality of the nation states lies at the basis of this social ontology as it produces the illusion of a state being abstracted from the international sphere, or from the structures of domination within global capitalism.

This very ontological position, as Jones has put it, results in the problem of 'blaming the victim' according to which '... the wealth or poverty, success or failure of the person or state is their fault and their responsibility, it is to be explained by their choices, attitude, commitment and so on.' [12] Jones discusses the issue with reference to an inherent characteristic of capitalist social relations: separation of the politics and economics which is fruitfully analysed in the writings of Wood.

With regard to the discussion here, such a separation means the existence of the 'surface appearances' of a complex phenomenon.[13] In that sense, to use Barthes' words, we tend to see the state failure as normal because of the mythology of the failed state. It indicates both an illusion (surface appearances) and reality. Yet, we tend to disregard the social context of the state failure, and think that the state failure fundamentally results from internal conditions of a country. Furthermore, the unacceptable violations of human rights committed by these failed states strengthen this vision. All in all, decontextualized from the social and historical conditions, and thus blamed for their own fault, the 'failed states' in Africa have been discursively produced to function as the legitimate as well as inevitable basis of Western intervention into the internal affairs of these underdeveloped and impoverished countries.

'Make Poverty History in Africa': The Real Story

The largest mobilization ever amassed in Scottish history occurred the Monday before the G8 leaders met in Gleneagles. Over 300,000 demonstrators packed the streets of the picturesque town of Edinburgh with quite a large part of the crowd being unable to march the route, after having waited up to three hours in line, because of the enormity of the demonstration's turnout.

The theme of the march, which was also the name of the NGO that temporarily formed to organize it, was 'Make Poverty History.' The most influential player of Make Poverty History (MPH) was Oxfam, a centrist NGO with close allegiance to the British government, in particular with

British Chancellor Gordon Brown's office. Working closely with the Commission for Africa, which is chaired by Bob Geldolf and run by Blair, Brown, and Britain's overseas aid minister Hilary Benn, the official MPH campaign ignorantly fell into supporting the neo-liberal agenda of the G8 leaders. Although the commitment toward ending the debt and fighting African poverty is genuine from the NGOs and rock stars, the assumptions and recommendations manufactured by the Commission for Africa would prove disastrous for Africa's workers, peasants, and the urban poor. These include the assumption that the impact of Western manoeuvres on Africa has been largely benign. There is a complete absence of criticism of the ongoing Western military interventions of the last half century, and the colonial exploits and brutality forced upon the peoples of African nations.

The other damaging assumption of the Commission revolves around the premise that free trade and privatization are somehow the key to liberation for Africans. The International Monetary Fund is viewed as being able to 'play an invaluable role' in clearing the way for 'private sector investors.' Private profit making is seen as the panacea to poverty: 'Successful growth will be led by the private sector.' The commission concludes that only by ridding themselves of barriers to free trade and exporting to the rest of the world can Africans work their way out of poverty.

In contrast to this whitewashing and sidestepping, the organizers of the G8 Alternatives and the Stop the War coalition won political battles and arguments, some lasting a year long, to lawfully protest at the fence surrounding the G8 meetings in Gleneagles, secure housing for protesters, and organize a counter-summit in Edinburgh. Importantly, the message of 'Fight Poverty, Not War' was stamped throughout the huge Make Poverty History demonstration critically inserting the obvious and necessary linkage between war and poverty a linkage many in Blair's government were trying to ignore. Thus, although Make Poverty History organizers were not confident enough or willing to draw out the connection, the British anti-war movement succeeded in proving that the hundreds of thousands marching against poverty were also marching against war and the system that creates both.

Blair and Brown's simplistic rhetoric of relieving Africa's debt instead masks the reality that there are massive and continuous flows of wealth out of Africa into the pockets of Western capitalists capitalists who are inextricably bound to the system that impoverishes millions, while the bankers and investors profiteer from the militarized budget. The Commission for Africa's agenda and the drive for free trade actually ties the mass of Africans into an exploitative neo-liberal system that has been bleeding them dry for decades.

A professor of development studies at the London School of Economics, Gavin Capps has researched the numbers behind the debt. In an article titled 'Redesigning the Debt Trap,' he explains the dangerous web that the debt, structural adjustment programmes, and capital flight creates in Africa. He cites Africa Action, a U.S.-based NGO, reporting in 2001 that the ratios of foreign debt to the continent's gross national product increased from 51% in 1982 to 100% in 1992. Africa's debt grew to four times its export income in the early 1990s. Its debt burden is twice that of any other region in the world, it carries 11% of the developing countries' debt, with only 5% of its income. The gross national product in Africa is $308 per capita, while its debt stands at $355 per capita.

The money spent paying back the debt and the interest on the debt expanded from an average of $1.7 billion from 1970-1979 to $14.6 billion from 1997-1999. Africa received a total of $540 billion in loans, paid back $550 billion, and still retained a debt of $295 billion between 1970 and 2002. In 1990 African countries paid out $60 billion more than they received in new loans, and by 1997, this increased to about 162 British pounds. In 2001, sub-Saharan Africa borrowed $11.4 billion, and paid back $14.5 billion.

This catastrophe is played out in the social service and health sectors. Shrinking African national budgets are being spent in greater proportions to repaying Western creditors at the expense of welfare or productive domestic investment.

During the 1980s debt service repayments averaged 16% of African government expenditure compared to 12% on education and 4% on health. A decade later, the situation remains appalling, as interest payments are prioritized over human needs. In 1999 the Zambian government was pressured to spend $14 million more in debt service than on its collapsing health care system, in the face of the AIDS pandemic reaching new heights. Also in 1999, 33% of Angola's gross domestic product was spent on debt repayments, as compared to 4.9% of gross national product on education and 1.4% on health. In the whole of sub-Saharan Africa in 2001, debt repayment amounted to 3.8% of GDP, as opposed to 2.4% spent on health care.

In tandem with the debt repayment crisis, capital flight and structural adjustment programmes tighten the fatal stranglehold on the African continent. Capital flight, the transfer of locally owned capital to the advanced economies, amounted to $187 billion during 1970 and 1996 in 30 sub-Saharan African countries. This flight of capital was inextricably bound with the accumulation of debt, as roughly 80 cents on every dollar borrowed by these countries flowed out as capital flight the same year.

When interest is added, the stock of capital flight of those 30 countries equals $274 billion, or 145% of the total debt owed by that group of countries in 1996.

Corrupt leaders skimmed from the top of these profits. But simply attributing capital flight to the greed of African politicians hides more than it reveals. The great powers, the leaders of the G8, propped up African dictators like Mobutu Seso Seko, of Zaire, now the Democratic Republic of Congo, in order to guarantee Western strategic interests during the Cold War. (Mobutu was installed in mineral-rich Zaire after the CIA-backed assassination of popular radical nationalist leader Patrice Lumumba.) Breaking the pathologyzing myth of corrupt black African leaders, apartheid South Africa enabled an average of 7% of annual gross domestic product to leave as capital flight between 1970 and 1988, a flight whose destination was into the coffers of major Anglo corporations. Such a move defied local capital controls and broke the international sanctions regime on apartheid. Thus, the private 'white' capitalists of South Africa and white European business leaders were also in lockstep support of capital flight.

The International Monetary Fund (IMF) and the World Bank consolidated their hold over Africa directly because of the debt crisis. They continue to ensure commercial banks are repaid by lending African states more money to service their private debts. And these U.S.-led institutions act as debt collection agencies for the Western powers, in addition to the IMF's insistence on even harsher repayment terms of the multilateral loans it makes. The charters of the IMF and World Bank specifically forbid debts that they hold to be rescheduled or written off, and most of these debts are charged at market rates. This is one of the main reasons why Africa's total debt has continued to grow while an even greater volume of its resources has flowed out of the continent.

The G8, Hypocrisy, and the Right to Protest

The logic of the G8's debt relief schemes is not an act of philanthropy, but a necessary manoeuvre in order to maintain the debt repayments to the private banks. First, only the poorest and most heavily indebted countries would be allowed to qualify; secondly, all participants would have to adopt structural adjustment programmes; and lastly, on no account would other debtors be offered any debt relief, and those that were could never have their debts written off. The retention of a large and costly debt after such 'relief' is entirely legitimate within this scheme, as the stated aim is to reduce the debt of the world's poorest states to 'sustainable levels.'

Calculations after structural adjustment programmes are imposed do not take into account the level of poverty in a country, only its ability to pay. Thus, on average, debt repayment of the poorest countries will only be cut by a third. Practically speaking, this means that after debt reduction, Mozambique, which had been paying about $120 billion a year in interest on the principal, will continue to spend $70 billion a year. Tanzania's debt reduction will only be about 10%. In Cameroon and Zambia, where one in five children do not live to the age of five and whose parents earn less than 60 cents a day, will be left with a debt of $5 billion.

Moreover, the debt relief pledged is only just that: pledged. The people of Southeast Asia who were devastated by tsunami destruction earlier this year received only 10% of the money the wealthy governments of the world pledged, governments which were shamed into pledging a respectable amount after their citizens' gave more generously than the governments themselves. It is for these reasons, for the G8's insistence that profits come before people's lives, that protesters swarmed the streets of Edinburgh, and then met at the gates of the posh hotel at an exclusive secluded golf course in Gleneagles.

Meanwhile, calling George Bush a 'sincere and passionate man,' resting his head lovingly on Tony Blair's shoulder while posing for the media cameras, Bob Geldolf joined Bono's tradition of delegitimizing the protesters and pandering to elite leaders, in particular two of the eight men who created the poverty in the first place.

Geldolf and Bono's actions not only dismissed the much more complicated and deeper critiques made by the protesters, but also implicitly condoned the hypocritical decisions of the corporate and government elites made during that week alone. The Scottish government punished members of Parliament who spoke out in favour of protecting protesters' rights to peacefully dissent in Gleneagles. For an entire month, these MPs were banned from government buildings and their salaries as well as the salaries of their staff were taken away. While Bono and Geldolf spoke from on high about saving the Africans, the rock stars took no action to pressure the UK government to let across the African protesters who were being denied entry into the country and denied participation in the events at which they had been invited to speak.

On a much more crude level, police rampantly lied the day of the Gleneagles mobilization, broadcasting over the mass media that the protest was cancelled, stopping dozens of buses and telling protesters the demonstration was cancelled and to turn back, stopping British MP George Galloway's car five times and searching it, and spreading general fear among townspeople that the protesters were violent, lawless, and ignorant.

None of these intimidations worked, as the ordinary people of Gleneagles waved, hung peace banners, and smilingly took photos of our buses as they passed through the streets. Despite the sometimes literal roadblocks erected by the Scottish government, over 15,000 protesters succeeded in reaching the fence at Gleneagles, demanding an end to poverty, war, and the crippling economic injustice spawned by the eight men toasting themselves inside.

Summary and Conclusion

Globalization was supposed to lift all boats, North and South. And the proliferation of democracies around the world would put the seal of good governance on this peaceful process. But globalization has also spawned multiple uncertainties. Players improvise the rules as they go along. Hedge funds and derivatives have left government regulators in the dust. And the fragilized states in Africa see their citizens' standard of living tumbling downwards. Many elements conspire to suggest that all African nation—states should have collapsed some time ago under the multiple assaults of their inadequacies as states, the extreme heterogeneity and polarization of their populations, and the dislocations of globalization and foreign domination. Yet, Africa has gone on defying such expectations and has continued to display a stunning propensity for resilience.

Why does Africa persist amid these overwhelming structural obstacles? State weakness, foreign invasions, the exploitation of its natural resources by transnational and informal networks, and the multiplicity of domestic rebellions linked to foreign interests have not managed to dent, however slightly, the generalized support that exists for the reproduction of all the states among its citizens, foreign political and economic interests, and the international community at large.

A collapsed state like Somalia is a failed state in its advanced stage. It is identifiable by three features, according to neo-liberalists. The first is its colonial legacy and ineffective post-colonial state-building. States formed from residual colonial rule may be confronted with insufficient love or loyalty to and from their artificially constituted population, with their domestic and international authority based not on legitimacy but on dominance, either economic or police/military. The historical process in accumulating centralized power in these states consists of subordination and assimilation that tend to maximize popular resentment, resulting in polarization derived from disillusionment and dissatisfaction by disfranchised minority or even majority groups and their elites. Thus neo-imperialists consider collapsed states to be the illegitimate children of anti-imperialism. In a way, collapsed states are juvenile delinquents of the international system left from the wreckage of the imperialist world order. The proper response to collapsed states is to re-colonize them, so argue neo-liberalists.

The second feature of a collapsed state is the withdrawal of superpower sponsorship/protection. The world order during the Cold War was a condominium of two superpowers. Local struggles and conflicts were frozen to avoid bringing the two superpowers into nuclear conflict. The end of the Cold War reduced both the legitimacy and the power of the client states of the sole remaining superpower to control domestic rival factions. The solution to this unhappy state of affairs is for the sole remaining superpower to assert its irresistible power by imposing a new world order according to its superior values, camouflaged as freedom and democracy.

This is the neo-conservative agenda. President George W Bush says that free and democratic states are peaceful states, notwithstanding the historical fact that World War II was launched by an expansionist German Third Reich born of a democratic process and the resistance by a British coalition government born through the suspension of elections. What Bush really means is that when the whole world subscribes to US values and accepts US power, not only out of fear but also out of respect for its power-backed legitimacy, the world will be peaceful. Adolf Hitler sang the same tune and failed. The US under Bush is attempting an ambitious undertaking of universal ideological control that even Christianity under the Holy Roman Empire failed to accomplish with the Thirty Years' War, having to yield finally to the Peace of Westphalia of sovereign states.

The third feature of a collapsed state is the impact on it from neo-liberal globalization. Unlike globalization in the past, which was implemented through an empire structure, neo-liberal globalization is imposed through a network of failed states by weakening a state's sovereignty and the role of the state in socio-economic arenas. Imperialist globalization of the past did not recognize the sovereignty of protectorates or colonies. In contrast, neo-imperialist globalization today employs weak client states with restricted sovereign rights as proxies of the strong market state to enforce its exploitative agenda worldwide. The use of Rwanda and Uganda in the Great Lakes region and Ethiopia in the Horn of Africa are eloquent examples

References

1. 'Failed States and the Failing States,' the Speech given by the Secretary Jack Straw at the European Research Institute, University of Birmingham, September 6, 2002. (Available at http://www.eri.bham.ac.uk/events/jstraw060902.pdf)
2. Zartman, W. (1995). *Collapsed States.* London: Lynne Reinner, p. 5.
3. Ignatieff, Michael. (2002). 'Intervention and State Failure,' *Dissent*, Winter, 2002. Available at: http://dissentmagazine.org/article/?article=641 (accessed on 1 November 2007).
4. Fukuyama, F. (2004). *State Building.* London: Profile, p. 125.
5. J. –G. Gross. (1996). 'Towards a Taxonomy of Failed States in the New World Order: Decaying Somalia, Liberia, Rwanda and Haiti,' *Third World Quarterly*, 17(3), p. 455.
6. Pupavac, V. (2001). 'Therapeutic Governance: Psychosocial Intervention a and Trauma Risk Management,' Disasters, 25(4), 2001, p. 368.
7. Wise, W. M. (2001). 'American Perspectives on the Threat Posed by Weak and Failing Asian States,' Paper presented in the US-China Conference on Areas of Instability and Emerging Threats, Beijing, February 23-24, 2004. Available at: http://www.isn.ethz.ch/pubs/ph/details.cfm?lng=en&ord61=alphaNavi&id=43638 (accessed on 4 November 2007)
8. P. Bilgin and A. D. Morton. (2002). 'Historicizing Representations of 'Failed States': Beyond the Cold War Annexation of the Social Sciences?,' *Third World Quarterly*, Vol. 23, No. 1., 2002, p. 66
9. Graham Allen& Roland Barthes.(2003). London and New York: Routledge, p. 34
10. Ibid, p. 36.
11. Ibid, p. 37.
12. Jones, . B. G. (2001). 'Blaming the Victim: Ideologies Arising from the Global Separation of the 'Economic' and the 'Political',' Paper presented at the conference on the Global Constitution of the 'Failed States': the Consequences of New Imperialism, University of Sussex, April 18-20, 2001.
13. Wood, E. M.(1995). *Democracy Against Capitalism.* Cambridge: Cambridge University Press, p. 28-32.

Chapter Eleven

The State in Africa and Civil Society in Historical Perspective

Overview

Concern with the nature and characteristics of civil society has increased greatly of late. This growth is in line with the growing tendency towards democratization in many parts of the world - in Africa, Latin America, Asia, Taiwan, and Korea - and, above all, with the collapse of the Communist regimes in Eastern Europe. It has been widely assumed that the successful institutionalization of a constitutional democratic regime is dependent on the existence and development of civil society, or that the existence of certain such nuclei is a prerequisite for the democratization of authoritarian and totalitarian regimes. Such an assumption, the validity of which, of course, must be critically assessed, demands a more thorough examination of the concept of civil society, or rather, of the reality which this concept purports to describe and its bearing on transitions to democracy and on the possible institutionalization of constitutional democratic regimes.

Historical Reprise

Certain historic and enduring facets of the modern European nation-state reached their most telling limits in the colony. A large part of the world under colonial rule, by the very same token, would also seem to have its political fate tied to histories that are intimately European. Among other institutions that arose in the particular context of Europe and sought their universal form outside Europe, the most fundamental was perhaps the modern form of statehood itself.

Crucial questions still remain on the nature of European state formation in Africa, away from the *terroir* of European politics, and on the conditions, limits, and *historia specifica* of various forms of political dominance implanted in the African colonial world in the period under consideration here. My observations draw on Gramsci's *Prison Notebooks* (1971), especially the chapter 'State and Civil Society,' where he considers the following question: To what extent can a state be identified with governance, thus underlining its basic political economic aspect—or, as Gramsci terms it, 'the economic-corporate form'—and creating a fortuitous confusion between civil and political society (262–63)? A general idea of the state, remarks Gramsci, must include elements of civil and political society joined together, a 'hegemony protected by the armour of coercion' (263).

It is tempting to describe the colonial state at the height of its powers as a coercive apparatus masked by trappings of hegemony. In many respects the ideology of colonial state formation straddled the line between acts of dominance and ambitions of hegemony. In order to resolve the seeming paradox of a state without a European-type civil society in the African colonial context, a certain concept of uncertainty and alienation between dominant and subordinate subjects needs to be elaborated. The colonial state created a unique set of relationships with the indigenous communities (Ekeh 1975; 1978;1983;1992; 1994; 1995) in its grasp, communities that were not represented by any direct means in the making or exercise of law. This fundamental disjuncture between native society and the dominant political structure implied that the colonial state-form, neither constituted by the subjects under its rule nor engendered fully through an indigenous history, could relate to that society only through a series of closures and limitations.

The first and foremost of these strictures derived from the right of conquest. For most modern European empires, argues Anthony Pagden (1995, 22–23), the Roman ideal cast a long shadow of both legitimacy and doubt. For Rome, *civitas* was perceived to be perfectly harmonious with the ends and means of the *Imperium*, giving the state a mandate to enslave, convert, and incorporate all who entered or were brought into its sphere. The Spanish occupation of the New World was justified principally on the grounds of what Pagden describes as the 'just war' of the Christian and righteous conquistador against the heathen Africans, sanctified through blood and the Crown's a priori prerogatives to seize native people, their goods, and their land as *encomiendas* (pp 91–95). In the case of the English conquests, articulated first in the context of North America, a major (ibid., p.395) premise of usurpation was the clause of *res nullius* (that is, all 'things,' such as land unsettled as common property of all mankind, that remained 'empty' until they were converted into the property of whoever worked and claimed them for use), drawn from Roman law.

The primacy of conquest notwithstanding, the notion of native groups' consent, acquiescence, or sufferance emerges as one of the most powerful moral conditions on which the state was erected in the colonial world. No history of attempted hegemony can be reduced easily to its bare bones of domination. Advocates and critics of empire bestowed a degree of both volition and agency to the victims of European ascendancy, and thus granted them, even if by default, a residual order of 'society,' 'civilization,' or at least 'culture' (to which I would add 'nationhood,' in the premodern sense of the word). Beyond the history of conquest, this acknowledgement led to the invention of a colonial society, somewhat in the spirit of what Jacques Donzelot (1984:20–21) has called 'faire du social,' especially the replacement of a society based on a given 'natural order' with a mutable society fabricated through human thought and action.

Colonial rule thus precipitated something like an apparition of civil society—a realm at times fictive, at times supposedly juridical—where the compliance of the subject population could be imagined and elicited. Conversions made possible a new society of the baptized under European imperial tutelage. The colonial moment in African history was a *parody* or a *distortion* of a quintessentially European modernity. One should tread carefully here to delineate where certain universal experiments that are associated readily with modernity took place, and it could very well be that just like the technology of Herschel's fingerprint, a few very intimate practices of the colonial state became available to the European Empires as instruments of universal discipline. But, the exogenesis of the colonial state form disrupted the effortless permeability of power in any given society that came under the shadow of imperial or colonial rule. In the case of Africa, colonial histories are thus always burdened with the cumulative legacy of the confrontations between the state and the indigenous society that it tries to shape.

Divergence between state and society, to be sure, is a familiar story, especially in the case of Europe, where the state had been involved for centuries in shaping and transforming social and cultural identities. The ability of the state and its agents to act *in the name* of the people, but not necessarily *for* them, has been illustrated very well by Philip Corrigan and Derek Sayer in *The Great Arch* (1985). My reflections on the colonial extensions of the English state spring from this very idea of the state as a live organ of society and culture, an entity that assumes a pivotal power to shape morality, law, property, gender, religion, and indeed all conceivable facets of everyday existence. The history of the creation of a modern society in England is of immense import to the history of the making of a colonial society elsewhere, and later a national society in any African colony. In asking such questions about the insularity of society as a concept, as much as a set of relations in the context of colonial Africa, one can only echo Eric Wolf's (1988) warning that the notion of a 'Society' immemorial, as a bounded and homogenous entity, can become a stumbling block in our search for further ethnographic—and by implication, historical—understanding. As Wolf saw it, it was crucial 'to recognize that the concept of Society has a history, a historical function within a determinate context, in a particular part of the world' (759). This question, recast in the historiography of (ibid. page 403) colonial domination in India, enables us to place the organic limits of the state from in a clearer perspective.

For the class of Europeans who came to rule Africa, an adequate translation of the morality of domination, to convince their African subjects, remained a perennial problem, most conspicuously exhibited through racial bars to the sharing of power later in the early twentieth century. As for the Africans, the unfathomable distance of the political idioms of alien rule only furthered the anarchic and the antinomian in their efforts at resistance and their search for autonomy.

Historically, therefore, the intermediate organizations that lie between the state and the household, that are formed voluntarily by members of society to protect and advance their interests and values, and that are separate from the state and largely autonomous, or call them civil society, were the forces that forcibly dislodged entrenched colonialism and post-colonial authoritarianism in Africa and brought about formal independence as well as the beginnings of formal democracy in the early 1990s. In fact, the continent's nascent civil societies were in the forefront (Lewis 1992).

Although external influences such as the fall of communism and pressure from foreign donors were important, it was often the resourcefulness, dedication, and tenacity of domestic civil society that initiated and sustained the process of transition. The opening of once-forbidden debate on new political directions; the decriminalization of dissent and the acceptance (however grudging) of pluralist politics; the convening of sovereign national conferences and constituent assemblies; preparations for competitive elections; and, in a significant number of cases, the eventual installation of elected governments—for all these things, civil societies can take a large share of credit. Civil society in Africa is alive and vibrant. What we need is knowledge about civil society in the face of continuing global recession. Will the present phase of the African crisis sharpen contradictions within the continent's states leading to a second African liberation? New paradigms have to be sought to explain the formations and realities of civil society in Africa.

Revisiting Literature on Civl Society and the State in Africa

Reviewing the literature on the state and civil society is necessary because scholarship is cumulative. No matter what one writes, one is standing on someone else's shoulders. Scholars must say something new while connecting what they say to what has already been said. That is why any review of the literature article considers the state and progress of current literature on a given topic or problem by organizing, integrating, and evaluating previously published books and articles. In short, a review piece is a critical evaluation of material that has already been published.

The State

In our case, we must note that conceptualizations of the state have been defined not only by the specific historical forms it has taken but also by ontological, epistemological, and methodological issues as well as differing ideological positions that colour the implicit and explicit elements embodied in the concept. Rakodi (1986, p. 426), in an attempt to grapple with the state in an urban context in Africa, identifies four broad ways of theorizing that delineate these differing ideological and methodological perspectives. Equally important to our understanding of the African context is the need to periodize the state in terms of its changing forms and the changes in social relations and politics that these involve (Doornbos, 1990).

Some formulations of the peripheral capitalist state conceptualize it as an 'institution of social and economic reproduction' and as 'the site of class interactions and struggles.' These conceptions assist scholars in seeing different patterns not only of state-economy relations but also of state-society relations. It must be pointed out that the state in Africa, even though it can be categorized as peripheral, 'underdeveloped,' and capitalist, does not have a single form of expression. A variety of forms and subcategories have emerged, determined by the specific history of the society under consideration. It is this complex expression that explains the multiple and often contradictory forms that state-society relations can take in any African social formation. Claude Ake (1989: 44) attempts to capture this when he points out that:

> [the state] is a specific modality of class domination... in which the system of institutional mechanisms of class domination are [*sic*] differentiated from the ruling-class and appears as an objective force standing alongside society. The essential feature of the state form of domination is that the system of institutional mechanisms of domination is autonomized and becomes largely independent of social classes including the hegemonic social class... the state really is... a contradiction of interests, of powers and of social forces. The dominant social forces struggle to maintain their domination and the subordinate social forces struggle against their subordination and related disabilities. This is the context in which public policies including development strategies are made.

This class character of the state raises the question of the interests represented and the implications for politics, public policy, and action. Apart from the conventional expression of the interests of dominant classes and their fractions, the very nature of the state and class formation in the African context allows the interplay and coming to the fore of interests and social forces not clearly located in the relations of production. Some of these interests are at the ideological and identity levels and are expressed as ethnic, racial, or religious interests.

Others are those of strategic groups located as parasites within the state apparatus, either military or bureaucratic. Thus there are specific instances when the state is dominated by racial interests, as in the Afrikaner example of apartheid South Africa, or by religious interests, as in the case of the Sudan. However, these interests are often linked with class domination, as expressed through the representations and actions of dominant classes and their fractions. There is also a need to distinguish between the state as a locale for the expression of class domination and the state apparatus, including agents of state domination, such as the police, the military, etc. These are part and parcel of the state, serve the state, but do not by themselves constitute the state.

At a different level of territorial concern is the 'local state,' that locates the institutions and agents of the state at a different spatial and administrative/political level. A troubled notion, the conceptual ambiguity embodied in it, centring on the extent to which the local state is autonomous from, rather than merely an agent of, the central state, has led not only to criticism but in some cases to outright rejection (Duncan and Godwin 1982; Bryne 1982). However, the notion opens up further space for the discussion of decentralization and participation in urban politics and management (Rakodi, 1986; Mabogunje 1990). In spite of the difficulties, the concept of an urban local state contributes to the understanding and evaluation of institutions and agents grounded in closer proximity to the concrete activities and lives of the variety of urban and rural actors.

Civil Society

Civil society is one of the 'hottest' concepts in all of the social sciences that touch on political life. As with most popular academic concepts, there is no universally accepted definition of either civil society or the related notions of a civic culture and social capital. Civil society is an unusual concept in that it always seems to require being defined before it is applied or discussed. In part this is because the concept was rarely used in African discourse before the late eighties and many people are therefore unfamiliar with it.

To be honest with my readers, civil society is part of a larger theoretical canvas and therefore needs to be looked at in the context of complex societal interrelationships. The overuse of the concept of civil society can lead to a loss of analytical rigor and conceptual clarity in contemporary theorization. What I mean here is when concepts lack these attributes, both the value and validity as politically relevant and worthy categories for action diminish considerably. However, time and time again, the ability of civil society to coalesce against the tyrannical—whether it is the state, the elites, or the powers that be—sends an important message about the power and desirability of civil society.

Unlike society, which sociologists broadly agree is the field of structured social relations and actions, notions of civil society are as varied and contested as those of the state. More recent use of the notion has tended to veil its pluralistic ideological and philosophical origins. In their concern with civil society as 'bourgeois' or liberal democratic society, or as the outcome of market-dominated economic development, they fail to see that this represents only one perspective (Bayart 1989; Cohen and Arato 1990; Gellner 1991; Fatton 1992) An interesting related dimension of the concept of civil society is its globalization both in practice and as an idea (Lipschutz 1992).

The concern with civil society has essentially been Eurocentric, and recent attempts at applying the concept in the African context have remained either ethnocentric or insufficiently rigorous and historically sensitive in their analysis. However, there has been an interesting application in the context of South Africa, where the concern is with the transition to a pluralistic democracy and uneasiness about an ANC dominated state. In the debate, the notion has had a wide range of use, from the banal and literal-meaning level to more theoretical debates between the neo-conservative, Marxist, and critical perspectives. See, for instance, Fine (1992), Simone and Pieterse (1993), Gouws (1993).

Mahmood Mamdani (1995a, b) and Abdel Kader Zghal (1995), in recognition of the limitations of these analyses, have recently offered a more Africa-relevant and non-Eurocentric application of the concept to contemporary Africa. Mamdani (1995a, p. 3), in an introduction to a recent book on social movements and democracy in Africa, asks:

What is civil society? Does it exist or is it emerging? Is it confined to the 'modern sphere,' whose organizations are predicated on a differentiation between the political and the social, the social and the economic? Or does it include the 'traditional' sphere where the organization of life process proceeds on the basis of a diffusion, and not differentiation, between the economic, the social and the political? Is the problem solved by making a distinction between 'modern civil society,' and 'traditional civil society.'.. Or is it thereby simply shelved? On the other hand, does the notion of a 'civil society' as a modern construct lead at best to a one-eyed vision of social and political processes?

The response to this questioning leads to a rejection of both the conventional and simplistic state-civil society dichotomy and the prescriptive modernization perspective that characterized development theory in the 1970s. It also rejects the romanticization and the denial of civil society in Africa. The informed response to this questioning links the concept politically with the notion and practice of social movements, in terms of their contribution to democratic politics, the defence of people's rights and livelihoods, popular participation, and empowerment. It is also recognized that neither society nor civil society must be idealized or conceived of as a homogeneous entity with consensual political direction. Rather plurality, polarization, contradictions, and conflict of interests are all aspects of the existence of civil society.

Furthermore, the relationship of civil society to the democratization process is not at all times progressive. Indeed there are often strong conservative trends. Civil society in this context refers to the sphere of social interaction that comprises the intimate sphere (family), associational life, social movements, and forms of public communication operating in the arena of the organized non-state, non-market sector with origins in both the modern and traditional bases of society (Cohen and Arato 1990). It is not synonymous with or inchoately distinguished from society at large but is a differentiated dimension of society with distinctive political functions (Harbeson 1992).

It is important to point out that the notion of 'associational life' extends beyond secular or modern voluntary associations and includes associations defined on more particularistic and at times primordial identities such as race, kinship, ethnicity, and religion. Civil society, of course, interacts with both the market and non-marketized elements of the economy and the state in the pursuit of its constituents' interests. Although Zghal (1995) has argued for the inclusion of unorganized and spontaneous protests in civil society, there is a need to exercise caution, because sustained and patterned existence seems to be important in the relevance of this arena to political life.

In one of its best brief attempts to sort through all the definitions, the British Library (2003) included the following characteristics:

All observers agree that civil society refers to *voluntary* participation by average citizens and thus does not include behaviour imposed or even coerced by the state.

- For some observers, it only includes political activity engaged in through nonprofit organizations such as nongovernmental organizations (NGOs). At the other end of the spectrum, some observers include all forms of voluntary participation, whether in the public or private sector, political or apolitical.

- Civil society includes not just the individuals who participate, but the institutions they participate in—sometimes called 'civil society organizations' or 'CSOs.' . Thus, civil society is strong to the degree that those CSOs are large and powerful.
- A civic culture is one in which most people think their government is legitimate and that their institutions (if not the leaders at any particular moment) can be trusted.
- Social capital is the human equivalent of economic capital. It is an intangible resource accumulated by civil society that can be expended when a society finds itself in crisis, as some argue occurred in the United States after September 11. (*Civil Society' - An Agreed Definition* (2003) available from http://pages.britishlibrary.net/blwww3/3way/civilsoc.htm; Internet.)

In its modern form, civil society means the active and organized formations and associations in the cultural sphere. These would include, among others, NGOs, academia, media, and Church groups, in contradistinction but not necessarily in opposition to the formal apparatus of governance in the political sphere and the web of business enterprises in the economic sphere. Business has economic power. Governments wield political power. But civil society uses cultural power. And, culture deals with the realm of ideas in its various diverse forms including worldviews, knowledge, meanings, symbols, identity, ethics, art, and spirituality, among others. The 'cultural sphere' of society is that subsystem of society concerned with the development of full human capacities and the generation of knowledge, meaning, a sense for the sacred, art, and ethics.

Indeed, culture is that social space where identity and meaning are generated. The two are inseparable. Both identity and meaning give human beings their cognitive, affective and ethical orientation. In short, it is the wellspring that determines and sustains all human behaviour. Loss of meaning results in a cluster of aberrant and destructive behaviours. Discovery of meaning results in greater creativity, compassion, and productivity. It is clear that the institution, in this case, civil society, which controls meaning and identity and, therefore, behaviour, will have a tremendous clout in the direction and affairs of national and world society.

I realise there are many definitions of civil society. The working definition of civil society used to inform this book's enquiry has three dimensions:

Civil Society as associational life

Civil society is the 'space' of organised activity not undertaken by either the government or for-private-profit business. It includes formal and informal associations such as: voluntary and community organisations, trade unions, faith-based organisations, co-operatives and mutuals, political parties, professional and business associations, philanthropic organisations, informal citizen groups and social movements. Participation in or membership of such organisations is voluntary in nature.

Civil Society as the 'good' society

The term civil society is often used as a short-hand for the type of society we want to live in and can therefore viewed in normative terms. It is often assumed that civil society is a good thing, but this is not necessarily true. For example, civil society associations can help strengthen democracy and improve the well-being of deprived communities as can they undermine human rights and preach intolerance and violence. The Enquiry is therefore especially concerned about the strength of civil society associations as a means through which values and outcomes such as non-violence, non-discrimination, democracy, mutuality and social justice are nurtured and achieved; and as a means through which public policy dilemmas are resolved in ways that are just, effective and democratic. A 'good' civil society needs to have constructive relationships with government, statutory agencies, the business sector and media. The actions of civil society associations alone cannot achieve a 'good' civil society.

Civil Society as arenas for public deliberation

Civil society is an arena for public deliberation and the exercise of active citizenship in pursuit of common interests. It is the public space in which societal differences, social problems, public policy, government action and matters of community and cultural identity are developed and debated. These public spaces might be physical in nature, such as community centres, or virtual, such as blogs. We may never share a common vision about what a 'good' society might look like and how it might be achieved, but can be committed to a process that allows people of all ages and backgrounds to share in defining how the different visions are reconciled.

To summarize, civil society is a goal to aim for (a 'good' society), a means to achieve it (associational life), and a framework for engaging with each other about ends and means (arenas for deliberation) in any society worthy of human habitation.

Why Is Civil Society Important?

In 'Reinventing Civil Society' (Civitas, 1993), David Green writes:

> 'Markets generate more prosperity, but 'more goods' do not make a good society.
>
> The challenge we face today is to identify a sense of community or solidarity that is compatible with freedom. Competitive markets coordinate the efforts of people who may be self-interested, even selfish, but they do not create solidarity.
>
> Contrary to the view attributed to Mrs Thatcher, that there is 'no such thing as society', there is indeed such a thing. But it is not synonymous with the state. It is the realm of 'activity in common', which is at once voluntary and guided by a sense of duty to other people and to the social system on which liberty rests.'

Unfortunately, not all observers agree that civil society is important at all. Marxists, in particular, argue that civil society and, especially, a civic culture tend to frustrate change and progress toward a more just and equitable society. However, there is growing agreement that civil society, civic culture, and social capital are all important for strengthening democracy and enabling conflict resolution. To be fair, the first academic discussions of civil society were naive, all but suggesting that any expansion of civic engagement was good for democracy. Anyone who has explored the rapid expansion of political involvement in such countries as the former Yugoslavia or Rwanda knows that any simplistic link between participation and democracy—let alone conflict resolution—is absurd.

Here, Robert Putnam's path-breaking (if controversial) book *Bowling Alone (2000)* provided an important breakthrough in our thinking. Putnam recalled that when he went bowling as a child in the 1950s, people bowled in teams. In the late 1990s, people went bowling just as often as they did in Putnam's youth. However, they bowled with a couple of friends or family members, not in leagues. For Putnam, 'bowling alone' is just one of dozens of indicators that Americans were less and less engaged in the rich social network of recreational and political organizations which his earlier research in Italy had suggested were vital for democracy. But Putnam did not fall into the naive trap of arguing that all social involvement helped democracy.

Indeed, Putnam distinguishes between 'bonding' and 'bridging' social capital, and only the latter unambiguously supports democratization. Bonding social capital develops when we get involved with people like ourselves. In my case, that would mean spending time with liberal, Jewish, middle-aged academics who like sports. If Putnam and scholars who have examined extremist nationalists are correct, bonding social capital can serve to reinforce our pre-existing beliefs including our prejudices. To cite the most tragic example, there is little doubt that the authorities fanned the anti-Tutsi hatred of the Hutu who flocked to the *Interahamwe* in Rwanda in the early 1990s and made them more and more likely to physically take their anger out on the Tutsi.

In bridging social capital, one becomes involved with people who are less like oneself. That may be as simple as getting involved in one's neighbourhood association. While only middle class families can afford to live in one's neighbourhood, one may be the only academic, the only Jew, and one of only a handful of liberals. Even more importantly, when one gets involved in trying to organize interfaith dialogues on divisive political issues, one spends time with people on the religious right, ultra-orthodox Jews, Muslims, Hindus, and atheists. In that work, one discovers not only the issues people disagree about, but also areas where they do agree and can work together. People then develop trust and toleration. Their community's social life literally becomes more civil.

This is important both for the building of democracy and for resolving conflict. The reason is that such values as trust and tolerance are important for both. No one has put this better than former U.S. President William Clinton (2003) in his 1994 speech to the United Nations General Assembly:

> 'A coalition for democracy—it's good for America. Democracies, after all, are more likely to be stable, less likely to wage war. They strengthen civil society. They can provide people with the economic opportunities to build their own homes, not to flee their borders. Our efforts to help build democracies will make us all more secure, more prosperous, and more successful as we try to make this era of terrific change our friend and not our enemy.'

Colonial State and Civil Society

The first crucial goal of the colonial state was to consolidate colonial control over African territory. At the Berlin Conference in 1884 and 1885, where diplomatic agreement was reached among imperial powers on major outlines of the partition, the principle of 'effective occupation' was enunciated. To confirm its title to a zone of African territory, a colonial power had to demonstrate to its European rivals that it exercised military control over the area; failing this, an imperial rival might snatch it away. 'Effective occupation' was to be achieved, however, with small outlays. Finance ministers and parliaments in Europe insisted that military commitments be kept small, and that the newly conquered territories pay for their own administration. Important consequences for the colonial state flowed from the twin imperative of consolidating hegemony and generating revenue.

Early African reaction to European intrusion into Africa in the late 19th century was not uniform. A few groups that had suffered from long-term warfare or slave raiding (such as in parts of East Africa) gave an uncertain welcome to European presence in their regions in hope that there would be peace. Other groups strongly resisted the coming of European political control. However, many people had no initial reaction to colonialism. This was because the early years colonialism had little impact on the lives of many rural African peoples. This situation changed as the impact of colonialism became more widespread and intense in the middle decades of the 20th century.

Throughout the period of the *Scramble for Africa*, European colonizers faced stiff resistance in many parts of Africa. It would take up too much time and space to present information on all instances of resistance. By the end of World War I, most of Africa had been effectively colonized. European colonialists had managed to *quell* the efforts by Africans to resist the establishment of colonial rule. The next two decades, the period historians call the inter-war years, were relatively quiet years in colonial Africa. This relative quiet, however, did not indicate that the colonized people of Africa were happy with colonial rule-that there was no opposition to colonialism. During the inter-war years opposition to colonialism was expressed in one of the following forms:

- *Demands for opportunity and inclusion*: Many Africans at this time accepted the reality of colonial rule but they did not accept the harsh discrimination and the lack of opportunity that was a central part of the colonial experience. Opposition to these aspects of colonialism was particularly strong among educated Africans. Educated Africans believed that 'all humans are created equal.' Discriminatory colonial policies and practice restricted economic opportunities and participation in the political process. During this period, educated Africans formed organizations to promote their interest for an end to discriminatory policies and for an increase in opportunities. However, these organizations had limited membership, and they did not make radical demands for the end of colonial rule. The South African National Congress and the West African National Congress (Nigeria/Ghana) are examples of elite African organizations.
- *Religious opposition*: A number of the early anti-colonial up-risings featured in the last section were led by religious leaders. The *Chimurenga* (Zimbabwe) and *Maji-Maji* (Tanganyika) uprisings were

led by African priests who were strongly opposed to colonial rule. This tradition of religious opposition to colonialism continued throughout the 20th century. However, unlike the earlier acts of religious resistance, the new opposition was led by African Christians. African Christians took seriously the Christian teachings on equality and fairness-values that were not practiced by colonial regimes. By the 1920s, some African Christian leaders were forming their own churches, sometimes called African Independent Churches. These churches that were formed in Southern, Eastern, Central and West Africa, provided a strong voice for justice. One of many examples is the *Kimbaguist Christian Church* formed in the Congo by Simon Kimbangu in the 1920s. In spite of Kimbangu's imprisonment for many years by the Belgians, the Kimbanguist church grew rapidly. When the Congo became independent in 1960, the church had a membership of over one million.

- *Economic opposition*: During this time period economic opposition was often not well organized. However, there were attempts in the 1920s and 1930s by mine workers in southern Africa and port workers in West and East Africa to organize into unions. While important, these activities had little impact on the majority of African peoples. Of greater impact were the less organized but more widespread efforts of African farmers to resist colonial demands on their labour and their land. A clear example here is how small scale African farmers in Mali quietly, but effectively, resisted the attempts by colonial officials to control the production of cotton.
- *Mass protests*: During the inter-war era, there were few mass protests against colonial policies. One of the most important and interesting exceptions was the *Aba Women's War* that took place in southeastern Nigeria in 1929. Ibo market women were upset with a number of colonial policies that threatened their economic and social position. In 1929, the women staged a series of protests. The largest protest included more than 10,000 women who had covered their faces with blue paint and carried fern-covered sticks. The women were able to destroy a number of colonial buildings before soldiers stopped the protest, killing more than fifty women in the process. Not surprisingly in contemporary Nigeria, the Aba Women are considered to be national heroes!

In sum, anti-colonial populism, such as 'people's power' movements and the like, frequently served to draw attention to inequity and distortions in the power structure, and then merely empower an ancillary class of civil-society activists and their self-generated agendas acting in opposition to state structures and other traditional authority. Thus, while at first glance, civil society activity grew greatly, and encouragingly so in colonial Africa, it involved a mass of the populace, but such mass participation in itself was no proof of mass empowerment. Time and time again, the ability of civil society to coalesce against the tyrannical—whether it be the state, the elites, or the powers that be—sends an important message about the power and desirability of civil society.

THE STATE IN AFRICA: Post-Colonial Authoritarianism and Civil Society

At the onset of independence, African leaders espoused Populism- African Socialism, Nationalism, Marxist-Leninism, and Capitalism, and these strategies had a lot of influence on the shaping of the post independence state and economies in Africa. Nationalist regimes were concerned with consolidating the nations' identities. They sought to maximize control over assets and sectors of the economy. Instead of the state taking over industry, nationalist regimes were concerned with the Africanization of private industry. The state was used as a catalyst to encourage foreign interest to sell to private indigenous interest. The governments sought to control or restrain foreign investors and markets.

Populism or African Socialism developed as a response to capitalism in most African nations that wanted to distance themselves from capitalism at least in rhetoric, because they had been the victims of capitalist imperialism. The main idea of populism best articulated by Kwame Nkrumah was self-reliance: reducing dependence on the world market, integration of markets, reduction of external dependency. Marxist-Leninist philosophy in Africa came out of the revolutionary movements in the Portuguese colonies of the mid-1970's. The proponents believed in greater state intervention in the economy than the populist. They believed in a command economy in the Soviet form, with state planning as a key. They stressed state administered farms and agriculture collectivism. The Capitalist countries such as Kenya encouraged foreign investment, entrepreneurship, and actively participates in the world market.

However, the day after independence, most African nations regardless of ideological belief sought to centralize state power. This varied in degree because of ideological belief but this was a common trait throughout Africa. African heads of state regardless of ideology generally sought to consolidate political power, build institutions of public administration, and state security military apparatus. The people had high expectations following independence; they expected prosperity to soon follow. Only the government could respond to the pressing needs of the people.

By consolidating political power, African leaders gave themselves and their single-party regimes vast amounts of power and as a consequence personalizing power. The personalization of power is unique to Africa; the leaders were essentially the state and not the institutions. More often than not this rule engendered a great deal of corruption. In terms of the economy, who is to say what is public money and what is the private money of the leader. His leadership is based upon his ability to satisfy, sedate certain groups usually through patronage and other types of gifts. Some times that group is the military as in Zaire in fact, most African nations allocate huge sums of funds to the military not enough on infrastructure and basic needs of the people. The state bureaucracy grew dramatically in post colonial Africa due to the pressing the demands imposed on the state. The state was forced to respond to the needs of the people with an ill equipped bureaucracy incapable of performing the difficult duties necessary for the daily administration of government. This greatly affects the ability to maintain a stable economy.

Also, depending on the philosophy of the state most African nations nationalized many of the industry's left by the colonial powers such as electricity and telecommunications Nkrumah did this in Ghana. This also led to the growth of bureaucracy and with the growth of bureaucracy came the growth of patronage and corruption. The ability to do another a favour whether that is getting them a job, government contract, or embezzle public funds, patron-client relations is the norm and not the exception in post-colonial Africa.

Finally, a state's ability to effectively run its economy lies in its legitimacy to the people this is the underlying political-economic theme that hovers around African politics. The very legitimacy of its borders, leaders and institutions of government must be taken into question in understanding what is going on in African politics and how it relates to the economy and society. The old-style personal dictatorships that ruled Africa with impunity are virtually nonexistent today. But, one remembers brutal rulers like Uganda's Idi Amin, Central African Republic's Jean-Bedel Bokassa, and Equatorial Guinea's Macías Nguema.

These are men who eliminated potential dissent with such brutality and ruthlessness that they earned international notoriety. Power in their dictatorships was virtually equated with the ruling strongmen. They personally directed the administration and political institutions, arbitrarily passed laws to suit their own purposes, banned independent political organizations, maintained power through various forms of patronage, and used the military as a personal army. They used the state to perpetrate violence against citizens arbitrarily with little regard for their own laws.

The authoritarian/personal rulers used the state to perpetrate violence against citizens arbitrarily with little regard for the law. In Uganda, for example, the orgy of murder that included the killing of the chief justice, Makerere University's vice chancellor, and the Anglican archbishop came to characterize General Amin's regime (1971-1979). Dr. Milton Obote's second government (1980-1985) was little better and state terror was more random, as the Youth Wing of the ruling party, Uganda People's Congress (UPC), searched villages for rebels. In fact, it is estimated that politically inspired violence caused the deaths of 800,000 or more Ugandans between 1971 and 1985.

There were also Afro-Marxist authoritarian regimes once found in Angola, Ethiopia, Guinea Bissau, and Mozambique. These regimes, on ideological grounds, suppressed challenges to the ruling 'vanguard' party. They organized various groups of women, youth, labour, and peasants into party-related organizations. Backed by Eastern-bloc countries and heavily reliant on the military, leaders of these regimes nationalized key private corporations and financial institutions, abolished private landownership, banned the hiring of labour, nationalized urban rental housing, and introduced other far-reaching social reforms.

Today, we also see few populist military oligarchies, as Ghana was under Jerry Rawlings in the early 1980s and Burkina Faso was under Thomas Sankara. Young military leaders who had come into power in the late 1970s and 1980s led such regimes. They used state-orchestrated mass mobilization organizations (e.g., people's committees, public tribunals, local councils) to establish what they claimed was a new egalitarian moral and social order. Despite the rhetoric of participation, elections were often suspended, and decision-making was carried out by an inner circle close to the president (Bratton and van de Walle 1997:80).

Indeed, they often manifested patterns of personal clientelistic rule reminiscent of African authoritarian regimes, with the executive holding a preponderance of power. These authoritarian regimes did not permit a changing of the guard through the ballot box. Some were run by military leaders, and may even held elections, but they did so under circumstances that could not be considered free and fair. Others might have been led by a one-party system (Eritrea) or create a multiparty context where electoral victories were accomplished through repression of the opposition, suppression of the media, and questionable electoral practices (Côte d'Ivoire, Cameroon, Gabon, Guinea, etc.). Sudan, which had one of the worst human-rights records in Africa, adopted a new constitution in 1999, permitting multiparty balloting and direct election of the head of state; however, civil and political liberties remained so restricted. It was thus difficult to imagine that elections under authoritarian regimes could be free and fair.

In sum, the cases of Nigeria, Cameroon, Senegal, Kenya, etc. are exemplary. Colonial rule in Nigeria or Kenya witnessed the emergence of a profoundly unbalanced institutional landscape, what Peter Ekeh (1983) calls a 'bifurcated state.' In this arrangement, all state capacity resided in a strong prefectural provincial administration. Political parties thenceforth remained underdeveloped. Sympathetic African elites during the colonial twilight were co-opted into the bureaucracy, the legislature and the private property-based economy. This scenario meant that the allies of colonialism and representatives of transnational capital were able to reap the benefits of independence.

In the late colonial period these elites not only attained the means of production, they also assumed the political and institutional capacity to reproduce their dominance. This explains why the post-colonial state must therefore be seen as a representation of the interests protected and promoted during the latter years of colonial rule. Under the Northern Oligarchy in Nigeria or Jomo Kenyatta in Kenya, the post-colonial state represented a 'pact-of-domination' between transnational capital, the elite and the executive. The ability of this coalition to reproduce itself over time lay in its capacity to brutally demobilize the civil society or popular forces, especially those elements of the nationalist movement that questioned both the social and economic cleavages of the post-colonial state. Whilst Kenya may have experienced changes to both the executive and legislature, the structure of the state itself has demonstrated remarkable resilience.

Failed/Collapsed States and Civil Society

A failed state is a state whose central government is so weak or ineffective that it has little practical control over much of its territory. The level of control required to avoid being considered a failed state varies considerably amongst authorities. (Patrick 2007). Furthermore, the declaration that a state has 'failed' is generally controversial and, when made authoritatively, may carry significant geopolitical consequences.

A state could be said to 'succeed' if it maintains, in the words of Max Weber, a monopoly on the legitimate use of physical force within its borders. When this is broken (e.g., through the dominant presence of warlords, paramilitary groups, or terrorism), the very existence of the state becomes dubious, and the state becomes a *failed state*. The difficulty of determining whether a government maintains 'a monopoly on the legitimate use of force' (which includes the problems of the definition of 'legitimate') means it is not clear precisely when a state can be said to have 'failed.' This problem of legitimacy can be solved by understanding what Weber intended by it. Weber clearly explains that only the state has the means of production necessary for physical violence (politics as vocation). This means that the state does not require legitimacy for achieving monopoly on the means of violence (de facto) but will need one if it needs to use it (de jure).

The term is also used in the sense of a state that has been rendered ineffective (i.e., has nominal military/police control over its territory only in the sense of having no armed opposition groups directly challenging state authority; in short, the 'no news is good news' approach) and is not able to enforce its laws uniformly because of high crime rates, extreme political corruption, an extensive informal market, impenetrable bureaucracy, judicial ineffectiveness, military interference in politics, cultural situations in which traditional leaders wield more power than the state over a certain area but do not compete with the state, or a number of other factors.

From a legal perspective, Daniel Thürer, writing for the *International Review of the Red Cross* December 1999, says 'Failing States are invariably the product of a collapse of the power structures providing political support for law and order, a process generally triggered and accompanied by *anarchic* forms of internal violence.' The former Secretary-General of the United Nations, Boutros Boutros-Ghali, described this situation in the following way:

> 'A feature of such conflicts is the collapse of state institutions, especially the police and judiciary, with resulting paralysis of governance, a breakdown of law and order, and general banditry and chaos. Not only are the functions of government suspended, but its assets are destroyed or looted and experienced officials are killed or flee the country. This is rarely the case in inter-state wars. It means that international intervention must extend beyond military and humanitarian tasks and must include the promotion of international reconciliation and the re-establishment of effective government.'
>
> 'States in which institutions and law and order have totally or partially collapsed under the pressure and amidst the confusion of erupting violence, yet which subsist as a ghostly presence on the world map,' Thürer says, 'are now commonly referred to as failed States or Etats sans gouvernements.'

Indicators of State Vulnerability

The index's ranks are based on twelve indicators of state vulnerability—four social, two economic and six political. The indicators are not designed to forecast when states may experience violence or collapse. Instead, they are meant to measure a state's vulnerability to collapse or conflict. All countries in the red, orange, or yellow categories display some features that make parts of their societies and institutions vulnerable to failure. Some in the yellow zone may be failing at a faster rate than those in the more dangerous orange or red zones, and therefore could experience violence sooner. Conversely, some in the red zone, though critical, may exhibit some positive signs of recovery or be deteriorating slowly, giving them time to adopt mitigating strategies.

Take the case of Nigeria under the Latest Obasanjo Administration. The restive military has remained in the barracks. Viewed from the perspective of former President Bill Clinton's two-day visit, it seemed that Nigeria had much to celebrate. But after what some saw as waffling by President Olusegun Obasanjo, a number of political worries tempered any optimism. Yes, things had changed. But the question was whether enough had changed. Little had been done to address serious and deep-rooted problems such as the unrest in the Niger Delta, secessionist demands from the southwest, high unemployment, the collapse of social services, and school closures.

With worsening economic conditions and government failures to deliver any benefit from democracy, popular fatigue provided fuel for communal violence at flashpoints throughout the country. The declaration by several northern states that Islamic Sharia law would be extended to criminal law sparked deadly clashes between Muslims and Christians. The uncertainty caused by all these problems seriously damaged the country's prospects for desperately needed economic rejuvenation and for sustaining and deepening its democracy.

Social Indicators

a. Demographic pressures

This includes the pressures deriving from high population density relative to food supply and other life-sustaining resources. The pressure from a population's settlement patterns and physical settings, including border disputes, ownership or occupancy of land, access to transportation outlets, control of religious or historical sites, and proximity to environmental hazards. For example, the property rights school, a dominant philosophy in development strategies pursued by Northern donor agencies, asks for the rapid legal institutionalization of private property that will theoretically move economies towards pare to efficient uses of resources and expand growth.

However, pursuit of property stabilization as a means to a growth strategy is deleterious, as brisk institutionalization of private property regimes proved disastrous in a development context and created additional social pressures leading to humanitarian catastrophes. Further, in the history of the countries that now comprise the developed world, property stabilization was an elongated, bloody transformation that accompanied hundreds of years of conflict, demographic shifts, intricate adjustment, and political alteration. To expect a swift, fastidious, and peaceful transformation during property rights stabilization in light of recent history in Rwanda, and across the developing world has shown to be not only myopic and intellectually dishonest, but dangerous as well.

b. Massive movement of refugees and internally displaced peoples

Forced uprooting of large communities as a result of random or targeted violence and/or repression, causing food shortages, disease, lack of clean water, land competition, and turmoil that can spiral into larger humanitarian and security problems, both within and between countries. At this moment, there are almost 9 million refugees in Africa, many of whom have escaped one dangerous place, only to find themselves in the heart of another conflict.

Today, Chad is a country rocked by its own protracted civil war, internal ethnic tensions, and widespread banditry. Still, it hosts some 500,000 Sudanese refugees fleeing indiscriminate attacks, summary executions, bombings, and the destruction of whole villages in neighbouring Darfur. The two conflicts are interrelated, and the human fallout can be seen in both countries. Still—inexplicably—the massive popular and political interest in Darfur stops at the Sudan/Chad border, and the international community has proven itself to be unwilling to take a regional approach to the resolution of these interlinked crises.

Ironically, the world has chosen to care about Sudan, and yet the ongoing crisis in Chad has been all but ignored by international policy makers. In contrast to this game of pick-and-choose that the international community has been content to play in the case of Chad and Sudan, the laws that protect refugees—the 1951 Convention relating to the Status of Refugees, and the Geneva Conventions—are built on the premise of common humanity, and the equal value of every human life. Similarly, the UN was built on the recognition that violent instability in any country represents a threat to international peace and security.

c. Legacy of vengeance-seeking group grievance

Based on recent or past injustices, this could date back centuries. This may include atrocities committed with impunity against communal groups and/or specific groups singled out by state authorities, or by dominant groups, for persecution or repression. That is, there is institutionalized political exclusion. Public scapegoating of groups believed to have acquired wealth, status or power as evidenced in the emergence of 'hate' radio, pamphleteering and stereotypical or nationalistic political rhetoric.

In Egypt, for instance, a range of institutions and associations are deeply engaged in battles for hegemony. While the Egyptian state may be dominant, it is not at all hegemonic. Violent opposition from Islamists, international and domestic economic pressures stemming from globalization and structural adjustment and the U.S. occupation of Iraq, an increasingly organized opposition movement, and cultural and moral critiques present challenges to the state and its legitimacy. Yet because the state and civil society are mutually constitutive of each other, though they may be analytically distinct, one cannot expect a strong civil society from a troubled state. Civil society cannot 'go it alone,' and no state can survive for long if wholly alienated from civil society (Walzer 1991:301).

d. Chronic and sustained human flight

Both the 'brain drain' and brain plunder of African professionals, intellectuals and political dissidents and voluntary emigration of 'the middle class.' Growth of exile/expat communities are also used as part of this indicator. There have been interesting trends in Senegal, Eritrea, and Somalia. In Senegal, the electorate rejected President Abdou Diouf in his quest for a fourth consecutive term. Following a highly competitive March,2000, election. Diouf peacefully conceded defeat to veteran opposition leader Abdoulaye Wade who took almost 60 percent of the votes cast. Diouf, head of the party that had governed Senegal since independence from France in 1960, became only the third elected African head of government to leave office following an election. Prior to the elections, Senegal set another precedent in February 2000, when a Senegalese court indicted Chad's exiled former dictator, Hissein Habré, on torture charges and placed him under house arrest. It was the first time that an African had been charged with atrocities in his own country by the court of another African country and represented a major step toward promoting the rule of law and breaking the cycle of impunity in Africa.

Economic Indicators

e. Uneven economic development along group lines

Determined by group-based inequality, or perceived inequality, in education, jobs, and economic status. Also measured by group-based poverty levels, infant mortality rates, education levels.

f. Sharp and/or severe economic decline

Measured by a progressive economic decline of the society as a whole (using: per capita income, GNP, debt, child mortality rates, poverty levels, business failures, a sudden drop in commodity prices, trade revenue, foreign investment or debt payments, collapse or devaluation of the national currency and a growth of hidden economies, including the drug trade, smuggling, and capital flight, failure of the state to pay salaries of government employees and armed forces or to meet other financial obligations to its citizens, such as pension payments.

Political Indicators

g. Criminalization and/or delegitimisation of the state

This attitude is characterized by endemic corruption or profiteering by ruling elites and resistance to transparency, accountability and political representation. It includes any widespread loss of popular confidence in state institutions and processes. Zimbabwe is the most dramatic illustration of a yearning for democracy and human rights, and of the dogged determination of civil society actors to engineer and orchestrate reform in Africa. Not so long ago the prospect of Zimbabwe's ruling party (ZANU_PF) losing a referendum vote and coming close to losing control of parliament would have bordered on the surreal. But that was precisely what happened. First, the Zimbabwean electorate voted down a government-sponsored constitution at a referendum in April, 2008, and two months later the ruling party-that had been thought unassailable-came close to losing its parliamentary majority were the elections to be 'free and fair.'

The June elections came in the wake of a period of unprecedented violence in which supporters of the ruling party reportedly killed nineteen people, including white farmers and opposition politicians, beat up hundreds more, raped dozens of women, and occupied more than one thousand commercial farms. At the vanguard of pressure for change was a coalition of nongovernmental forces that confronted the powers that be, questioning not only their efficacy but also their legitimacy. This was an insurrection of courageous academics, high school teachers, priests, students, lawyers, judges, citizens, all seeking to move their country closer to the ideals of democracy and respect for human rights and the rule of law. They rose to that task very effectively and pulled off a people-power revolution that achieved astonishing gains in a short span of time.

h. Progressive deterioration of public services

The deterioration is marked by a disappearance of basic state functions that serve the people, including failure to protect citizens from terrorism and violence and to provide essential services, such as health, education, sanitation, public transportation. This also entails using the state apparatus for agencies that serve the ruling elites, such as the security forces, presidential staff, central bank, diplomatic service, customs and collection agencies. South Africa is not out of the woods. The growth, employment, and redistribution (GEAR) programme implemented in previous years still failed to bring economic growth to some sectors of society, which had barely benefited or had even fallen further behind since 1994, leading to disagreement between the African National Congress (ANC) and its allies in the labour movement.

In particular, joblessness remained intractably above 30 percent. There were other major problems: crime rates remained shockingly high; 'taxi violence' between competing operators of minibus taxis remained a crime control riddle; violence against women, including sexual violence, remained alarmingly uncontrolled, with very high numbers of reported rapes; reports of police corruption and brutality were common during the year; and, despite over-congested prisons, the criminal justice system seemed unable to cope. Despite policies and laws designed to bring transformation to all sectors, implementation sometimes seemed a distant dream.

i. Widespread violation of human rights

One witnesses this in an emergence of authoritarian, dictatorial or military rule in which constitutional and democratic institutions and processes are suspended or manipulated. There are outbreaks of politically inspired (as opposed to criminal) violence against innocent civilians. A rising number of political prisoners or dissidents who are denied due process consistent with international norms and practices are commonplace. Any widespread abuse of legal, political and social rights, including those of individuals, groups or cultural institutions (e.g., harassment of the press, politicization of the judiciary, internal use of military for political ends, public repression of political opponents, religious or cultural persecution.)

j. Security apparatus as 'state within a state'

The emergence or raising of elite or praetorian guards that operate with impunity are an integral aspect of such 'National Security' states. One finds an obvious emergence of state-sponsored or state-supported private militias that terrorize political opponents, suspected 'enemies,' or civilians seen to be sympathetic to the opposition. There is an 'army within an army' that serves the interests of the dominant military or political clique; and, an emergence of rival militias, guerrilla forces or private armies in an armed struggle or protracted violent campaigns against state security forces.

k. Rise of factionalized/fractionalized elites

There is a visible fragmentation of ruling elites and state institutions along group lines. Any use of nationalistic political rhetoric by ruling elites, often in terms of communal irredentism or of communal solidarity (e.g., 'ethnic cleansing' or 'defending the faith') is welcome by elite factions. War-torn Angola has also showed signs of pressure for change. With an eye to forthcoming elections, seventeen minor opposition parties met in May, 2008, to fashion an alliance to foster opposition to the war, and advocate free and fair elections. Concurrently, Angola's churches-known to command the largest base of support in the country-formed a joint body to champion peace and national reconciliation. In Sudan too, in the face of overwhelming security obstacles, the New Sudan Council of Churches' 'People-to-People' reconciliation process held a meeting in May in conflict-ridden southern Sudan, of people on the east bank of the Nile, despite overwhelming ethnic and military impediments. The May meeting sought to build upon the positive results of the West Bank March 1999 meeting.

l. Intervention of other states or external factors

The situation attracts military or Para-military engagement in the internal affairs of the state at risk by outside armies, states, identity groups or entities that affect the internal balance of power or resolution of the conflict. Intervention by donors becomes evident, especially if there is a tendency towards over-dependence on foreign aid or peacekeeping missions.

The Democratic Republic of Congo, for instance, is the story of the deadliest war since Adolf Hitler's armies marched across Europe - a war that has not ended. But it is also the story of a trail of blood that leads directly to the whole world: to one's remote control, to one's mobile phone, to one's laptop and to one's diamond necklace. This war has been dismissed as an internal African implosion. In reality it is a battle for coltan, diamonds, cassiterite and gold, destined for sale in London, New York and Paris. It is a battle for the metals that make the technological society vibrate and ring and blind, and it has already claimed some six million lives in five years and broken a population the size of Britain's.

In Zambia, a less dramatic but nonetheless crucial development took place during the country's World Bank Consultative Group (CG) meeting. For the first time in Africa, a transparent CG meeting where all deliberations were open to independent human rights and civil society activists was convened in Lusaka in July, 2008. Building upon the experience of a previous CG meeting in Malawi when a select number of NGOs were invited to a session on human rights and governance, the Bank and a number of bilateral donors used it as a precedent to persuade the Zambian authorities of the benefits of opening up the discussions.

After strenuous objections to the participation of human rights and civil society activists, Zambia's Minister of Finance Katele Kalumba relented and agreed to have the entire meeting opened to civil society groups, both local and international, including traditionally tightly closed sessions. The human rights performance of the government was openly discussed during the meeting in the presence of NGOs. This was a significant opening given the strategic importance of a World Bank Consultative meeting to an aid-dependent government like Zambia. Seemingly, the success of the Lusaka meeting was due to good teamwork between Zambia's bilateral donors, and a new, more open team at the World Bank-reflecting a softening of the World Bank's compartmentalization of poverty reduction versus human rights, and some risk-taking by the Zambian government.

By way of a summary by the British Broadcasting Corporation (BBC)'s, 'Failed States Index 2006,' *Fund for Peace (May 2), 11* of the 20 most failed states of the 146 nations examined are in Africa. The second annual 'failed states index' was based on 'tens of thousands of articles' from different sources gathered over several months in 2005 and reviewed by experts. Each nation was given an overall score based on the 12 criteria: mounting demographic pressures; massive movement of refugees and internally displaced peoples; legacy of vengeance —seeking group grievance; chronic and sustained human flight; uneven economic development along group lines; sharp and/or severe economic decline; criminalization and delegitimization of the state; progressive deterioration of public services; widespread violation of human rights; security apparatus as 'state within a state'; rise of fragmented and factionalized elites; intervention of other states or external actors.

'Democratizing' the State in Africa and Civil Society

The post-colonial period in Africa saw nationalist aspirations for development entangled with the quest for industrialization. However, the national experiences of industrial and economic development in this era have been marked by varying degrees of disappointment. Oil-rich Nigeria (Onimode,1982) or Gabon, etc., like much of Africa, has failed to engender the levels of industrial growth and subsequent levels of development to which it aspired. Much of the explanations for Africa's disappointing record of industrial development have focused on two central factors: the structural constraints on industrial development and the policies that were pursued by THE STATE.

In many ways, these factors are inherently linked to a colonial state legacy. Africa's disappointing record of industrial and economic development cannot be divorced from its historical context. It is thus necessary to consider the extent to which the structures that were in place at the end of colonialism predetermined the pattern of development democracy that would emerge in the post-independence era. When evaluating the post-independence experience of industrial development and democratization, two specific colonial legacies stand out as decisive: 'colonial under-development' and the 'policy inheritance' of undemocratic political exclusion.

If the twentieth century was dominated by the rise and reach of the state, its close has been marked by the ascendance of civil society. Yet this long-overdue recognition of the importance of civil society has too often evolved into a simplistic equation of democracy with a strong civil society. A strong civil society, however, may not necessarily be a democratic one. For example, popular social forces have recently sought to undermine democracy in Kenya (Leys 1975) and Zimbabwe, and democratic voters have returned former authoritarian leaders to power in Uganda and Benin. Even a democratic civil society does not ensure a democratic state, but the latter is unlikely to be sustainable without the former. Democratic deficits within civil society jeopardize its ability to perform its proper social functions—and its legitimacy at home and abroad. Democracy requires not just more civil society, but better civil society.

As normal politics replaces crisis, however, civic groups that are unrepresentative or unaccountable will often lose legitimacy, become ethicized, split into factions, or simply fail to adapt to changing political circumstances—as occurred with one segment of Cameroon's human rights movement. At the system level, studies of consolidation suggest that institutionalizing civil society is a key condition for stabilizing democratic regimes. In contrast to the prevailing Cameroon norm of ethnic factionalism, Benin, a country once known as Dahomey, in West Africa is one of the few exceptions, that seems to have proceeded to legalize hence legitimate the struggle against tyranny and particularly to stand up against *coup d'états*. See art. 66 of 1990 Constitution of Benin which provides:

In the case of a coup d'état…any member of the constitutional agency shall have the right and duty to make an appeal by any means to re-establish the constitutional legitimacy…In these circumstances, for any Beninese to disobey and organize himself to put a check to the illegitimate authority shall constitute the most sacred of …duties.'

Thus promoting democracy means not only empowering civil society but also democratizing it. To proceed further, we must clearly define both civil society and democratization. A typical policy maker's definition is that civil society comprises 'human activity outside the market and the state . . . non-governmental organizations, people's organizations, trade unions, cooperatives, consumer and human rights groups, women's associations, youth clubs, the media, neighbourhood or community-based coalitions, religious groups, academic and research institutions, grassroots movements and organizations of indigenous peoples.' Yet can this motley assortment of groups—from mosques to bowling leagues, food co-ops to chambers of commerce—play a coherent political role? How can purely private groups play a democratizing role? On the other hand, if civil society is not separate from the government, how can governmental and partisan activity be disentangled from the civic realm? Where is the fine line between a political party, a social movement, a lobby, and an NGO?

Some of these issues can be resolved if we define civil society in terms of its civic role rather than its social identity: Civil society is *public* and *political* association outside the state, not a residual category or a list of types of actors. Its political role is not just to aggregate, represent, and articulate interests, but also to create citizens, to shape consciousness, and to help define what is public and political. Civic actors build 'social capital,' serve as intermediaries between the state and private citizens, and sometimes exercise delegated authority in specific issue areas (such as education, development, and resource management). In Africa, for example, the Catholic Church plays a wide range of social roles, from conflict mediation to education to human rights monitoring to lobbying for its own institutional or theological interests.

Within these bounds, civil society is often analysed by its sociological form (for example, union, NGO, or sect) rather than its political function: mobilization, contention, or institutionalization. These functions, in turn, play different roles in democratization: developing citizenship, shaping the public agenda, or changing institutions through collective action. In general, traditional social sectors such as tribes and churches shape and represent identities—developing citizenship and sometimes shaping the public agenda. Social movements are less institutionalized, but more contentious and disposed to collective action. NGOs and service providers tend to be less mobilized, but may play a greater role in building democratic institutions. Political parties, trade unions, and lobbies are generally the most mobilized, contentious, institutionalized, and oriented toward state action.

The types of organizations that have stepped in to mobilize disenfranchised workers have more voluntary membership and contentious mobilization than the corporatist unions, and often draw on a more encompassing identity base. Such organizations include binational ethnic associations for Indian migrant labourers, social movements of female garment workers, and independent teachers' unions campaigning for electoral reform.

Democratization

If civil society is more than association, democratization is more than participation. Otherwise, the democratization is 'under siege' (Mentan 2007a). The same local communities that are charged by shrinking states with taking on more responsibility for development and local governance are lynching suspected criminals in Africa (and burning alleged witches in southern Africa). Supporters of social movements that unquestionably contribute new issues and voices to the wider arena (such as ethnic-rights organizations) seldom query these movements' relationships to their own constituencies.

In other words, civil society is an important aspect of the democratic process, providing a vital link between the citizens and the state. One of the principal functions of civil society is to maintain a watchful eye on the activities of public officials. On the role of civil society movements (Rakoy 2008) in Africa where the geopolitical situation is changing rapidly, some interesting points and questions also come up, including:

- How is the position of NGOs justified, since, unlike governments, they are not elected? The answer seems to be that their role is not generic, but specific to problems affecting citizens, so it is the right of the citizens to speak up and act on them.
- Where is the possible impact of civil society?
- What is the identity of civil society?
- Civil society needs also to become more transparent and broaden its base.

Democratic Deficits Within Civil Society

One electoral process after another stumbled into difficulty. Electoral manipulation, government spending to support its own candidates, and the pervasive pro-government bias of most local media left electoral landscapes badly tilted in favour of incumbents-despite the now ubiquitous presence of election observers and their ritualized post-election reports. Angola, Ethiopia, Eritrea, Guinea, Ivory Coast, Kenya, Liberia, Sierra Leone, Sudan, Uganda, and Zambia saw stagnation or regression.

Which features of civil society impede democratization? Systematic problems of representation and accountability are present in even the most idealistic and widely supported social movements. As the stories of Rigoberta Menchú and Winnie Mandela suggest, these shortcomings are, in part, the result of the fragility of charismatic leadership and of opposition movements forged under repressive regimes. In broader terms, civic 'democratic deficits' include unclear representation, unaccountable leadership, lack of autonomy (from the state, political parties, or international forces), and lack of respect for universal human rights. While these problems should not be used as an excuse for failing to provide support for civil society, they should be taken into account when designing and implementing public policy in this area.

Representation

Whom and what do civic organizations represent? It would be unreasonable to expect an NGO to include within its membership the entire constituency that it represents. Yet there is no standardized mechanism for selecting civic leaders such as elections with universal suffrage provide for states. Civil society's constituents depend on 'political entrepreneurs,' social leaders, or outside allies to represent them. States, firms, and international organizations sometimes develop protocols to determine whether certain civic organizations are representative, such as certifying union elections. The UN's procedure for granting official recognition to NGOs examines the autonomy—but not the representativeness—of civic groups. More often, however, recognition is based on the policy maker's political goals rather than on a systematic evaluation of how well a given organization represents its constituency.

Since civic groups have no designated sphere of authority, geographically or functionally overlapping organizations may claim to represent the same populations. In one Indian region of the Ecuadoran highlands, there have been as many as 26 NGOs per community. Recently, there have been conflicts between transnational and local social movements over which of them truly represents their constituents. Exiles and locals battle for leadership of transnational campaigns for human rights in countries like Chile. Latin American environmental movements have been particularly plagued by tensions between international ecologists with global conservationist agendas and local residents with urgent development needs. Even transnational networks established to contest development projects such as World Bank dams often founder on North-South representation issues.

Furthermore, the way civil society is constructed has an influence on which social issues and identities are seen as public and political. Many civil societies privatize women's lives, in effect denying democratic representation to half the population. The deep agenda-setting power of civil society in this regard is manifest when even external democratizers led to ask why there are so few women in trade unions instead of asking why there are no public associations for women whose labour is 'privatized,' such as maids or prostitutes. Outside assistance may also have the effect of making civil society less representative by creating a gap between groups that receive assistance and those that do not. As a result of these disparities, there are differences in levels of organization, mobilization, and even identity among entire social sectors. Even among indigenous peoples' movements, for instance, small, poor rainforest populations heavily penetrated by anthropologists, missionaries, and aid workers are often more politically mobilized and visible than larger highland Indian groups categorized by states and outsiders as 'peasants.'

Accountability

If the representativeness of civil society is sometimes open to question, the accountability of its leaders is also problematic. Social movements, NGOs, and religious and ethnic groups are especially prone to personalistic leadership. This is more than just the result of the 'iron law of oligarchy'—it also reflects the small size of these organizations, the power of charismatic leadership, and the limited leadership pool. The requisites of mobilization tend to concentrate leadership quickly, especially in less developed democratizing countries, where skills and availability are scarce (Fox et al. 1989: 8-15). Civic leaders who emerge in the struggle against authoritarian rule are often less than democratic in the way they act within their own organizations; the moral certainty, persistence, resolve, and discretion necessary for survival as dissidents are not conducive to open, pragmatic, and fluid consensus-building.

Worse still, personalism makes civic groups more vulnerable to state attack (by discrediting their leaders) and more susceptible to corruption, cooptation, and partisanship. Corruption can also be a problem in civil societies. Personal venality is probably the least common form of corruption, moral or otherwise, but it is the most inimical to an organization's representativeness; when organizational resources are diverted to the leadership, legitimacy is sacrificed and civic goals may be distorted. The role of the Church, especially the Catholic Church in challenging structural problems of the state in Africa, particularly in extremely repressive periods of the 80s and 90s, requires respectful attention. The leadership provided by religious personalities such as Desmond Tutu in South Africa, Father Kaiser and Alexander Muge in Kenya, Bishop Luwum in Uganda's Idi Amin among others are deserving of mention.

Autonomy

Civic organizations can also be co-opted by their targets, thereby curtailing their capacity for contestation, interest articulation, or even mobilization. Cooptation is most commonly pursued by the state; for some regimes (like Uganda's), it is the characteristic response to challenges from civil society. In a number of states, the creation of government-sponsored NGOs confuses representation and autonomy.

THE post- colonial STATE IN AFRICA is still heavily averse to independent and autonomous agency action. Predominantly, thus such groupings have to contend with high handed state repression or subtle state manipulation. Either of such strategy is designed to mute the impact of such groupings. In particular, states in Africa are most restive when issues in the nature of civil and political rights (Mutunga and Mazrui, 2002) are raised. The states apparently prefer issues that focus on economic, social, and cultural rights. The pursuit of solidarity rights however, seems to draw the greatest measure of targeted state resistance in so far as they are seen as implicating 'national and international development' or so-called 'national security'. These solidarity rights pursuits tend and invite the state to stand in the dock on charges of totalitarian control, the reverse side of the creeds of the democratization discourse mouthed by state agents to attract foreign sympathies and aid (Mentan 2004).

Cooptation is also practiced by corporate targets of labour, environmental, or human rights mobilization. For example, one Ogoni rights group is now funded by the oil company (to secure off-shore carting away of oil unnoticed by the Nigerian authorities) against whose incursions it was originally formed to protest. Civic groups that lack internal democracy are the most vulnerable to cooptation, since capture is most likely when leadership is personalistic and unaccountable. As with organizational hypertrophy, cooptation hinders representation most when the group's goals include contestation and least when they centre on the provision of services.

Dependency

Today, authoritarian regimes in Africa increasingly are being challenged across the continent. Nevertheless, emerging democratic governments confront a legacy of poverty, illiteracy, militarization, and underdevelopment produced by incompetent or corrupt governments. New demands being placed on African nations by international donor institutions as well as heightened individual expectations for better lives are difficult to be met by the nascent democracies.

This is why contemporary authoritarian regimes in Africa have taken a number of forms. They fall within the general models of one-party systems, personal dictatorships, and military regimes. The postcolonial trend toward one-party systems in Africa was justified on a number of grounds, including the alleged tradition of a single unchallenged chief, the idea of a democratic majority expressed through a single party, and the need for unity in the face of ethnic, linguistic, and cultural differences. Competitive politics was rejected as an imported luxury neither needed nor affordable in developing countries. In Malawi, for example, the idea of an opposition was rejected on quasi-theological grounds: 'There is no opposition in Heaven. God himself does not want opposition…'

One concern is dependence of African civil rights movements on international support. Yet while states may cite the potential threat to sovereignty from civil society's international ties, this objection is valid only if states themselves eschew foreign assistance, and only insofar as foreign support threatens the state's monopoly of coercion. More often, global civic links merely affect the state's monopoly of information, development resources, or representation. This diversification of access to information, resources, and organization is a crucial component of democratization.

Furthermore, international support may be necessary for democratization under two sets of circumstances. First, when domestic groups do not have the resources to mobilize effectively to articulate citizen interests, international resources may be needed to 'level the playing field' between citizens and the state. Without the support of foreign funders such as Global Exchange, the Honduran peasant movement would not have the resources needed for transportation to regional organizing meetings, government offices, or squatter sites. In this kind of situation, foreign support would lead to dependency only if it distorted an organization's goals or exerted an undue influence over its decision making.

Second, civic groups and their goals are increasingly transnational. It is natural and proper for a border-spanning ethnic group or environmental NGO addressing global issues to mobilize transnationally—there are both environmental and Indian rights groups that appropriately span the Amazon basin. More generally, the resources, goals, and decision making of civic groups may be intertwined with those of foreign supporters through transnational networks and global memberships (.Margaret E. Keck and Kathryn Sikkink, 1997). This will produce interdependence rather than dependence: The transnational network may include peer groups (like Hillaire Kamga's pan-African good government group, *Conscience Africaine, in Cameroon*), and the Southern partners in North-South alliances may provide some resources and exercise some control (as in Oxfam partnerships).

Partisanship

Party affiliation poses another dilemma for civic organizations, since it enhances effectiveness while diminishing public legitimacy. Although there is nothing inherently illegitimate about party affiliation, there is always the danger that partisan ideology will subsume civic goals or representation—especially when party connections are unacknowledged. To some extent, these fears flow from Cold War histories of covert civic sponsorship on both sides. When civic groups are tied to ruling parties, the issue of partisanship is akin to that of cooptation. Support from foreign or transnational political parties raises the spectre of dependency.

Even NGO support for (or from) domestic opposition parties can be tainted by these parties' role as contenders for state power. Yet civic goals may naturally lead to or flow from a larger critical consciousness associated with a universal ideology. Human rights activists, for example, may adopt a leftist analysis linking repression to underlying structural inequalities. And social movements that found their own parties—like the European Greens, the Brazilian Workers' Party, or the Bolivian Indian rights movement (the Katarista party)—are generally applauded.

Human Rights

Failure to respect universal human rights mars the democratic character of civil society. Some civic groups may be representative of constituencies whose goals are in some way anti-democratic: discriminatory, exclusionary, hegemonic, or even violent. What about a military officers' club that lobbies against human rights reform? A coca growers' union that blockades police? A radical student group that promotes political change 'by any means necessary'? An exile group that monitors human rights at home but funds violence abroad? Should civil society be held accountable to the same human rights norms as states? What if deviations from universal norms reflect cultural differences and the heritage of the group represented (as is often claimed by indigenous activists)?

Democracy rests on pluralism, and respect for universal human rights enhances both the experience and the pursuit of pluralism. For this and other reasons, a growing international consensus subjects all political actors to universal human rights standards. International human rights monitors now include the behaviour of rebel movements in their assessments. Even citizens engaged in wholly private behaviour must respect human rights, though the state bears ultimate responsibility for regulating their behaviour (as a legitimating condition of its monopoly of coercion). Thus self-determination for citizens, as for states, is always limited by human rights standards. These standards, however, apply to behaviour, not to political opinion or identity.

Finally, it is important to recognize that there are frequent, and perhaps inherent, contradictions among the various democratizing roles of civil society. Larry Diamond (1995: 48) lists a spectrum of desirable roles that includes scrutinizing the state, educating citizens, increasing participation, promoting tolerance, representing interests, training leaders, monitoring elections, and 'generating democratic constituencies for market reforms.' As we have seen, however, representing interests may not promote tolerance, and training leaders may be at odds with increasing participation. As market reforms generate increasing resistance and 'IMF riots' among impoverished majorities throughout Africa, broad representation and popular accountability may often conflict with economic liberalization. Pluralist optimists can envision a healthy division of labour in which different civic groups promote distinct democratizing goals, but civic stalemate and polarization are equally likely outcomes. In the era of democratic consolidation, the old image of relatively unified societies coming together to challenge the state must be modified to incorporate these civic contradictions.

Despite its shortcomings, civil society is a key site for democratization, and civic actors are growing in importance. International agencies, national governments, foreign funders, and transnational NGOs are already involved in shaping civil society through funding, regulating, training, and subcontracting with civic organizations. How can these supporters of civil society help to democratize it? They can do so by strengthening the same qualities in civil society that build democracy at the state level: *transparency, accountability, checks and balances, periodic consultation with constituencies, pluralistic goals,* and *respect for human dignity.* To be truly democratic, such measures should also incorporate the greatest possible level of participation from African organizations in standard-setting, monitoring, popular education, and implementation.

Transparency

The first requirement for deepening democracy within civil society is to secure better information about civic organizations and local cultures. In many cases, a simple mapping of organizations, their membership, and their claims to be representative is a necessary prerequisite. In Africa, Welch (1995: 184) observes:

'Millions of refugees and displaced persons eke out wretched lives in squalid camps. African women continue to labour longer and with far less reward than African men…Clogged court systems seem to apply one brand of justice for the few who can afford lawyers, another brand of justice for many with limited funds or knowledge. Despite veneers of democratization, transparency and accountability in government operations remain limited.'

For funders, statements of NGO goals and lists of accomplishments should be supplemented by analyses that emphasize the *quality* of participation, mobilization, or services. Above all, civic groups' budgets and funding sources must be public, clear, and widely accessible to all parties. This may include outside audits of civil groups (perhaps by transnational organizations like Transparency International). Funders may combine such scrutiny with incentive plans that recognize the challenges of civic mobilization in diverse environments. To this end, supportive states, funders, and transnational networks should make it a priority to improve civic groups' capacities to receive, gather, and transmit information, both internally and externally. In this respect, freedom of the press and the alternative media play a crucial role in deepening democracy.

Accountability

Democracy also requires clear and consistent standards of accountability. The articulation of such standards must eventually be linked to consequences for organizational funding or recognition, but even initial standard-setting provides a useful benchmark as well as a starting point for dialogue between outsiders and civic organizations. The democratic character of civic groups, like that of other political organizations, can be assessed by their autonomy, breadth of representation, accountability to constituents, and institutionalization. Assessment of these characteristics may be useful when civic groups contend for outside recognition by intergovernmental organizations, funders, or foreign counterparts.

Nongovernmental international networks could provide universal norms and peer monitoring for internal leadership-selection processes (a civic version of election monitoring or union certification). This would merely systematize and publicize a process that already occurs among international NGO networks, which informally rely on local gatekeepers such as the Catholic Church, transnational groups like Cultural Survival, and Northern academics to assess the effectiveness and democratic character of Latin American civic organizations. Another useful measure would be to supplement leadership training with membership training, in order to develop an internal constituency for civic accountability.

Checks and balances

Introducing civic checks and balances requires diversifying social forces without splintering them. To minimize clientelism, funders, state agencies delegating tasks, and advocacy networks seeking local partners should strive to emphasize issues rather than relationships. This will mean greater and more transparent competition, especially in urban and more developed sectors. The least developed countries and weakest social sectors, however, may be barely capable of generating a single association to address any given issue. Moreover, frequent changes or even frequent reassessment of relationships may jeopardize programme goals in environments with low 'social capital.'

An example of an unexpected 'civil society' reaction to attempts to limit communication, by fate or design, could serve to illuminate the issue of expansion of political space by such mass action through popular checks and balances. On 19 September 2003, mobile phone subscribers in Nigeria took the unprecedented step of switching off their handsets en masse. The subscribers took this symbolic step in protest against perceived exploitation by the existing mobile phone companies. Among other things, they were angered by allegedly exorbitant tariffs, poor reception, frequent and unfavourable changes in contract terms, and arbitrary reduction of credits.

Among other critical questions, the protest helped bring into focus the following: How is (mobile) technology shaping the democratic momentum in Nigeria? How useful is technology as a mechanism for socio-economic empowerment? The boycott can be appraised, first, in the context of existing mistrust between citizens and transnational big business in Nigeria; and second, against the background of difficult state-society intercourse which has mostly been characterized by the latter's suspicion of the state's connivance with the corporate establishment. Furthermore, because it gives 'civil society' a combined cause and instrument of protest, mobile phones in the Nigerian context appear to presage the emergence of a new social space of politics and agitation. This example underscores an ordinarily subsumed 'class' dimension to the protest. It eloquently illustrates how a struggle about the interests of a section of 'civil society' may have a potential for enlarging the larger 'political space'.

Pluralism

A more constructive policy for funders may be the direct promotion of civic pluralism, focusing on areas where greater diversity of associations or approaches will contribute the most to democratization. For example, outsiders may help to level the playing field *within* civil society by providing preferential support to new vehicles for historically underrepresented sectors, as the Inter-American Foundation did in its cultural-promotion programmes. Democratizers can also provide grassroots-oriented leadership training to diversify the pool of civic organizers and broaden the base of existing organizations.

Consultation

Outsiders should encourage NGOs to engage in periodic consultation with their constituencies on such matters as leadership, goals, strategies, and representative status. This will help moderate the tendency toward personalistic leadership and generally improve accountability and legitimacy. Funders may even require such consultation as a condition of support, as long as such conditionality is universal and designed in partnership with civic organizations. Yet only a few African states seem likely to enforce such a requirement in a credible, non-discriminatory, and no repressive fashion, so it is not yet appropriate to incorporate civic consultation in the criteria for state recognition. Efforts at civic grassroots consultations are essential. And, where possible, such consultations should be monitored and incorporate constituencies beyond the direct membership.

Summary and Conclusion

THECOLONIAL STATE IN AFRICA made three major claims.

- In its framework of local administration and justice, carried out by African intermediaries under European supervision, the colonial state purported to supply 'good government.'
- The colonial state asserted its performance of a 'civilizing mission,' in sponsoring introduction of European culture. The culture-dispensing function was in good part carried out by Christian missions, except in Islamic zones where their presence was unwelcome.

- The colonial state, as self-appointed trustee for the subjugated populace and mankind in general, charged itself with developing the natural resources. This responsibility was entrusted to the metropolitan private sector, often induced by large concession, state-assured supply of labour, and fiscal advantages.

After World War II, colonialism in Africa was placed on the defensive by nationalist forces and the international environment. Global politics was now dominated by the Soviet Union and the United States, who had no ultimate stake in perpetuating European rule. The colonial experience in Africa was distinctive in several ways. Africa was the last continent to fall under direct European rule; colonial administrations were organized at a historical moment when the state had far greater resources (communications, military technology, professional bureaucracies) than had been available in earlier centuries. The revenue imperative and absence of established fiscal machinery (like the land tax, which supported colonial administrations in Asia), led to forcible restructuring of rural economies, to compel or induce African labour into a cash economy that could provide subsistence for the colonial state. Culturally, Africa was held in low esteem by its colonizers. Colonial conquest of Africa coincided with an outburst of evangelical fervour in Europe and North America. Usually supported by the colonial state, the Christian mission societies deployed more personnel than the state administration, and had profound influence as vehicles not only for proselytizing, but also for diffusing European cultural values.

Although broad similarities marked colonial influence, there were important variations. The several colonial powers in Africa applied somewhat different doctrines of administration. These reflected the political culture of the home country and the character of its own state institutions. For France, Germany, and Belgium the concept of the state was shaped by the absolutist tradition, which stressed centralization, hierarchy, and bureaucratic dominance. At home, this culture was overlain with nineteenth-century notions of constitutionalism, which were stripped away in designing state structures for conquered African domains. The British state had a distinctly different texture, with looser structure, greater diffusion of power, and more regional variation and autonomy.

A second major legacy of the colonial state was organized as a structure of institutionalizing alien rule; its vocation was domination of a subjugated population. A command mentality, a paternalistic mode of rule, a hegemonic relationship with the populace: these attributes of the colonial state are deeply ingrained in the daily routines of administration. Legally and practically, the colonial state considered the indigenous populace as subjects, not citizens.

A third crucial effect of the colonial state lay in the process by which it yielded power to African successor regimes. One by one, in the three decades following World War II, colonial powers became persuaded that nationalism was an irresistible force. In a handful of cases, this conclusion was forced upon the colonizer by prolonged armed struggle (Algeria, 1954 to 1962; Guinea-Bissau, 1961 to 1974; Mozambique, 1964 to 1975; Angola, 1961 to 1975; Zimbabwe, 1973 to 1979). In most instances the withdrawing power recognized the need for accommodation with nationalist forces by negotiation. Once this conclusion was reached, the colonial power retained considerable means to influence the terms and method of decolonization in the face of a rising tide of nationalist protests in Africa that vigorously and at times violently challenged the legitimacy of alien occupation.

The formula for decolonization generally called for creating political institutions closely modelled on the colonizing power's constitutional structure (Mentan 2007). The formal institutions of constitutional democracy-elected parliaments, competitive parties, and politically recruited cabinet-were hastily grafted onto the authoritarian bureaucratic colonial state. Yet in the home countries this process was a long and gradual one, before constitutional democracy was institutionalized. African states were asked to make an instantaneous transition from colonial subjugation to representative democracy. Enormous difficulties arose, and in most the initial constitutional structures failed to survive. It is no accident that popular commitment to democratic values and insistence on a competitive party system appear most strongly rooted in Nigeria, where African political participation and expression began early.

The French, in keeping with the centralist ideology of the French state, permitted modest but very visible African representation in the French National Assembly in Paris long before an African voice was tolerated in Africa itself. A Senegalese leader, Blaise Diagne, entered the French Parliament in 1913 and served as junior minister in four French cabinets. Not until 1956 were territorial assemblies with significant power created in French-ruled tropical Africa. The Belgians prohibited African political activity until urban elections in 1957 and parties were not tolerated until 1959, the year before independence. The African leadership that succeeded to power has, to varying degrees, endeavoured to eradicate this heritage. the inertia of the colonial state tradition is powerful, however, and continues to colour state-society relationships.

The Kenyan case is worth mentioning here. In November 2005 Kenyans went to the polls to vote for or against a draft constitution, a majority rejecting the proposed document. This marked the most recent stage in a long-drawn-out process. Kenya's (still) existing constitution had been drawn up at its own Lancaster House Conference in London in 1962 and had been in force though under threat at some crisis moments since Independence in 1963. The only significant amendments to it were the move to a one-party system in the 1970s and then, under after widespread demonstrations and sustained pressure from civil society - and from international donors' threats - the amendment in 1992 to allow registration of other parties. This latter change heralded in a new period of civic political activity and competitive parliamentary and presidential elections in 1992, 1997 and 2002. But like the other few changes it only amended one small part (Section 2A in this case) of the overall document.

Decades after independence, and despite the 'development agendas' of the State, a majority of African citizens have been untouched by the economic progress and social reforms boasted by State institutions. The fault lies with the institutionalization of the patrimonial/neo-patrimonial/personalist rule. Moreover, civil society is still mired in the hierarchical feudal relationships that define the stagnation of the social arena. Modernization has been restricted to the economic arena, with socio-cultural and political reform absent.

The State today, wherever it exists, is still powerful, and civil society looks to it for guidance. During the post–independence era, the state appropriated many functions of civil society and it is now loath to let go for fear of diminishing its stature. Having lost its creative and associational edge, civil society must work hard to rebuild it. The reason is simple. The patrimonial/nationalist/welfare state is not a neutral actor that can be taken to task and brought back to play its role more efficiently without any reference to the social setting in which it operates. Civil society in Africa is not inherently virtuous; it is also fractured from within on class/ethnic lines. Good governance thus does not only mean reforming the state; the reformation of society and economy also need to be simultaneously undertaken.

Although on May 13, 2000, the *Economist*, the venerable and influential magazine of the global English-speaking political classes, dubbed the continent 'Hopeless Africa,' yet beyond the ubiquitous images of mayhem, positive, though less 'newsworthy,' changes have been evolving at the societal level. Thanks to discernible changes in public attitudes and less willingness to accept the inevitability of authoritarian rule, it was at the grassroots that the most promising battles were being waged for a more humane Africa.

Human rights groups, churches, academics, and other civil society activists demonstrated an uncommon resolve, courage and willingness to put their lives on the line to resist repression and lead the push among nongovernmental actors for transparency, participation, and accountability. None of the authoritarian/patrimonial/personalist and anti-democratic forces seem likely to blunt the fundamental forces that had driven the switch from criminalized rule to democratic civilian government. The passage to democracy is certainly rough but would stay the course, even in Egypt, Zimbabwe, Algeria, Cameroon, Gabon, etc.

Section Four

The Future as Epilogue

Preview

History has stripped Africa's people of the dignity of building their nations on their own indigenous values, institutions, and heritage. The modern African state is the product of Europe, not Africa. To attempt at this late date to return to ancestral identities and resources as bases for building the modern African nation would risk the collapse of many countries. At the same time, to disregard ethnic realities would be to build on loose sand, also a high-risk exercise. Is it possible to consolidate the framework of the modern African state while giving recognition and maximum utility to the component elements of ethnicities, cultures, and aspirations for self-determination?

There is a general consensus that Africa entered the twenty-first century plagued by multifaceted crises of underdevelopment evidenced by, among other things, abject poverty, the inadequacy of basic human needs, social stresses and tensions in the various major urban centres, environmental degradation and the devastating effects of violent civil conflicts. While there is no doubt that slavery and colonialism have contributed to the continent's predicament, the failure of the neo-colonial state, its custodians and the other sectors of the African ruling classes to formulate and implement a pro-people, pro-development and pro-democracy national development agenda is the proximate cause of the region's precarious conditions. Clearly, in order to reverse the negative effects of Africa's peripheral status and role in the global order during the previous millennia and to set the continent on the path of holistic democracy and development, the neo-colonial state must be demolished.

Chapter Twelve

Future of the State in Africa in an Era of Neoliberal Globalization

Overview

Capitalism has always had a world–wide dimension, whose forms are historically determined. The notion that the present historical phase is one of nomadic, de–territorialized and global capitalisms distorts reality, and constitutes the global projection of neo–classicism. The 'Fordist' era is thus reduced to the sum of national economies, while the world–wide dimension is now supposed to be an immediate, reified datum. The world–wide dimension is, on the contrary, an uneven and unstable process, generated by the articulation of different spatial levels, by the contradictions, crises and conflicts shaping them.

That is why one should also pinpoint the internal, class–conflict related reasons which drove the dominant States down the road of financial and commercial liberalization, of a re–definition of social and economic policies, and of the creation of regional areas. The reason why 'globalization' is neither an absolute nor an irreversibly total datum is also related to contradictions surviving in liberalization processes and between imperial States and subordinate areas. Due to unequal and combined development, 'Nation'–States, especially those in Africa, are still the main arena of social conflict: there is still room for politics, precisely because capitalism is not an abstract, de–territorialized and immediately global quantity. This is the growing role of the African Nation–State, as a process leading to the latter's marginalization in relation to emerging new 'global' functions of control and regulation by global capital. The state in Africa should thus be viewed in the context of the processes and cyclical interpretation of capitalism's dynamics, shaped by phases of deep restructuring and phases of stabilization, diffusion of new relationships, and periods marked by different roles played by the client African State and its machinery.

Introduction

Any state exists in relationship to the social formation which it serves to reproduce. However, it is evident that a state can take a number of different forms. Hence, Fernando Enrique Cardoso has proposed a conceptual distinction between state and regime. A regime refers to the 'rules of the game' which link political institutions and govern the ties between citizens and rulers. A state, on the other hand, refers to the basic alliance or 'pact of domination that exists among social classes or fractions of dominant classes and the norms which guarantee their dominance over the subordinate strata.'

The state's pact of domination determines which social forces control and whose interests prevail in a given political order; the regime form merely establishes the political procedures and institutions through which the dominant coalition exercises its power. It is thus possible for any state—that is, any pact of domination—to become reified under a number of different regime forms, including democracy or authoritarianism, depending upon the requisites for maintaining the structure of domination.

States in Africa are by nature dependent and capitalist. They emerge from and reproduce the social formation of dependent capitalism, which shapes the underlying pact of domination. The dominant coalition of dependent capitalism is composed principally of foreign capital and the national bourgeoisie, in particular that sector of the national bourgeoisie with the strongest links to international financial and industrial capital. Under an authoritarian regime form, the dependent capitalist state forcibly excludes and subordinates other social sectors; under democratic forms, the political order is more inclusive, and subordination more veiled and subtle.

Generally, the preferred form of the dependent capitalist state in Africa today would be electoral democracy, whereby the pact of domination would be less evident than under authoritarianism. Authoritarian repression is an inherently blunt and unwieldy instrument with which to enforce the political and economic exclusion of subordinate social strata. Such manifest exclusion makes it virtually impossible to legitimize the regime within the subordinate strata of society, leading to the creation of a permanent regime opposition, and the reliance upon coercion and repression may well undermine the legitimacy of the state's dominant coalition itself. Ideally, electoral democracy would allow a less blatant, more subtle, and more legitimate form of domination. Indeed, the reality of domination may be obfuscated by the forms and procedures of electoral democracy—formal equality before the law, open electoral competition for the staffing of government, and liberties for the articulation and organization of dissenting positions.

To be stable, a democratic regime form would have to be capable of containing threats to the dominant coalition of the dependent capitalist state. The policies of political parties that prevail in electoral contests would have to be compatible with the interests of the dominant coalition, in particular respect for private property and the maintenance of conditions conducive to accumulation. Parties transcending such parameters would have to be kept at a minority status, and their mobilization of subordinate strata contained at a level short of that required for electoral victory or substantial influence over policy formation. Additionally, strikes, demonstrations, property seizures, and other types of popular mobilization and pressure would have to be contained at a level where they would not threaten political order or capital accumulation.

Such stability would appear to be predicated upon the existence of one or both of the following conditions. First, the prevailing social formation would allow the dominant coalition to represent a broad spectrum or even an absolute majority of the total population. That is, the dominant coalition would not be restricted to a tiny, isolated elite sector of society, thus facilitating domination of the electoral process. Second, subordinate social sectors would grant legitimacy to the social formation and its established hierarchy. In Gramscian terms, the dominant coalition would exercise 'ideological hegemony' over subordinate social sectors; lower classes would believe that the prevailing order is just and proper, or that their own interests could be advanced, either as individuals or as classes or class fractions, within the established social formation. As such, subordinate sectors would relinquish opportunities to alter the basic social structure through the electoral process or other forms of democratic mobilization.

A mixture of these conditions is generally present in advanced capitalist societies with relatively stable democratic regimes. In these societies, although the means of production may be highly concentrated in a few hands, large middle classes with political, economic, and ideological ties to the bourgeoisie serve as a buffer between the dominant and subordinate sectors. The industrial working class represents a minority of the population, and substantial sectors of the working class fall under the ideological hegemony of the bourgeoisie. Therefore, democratic procedures pose little threat of altering the social formation or the state's dominant coalition, and political order is relatively easy to maintain.

However, conditions are much different within the social formation of dependent capitalism in Africa. The dominant coalition tends to be tiny internationalized elite, and national legitimacy may be undermined by external linkages or domination. The middle class is generally small in comparison to the working class, the peasantry, and rural and urban marginalized sectors. The ideological hegemony of the dominant coalition is often tenuous; ideological currents hostile to the social formation of dependent capitalism are common among students, intellectuals, and sectors of organized labour, and even filter down on occasion to the peasantry. Additionally, some sectors sympathetic to a capitalist social formation may nevertheless reject the prevailing dominant coalition of the dependent capitalist state, particularly if the traditional landed oligarchy of foreign capital are prominent members of the coalition.

Hence, the dominant coalitions in Africa's dependent capitalist societies have been less successful than their counterparts in advanced capitalist societies at preventing threats to their hegemony from emerging within the democratic process. Frequently, the liberties associated with democratic procedures—the opportunities for the mobilization and articulation of lower class demands and channels for electoral influence—have come to be viewed as threatening by the dominant coalitions. Frequently, they have been able to find allies within the military establishments and the middle classes when popular mobilization and demands threaten social and political order. Where lower-class mobilization, political turmoil, or ideological radicalization have threatened the reproduction of the dependent capitalist social formation or its structure of domination, democratic procedures have been quickly discarded to enforce the political and economic deactivation of the popular sectors. The structure of domination which underpins the dependent capitalist state is thus maintained by shifting from a democratic to an authoritarian regime form.

The wave of authoritarianism which struck Africa in the 1960s and 1970s—with a few exceptions, such as the reformist military government which came to power in Ghana and Nigeria in 1966—was directed toward such a deactivation and exclusion of the subordinate strata, and hence toward the reinforcement of the states' dominant coalitions against pressures from the lower classes. The process of lower-class exclusion and deactivation was the common denominator which linked such diverse forms of authoritarianism as the bureaucratic authoritarianism of the relatively modernized societies of Eastern Africa like Kenya and the traditional military dictatorships in the less developed societies of Central and West Africa.

Throughout Africa, industrialization and social modernization in the post-World War II era led to the emergence of new middle- and working-class sectors which demanded the right to participate in the political life of their societies. Furthermore, their demands for land and income redistribution, higher wages, and social programmes threatened the property rights and accumulation potential of the dominant coalitions. Populist democratic regimes in such countries as Guinea, Congo, and Zaire were buffeted by high inflation, serious balance of payments deficits, and economic stagnation. Populist political parties, peasant and labour unions, and progressive sectors of the church encouraged the mobilization of the lower classes; authoritarianism served as the bulwark against the capture of the state by such forces through the mechanisms of popular democracy, and helped to restore the conditions of social and political stability that were requisites for capital accumulation and economic growth.

Future of the Client-collaborator State in Africa

Under the impact of diverse processes referred to as 'globalization' states cede authority to supra-national and sub-national levels of government as well as to non-hierarchical spheres of governance. But states also take on new functions in organizing and steering the emerging trans-border governance processes. A restructured territorial state, which is no longer of the Keynesian national welfare type, remains central to the management of capitalism.

Lively debates over the future of the nation-state resurfaced in the 1980s as scholars and politicians began to suggest that it was now too small to solve the world's big problems and too big to solve its little ones. Among the most frequently cited problems were: (1) the rise of an uncontrolled and possibly uncontrollable global capitalism, (2) the emergence of a global risk society, (3) the challenge to national politics from the politics of identity and new social movements based on local and/or transnational issues; and, more recently, (4) the threat of new forms of terrorism and decentralized network warfare.

But there is little agreement about what these problems mean for the state— especially as such challenges are politically constructed and contested. Prognoses include the rise of a single global Empire; a western conglomerate state centred on the United States; a series of supranational states modelled on the European Union; the rise of a fragmented neo-medieval state system; a shift from largely state-based government to network-based governance; the re-scaling of the powers of the national state upwards, downwards, or outwards; and minor incremental changes in secondary aspects of the nation-state that leave its primary features intact. This paper reviews some major changes in the postwar state in advanced capitalist societies and relates them to other changes, including the increasing integration of the world market. But it first offers six clarifications regarding what is really at stake in the debate over globalization and the future of the state.

Some Clarifications

First, all forms of state are based on the territorialization of political power. A formally sovereign national state exercising control over a large territorial area is only a relatively recent institutional expression of state power. It results from a specific, socially constructed division of the global political order into many territorially exclusive, mutually recognizing, and mutually legitimating, sovereign states.

Other modes of organizing political power on a territorial basis existed before the rise of this Westphalian system (e.g., city-states, the medieval state system, absolutism, and traditional empires); and other modes have co-existed with it and/or may be superseding it (e.g., modern imperial-colonial blocs, supranational alliances such as the European Union, or complex post-national polities associations with variable geometries). Thus, even if we accept that globalization challenges the national state as one mode of territorialization of political power, it does not follow that political power will cease to assume some territorial form or another. Indeed, rather than simply withering away or being entirely superseded by non-territorial forms of organizing political power (e.g., a series of global or international regimes addressed to specific functional problems), the evidence points to continuing attempts to redesign and/or rescale territorial statehood in response to current challenges.

Second, we should distinguish between the national state and the nation-state. The territorial organization of power long preceded nation-formation and, whereas territorial statehood is now almost universal, nation-statehood is not. The latter can also have different, potentially overlapping, sometimes antagonistic bases. These include ethnic identity, based on a socially constructed ethnonational community (e.g., Germany); a cultural nation based on a shared national culture that may well be defined and actively promoted by the state itself (e.g., France); and a civic nation based on patriotic commitment to the constitution and belief in the legitimacy of representative government (e.g., the USA).

These three forms can reinforce each other (e.g., Denmark), be combined in a hybrid multinational state (e.g., mainland Britain), or provoke conflicts over the proper basis of the nation-state (e.g., Canada, New Zealand). Pressures exist to grant significant autonomy to regionally-based national minorities (e.g., Spain) or institute consociational ' forms of government to share power between nations in a given state (e.g., Belgium, New Zealand). Initially, then, we should consider how these challenges affect the national state form rather than different forms of nation-state.'

Third, addressing the future of national and/or nation-states requires us to look beyond the state. The latter does not normally exist in majestic isolation overseeing its own society but is more or less embedded in a wider political system, other institutional orders, and civil society. Thus state transformation involves the redrawing of the multiple „lines of difference between the state and its environment(s) as states (and the social forces they represent) redefine their priorities, expand or reduce their activities, rescale them in the light of new challenges, modify the relation between different branches and apparatuses, seek greater autonomy or develop forms of power-sharing, and disembed or re-embed specific state institutions and practices within the social order. This holds for the international as well as national dimensions of state relations. Even the dominant, neo-liberal form of globalization continues to depend heavily on state institutions and practices at many different territorial scales.

Fourth, and relatedly, even in the most liberal economies, states are actively involved in shaping economic life. There is no absolute institutional separation between the political (the domain of the state) and the economic (the domain of the market). The market economy is also embedded in an ensemble of extra-economic institutions and practices that are essential for its operation. The state plays a key role here not only in securing the general institutional framework for profit-oriented, market-mediated economic activities but also in shaping their specific forms, organization, and overall dynamic. This is reflected in growing academic and practical interest in the intimate relation between forms of state and political regime and varieties of capitalism and in the various complementarities and contradictions among these different local and national varieties within a changing global economy. Thus even the dominant, neo-liberal form of globalization continues to depend heavily on state institutions and practices at many different territorial scales and in many different functional areas and on the survival of other ways of organizing capital accumulation both within and beyond the dominant neo-liberal economies.

Fifth, globalization is not a single causal mechanism with a universal, unitary logic but is multicentric, multiscalar, multitemporal, multiform, and multicausal. It is better seen as a hypercomplex, continuously evolving product of many processes. As such it does not generate a single, uniform set of pressures on all states but affects them in different ways. Indeed, it is not the State as such (sovereign or otherwise) that is pressured by globalization (or other challenges). For the many social forces and mechanisms that generate globalization can only exert pressure on—or, indeed, strengthen— particular forms of state with particular state capacities and liabilities. Moreover, in so doing, they modify the balance of forces within states and create space for, and prompt, struggles to reorganize state forms and capacities in order to meet these challenges.

Sixth, and consequently, questions about globalization and the state should not be posed in zero-sum terms. At its worse, this involves an untenable contrast between a singular, emergent, borderless flow-based economy able to operate globally in real time and a plurality of formally equivalent traditional national territorial states qua 'power containers' that operate within defined territorial frontiers and according to heavily time-consuming political routines. This contrast errs in two ways. On the one hand, it misrepresents the actual complexities of globalization, ignores the extent to which it depends on changing place-based competitive advantages, neglects the general dependence of economic activities on extra-economic supports that are place—and time—bound, and, of course, overstates the extent of the global economy, even in regard to financial capital, let alone industrial and commercial capital. It also ignores the significant degree to which the unfolding economic logic (and illogic) of globalization constrains individual firms, branches, and clusters as well as the operations of the political system.

On the other hand, despite the formal equivalence among sovereign states in the modern state system, as signified, for example, by membership of the United Nations, not all states are equally capable of exercising power internally and/or internationally. They face different problems at home and abroad; have different histories; have different capacities to address these problems and reorganize themselves in response in international as well as domestic matters. Moreover, just as the economy has important territorial dimensions (reflected in concepts such as industrial districts, agglomeration economies, global cities, and regional or national capitalisms), so states also operate as power *connectors* within various global systems as well as power *containers*.

And, while not even the USA has an effective global reach and the ability to compress its routines to match those of hypermobile capital, many states have proved capable of reorganizing their routines to modify the impact of economic processes. Given these arguments, we should focus on the changing organization of politics and economics and their respective institutional embodiments and see frontiers and borders as actively reproduced and contingent rather than as pregiven and fixed. I will illustrate this approach by exploring:

- changes in the form of postwar state typical of postwar western capitalist economies;
- broad changes in six key dimensions of the state;
- and the temporal pressures currently facing the state and its responses thereto.

The Keysian National Welfare State

This essay cannot consider recent changes in all forms of state in the interstate system. Instead it focuses on changes in the Keynesian national welfare state (or KNWS). This is the form of state that became dominant in North Western Europe, North America, Australia, and New Zealand during the 1950s to 1970s and that was closely linked with the postwar Fordist growth dynamic based on mass production and mass consumption. Obviously, there are important differences among the states in these countries but there are enough similarities to justify describing them in terms of an ideal-typical (or stylized) state form.

Each term in this four-dimensional ideal type refers to a major aspect of state involvement in securing continued capitalist expansion and, in this sense, it interprets the state from a broadly economic perspective. This is not the only way to examine changes in the state; adopting alternative entry points would highlight other aspects of state transformation or, indeed, reveal some continuities in state forms. But my approach does provide a benchmark for assessing some key recent changes.

First, in promoting the conditions for profitable economic growth, the KNWS was distinctively *Keynesian* insofar as it aimed to secure full employment in a relatively closed national economy and did so mainly through demand-side management and nationwide infrastructural provision. Second, in contributing to the day-to-day, lifetime, and intergenerational reproduction of the population, KNWS social policy had a distinctive *welfare* orientation insofar as it (a) instituted economic and social rights for all citizens so that they could share in growing prosperity (and contribute to high levels of demand) even if they were not employed in the high-wage, high-growth Fordist economic sectors; and (b) promoted forms of collective consumption favourable to the Fordist growth dynamic.

Third, the KNWS was *national* insofar as these economic and social policies were pursued within the historically distinctive matrix of a national economy, a national state, and a society seen as comprising national citizens. Within this nationally-organized matrix it was the national territorial state that was mainly held responsible for developing and guiding Keynesian welfare policies. Local and regional states acted mainly as relays for policies framed at the national level; and the leading international regimes established after WW2 were mainly intended to restore stability to national economies and national states. And, fourth, the KNWS was *statist* insofar as state institutions (on different levels) were the chief supplement and corrective to market forces in a 'mixed economy' concerned with economic growth and social integration. Whereas denationalization concerns the territorial dispersion of the national state's activities, destatization redraws the 'public-private' divide and modifies the relationship between organizations and tasks across this divide on whatever territorial scale(s).

There was never a pure KNWS. It assumed different national forms within the broader international framework of Atlantic Fordism. This is reflected in distinctions between, for example, Germany's 'flexi-Fordism,' France's statist Fordism, and Sweden's social democratic Fordism. Nor has there been a generic crisis that affects all national cases in the same way. Nonetheless, they have all faced similar pressures. The first signs of crisis in Fordist growth emerged in the mid-1970s and worsened in the 1980s. In addition, the structured coherence of a nationally-scaled economy-state-society was weakened by changes associated with globalization, internationalization, the rise of multi-tiered global city networks, the formation of triad economies (such as European Economic Space), and the re-emergence of regional and local economies. The unity of nation-states (as opposed to national states) has also been weakened by the (admittedly uneven) growth of multiethnic and multicultural societies and of divided political loyalties (with the resurgence of regionalism and nationalism as well as the rise of European identities, diasporic networks, cosmopolitan patriotism, etc.). Because many of these changes are not directly related to globalization, we should not focus one-sidedly on the latter as the decisive causal mechanism in recent political transformation.

Restructuring the Keysian National Welfare State

Taking the postwar KNWS as our benchmark, the current reorganization of the state and its capacities can be summarized in terms of six analytically distinct but empirically interrelated trends. Each trend is also linked to a countertrend that both qualifies and transforms its significance for the state's form and functions. These countertrends can be viewed initially as specific reactions to the new trends rather than as survivals of earlier patterns. This is why they are presented as countertrends rather than as additional trends.

Denationalization of Statehood

This involves the transfer of powers previously located at the national territorial level upwards to supra-regional or international bodies, downwards to regional or local states, or outwards to relatively autonomous cross-national alliances among local, metropolitan or regional states with potentially complementary interests. In addition, new state powers have been allocated to scales other than the national. This re-allocation of specific state powers weakens national states qua mutually exclusive, formally sovereign, spatially segmented instantiations of the modern interstate system. Given the primacy of the national scale in the KNWS, this trend is sometimes termed the 'hollowing out' of the national state. But this is misleading because it focuses on the transfer of specific tasks, ignores the assumption of new tasks by the national state, and, above all, overlooks the real extent to which this re-arrangement of state functions may be undertaken by state managers to enhance their operational autonomies and strategic capacities.

De- and Re-Statization

This involves redrawing the boundaries between state and non-state apparatuses and activities within the political system. Whereas denationalization concerns the territorial dispersion of the national state's activities, destatization redraws the 'public-private' divide and modifies the relationship between organizations and tasks across this divide on whatever territorial scale(s) the state in question acts.

In other words, some of the *particular* activities (technical, economic, fisco-financial, juridico-political, ideological, etc.) performed by states (on any scale) have been transferred entirely to, or shared with, parastatal, non-governmental, commercial, or not-for-profit actors, institutional arrangements or regimes. This is often described as a shift from govern*ment* to govern*ance* but this slogan is misleading insofar as it depicts the shift as unidirectional. There is also reverse traffic as states on different scales undertake new tasks that were previously undertaken, if at all, by the market or civil society.

Overall, this trend involves the increased importance of quite varied forms (and levels) of public-private partnerships in managing economic and social relations. The state is often only first among equals in these relations. This blurs the division between public and private, expands and reinforces the principle of subsidiarity, strengthens the informal sector as well as private enterprise (especially in delivering welfare and collective consumption), and reinforces mechanisms such as 'regulated self-regulation' and 'private interest government.' It is also linked to the state's growing involvement in decentred societal guidance strategies based on growing recognition of functional interdependencies, the division of knowledge, and the need for mutual learning, reflexivity and negotiated coordination. This need not entail a loss in the overall power of government, however, because resort to governance could enhance the state's capacity to project its influence and secure its objectives by mobilizing knowledge and power resources from influential non-governmental partners or stakeholders.

The Retreat of the State

This involves the rise of modes of exercising political power that are formally independent of state borders, even if re-scaled. This process weakens territorial 'power containers' on any and all scales relative to non-territorial forms of political power. As such it is often subsumed under the shift from govern*ment* to govern*ance* but it is distinctive because it dissociates the exercise of political power from imagined political communities whose interests are tied to territorialized state power. De-statization involves public-private partnerships in which the state devolves responsibilities to the private sphere but attempts to remain primus inter pares.

In contrast, this trend involves the self-organization of functional forms of power that by-pass or circumvent state power—perhaps at the behest of state managers. The increasing importance of international regimes for the relative stabilization of a globalizing economy and the rise of networks in an extra-territorial cyberspace that is allegedly beyond state control are two contrasting examples of this third trend.

Re-articulating the Economic and Extra-Economic

The division of labour between the political and economic systems is being redefined to take account of changed understandings of the economy and the conditions that make for sound economic performance. The economy is no longer interpreted in narrow terms but now includes many additional factors, deemed „non-economic' under the KNWS regime that affect economic competitiveness.

This is reflected in ideas such as „structural competitiveness (the OECD) 'systemic competitiveness'**1**, or the „competitive advantage of nations'**2** (Porter 1990). It requires attention to a growing range of social practices, institutions, functional systems, and domains of civil society that affect competitiveness. This has two interesting and paradoxical effects on states and politics. First, whilst it expands the potential scope of state intervention for economic purposes, the resulting complexity renders the typical postwar forms of top-down intervention less effective – requiring that the state retreat from some areas of intervention and redesign its institutional forms and functions in order to intervene more effectively in other areas.

And, second, whilst it increases the range of stakeholders whose cooperation is required for successful state intervention, it also increases pressures within the state to create new subjects to act as its partners. Thus states are now trying to transform the identities, interests, capacities, rights, and responsibilities of economic and social forces so that they become more flexible, capable, and reliable agents of the state's new economic strategies – whether in partnership with the state and/or each other or as autonomous entrepreneurial subjects in the knowledge-based economy.

Re-Ordering Political Hierarchies

Political hierarchies are also being re-ordered. The nested hierarchy of state power within territorially exclusive sovereign states and formal equality among such states was never fully realized in the modern interstate system; but it did provide the institutional framework within which forces struggled to control state power and/or modify the balance of international forces. Many of the above changes weaken the coherence of this nested hierarchy and produce increasing unstructured complexity as different scales of economic and political organization proliferate and different strategies are pursued to link them. This is reflected in the internationalization of policy regimes.

This means that the international context of domestic state action (whether national, regional or local) has expanded to include a widening range of extraterritorial or transnational factors and processes; that the international context has become more significant strategically for domestic policy; and that key players in policy regimes have expanded to include foreign agents and institutions as sources of policy ideas, policy design and implementation. This trend affects local and regional states below the national level as well as supranational state formations and international regimes. It is also evident in the development of the interregional and cross-border linkages connecting local and regional authorities and governance regimes in different national formations.

Re-Imagining Political Communities

The political communities (or publics) around which forces in the political system orient their actions are being re-imagined in various ways. Among them are new 'imagined nations' seeking autonomy within and/or control of a defined territory below, above, or transversal to existing national states; a global civil society based on cosmopolitan patriotism, the primacy of human rights over national citizenship, or some other global identity; new „communities of fate' defined by shared risks regardless of specific territorial location and, perhaps, global in character (e.g., global warming); and new communities of interest defined by shared identities, interests, and values regardless of specific territorial location (e.g., cybercommunities). Such new territorial or extra-territorial conceptions of political community are linked to struggles to redefine the nature and purposes of the state, find alternatives to territorialized forms of political power, and redefine the imagined general interest which political power, whether territorial or not, should serve.

Some Counter-currents

Countering the denationalization of statehood and the re-ordering of political hierarchies are the continuing attempts of national states to control the relation between different spatial scales and the transfer of powers between them. It might seem that little has changed here but the denationalization of statehood has introduced two major discontinuities. First, it enhances the need for supranational coordination and opens the space for subnational resurgence.

And, second, it radically extends the scope for national states to mediate between an increasing numbers of significant scales of action. Thus, while the national state may have lost some formal sovereignty through the rescaling of state powers, it seeks to play a central role in interscalar articulation. This is especially clear in the complex politics of the European Union as the most advanced form of a new supranational political system in which national states regularly engage in meta-constitutional deliberation about the appropriate competencies and the appropriate balance of powers between different apparatuses and levels of government and governance in relation to their substantive economic, political, and socio-cultural objectives.

In addition, national states have an important role in producing and regulating extra-territorial spaces, such as offshore financial centres, export-processing zones, the 'flagging out' of merchant shipping, and tax havens. They are also involved in developing the new *lex mercatoria* governing international economic relations in the effort to benefit their own economic spaces. The same holds for the governance of cyberspace and its new *lex cybertoria.*

Nor does the dual shift from government to governance included in the second and third trends noted above make the state redundant. It retains an important role precisely because of these trends. It is not only an important actor in many individual governance mechanisms but also attempts to manage these mechanisms in the light of the overall balance of forces and demands of social cohesion. These attempts can be described in terms of a shift from government to meta-governance.

Even as states cede their claim to formal juridical sovereignty in the face of growing complexity and interdependence among different functional systems and seek to enhance their political capacities by participating in public-private partnerships and/or delegating public responsibilities to private institutions and actors, they are also becoming more involved in organizing and steering the self-organization of partnerships, networks and governance regimes. This shift from governance to metagovernance should not be confused with the survival of state sovereignty as the highest instance of government nor with the emergence of a 'megapartnership' that subsumes all other partnerships.

Instead, it involves a shift from the top-down political organization typical of sovereign states to an emphasis on steering multiple agencies, institutions and systems that are operationally autonomous from one another and yet coupled through reciprocal interdependence. Thus states are increasingly involved in facilitating collective learning about functional linkages and material interdependencies among different sites and spheres of action. And politicians are developing the shared visions that can link complementary forms of governance and maximize their effectiveness. States undertake such tasks not only to promote particular state functions but also to ensure political stability and social cohesion.

Even as states cede their claim to formal juridical sovereignty in the face of growing complexity and interdependence among different functional systems, they are also becoming more involved in organizing and steering the self-organization of partnerships, networks and governance regimes. The expanded definition of the economic at the expense of the extra-economic clearly involves a key role for states (on whatever scale) in redefining their relations, steering the (re-) commoditization of social relations, and dealing with the repercussions of the increasing dominance of economic logic in the wider society.

Moreover, whereas promoting the micro-social conditions for economic competitiveness in these changing circumstances may well be better handled at other levels than the national, problems of territorial integration, social cohesion, and social exclusion are currently still best handled through large national states. Large and rich states still have significant fisco-financial powers and redistributive capacities for these purposes — whether they choose to exercise these powers is another matter. Smaller national states require far greater cohesion to deal with the pressures resulting from globalization and, without this, they have strong interests to form strategic alliances with other states and/or enter supranational blocs.

The emergence of new imagined political communities is too complex to discuss here because it is shaped by a wide range of processes from technological change and economic globalization to crises of class and national identity and the rise of new social movements. Nonetheless it has led states to introduce policies to counteract the newly perceived problem of social exclusion and to seek new bases of legitimation to counteract threats posed by growing political disenchantment with the prevailing forms of state. These policies are pursued across different scales and involve multiple agencies but the national state generally retains the leading metagovernance role in these areas.

Time and Politics

A key dimension of state capacities is their temporal sovereignty, i.e., their ability to make decisions according to their own political routines rather than the temporal rhythms of other systems. Much of the pressure that state managers feel in the current global era has more to do with the compression of time than the spatial extension of economic (or other) activities. This affects politics as the 'art of the possible'

States increasingly face temporal pressures in policy-making and implementation due to the acceleration of time and the shortening of time horizons in other social spheres. In particular, as economic routines of superfast and/or hypermobile capital accelerate, the time available to states to determine and co-ordinate political responses to economic events shrinks. This puts pressure on states to adapt by withdrawing from areas where they are too slow to make a difference (this pressure is independent of calls from certain forces to withdraw from such areas), speeding up their routines through fast policy and fast tracking, or seeking to slow down economic movements.

A laissez-faire retreat could reinforce the impact of deregulated financial markets, however, especially when market forces provoke economic crises and states cannot respond quickly. The acceleration of politics is reflected in the shortening of policy development cycles, fast-tracking decisions, rapid programme rollout, continuing policy experimentation, an institutional and policy Darwinism in which only the quick and effective survive, and a relentless revision of guidelines and benchmarks. This acceleration privileges those who can operate within compressed time scales, narrows the range of participants in policy-making, and limits the scope and time for deliberation, consultation, and negotiation. This can significantly affect the choice of policies, the initial targets of policy, the sites where policy is implemented, and the criteria for success.

Fast policy privileges the executive over the legislature and the judiciary, finance over industrial capital, consumption over long-term investment. It is likely to increase the chances of making decisions on the basis of unreliable information, insufficient consultation, lack of participation, etc. It also tends to destroy institutional memory and to discourage long-term planning. Hence the present is extended at the expense of both past and future; and politics is lived in the mediatized world of spin and presentation, the quick fix, rapid churning of policies, and plebiscitarian forms of democracy.

Rather than compressing absolute political time, states could create relative political time by slowing the circuits of capital. The most celebrated, if not yet implemented, example of this strategy is the Tobin tax, which would decelerate the flow of superfast and hypermobile financial capital and limit its distorting impact on the real economy. Other examples include a tax on fossil fuels to slow the exhaustion of non-renewable resources and global warming, inclusion of recycling and disposal costs in the pricing of goods, and resort to prudential principles in the introduction of new technologies.

For these could tilt the balance away from globalization in favour of regional and local economies, slow the rate of environmental destruction, and allow proper evaluation of the likely consequences of technological innovation. This could be supplemented by a fourth political time-management option. This is to establish the institutional framework for guided self-regulation on various scales based on the principle of subsidiarity as well as for continuous monitoring of how well such self-regulation is operating in the light of agreed criteria. This strategy of reflexive metagovernance would enable the state to retain the capacity to co-ordinate activities across different time zones and temporalities without the risk of overload.

Summary and Conclusion

I conclude this review of recent changes in the state with two main sets of arguments. First, in most advanced capitalist economies, the Keynesian national welfare state is being tendentially replaced by a Schumpeterian post-national workfare regime (SPWR). The latter can be presented along the same ideal-typical lines as the KNWS. Thus, regarding its economic functions, the new state form is *Schumpeterian* insofar as it tries to promote permanent innovation and flexibility in relatively open economies by intervening on the supply-side and to strengthen their structural and/or systemic competitiveness.

This invokes Schumpeter, the theorist of innovation, entrepreneurship, and competition, rather than Keynes, the theorist of money, employment, and national demand, as its emblematic economist. Likewise, as a *workfare* regime, the SPWR subordinates social policy to the demands of labour market flexibility and employability and to the demands of economic competition.

This includes putting downward pressure on the social wage qua cost of international production but, given the economic and political limits to welfare cuts; it also involves the reorientation of the inherited welfare state to economic interests. In more neo-liberal economies this leads to the partial dismantling of the welfare state and increasing polarization and social exclusion; but it is consistent with a more incremental redesign, reorientation, and rescaling of welfare in other -types of economic regimes. In relation to its economic and social functions, attempts are also made to create appropriate subjects to serve as partners in the innovative, knowledge-driven, entrepreneurial, flexible economy and its accompanying self-reliant, autonomous, empowered workfare regime.

Regarding the scale on which these functions are performed, the SPWR is '*postnational*' insofar as the national territory has become less important as an economic, political, and cultural 'power container.' This is associated with a transfer of economic and social policy-making functions upward, downward, and sideways. On a global level, this can be seen in the growing involvement of a growing number of international agencies (such as the IMF, World Bank, OECD, and ILO) and intergovernmental forums (such as the G8) in the shaping of current social as well as economic policy agendas.

Other scales of political organization are also increasingly active in this redesign— including the European Union as an emerging post-national polity, the emerging global hierarchy of networked cities, and a growing number of cross-border regions. Finally, the SPWR relies increasingly on forms of governance rather than sovereign state capacities to compensate for market failures and inadequacies. There is an increased role for non-state mechanisms in shaping and delivering state-sponsored economic and social policies. One aspect of this is the increased importance of private-public networks to state activities on all levels from the local to the supranational.

The shift from govern*ment* towards govern*ance* means that traditional forms of intervention are less important now in economic and social policy. This does not mean that law and money have disappeared, of course; instead, active economic and social steering now tends to run more through soft regulation and reflexive law, additionality and private-public partnerships, organizational intelligence and information-sharing, etc. A key role is also played by 'meta-governance,' i.e., the organization of the institutional framework and rules for individual modes of governance and the 'calibration' (or re-balancing) of different modes of governance.

The early stages of Europolity construction were shaped by a tension between strategies to develop a supranational European state and strategies to confine it to a limited, goal-oriented, and revocable mechanism of intergovernmental collaboration. We are now witnessing the emergence of the European Union as a complex, self-organizing system of multi-level meta-governance.

My second conclusion relates primarily to the European Union as the currently most advanced form of post-national political regime that is committed to a broad range of economic and social tasks within a more or less integrated political territory. On the one hand, the EU has key roles in organizing the transition to a Schumpeterian post-national workfare regime in Europe, in promoting the competitiveness of European economic space in a globalizing knowledge-based economy, and in restructuring and defending the European social model in the face of pressures emanating from more evangelistic neo-liberal economies (most notably the United States).

Moreover, corresponding to the increasingly post-national nature of contemporary political economy, the EU also acts both as a relay and a filter for the agenda-shaping efforts of international agencies (such as the WTO and OECD) at the same time as it attempts to shape the emerging global economic, political, and social agenda and to promote a distinctive European agenda in regions and countries beyond its borders. On the other hand, corresponding to these changing economic and political functions, their expanding territorial scope, and their increasing functional interdependence, the EU is being reorganized politically as part of the more general transformation of statehood and politics on a global scale.

The early stages of Europolity construction were shaped by a tension between strategies to develop a supranational European state and strategies to confine it to a limited, goal-oriented, and revocable mechanism of intergovernmental collaboration. We are now witnessing the emergence of the European Union as a complex, self-organizing system of multi-level meta-governance. This involves a variety of state and non-state political actors and a variety of non-political actors in a continuing process of meta-constitutional design and meta-governance practices.

This process is concerned to produce appropriate forms of government *and governance* that have variable territorial and functional geometries but are also compatible with the pursuit of longer term economic and political projects and with some overall coherence and cohesion of the emerging European regime. This involves complex processes of interscalar management and the calibration of activities on different scales with careful attention to what tasks are allocated to which scales and the balance among different modes of governance. This is a distinctive feature of the European Union and excludes any easy generalization from the EU case to the other two triads — or vice versa. It is itself a sign that one should not push globalization too far as a general explanatory framework of recent changes.

Finally, while globalization and the other challenges mentioned in the introduction to this essay have undermined the effectiveness of the Keynesian national welfare state, a restructured national state remains central to the effective management of the emerging spatio-temporal matrices of capitalism and the emerging forms of post- or transnational citizenship. For national states have become even more important arbiters of the movement of state powers upward, downward, and lateral; they have become even more important meta-governors of the increasingly complex multicentric, multiscalar, multitemporal, and multiform world of governance; and they are actively involved in shaping the forms of international policy regimes.

This is especially clear even in the most advanced case of state transformation, namely, the emergence of the Europolity as a complex multi-level meta-governance regime. National states are also responding more or less effectively to the crisis in traditional forms and bases of national citizenship. Their activities in these respects have far less to do with globalization in the strongest sense of this polyvalent, promiscuous, and controversial word (i.e., the emergence of a borderless planetary economy—an entity widely and rightly regarded as mythical) than they do with the more general spatio-temporal restructuring of contemporary capitalism. And in this regard it is just as important to pay attention to the temporal dimensions of these transformations as it is to consider their spatial aspects. For the effectiveness of the exercise of state powers depends on its command of time as well as space. The changes in the state reviewed above reflect the complex interrelations between both aspects.

References

1. Messner, D. (1996) *Die Netzwerkgesellschaft*, Köln: Weltforum Verlag.

2. Porter, M. (1990) *The Competitive Advantage of Nations*, Basingstoke: Macmillan.

Chapter Thirteen

An African State is Possible: Looking Back in Order to Look Ahead

Overview

Before the onslaught of globalization, 'the system' of governance in Africa was sometimes hard to recognize in its diverse manifestations and policies. Abstract Western critical theory was confronting an abstract multifaceted system. But the reduction of diversity in the corporate landscape and the concentration of power within international institutions, such as the International Monetary Fund (IMF), the World Trade Organization (WTO) and the financial markets, has clarified things and offered a focal point for protest and opposition.

It is a lot easier to oppose concentrated uniform power than diverse and flexible forms. As power heads further and further in this direction, those opposing it seem to become more and more diverse and fluid, and hence much harder to diffuse and undermine. As the capitalist elite, their transnational corporations and their puppets the IMF, World Bank, WTO and client states impose 'free market' policies on every country on the planet, they are unwittingly creating a situation where diverse movements are recognizing each others' struggles as related and are beginning to work together on an unprecedented scale.

The global race to the bottom in which workers, communities and whole countries are forced to compete by lowering wages, working conditions, environmental protections and social spending, all to facilitate maximum profit for corporations, is stimulating resistance all over the world. People everywhere are realizing that their resistance is pointless if they are struggling in isolation. For example, say your community manages, after years of tireless campaigning, to shut down your local toxic waste dump, what does the transnational company that owns the dump do? They simply move it to wherever their costs are less and the resistance weaker—probably somewhere in Africa, other Third World societies or Eastern Europe. Under this system, communities have a stark choice; either compete fiercely with each other or co-operate in resisting the destruction of their lives, land and livelihoods by rampaging capital.

The era of globalization has thus made the economy increasingly transnational, so too has the resistance to its devastating social and ecological consequences. The June 18th (J18) International Day of Action in financial and banking districts across the world was probably the largest and most diverse day of action against global capital in recent history. Hundreds of actions took place in over 30 countries on every continent, all in recognition that the global capitalist system is based on the exploitation of people and the planet for the profit of a few and is at the very root of our social and ecological troubles. But where did this extraordinary show of international solidarity spring from? And how and why should such diverse groups in Africa and beyond build global networks of struggle to counter the globalization of misery under capitalism as it was the January, 2007, case of the emergent *World Social Forum* (*WSF*) in Nairobi, Kenya?

Introduction

The socio-political economic past of Africa since the 19th century is one of foreign domination and Western imperialist influence. Such features as exploitation, extraction, and exportation of natural resources and raw materials have become permanent features in the interaction of Africa with the West and other developed nations, with the former, of course at the receiving end. Down through the ages, Africa, the so called 'Dark Continent' has passed through such metamorphic processes as slave trade, colonization and the subsequent rise in nationalistic struggles that led to the wave of independence across the continent. Due to the obvious negative legacies of colonization (witnessing the looping together of loose contraption and strange 'bed-fellows' as nation states), Africa relapsed into differing features of neo-colonialism—Europe and America still manipulating the stranglehold.

Terms and institutions as SAP (Structural Adjustment Programme), economic Liberalization, WTO, IMF the World Bank, which, in fact, are aspects of globalization, gradually evolved as tools for steering Africa's relationship with the West. What has been the lot of Africa in the era of globalization? Are there obvious economic and cultural challenges for the continent in this era of globalization or is it merely tagging along as the policies are being formulated in the developed economies? This section reveals a gradual erosion of values which has left the nations of Africa economically comatose and culturally bankrupt or call them 'failed/weak/collapsed states.'

The state in Africa today is in the midst of an anti-democratic counter-revolution in which globalization and its imperatives are being used to weaken popular and elected authority in favour of a system of domination by super-citizens, the TNCs. This process sows the seeds of its own destruction, as it serves a small global minority, damages the majority, breeds financial instability, and exacerbates the environmental crisis. Its destructive tendencies are likely to produce an explosion if the process is not contained and democracy is not rehabilitated. The reason is that the current African institutions fail to adequately constrain the predatory client state, stunt all sorts of people-centred development, disregard any sustainable indigenous entrepreneurship, discourage peaceful coexistence of African groups, and fight back any creation of wealth by the indigenous private sector.

Halting this anti-democratic juggernaut will be difficult, not only because of the power of its foreign-sponsored beneficiaries, but also because it operates within the framework of nominally democratic structures and musters plausible arguments. But these arguments are self-serving and wrong, and should be vigorously contested. An agenda should be advanced that serves ordinary citizens rather than the TNCs and vampire financial institutions.

Negatively, this agenda will include strenuous opposition to all supranational arrangements that take power out of the hands of democratic governments to serve some alleged economic need. Positively, the agenda requires support for the imposition of serious limits and responsibilities on TNCs, including capital controls and other deterrents to financial speculation. Pursuit of this agenda is going to require a combination of understanding and effective organization of the large majority who are the victims of globalization. Why?

The Issue: Globalized Imperialism

British Prime Minister Gordon Brown, was arrogantly direct in his unapologetic defence of imperialism. 'The days of Britain having to apologize for its colonial history are over,' he said during a tour of Africa, 'We should celebrate much of our past rather than apologize for it.' This statement was quoted in John Pilger, 'Iran may be the greatest crisis of modern times,' *International Socialist Review* 53, May–June 2007.What is amazing is that for centuries, beginning with the slave trade, the West has ruthlessly exploited the African continent by using the state as a source of violence directed against Africans, an engine for the forcible appropriation of African wealth with no compensation, laws restricting voluntary activities by Africans at both national and international levels, and imposes divisive regulatory economic legislation that places Africans at a disadvantage .

As Karl Marx (1977, p.915) described it, 'the turning of Africa into a commercial warren for the hunting of black skins' was one of the chief sources of 'primitive accumulation' that 'signalled the rosy dawn of the era of capitalist production.' But the abduction and enslavement of millions of Africans was only the start. In the late nineteenth century, in what became known as the 'scramble for Africa,' the continent was arbitrarily carved up into colonies by the leading European powers, which violently subjected its people and plundered the continent of its rich natural resources. In the post-independence eras, African states became weak pawns in the world economy, subject to Cold War rivalries, their path to development largely blocked by their debilitating colonial past. More recently, the West has choked Africa with an onerous debt regime, forcing many nations to pay more in interest on debts to the World Bank and International Monetary Fund (IMF) than on health care, education, infrastructure, and other vital services combined.

The legacy of Western domination has left Africa devastated with crippling rates of poverty, hunger, and disease. The continent today has a gross national per-capita yearly income of $829—below that of the 1950s and 1960s in most African countries—and an average life expectancy of only fifty years. Sixty-two percent of Africans have no access to standard sanitation facilities, and two-thirds of the total world population suffering from HIV/AIDS (25.8 million people) lives in Africa. It remains a continent abundant in human and natural resources, but these manage to enrich only a handful of African rulers and foreign capitalists.

This is the historical legacy, in the words of Patrick Bond (2006, p.2), 'of a continent *looted*':

> [T]rade by force dating back centuries; slavery that uprooted and dispossessed around 12 million Africans; precious metals spirited away; the 19th century emergence of racist ideologies to justify colonialism; the…carve-up of Africa into dysfunctional territories or so-called states in a Berlin negotiating room; the construction of settler-colonial and extractive-colonial systems—of which apartheid, the German occupation of Namibia, the Portuguese colonies and King Leopold's Belgian Congo were perhaps only the most blatant…; Cold War battlegrounds—proxies for U.S./U.S.S.R. conflicts—filled with millions of corpses; other wars catalyzed by mineral searches and offshoot violence such as witnessed in blood diamonds and coltan; poacher-stripped swathes of East, Central and Southern Africa…; societies used as guinea pigs in the latest corporate pharmaceutical test; and the list could continue.'

One would be dead wrong to think that Western powers are sorry for their violent exploitation, repression and underdevelopment of Africa. For example, Robert Calderisi, a former World Bank Africa chief and author of *The Trouble With Africa: Why Foreign Aid Isn't Working* (2006) offers diagnoses and prescriptions for Africa that are no less paternalistic than those given by the colonialists of old:

> [Some Africans] believe all of Africa's problems are basically rooted in Western nastiness: colonialism, slavery, debt, and the like. But my own sense is that opinion has shifted tremendously in Africa over the last ten years, that there's greater openness to accepting that African problems have roots in Africa.... [O]ne of the good legacies of colonialism [is that] there are Western nations that could have turned their backs on Africa a long time ago if they didn't have some historical, economic, and sentimental connection.... For me to suggest that we reduce rather than increase aid to Africa will sound to many people like spitting in the face of a dying man, but I see it as analogous to dragging a dope addict to his feet and bringing him to a rehabilitation clinic (Weinstein 2008).

A new scramble for Africa marks the beginning of the latest chapter in the plunder of the continent. The United States and Europe, but also rising powers like China, seek to consolidate their grip on Africa's oil, its minerals, and other resources, all worth more every day because of a massive boom in the price of oil and raw materials. Like the earlier scramble for Africa, the new scramble for Africa is not only about profits, but also control of strategic resources, chiefly oil. The United States in particular is concerned about threats to its hegemony in the region. And, as in the Middle East, the defence and expansion of that hegemony also involves military intervention, justified under the rubric of fighting terrorism. As author Michael Watts writes (2006), 'The strategic interests of the United States include not only access to cheap and reliable...oil imports, but also keeping the Chinese (for example in Sudan) and South Koreans (for example in Nigeria)...and Islamic terror at bay. Africa is, according to the intelligence community, the 'new frontier' in the fight against revolutionary Islam. Energy security, it turns out, is a terrifying hybrid of the old and the new: primitive accumulation [i.e., looting] and American militarism coupled to the war on terror.'

Transnational State Mobilization from Above

So what is to be done? Smash the TNS and attempt a return to nation-state projects of popular social change? The problem with such propositions is that globalization, although it involves agency as much as structure, is not a project conceived, planned and implemented at the level of intentionality. I think we need to look forward rather than backward. Such historic processes cannot be reverted as such, but they can be influenced, redirected, and transcended. This returns us to my opening affirmation that historical materialism is emancipatory precisely because it reveals the historical specificity of existing forms of social life. Emancipatory projects operate in history. As Marx would have us recall, we do make our own history, but we do not make it just as we please, 'but under circumstances directly found, given and transmitted from the past.'

It is not inevitable that new transnational elite will consolidate its economic and political hegemony. A major economic crisis or collapse could stymie the process or push it into unforeseen directions. Transnational capital currently enjoys an unprecedented structural power over popular classes worldwide, but this is an historic conjuncture and not a fixed feature of the system. The confidence exuded by the transnational bourgeoisie in the latter decades of the 20th century - with its 'end of history' thesis and so on - is giving way to fear of looming crisis as contradictions internal to global capitalism have become increasingly manifest. The world recession of the 1990s exposed the fragility of the world monetary system and caused rising alarm and growing fissures in the inner circles of the global ruling class. As the decade drew to a close a rising chorus of voices from within the global elite called for centralized global financial regulation and numerous proposals were put forward for achieving it, ranging from the creation of a world central bank to the transformation of the IMF into a veritable 'lender of last resort.' These developments highlight the attempt by the transnational capitalist class to achieve some regulatory order given the inability of an incipient TNS to stabilize the system.

Capitalism has always been a violent and unstable system fraught with contradictions. All of the contradictions germane to the capitalist system are rising to the surface in the new epoch of globalization, in particular, overaccumulation and worldwide social polarization. In the past, these contradictions have led to periodic crises that tend to result each time in a reorganization of the system. Imperialism, for instance, allowed core countries to displace to the colonial world, momentarily, some of the sharpest social antagonisms that capitalism generated, while Keynesian absorption mechanisms such as credit creation postponed overaccumulation crises.

But many if not all of capitalism's recurrent crises have been mediated by the nation-state. Under globalization the national-state is less able to address these manifold crises, yet the emergent TNS is similarly ill-equipped to resolve them, especially those of overaccumulation and social polarization. Even if the global financial system can be brought under regulation, the mechanisms simply do not exist for absorption strategies, nor does the system provide a material basis for a project of legitimation.

It is not clear in the new epoch how the contradictions of the system will be played out, but certainly new opportunities for emancipatory projects are on the horizon. To speak of globalization as the culmination of capitalism's extensive enlargement and its accelerated conquest of pre-capitalist spheres is to posit that there are a series of world historic dynamics and of contradictions that are being modified or supplanted by these new circumstances. The system will not be defeated by challenges from outside its logic such as those of the former Soviet bloc countries and Third World liberation movements. Rather, defeat will be from within the global system itself. The contradictions between capitalist and pre-capitalist classes, for instance, are increasingly irrelevant. Resistance to capitalist colonization from without is giving way to resistance to capitalism from within. The universal penetration of capitalism through globalization draws all peoples not only into webs of market relations but also into webs of resistance.

To defend the relevance of Marx and the continuing vitality of historical materialism is not to say all of what Marx had to say is still applicable to the conditions humanity faces in the new millennium. To the contrary, any such proposition becomes dogma, intellectually sterile and politically disenabling. Marx's and Engel's argument that 'the proletariat of each country must, of course, first of all settle matters with its own bourgeoisie,' is now outdated. 'Its own bourgeoisie' is now transnational; each 'national' bourgeoisie is as well the bourgeoisie of the proletariat of numerous countries. Popular classes in the age of globalization need to transnationalize their struggles. The mobilization of the transnational bourgeoisie from above can only be countered by a transnational mobilization from below. Working and popular classes whose fulcrum has been the nation state need must transpose to transnational space their mobilization and their capacity to place demands on the system. This means developing the mechanisms - alliances, networks, direct actions and organizations - that will allow for a transnational resistance. It also means developing a transnational socialist ideology and politics, and targeting the TNS as contested terrain.

Which Way Africa?

The new apologists for colonialism, the erstwhile Bush administration in the USA included, operate as if the only solution for poverty, crisis, and civil war in Africa is to back up Big Oil and mineral-exploiting Trans-national corporations with more privatization and military force. The Somali, Sudan and Congo debacles are eloquent examples. Even many NGOs are resigned to promoting limited reforms that fall far short of challenging the murderous terms dictated by global corporations and Western imperialism. But these are not the only alternatives. Africa has a long tradition of militant struggle. Mass movements in the anticolonial period, supported by millions of workers and peasants, shattered the political control of European powers on the continent. Left-wing national liberation movements and African socialism—new heads of state such as Nkrumah, Lumumba, and Nyerere—inspired movements elsewhere around the globe, including Black liberation struggles in the United States.

Imperialism's relentless super-exploitation and oppression of the people of the neo-colonial world has steadily reduced the 4.75 billion human beings in Africa, Asia, and Latin America down to the lowest depths of poverty. That means that the great majority of this planet's 6 billion souls live as though scientific, technological, and economic development had stopped hundreds of years ago. Terrible as these simple statistics may be, all too many people think that imperialism is so powerful that it can reign supreme over its empire indefinitely. The evidence we shall present below, however, suggests otherwise.

Despite the awesome power of imperialism: its weapons of mass destruction and the enormous accumulation of wealth at its disposal, it is becoming ever more difficult for the world's capitalists to maintain control over their vast empire. Lately the capitalist mass media has been agonizing over the failure of imperialism's so-called 'peacekeepers' to bring peace to an increasingly miserable and thus ever more ungovernable Africa. The appalling misery suffered by the peoples of Africa after more than 500 years of imperialist enslavement is comparable only to history's most draconian holocausts. Media headlines are focused on the civil war in Sierra Leone and the 'senseless war' between Ethiopia and Eritrea.

Meanwhile, civil war in the Congo continues without let-up; and landless veterans of Zimbabwe's war for independence from Britain continue their struggle for a place in the sun by occupying over 700 white-owned farms. And Black South Africa, despite its victory over apartheid, continues to suffer undiminished super-exploitation by the country's white capitalist class. The main change is that the oppressive force of the South African capitalist state now wears a Black face.

These newly emerging African economies, however, were not able to fulfil the aspirations of their populations after the era of liberation. Those that attempted to insert themselves into the world market, or break free from it, met increasing resistance as the global recession of the 1970s intensified competition. Widespread illusions that political independence would create the conditions for rapid economic development were undermined. Africa's new national states were so small and economically weak that they could not, without giant loans, even begin to embark on the policy of national development they eagerly promised. Hobbled with weak infrastructures inherited from the colonial regimes, and insufficient capital to technologically advance, these economies fell increasingly behind. The new nationalist elites, meanwhile, were forced into the mould of all ruling classes: exploiters of workers and peasants, driven by the logic of international competition.

But these few cases are only the tip of the iceberg. According to the *Financial Times* of London, there are 20 wars going on in Africa at the present time. This is a clear indication that the misery of the masses of indigenous Africa is getting worse and the victims are fighting back however they can-most often ineffectively, because of misleadership. In Africa today, wars between nations and within nations have not only proliferated; they have degenerated from a generalized struggle of the exploited and oppressed against their imperialist oppressors into a desperate and hopeless struggle among the victims of imperialism for bare survival. What we see in Africa today are for the most part wars between ethnic groups, clans, and tribes without a clear vision of the road to freedom from super-exploitation and oppression.

The big question is not what and who is responsible for the terrible tragedy of Africa at the end of the second millennium. There are few if any in the neo-colonial world, at least, who don't know that imperialism is solely responsible. The main question is why the struggle of Africa's peoples against imperialism has degenerated into a blind fratricidal struggle for survival by its victims. But before we can begin to answer this question, let's see what Africa's problem looks like today. What we will see-we intend to show-reflects the more general problem that afflicts global capitalism.

Obstacles to African Liberation

What is it that has stood in the way of the neo-colonial world's ability to carry their many attempts at revolution to a successful conclusion? While there certainly have been successful struggles to achieve political independence from imperialism, independence alone is not a solution to the problems Africans face.

A real solution is much more than the conquest of military and political power. That's only a very first step toward real freedom. Only the industrial and economic transformation of a backward economy into an advanced industrial economy can bring the inhabitants of the neo-colonial world up to 21st century living standards. Short of that, there is no end to the misery that comes from not having enough of the necessities of life for everyone.

Moreover, it should be understood that the truce that comes after a partial victory by the oppressed against the oppressor is not an end to the struggle. When capitalists lose a battle or a war, they don't give up. They are only forced to bide their time and wait until the upsurging movement that led to a partial victory recedes and its force is spent. Then the oppressors invariably launch their counterattacks to take back whatever concessions they were forced to make-including even the trappings of independence.

In the meantime, history shows, the imperialists assiduously use their monopoly over capital-without which economic development is impossible-to block the road to real freedom. This is what they did in every case from South Africa to Algeria, and from the Russia to Cuba. And if that's not enough, world imperialism uses its monopoly over the world market to more or less completely block the road to development in Africa and elsewhere. In other words, the preconditions for economic development-access to capital and to the world division of labour-can be achieved by the neo-colonial countries only if they have socialist revolutions. And no less important, even a socialist revolution must be conceived as incomplete until it is extended to the most advanced industrially developed capitalist countries.

Only a workers' socialist revolution in major industrial countries like Germany, France, Britain, or the United States would begin to help bring the neo-colonial countries into the 21st century by providing them with the capital and other material assistance needed for the development of the industrial infrastructure of their national economies. Such help will never come from imperialism. A socialist United States or a socialist Germany, France, or Britain would have nothing to lose and everything to gain by helping their class brothers and sisters in Africa, Asia, and Latin America to become equal members of a Socialist United States of the World. Such a united socialist world order, of course, won't come all at once.

But once the socialist revolution is extended to one of these major industrial powers, it becomes virtually unstoppable, because such a nucleus of a world socialist order will begin raising living standards almost instantly. Of course, it goes without saying that a new leadership is needed in the world today-everywhere, in developed and undeveloped countries alike. The world needs leaders that understand history's lessons-starting with the fact that the bourgeois-democratic revolution against imperialist domination in the world as it is today is impossible.

Global Apartheid

Global apartheid is a pervasive system of inequality and international minority rule, where access to wealth, power and basic human rights are dictated by one's race, gender and place. For instance, recent decades have exposed the disastrous impact of Western global financial institutions, such as the IMF and World Bank, on African societies. After independence, African ruling classes emphasized state investment and national development based on import-substitution industrialization. The concept was that the West would lend funds through the World Bank to help nations build infrastructure, grow domestic industries, cut reliance on imports, and boost exports. One of the chief concerns of the World Bank and IMF was to keep nation states in Africa out of the Soviet orbit by promoting Western-led economic development.

These loans from the World Bank were the origin of Africa's debt—debts incurred to create large numbers of unproductive state enterprises heavily subsidized by government, investment codes that restrict the free movement of African capital, high marginal taxes, poorly specified and even unenforceable property rights regimes, excessive regulation of the international trade sector, fiscally discriminatory statutes, resulting in the transfer of wealth from the poor to the rich. Such industrial sectors were such that could not effectively compete on the world market. Respectable growth rates of 4–6 percent in the 1960s gave way to stagnation and decline in the 1970s, as most African states proved, as latecomers to industrialization, unable to marshal sufficient capital resources, even with state intervention, to overcome the legacy of colonialism. Beginning in the late 1970s, the dogma began to change; the World Bank and IMF mandated a shift away from industrialization toward economies based solely on the export of raw materials and agricultural products. Loans were now to be used as leverage to impose what were called Structural Adjustment Programmes (SAPs)—programmes that mandated slashing social spending, eliminating price subsidies and trade tariffs, and privatizing government-owned industries and services—all in order to pay down foreign debt.

This approach flowed from a need to spur world trade and helps restore profitability in the advanced capitalist countries following a series of recessions starting in the 1970s. Industrializing African nation states were cornered into growing their economies by focusing on producing commodities that could be exported to the rich countries while importing the latter's finished goods. In practice, this had the effect, as under colonialism, of turning Africa back to a one-way conveyor belt of raw materials. Africa today exports the bulk of its natural resources.

The strategy has had disastrous consequences. For one, it stultified its developing economies: rather than building diverse industries, economies became entirely reliant upon the West for imports to meet domestic needs. Further, economies reliant on a handful of exports are more vulnerable: if the price of one commodity falls, it sends the entire nation into recession. In the telling words of Toussaint (2005: 279), 'Sub-Saharan Africa has seen the terms of exchange of its export products on the global market deteriorate since the 1980s.... [T]he value of a basket of goods exported by Africa has lost half its value compared to products imported by the North.'

The effects of such global apartheid can be seen not only on an international level, but also within national and local communities. As a result, we see communities of colour in the U.S. and globally denied equal access to education, healthcare, housing, and other essential services. Through this system, disparities in wealth, living conditions and life expectancy become entrenched, as wealthy and powerful elites continue to control global decision-making bodies and to preserve centuries-old patterns of inequality. Global apartheid persists based on the assumption that it is 'natural' for certain populations to have different expectations of life.

Global apartheid manifests itself in many ways. We see it in the Global South being dominated financially through overwhelming debt burdens, which decimate access to social services such as education, or through unfair trade policies that stunt economic growth. It is obvious in the low international funding levels for major health priorities such as malaria and HIV/AIDS, neglected as problems primarily afflicting the world's most poor and vulnerable. Again, it appears in the undemocratic systems of global governance and the international financial institutions, wherein the majority of the world's voices are unheard and undervalued, despite the fact that it is the impoverished majority that bears the impact of decisions made by these institutions.

The World Bank and IMF launched the Highly Indebted Poor Country (HIPC) plan in 1996, which effected a miniscule reduction in debt. And the UN launched a set of targets for 2015 called the Millennium Development Goals for child mortality, disease, and environmental sustainability. But the actions of the U.S. and the EU give lie to the lip service they pay to these goals. New trade deals that force African countries to eliminate tariffs will cut 25 percent of their income—the equivalent, for example, of Zambia's yearly budget for dealing with AIDS (Cronin 2007).

Meanwhile, such so-called reforms come with requirements for 'good governance,' the favourite buzzword for new conditions imposed on African nations for aid. But Western powers' concern over political instability in Africa is sheer hypocrisy, given that they have supported the worst, blood-soaked rulers in Africa when it suited them, while backing deregulation and privatization that 'stripped the African states of what little control they had previously exercised over…foreign firms'(Capps 2005).

Neoliberal African-based reforms, like the New Partnership for Africa's Development (NEPAD) and the African Union, championed by South Africa's Thabo Mbeki and former Nigerian president Olusegun Obasanjo, are no solution to African inequality and poverty as they merely create opportunities for more African ruling-class involvement in trade policy(Henning Melber, 'The new scramble for Africa's resources,' -*Pambazuka News*, February 8, 2007). NEPAD helps to create favourable conditions for Western investment through (African-imposed) requirements for privatization, cuts in social spending and 'good governance,' i.e., subjecting African policy-making to the political will of Western imperialism and its allies. The response to this African 'partnership' highlights the tremendously uneven benefits of neoliberal policy across classes and nations.

In 2002, members of some forty African social movements, trade unions, youth and women's organizations, non-governmental organizations (NGOs), religious groups, and others rejected NEPAD in the African Civil Society Declaration on NEPAD (The full declaration can be found at http: //www.ifg.org/wssd/acsnepad_decl.htm). Ultimately, whether African elites are at the table or not, the priorities for Africa are set by the needs of global capital rather than the needs of ordinary Africans. These are fundamental global injustices that create a space for Africans to devise alternatives to the current system. Alternative visions emerging from Africa, as the continent most affected by the dynamics described above, must be integrated into the search for global solutions.

Promises of Past Revolutions Unfulfilled

The victory of the Russian socialist revolution at the end of World War I also saw the birth of the kind of leadership needed in the world today. That first successful conquest of state power by the Russian working class became the model for world socialist revolution and provided living proof of the promise of revolutionary Marxism.

However, the Russian Bolshevik leaders in the time of V. I. Lenin and Leon Trotsky fully understood that the revolution had a permanent character and could only be completed and made absolutely irreversible by its extension to the advanced industrial countries. But even the Great Russian socialist revolution was unable to realize its historic promise for three main reasons:

1) The backwardness of Russia-its lack of a fully developed industrial infrastructure and its largely illiterate population.
2) The irrepressible counter-revolutionary efforts of world imperialism.
3) The betrayal of the Stalinist bureaucracy that usurped the leadership of the party of Lenin and assassinated virtually all of Lenin and Trotsky's co-thinkers, including Trotsky.

It's no accident that Stalin's betrayal began with his slogan of 'Socialism in One Country.' This was much more than a mere tactical slogan; it turned out to mean 'socialism' only in one country! And that meant socialism nowhere since, as indicated above, socialism is impossible without access to the world market, its resources and the world division of labour. And, as we now are all too aware, the Stalinist bureaucracy ultimately capitulated completely to imperialism and are now scrambling as fast as they can to become capitalists. However, that is only one side of a very contradictory world situation. One must keep in mind that history wields a double-edged sword. On the one hand, history has put powerful reactionary forces into the hands of world capitalist imperialism.

On the other hand, all things, in time, turn into their opposites. And capitalism, which once played an enormously progressive role in history, has long ago outlived its usefulness. From a creative force that accelerated the development of the productive forces of humanity, capitalism has become an obstacle to further development-and worse. If it is not overthrown and replaced by a rational social system in which the guiding principle is to serve the needs and interests of all, not the profits of the few, the current descent by world capitalism toward a world of a multitude of little wars will not stop until one big war ends everything.

World capitalism, as Africa can testify to in this era of its recolonization (Mentan, 2007b), is driven by its need to extend its domination to every corner of the globe. Capitalism goes everywhere only to feed its insatiable appetite for higher rates of profit. Not only does it drive the peoples of its captive nations ever further down into ever lower depths, but it must also squeeze every last ounce of blood and sweat out of its own working classes. But this world is finite. Capitalism has nowhere to sell the increasing supplies of goods produced with more machines and less workers to buy them. It is doomed to choke on an ever-mounting flood of unsold goods flowing from its increasingly productive technology. Those in charge of regulating the economy are desperately trying to ease it down before it comes crashing down. They do so because they know that sooner or later the invisible hand of capitalist market forces will have its way and not so gently bring the productive forces to a stop, as it has throughout the history of capitalism.

Karl Marx noted long ago that being determines consciousness. And the relative stability of world capitalism in its imperialist strongholds has kept the living standards of most workers within tolerable levels for an amazingly extended period of over half a century. But no one, not even the Alan Greenspans of capitalism, can cheat history forever. Everything comes to an end, and this too will end. When it does, the long-slumbering workers of the world will have no choice but to make up for all the time that was lost-and with a fury and combativity that must surpass its greatest moments in world history.

What Can Be Done?

In defining strategies to engage with the Neoliberal State in Africa, it is critical to ensure analytical clarity about the issues at stake. A historical perspective is required in order to expose the flaws in the neoliberal discourse which presents globalization as an ahistorical and benign process. We must make the point that globalization builds on a history of slavery, racism, colonialism, exploitation and discrimination, especially against women. Therefore, we must use a gendered class analysis to identify the issues around which we are going to strategize.

The fight in which we have to engage together is primarily about ideas. It is about neoliberal ideas that deprive us of our humanity and reduce us to consumers in the « free » global market. It is about ideas that treat our labour as an input, on the same footing as machinery or raw materials. It is about ideas that consider women's labour as free and infinitely elastic, so that it can be exploited forever to sustain society in the global village. In this fight, it will be critically important to build strategic alliances between workers and African intellectuals. These intellectuals have a specific responsibility in providing the knowledge base for social transformation. African research must have policy relevance and serve the interests of the dispossessed and oppressed under globalization. Research should contribute to progressive and equitable social transformation.

We have to forget about collaboration with the neoliberal system. History tells us that this has never worked. The trade unions in different countries have experienced more disempowerment in this process, than progress towards the full realization of workers' rights. The market-based growth that the neoliberal State wants to promote is basically biased against women, because much of their work is non-market work. Therefore it is critically important for women workers and organizations to engage with the neoliberal State and to challenge the hold of patriarchy that prevents them to have access to the male-dominated public sphere where the power and resources are mainly located.

We need to unite with other civil society organizations and progressive forces in order to ensure broad-based support for a different vision of society. We need to establish a new social contract by which economic policy making and processes will be democratized, and the State held accountable for its economic policies. We have to re-think our way of organizing and go beyond our differences and national borders to build strategic alliances around our common concerns. More than ever, solidarity is crucial. It is crucial in itself as a value that we must uphold in order to confront the ideology of profit. It is crucial as a strategy if we want to capture and influence the neo-liberal State.

African Union Mobilization from Below

I would like to start with a reference to the *Communist Manifesto* of Marx and Engels, which contains a remarkable and prophetic diagnostic of capitalist globalization. The capitalist system, insisted the two young authors, is embarking upon a process of cultural and economic unification of the world : 'By exploiting the world market, the bourgeoisie has made production and consumption a cosmopolitan concern for every country. To the great regret of reactionaries, it has removed industry's national base.[1] The self-sufficiency and regional and national isolation of the old days have been replaced by a widespread circulation and a widespread interdependency between nations. This is as much the case for material production as for intellectual production'.[2]

It is not just a question of expansion, but also of domination : the bourgeoisie 'compels all nations, if they do not want to head for their own undoing, to adopt the bourgeoisie's mode of production ; it compels them to introduce in their own countries what is considered to be civilization - that is to become bourgeois. In a word, it has created a world in its own image'.[3] For example, the disinformation by the global financial dailies as to the cause of the global financial tsunami, serve the same purpose as the global mass media when they perpetuated the lies that lulled the people to support the war criminals to launch the barbaric war against Iraq and Afghanistan which resulted in the genocide of millions, the mutilation of hundreds of thousands, physically and psychologically, and the devastation of an entire nation. The wars unleashed thus far, specifically the 'War on Terror' were launched to preserve the shadow money-lenders' political and military power.

This 'War on Terror' is the greatest military sideshow that distracted the American people from the financial rape and plunder of their economy and the destruction of their Constitution. Since the Summer of 2007, we have witnessed a concerted effort by the world's central banks and global commercial and investment banks to preserve the shadow money-lenders' financial power, one that is founded on fraud and structured in every detail as in the infamous Ponzi scheme. In the last several years, the Ponzi scheme was globalised by the Shadow Money-Lenders, siphoning hundreds of billions from so-called sophisticated investors and sovereign wealth funds. At its peak, the Ponzi scheme was estimated to be worth over $500 Trillion, with the Credit Default Swap (CDS) portion just under $60 Trillion (For more about the Ponzi schemes See Wikepedia, 2005).

In the discussion of the future of African nation states there are two mistakes that must be avoided : the first is to consider nation states as institutions that are in decline or disappearing, or that they are losing all political or economic power as a consequence of the process of capitalist globalization ; and the second is to believe that the defence of a nation and of national sovereignty is the only, or the principle, line of defence against the catastrophes brought on by the globalised market. Let us start with the first point: contrary to what is often said, nation states continue to play a decisive role in political and economic fields. Nicos Poulantzas was correct in writing that in imperialist countries, 'the national state... is undergoing important modifications in order to take over the internationalization of capital. On the other hand, the current phase of imperialism and this internationalization removes nothing (we often wrongly think this however) of the pertinence of the role of the national state in this process'.[4]

Let us remind ourselves that it is the governments of dominant capitalist countries that, through their representatives, determine the neoliberal politics of the G-7, the IMF, the World Bank and the WTO. It is these same states that, through the use of their military instruments such as in particular NATO, impose their order on a world scale, as demonstrated by the wars of imperial intervention in the Gulf and in Yugoslavia. Finally, the North American nation state, unique super-power in today's world, practices an undoubted economic, political and military hegemony.[5]

As far as southern hemisphere countries are concerned, nation states have never stopped playing an important role: allowing for exceptions, they tend to function as a driving belt for the system of imperial domination. They submit themselves unhesitatingly to the demands of financial capital and to the dictates of the IMF, make the payment of the exterior debt a priority for the national budget, and put into practice—

with zeal—the neoliberal policies of 'structural adjustment'. After all, Napoleon Bonaparte made this point by saying that *'When a government is dependent upon bankers for money, they and not the leaders of the government control the situation, since the hand that gives is above the hand that takes. Money has no motherland; financiers are without patriotism and without decency; their sole object is gain.'*

How can Africans put up a resistance against capitalist globalization, with its neoliberal policies that produce brutal social inequalities, ecological disasters, social regression, 'economic horror', and an aggravation of debt and dependency for third world countries ? It is obvious that the nation—state has a role to play in this resistance, and the first requirement for any anti-systemic movement—to use the pertinent terminology of Immanuel Wallenstein—is that a country's government should break away from the orientations imposed upon it by the IMF, declare a moratorium on its external debt, and re-direct production towards the needs of the interior market. However it would be a dangerous illusion to believe that salvation lies in purely 'national' resistance. It is, insists Nicos Poulantzas, above all important not to fall into the trap of «the line of defence of one's 'own' national state against 'cosmopolitan institutions.'[6] An efficient combat against the empire of multi-national capital cannot limit itself to the nation state and this for several reasons:

1) Victories obtained on a national level are limited, precarious and constantly menaced by the powers of the world capital market and its institutions.
2) A narrow national perspective does not allow for the formation of alliances or for the constitution of an alternative world focus of attention. Only a coalition of international forces is capable of affronting and forcing a retreat upon global capital and its instruments such as the IMF and the WTO.
3) The nation state is not a homogenous social space. Class contradictions, social conflicts and the fracture between an oligarchy and the working masses, between the privileged élite and the multitude of the poor and excluded, cut across national barriers.
4) The legitimacy of progressive and emancipating national movements such as those of the Kurds, the Palestinians and the inhabitants of East Timor cannot be denied, neither can it be denied that nationalism, in today's world, tends to take on essentially supremacist forms. Inter-community massacres, national or religious wars, 'ethnic purification' and even genocides, have become characteristic of the last decade of the 20th century.

5) The most urgent problems of our era are international. The third world debt, the imminent threat of ecological disaster, the necessity of controlling financial speculation and suppressing tax havens, are all global problems that demand global solutions.

In order to fight the system efficiently, it is necessary to act simultaneously upon three levels: local, national and global. The Zapatist movement is a good example of this dialectic: deeply rooted within the indigenous communities of the Chiapas and in their demand for autonomy, it is at the same time fighting the world hegemony of neoliberalism. This is also the case for the peasants' land rights movement (MST) in Brazil, which has its social base in a local mobilization and land occupation, and offers a project for alternative development for their country, but without neglecting to participate in all the international mobilizations that exist against liberal globalization.

It is not a question of fighting 'globalization' as such, in the name of some retrograde defence of 'national sovereignty', of the nation state, or of (capitalist) national industry, but more a question of opposing the imperialist globalization that 'really exists' with another global project of emancipation, democracy, equality and freedom. This does not mean that the movement for radical social change should not begin on the level of one or several nations. Nor would one say that those movements for national liberation are not legitimate. But contemporary struggles are, to a degree without precedent, interdependent and linked from one end of the planet to the other.

In reaction to the ravages of globalization, we observe here and there the appearance of the first seeds of a new internationalism, independent of states and of particularized groups of interest. These are the bases of what will one day become the 'Resistance Internationale' against the neoliberal capitalist offensive. This renewal of internationalism has not just come to be through the most radical trade union and political forces of the socialist and workers' movement (grouping all constituents from Marxists to libertarians). New internationalist leanings also appear in the social movements that have a planetary vocation such as feminism and ecology, in anti-racist movements, in the theology of liberation, in the associations for the defence of human rights or for solidarity with third world countries, and, more recently, in the teeming network of movements fighting the 'merchandizing of the world' Not to speak of well-known intellectuals such as Pierre Bourdieu or Jacques Derrida, who consider the foundation of a Resistance Internationale as today's most urgent tasks.

If certain international NGO's function simply as 'lobbies', adapting themselves to the dominant neoliberal framework and limiting themselves to giving 'advice' to the IMF and to the World Bank, others such as the committee for the abolition of the third world debt (Comité pour l'Abolition de la Dette du Tiers-Monde), in Brussels ; the alternative economic Forum launched on an initiative taken out by Samir Amin ; the People's Conference against free-exchange and the WTO, in Geneva ; or the international association ATTAC (association pour la taxation des transactions financières et l'aide aux citoyens: the association for the taxation of financial transactions for aid towards citizens), have a clearly anti-imperialist vocation.

Radical Christians are an essential component, be it those making up third world social movements - often inspired, notably in Latin America, by the theology of liberation - be it European associations aiming at solidarity with the struggles of poor countries. Inspired by a humanist and ecumenical Christian ethic, they offer an important contribution to the elaboration of a new internationalist culture. The new movement of farming communities, organized on a world scale in the case of the association Via Campesina, also occupies a strategic position in the process of international resistance in the sense that it is the hinge between agrarian struggles, ecological struggles and the battle against the WTO. The organizations such as the landless rural workers movement (MST) in Brazil and the Confédération Paysanne in France are at the avant-garde of the resistance against the huge capitalist agricultural industry that threatens the planet with its pesticides and its genetically modified organisms, and destroys forests - the guardians of the planet's ecological equilibrium - with its policy of 'profitability'.

A selection of the most active representatives of these various tendencies, from both the north and the south of the planet, from the radical left or from modern social movements, joined in a united and fraternal spirit in July 1996 in order to attend the Intergalactic Conference for Humanity and against Neoliberalism in the Chiapas mountains of Mexico, called together by the Zapatist National Liberation Army. It was a first step, modest, but in the right direction: towards the reconstruction of an international solidarity.

The events in Seattle in 1999 saw an impressive rallying of trade union, ecological and anti-capitalist forces that succeeded in thwarting the plans of the World Trade Organization—the number one instrument of neoliberal globalization—and revealed the potential in North America for fighting against the merchandization of the planet. In Europe, also, the movements of resistance to neoliberalism are far from negligible, as demonstrated by the recent mobilizations in Millau in the year 2000, in which 100,000 people assembled in solidarity with José Bové and his combat against the WTO ; or in Prague during the meeting of the International Monetary Fund and the World Bank. The International Meeting in Paris, in December 2000, and the World Social Forum which took place in January 2001 in Porto Alegre, are the most recent high points of this planetary mobilization which—above and beyond necessary protest—is searching for radical alternatives to the existing order.

Three constituents participate in the construction of this 'Resistance Internationale' : I) the renovation of the anti-capitalist and anti-imperialist tradition of proletarian internationalism, rid of the authoritarian scoria of the past (the Stalinist inheritance of blind submission to a state or a 'camp') ; II) the humanist, libertarian, ecological, feminist and democratic aspirations of the new social movements; and, III) the new networks fighting neoliberal globalization, which mobilize not only critical researchers but young people who wish to do battle with the institutions of the international commercial and financial system.

In the mobilizations of the last few years we are witness to a joining of these forces. This is not just a question of a juxtaposition of social actors with very different traditions and political cultures, but of the beginning of a reciprocal apprenticeship in the face of a whole series of questions. We see, for example, trade unionists beginning to take an interest in ecology, and the defenders of the environment taking into consideration workers' struggles; Marxists who learn from the feminists, and vice-versa. It is from the convergence of and the interaction between these different positions that a universalist and liberating internationalism will spring in the 21st century.

What Would 'An African Developmental State' Look Like?

THE STATE IN AFRICA has been essentially a bunch of RENTIER STATES. These rentier states have been delivering small amounts of resources to fragmented societies through informal personalized networks. They have survived because of their access to external resources from the IMF, World Bank, Club de Paris, etc. for holding themselves and their societies together, even by brute force. But, they have failed to act as developmental states or agents of national development because they cannot gather resources from society for any productive investment in national development.

This existential situation has pushed Africa to the brink of disaster and warlordism. And, one would readily agree with Claude Ake (1996: 79) that Africa has therefore become 'so marginal now that it is difficult for non-Africans to bring themselves to care about what happens in the continent...particularly when it entails some cost.' However, Ake sees a silver lining in the challenges and opportunities brought by globalization in that Africa's 'marginalization, so often decried, is what Africa needs right now.' As he points out clearly:

> For one thing, it will help with the evolution of an endogenous development agenda, an agenda that expresses the aspirations of the people and can therefore elicit their support...(W)hat Africa has (now) is a confusion of agendas, reflecting the demonstrated failure of an exogenous agenda that its promoters do not acknowledge and the unfulfilled promise of an endogenous agenda that African leaders are too dependent and too diffident to push through. The marginalization of Africa in the world economy could be useful in another important sense.
>
> Insofar as it leaves the development of Africa to Africans, it offers a chance of breaking out of another major development trap-the dissociation of development strategy from social experience (p.79).

These three scenarios are present in Africa's current political experimentations with globalization. Despite the ingrained injustices within the global world power politics, the common principles of the African liberation point the way towards a different set of possibilities. These alternatives underscore our common humanity and aspirations towards a new people-centred system. This vision would incorporate democracy at every level—not just in name, but also in practice—and would allow equal opportunity for all global perspectives to be heard. In this 'other Africa,' equal access to wealth, power, basic human rights and social services would be a reality. The following sections describe the visions elevated by various African civil society and community-based organizations so that the globalizing world can be stopped from pulling further ahead and apart from Africa. This path of globalization that is becoming steeper on a daily basis can only be contained by an AFRICAN STATE that can start from their limited resources and under-tapped creativity and evolve a new model for Africa predicament in areas such as:

Health

Structural and ideological challenges stand in the way of access to comprehensive care for most people in Africa. Despite the urgency of many health crises around the continent, global and national initiatives are hamstrung by failure to acknowledge broader economic issues, by a lack of funding, and by ideological biases that prioritize profits over people.

Discussions among global and national officials should not only concern the best means of tackling various challenges, such as HIV/AIDS. This approach runs the risk of perpetuating an excessively narrow focus. Much debate should revolve around issues of prevention of HIV/AIDS or how to deal with the delivery of much-needed treatment in low infrastructure settings. The weakness of this approach lies in its failure to place the response to specific conditions in the larger framework of general health and wellness.

Advocates need a more holistic approach to the treatment of illnesses such as HIV/AIDS, with a new focus on food security and adequate nutrition. These pressing priorities, when unmet, can stand as serious obstacles in the treatment of other illnesses and the attainment of good health. Broadening the framework of this discussion will require a removal of the distinction between health and economic security and the leadership of the communities dealing with these challenges.

The Abuja Declaration on governmental spending on health, signed in April 2001, as a target for civil society and community activism is imperative. This declaration marked a commitment by African governments to devote 15% of their budgets to improving the health sector. In local efforts to hold national governments accountable to good governance standards, the target of increased health spending be an integral component of such demands. Stressing health as a basic human right the international community should be held to account for its failure to prioritize people over profits. Specific reference should be made to the threats against generic medications for HIV/AIDS made by financial institutions and pharmaceutical companies seeking to protect intellectual property rights.

Economic Justice

Creating a fair and equitable international financial system, in which borrowers stand on equal footing with lenders in negotiations, will require radical restructuring. First priority must be the cancellation of Africa's unjust debt burden. The LAGOS PLAN OF ACTION for Africa's economic liberation should be implemented immediately (Ejigiri 1991).

The origins of these debts are tangled in histories of dictatorial regimes and the complicity of international financial institutions such as the World Bank and International Monetary Fund (IMF). Moreover, the effects of persistent and overwhelming debt payments by African governments can be seen in the declining standard of living in many countries, in social service cutbacks, and the waning availability of national resources for economic development.

A renewed international financial system must have oversight in place to prevent new odious debts. One solution would be to re-channel funding for development through the United Nations (UN) or bilateral avenues, and away from the World Bank and IMF. Charges levelled against these institutions emphasize that they have neglected to prioritize internal re-organization to allow for adequate democratic participation. The issue of international trade in protest against the Economic Partnership Agreements (EPAs), which seek to create Free Trade Areas (FTAs) between the European Union (EU) and many member nations of Africa should be reviewed. Such agreements were not in the best interests of the African continent and maintaining an unbalanced trade relationship by allowing industrialized countries to exploit the natural resources and raw materials of their African counterparts. Demonstrations against these unfair agreements should emphasize that respect for the economic sovereignty of all Africans must be a cornerstone of restructured international trade.

Human Rights

Recent years have seen augmented levels of global activism for the protection of human rights wherever violations may occur. Connections have been made across borders to create international constituencies for action. Increasingly, this trend is visible in Africa and should be promoted. For example, organized marches and sign-on letters, expressing concern about the crisis in Darfur, genocide in Rwanda should highlight the vibrant African constituency to counter human rights abuses on the continent and to assert the international responsibility to protect. As this constituency grows, we witness an increasing capacity of Africa's citizens to mobilize pressure to ensure these rights.

Women's Rights

African women continue to be most affected by global injustice, especially as it plays out on a local level. They are disproportionately affected by the global HIV/AIDS pandemic and face overwhelming levels of poverty and economic vulnerabilities. Furthermore, women are marginalized in decision-making processes, denying them the opportunity to exert control over their lives. African women's organizations should be allowed to participate actively in their community's social, economic and political affairs, and be recognized for that participation.

How Are these New Alternatives Emerging?

Due to the politics of pauperization of the populace by predatory African regimes, the central institutions of civil society are both fragmented and quiescent in most African countries. Nevertheless, churches, lawyers unions, students, contagious women's grassroots organizations in some countries are blowing down feudal walls of political monolithism and paving the way for popular participation in the democratic process. Examples are no longer in limited supply in Algeria, Zambia, Nigeria, Kenya, etc.

Our premise is therefore that capitalism has always had a world–wide dimension, whose forms are historically determined. The notion that the present historical phase is one of nomadic, de–territorialized and global capitalisms distorts reality, and constitutes the global projection of neo–classicism. The 'Fordist' era is thus reduced to the sum of national economies, while the world–wide dimension is now supposed to be an immediate, reified datum. The world–wide dimension is, on the contrary, an uneven and unstable process, generated by the articulation of different spatial levels, by the contradictions, crises and conflicts shaping them.

That is why one should also pinpoint the internal, class–conflict related reasons which drove the dominant States down the road of financial and commercial liberalization, of a re–definition of social and economic policies, and of the creation of regional areas. The reason why 'globalization' is neither an absolute nor an irreversibly total datum is also related to contradictions surviving in liberalization processes and between major States and areas. Due to unequal and combined development, even African 'Nation'—States are still the main arena of social conflict: there is still room for politics, precisely because capitalism is not an abstract, de–territorialized and immediately global quantity.

Tens of thousands of activists and advocates from around the globe gathered in Nairobi, Kenya for the seventh World Social Forum (WSF) in January. The rallying cry, 'Another world is possible,' served as a catalyst for debate and mobilization: what might this new world look like, and how are we to achieve it? The agenda was expansive. It included discussions on many campaigns and challenges across the spectrum of social, political and economic justice issues. Notably, the 2007 WSF marked the first time that the gathering was hosted in Africa, shedding new light on the role of African civil society in the work towards global justice.

The WSF produced several key frameworks for educating and mobilizing the impoverished majority to drastically improve the current global system. Numerous tactics are being utilized to implement new African alternatives to the current global economic system. Coalition building between local and international organizations with overlapping issue areas was displayed as a driving force within these emerging strategies. The following are examples of how coalition-building, new grassroots mobilization tactics, and a strong effort to democratize the movement itself appeared at the forefront of the effort to transform economic, social, and political systems to achieve sustainable development and social equality.

International Collaboration

The WSF created numerous opportunities for international coalition building, specifically on Africa Action's campaign areas of HIV/AIDS, debt cancellation, and Darfur. Many grassroots organizations, including the Tutlano AIDS Organization, which focuses on the plight of women in Malawi, the Kenyan Debt Relief Network (KENDREN), and Darfur activists from Uganda, sought to join forces with U.S.-based efforts. Beyond these projects, linkages are emerging between social and economic struggles in Africa, Asia, Central America, and South America. The Catholic Economic Justice Network and Jubilee South were present at the WSF as illustrations of coalitions that advocate for debt cancellation in the Global South.

Various women's groups pledged that relationships between the North and South must be strengthened in advocating for the human rights of women worldwide and that men also play a significant role in the implementation of that process. A travelling quilt, on which national representatives had sewn each patch to show continued unity in the gender equality struggle was presented at the WSF as a symbol of reinvigorated solidarity between women's groups worldwide. One example of the many attempts to collaborate was led by the African Forum on Debt and Development (AFRODAD), with a workshop on 100% debt cancellation focusing on the Democratic Republic of the Congo (DRC) and Liberia. During this workshop, panellists representing advocacy work in Sierra Leone, Liberia, and the DRC discussed the destabilizing impact the current massive debt burdens have had in every sector of the economy. After the panellists described local efforts, other participants shared their initiatives with AFRODAD and other Africa-based activists. Among them, the Jubilee USA Network announced their 'Have a Heart, Cancel Liberia's Debt' campaign, in which thousands of Valentines were collected across the U.S., asking U.S. Treasury Secretary Henry Paulson to cancel almost $4 billion of Liberia's debt.

Africa Action also contributed to the discussion by announcing efforts to engage the African immigrant community in the U.S. and to continue mobilizing people within the religious and student activist communities to join the global movement to cancel Africa's debt. The workshop closed with a call for more frequent dialogue to foster closer-knit relationships within the global advocacy community and to create more long-lasting partnerships.

Art as a Public Education and Mobilizing Tool

The WSF also created a space where budding artists within the areas of film, theatre, poetry, and performance could display their mobilization strategies. For instance, there was a tent dedicated to screening documentaries on the issue of economic disparities perpetuated by the system of global apartheid. One of the new films shown in the tent, Kieran Kid, documents the daily life of a Kenyan child living in Africa's largest slum, an illustration of a result of Africa's colonial legacy.

A night of spoken word and song served as a powerful tool in bonding, reenergizing and reminding the global advocacy community of the history of social movements. Art also played the role of reassuring the community of future success in our work, as long as consistency and commitment persist. Dennis Brutus, a long time anti-apartheid activist performed a powerful spoken word piece, revealing the intergenerational and diverse composition of Africa's activist community. The response of participants to the various art forms, including up-and-coming Zimbabwean singer Chiwoniso and Vibe Culture, demonstrated the power that art possesses in making local and global connections in societal struggles.

Democratizing the Movement

Kenyan media outlets reported how coalition building within the WSF process was not limited to the transformation of economic systems but also social and human rights struggles. For instance, the 'Q Spot' tent was designed to connect the lesbian, gay, bisexual, transgender and questioning (LGBT) community. East African LGBT groups led workshops, representing a region of the world where advocating for the rights of these minorities is largely taboo, even within some parts of the African activist community. The area provided the opportunity to challenge concerns within the community with a focus on stigma, awareness, and human rights issues.

Women and youth-focused workshops displayed the emerging tactics led by some of the most underrepresented members of society. One Tanzanian youth-led HIV/AIDS organization demonstrated how it has been educating youth on practicing abstinence, and redirecting sexual energy towards learning Tai Chi. Kenya-based organizations FEMNET and Daughters of Mumbi, as well as other women's groups, led workshops that tackled strategies combating violence against women and female circumcision, two very sensitive issues on the continent.

Rallies during the WSF demonstrated tactics used by activists around the world to move policy makers. The most captivating rally spoke to the economic and living situation of local Kenyans and to specific weaknesses of the WSF process. A group of local residents, effectively barred from the WSF due to high registration fees, stormed the WSF main office in an attempt to bring attention to this and other issues that had been overlooked. In addition, they protested the exclusion of local vendors from the WSF site in favour of food and service-providing companies.

This exclusion had the effect of preventing local Kenyans with less buying power from gaining access. The protest resulted in the elimination of fees for Kenyans during the final days of the WSF and in the opening of the WSF to local vendors. In this case, underrepresented voices were acknowledged, and solutions were implemented. The actions that were taken as a result of this rally exemplified what activists, as part of the WSF, strive to accomplish within the global community.

Opportunities to Improve Africa's Civil Society Solidarity

New alternatives to the current global economic system are emerging through the growth of coalitions worldwide. The WSF represents one way for the U.S. advocacy community to begin building solidarity movements with counterparts in the Global South. At the same time, the WSF also highlighted an additional option for advocates focused on Africa. The Africa Social Forum gives activists the opportunity to strengthen dialogue between those working diligently on these issues on the ground. The last meeting was held in Dakar, Senegal in December 2006 and tackled debt, free trade, democratization and gender equality, among other pertinent issues on the continent.

Representatives from the Africa Social Forum were in Nairobi and solicited membership and partnership from the global advocacy community. Members of civil society and activists working on various issues can use this forum as an opportunity to strategize and implement new ways to battle marginalization and social injustice.

Summary and Conclusion

Today, the world is witnessing a new phase of capitalism, with new forms of power and new forms of resistance. The hidden power is almost indestructible because throughout the ages, any attempt to unveil their hidden agenda and to expose the men behind the screen has been labelled 'a Conspiracy Theory' and those who risk their wealth and reputation to expose this power are accused of being 'Conspiracy Theorists.'

The key characteristic of this new epoch is the rise of truly transnational capital and a new globally integrated production and financial system. Production has become fragmented into countless and constantly changing phases that are decentralized and dispersed across the planet. In turn, the distinct segments are functionally integrated into vast global chains of production and distribution. Each autonomous national economy has been restructured and externally integrated, so that each 'national' economy becomes a constituent part of the larger global production system.

We also now have a truly global financial system. American President James Madison exposed money power by stating that '*History records that the money changers have used every form of abuse, intrigue, deceit, and violent means possible to maintain their control of governments by controlling money and its issuance.' And* President Abraham Lincoln opined: *The money power preys upon the nation in times of peace and conspires against it in times of adversity. It is more despotic than monarchy, more insolent than autocracy, more selfish than bureaucracy.*

Today, there is no longer any such thing as a national financial system. In fact, finance capital is the most mobile and the most transnationalized fraction of capital. This has major implications. Money capital exists in cyberspace, where it recognizes no borders and faces few, if any, state controls in Africa. Money capital subordinates fixed capital. Those who control money capital can appropriate values anywhere in the world by financial manipulation and relocate them on an ongoing basis to anywhere else in the world. This globally-integrated production and financial system underscores the increasing interpenetration of capital in all parts of the world, organized around the giant transnational corporations that drive the global economy.

There are important new mechanisms that facilitate this transnationalization of capital. The spread of stock markets, for instance, from the principal centres of the world economy to many if not most capital cities around the world, combined with 24 hour trading, facilitates an ever greater global trading and hence transnational ownership of shares. The global integration of national financial systems and new forms of money capital, including secondary derivative markets, has also made it easier for capital ownership to transnationalize.

Other mechanisms of integration are the sharp rise in foreign direct investment and the spread of TNC affiliates, the phenomenal increase in cross-border mergers and acquisitions, the growth of transnational interlocking of boards of directorates, the spread of cross-border strategic alliances of all sorts, and the mounting influence of transnational peak business associations. In this way, a transnational capitalist class has come into existence as the manifest agent of capitalist globalization promoting external domination through domestic control of THE STATE IN AFRICA.

However, there is a new type of class fractionation between local and national fractions of capital, on the one hand, and transnational fractions on the other. Transnational capital is now the hegemonic fraction of capital on a world scale. Trasnationally-oriented capitalist groups and elites are present now in all countries around the world, including THE STATE IN AFRICA as their loyal agent. These fractions, or their bureaucratic allies, exercise considerable influence if not outright control within most of the state apparatuses in Africa and around the world. They often dictate policy.

Indeed, capitalism has been reorganized into a new network structure, so that the system functions through interconnected webs that stretch across the globe. This is important because the old corporate dinosaur vertical structures are extinct. Now capital functions through vast networks of subcontracting and outsourcing, through numerous forms of alliance between different capitalist groups and other economic agents. It is transnational capital that stands at the pinnacle of these global networks. This means that there still may be local and national capitals but they cannot compete with transnationally mobile capital. If they want to remain competitive, if they want to continue playing the game, they must link up with transnational capital, and they must do so, structurally, in a way that subordinates them to transnational capital.

The visible element is there is a global working class that runs the factories, farms, and offices of the global economy. Their ranks can be found in the *maquiladoras*, in the agro-industrial complexes around the world, among the armies of service workers in global cities. However, the global working class is internally stratified. It is divided along national - as well as racial, ethnic, and gender - lines. The continued existence of the nation-state system in Africa serves to distort the consciousness and subjective experience of the global as well as African working class.

In distinction, the transnational capitalist class is a class group with a subjective consciousness of itself and its interests. Its members increasingly socialize together in their private institutions such as the World Economic Forum in Davos and develop a transnational class consciousness. In this sense it is a class-for-itself, to use Marx's language on this matter, whereas the global working class is a class-in-itself but not yet for-itself.

One may ask: where does actual political power rest in this new form of global capitalism that you describe? The answer is clear. There is a new transnational configuration of power. In part, this is where a transnational state comes into play, which is another novel aspect of the new epoch. The question is how can the transnational capitalist class exercise its political authority? Well, one way is through utilizing existing state apparatus in each country, and we have seen plenty of that. Another is through the transformation of existing international institutions, such as the old Bretton Woods institutions or the agencies of the United Nations system, and the creation of entirely new ones, such as the World Trade Organization. Transnational capital attempts to convert the structural power of the global economy over individual countries and over working classes in each nation-state into direct political authority or influence through this transnational state apparatus.

Transnational institutions attempt to coordinate global capitalism and impose capitalist domination beyond national borders. The IMF, for instance, by imposing a structural adjustment programme that opens up African countries to the penetration of transnational capital, the subordination of local labour, and the extraction of wealth by transnational capitalists, is operating as a transnational state institution to facilitate the exploitation of local labour by global capital. Although it is true that nation-state power and autonomy has declined/failed/collapsed, etc. in relation to transnational power structures, this image is somewhat misleading since these transnational power structures are localized within each African country by concrete social forces that are materially and politically part of the emergent transnational power bloc.

In this context, many may wonder about how America struggles for hegemony and global expansion? We cannot understand global hegemony, or the role of the U.S. state in the world, from a nation-state/interstate framework. Nation-state centric analyses of inter- and transnational relations fail to appreciate the integrative character of global capitalism. If by imperialism, we mean relentless pressures for outward expansion of capitalism and distinct political, military and cultural mechanisms that facilitate that expansion, then, yes, we are obviously seeing ongoing imperialism in 21st century. But there is nothing in this 'new' imperialism to suggest it is a U.S. drive for empire in competition with other nation-state capitalists. Those who make this argument have frozen their historical analysis in an earlier moment. They are trapped in the world of late 19th and early 20th century. They see world capitalism as still in its national 'monopoly' stage of Lenin's and Hilferding's day, so that U.S. interventionism can only be a drive for 'U.S.' hegemony over other states.

Recent U.S. policies such as the imposition of neo-liberal structural adjustment programmes and sponsorship of free trade agreements have served to further pry open regions and sectors around world to global capitalism, to transnational capital. The IMF and other transnational state agencies have not acted as simple instruments of 'U.S.' imperialism. I know of no single IMF structural adjustment programme that creates conditions in intervened country that favours 'U.S.' capital in any special way, rather than opening up the intervened country, its labour and resources, to capitalists from any corner of world. The first thing the U.S. occupation forces did after the invasion of Iraq was not to seal off country to all but its own capital but to decree a foreign investment law that invited capitals from any corner of the world to invest.

The U.S. state has attempted to play a leadership role on behalf of transnational capitalist interests. That it is increasingly unable to do so points not to heightened national rivalry but to the impossibility of the task at hand given the crisis of global capitalism. In this sense, interventionism and militarized globalization are less a campaign for U.S. hegemony than a contradictory response to the crisis of global capitalism—to economic stagnation, legitimation problems, and rise of counter-hegemonic forces.

There are specific, new problems posed by the new globalism. The system is in chaos; its contradictions are explosive and, frankly, humanity is in grave danger. The global crisis is one of social polarization and social reproduction, reflecting the deeper structural problem of over-accumulation. The crisis is also of sustainability. An ecological holocaust has already begun. If we do not pull back from the precipice, and very soon, we could well be facing catastrophic consequences.

One may need to step back and see the big picture. The 1980s saw a recovery of profits following the decline of the 1970s. There was a massive wave of transnational investment in the 1980s and the 1990s, leading to overcapacity and overproduction. Capital began increasingly to seek an investment outlet through financial speculation - the notorious 'casino capitalism.' The volatility of financial speculation in the face of over-accumulation led to the 1995 Mexico peso crisis and its 'tequila effect' elsewhere, followed by the 1997-98 Asian financial meltdown, the Russian, Turkish, and Brazilian crises, and worldwide recession from 2001-02.

It is at this point that structural and political pressures building up in the system lead towards a militarization of global accumulation. The U.S. state as the guarantor of the system sought to open up new outlets for the global surplus through a military Keynesianism and a war mobilization, through the 'creative destruction' of war. From the 1990s to date we seen a shift in the axis of accumulation, from computer and information technology as the cutting edge, along with financial speculation in stocks, real estate, and so forth, to a military-industrial-petroleum-construction-engineering complex.

States in Africa, created and sustained by capitalist imperialism, are responsive to the demands of transnational capital yet are unable to capture and redistribute surpluses, to regulate the circuits of accumulation, and therefore to fulfil social functions. These fragile States in Africa cannot absorb popular demands and resolve contradictions. All this leads to crises of legitimacy and governability, to chronic instability, to waves of crime, social decomposition, spreading anomie.

The problem of social control in the global capitalist order becomes primordial. This was symbolized in the late 2005 insurrection of the excluded in Paris, Ogonis in Nigeria, etc. We are seeing a transition from social welfare to social control states, the rise of police states in Africa that manage prison-industrial complexes to contain the excluded population, new forms of social and spatial apartheid, social cleansing, Katrina-type militarized control responses to disasters and other stresses. We may be heading more generally towards a global police state.

To claim that globalization has led many nations out from underdevelopment is to phrase the question within a misleading nation-state framework of analysis, as if what 'develops' or what is 'underdeveloped' is a nation-state. This ignores class polarization, power relations, and social inequality within each nation-state. Globalization has turned many people in the South into participants—consumers—in the global marketplace - and spread the culture of global capitalism, with its individualism, consumerism, escapism and banality. But it has generated downward mobility, marginality and immiseration for many more.

Inequalities worldwide have reached unprecedented proportions. The pattern is a polarization between 20 percent of the population that is advancing, on the one hand, and 80 percent that is falling behind, on the other. There are new transnational class inequalities that cannot be understood within the North-South divide. The global South is increasingly dispersed across the planet so too is the global North. India now has 200 million middle class consumers who participate in the global market, as does China, even while majorities in those countries sink into destitution. Global social polarization is cutting across national lines in new ways.

What viable African or global strategies are available for challenging transnational capitalism? Social justice requires a measure of transnational social governance over this global production and financial system as a necessary first step in a radical redistribution of wealth and power to poor majorities. What would such a new redistributive component involve and how would it come about? Certainly it would require a reversal of neo-liberal policies at the nation-state level. But redistribution is not enough. It must be linked to the transformation of class and property relations. Local class and property relations have global implications. Webs of interdependence and dependence link the local to the global.

Pockets of counter-hegemony are now emerging more clearly, for example, in the rise of an anti-neo-liberal power bloc in Latin America centred on Venezuela. Nonetheless, the challenge is how to convert a reactive global resistance into a proactive global programme. The recent experiences of Venezuela, Brazil, South Africa, and Haiti, among others, make clear the limitations to reintroduction of a redistributive project at nation-state level alone.

Any challenge to capitalist state power must involve a major transnational component. Struggles at African nation-state level are far from futile. They remain central to the prospects for social justice and progressive social change. But any such struggles must be part of a more expansive transnational counterhegemonic project and a programme to rein in on the global market and the power of global capital. An alternative to global capitalism must be a transnational project, involving transnational trade unionism, transnational social movements, transnational political organizations, and so on.

What we can see in all of this is globalized states in African peripheral countries acting in the service of transnational capital even at the expense of their own national populations. The state's historical function of preserving the social order is increasingly accomplished with no more than a passing glance at the form of justice that had once ensured governability. Here, I have in mind a Gallup International poll of 50,000 people in 68 countries found that 65% do not think their country is governed by the will of the people, even though 47% thought their elections were free and fair, according to a BBC World Edition report, http://news.bbc.co.uk, (accessed September 14, 2005). The governance exercised by globalized states amounts to providing macroeconomic and political stability while enforcing on its population norms established at the transnational level.

This last point is well illustrated by NAFTA, etc. negotiated by technocrats for the three major states of the North American continent. It gives corporations the right to sue governments to recover lost future profits resulting from state action, even if that action was undertaken to promote the common good of its nation, e.g. protect health, the environment, working conditions, income levels, etc. Further, such suits are adjudicated not in national courts, but by a transnational body of experts operating in secret. States are expected to enforce its decisions on its own nation's taxpayers. This privileging of investor rights (i. e. the interests of transnational capital) over the democratic rights of an African nation, agreed to by its own state, shows the extent to which that state is no longer a nation-state but a globalized state.

States, even globalized states, require some measure of legitimacy in order to be able to govern. That means that political elites have to respond to concerted popular pressures, even those that oppose the agenda of transnational capital. The opposition to MAI was moved by the realization that its adoption would deny them the opportunity to protect their own interests against foreign capital. It was born of a nationalistic concern to preserve sovereignty in hopes that democratic pressure would be able to make the state an instrument of the popular will. They were unwilling to surrender to transnational capital the last, best means for protecting the national interest—the nation-state.

This suggests a multi-pronged strategy in opposition to transnational capital: 1) a popular struggle for the democratic retrieval of the state by the nation, and 2) resistance at every turn to the efforts of transnational capital to consolidate its global rule. These ccomponents of a multi-pronged strategy include:

a. expose and disrupt the emerging transnational governance structure
b. democratic retrieval of the state by the nation
c. build a global civil society as a future global nation with popular democracy (cross-border solidarity leading toward transnational power of popular classes no longer mediated by nation-states)
d. alterglobalization from below: a global Lilliputian strategy of cooperative localism

To date, the anti-corporate global justice movement has focused primarily on the second of these strategies. But it should not forgo the powerful appeal of an enlightened nationalism to the popular classes to 'take back the state' from the globalizing elite who have betrayed the nation. The nation-state remains an important terrain of political struggle even in a globalizing world.

As we have seen, a state may serve either the interests of a dominant class or popular classes. Which it is, depends on the political activity of the various classes and the leadership they throw up. Globalized states are led by political elites beholden to transnational capital. They have put forth a neo-liberal project that identifies the interest of the nation with that of capital, and especially transnational capital. But this identification has worn increasingly thin as economic inequalities have widened within nations and between them as well. In response, radical social movements have emerged. Some, as the *piquetero* movement in Argentina and the popular and indigenous movement in Bolivia, have even been able to topple neo-liberal governments.

The social movements of Latin America are putting forth alternative projects for nations and even redefining what the nation is. Some have been anti-state while others have recognized that to the extent the state can be captured by popular forces, it can be a powerful instrument against transnational capital. Witness *Chavismo* (Gindin 2005:27-29) in Venezuela, which has given rise to participatory leadership and power in poor communities in a kind of 'nationwide social movement-cum-political party.' This kind of extension of a revolutionary state into civil society and extension of civil society into the state is similar to the early development of Committees for the Defence of the Revolution or CDRs in revolutionary Cuba. In other cases social movements remain outside the state, thereby avoiding cooptation by entrenched political elites and preserve the ability to act independently through civil society to affect state policy, as for example, *Movimento dos Trabalhadores Rurais Sem Terra or MST in Brazil.*

Often social movements are better able to represent the general interest of a nation than political elites, tied as the latter are to the particular interests of dominant classes. This is because in order to grow to the scale of a mass social movement, they must universalize their agenda in order to attract broad support and build alliances. It is even possible for a social movement to build a kind of parallel power to the state and the dominant class. This can be done by creating alternative economic institutions (e.g. cooperatives as in Mexico's Yucatan or occupied factories in Argentina) and autonomous participatory structures of governance (e.g. the Zapatista's *Juntas de Buen Gobierno* and their *Caracoles*), that strengthen civil society as an alternative to a globalized state. In this way, popular forces can literally reshape the nation out from under the control of the state. Which of these various relations between social movements and the state is optimal depends on conjunctural factors such as the country's political leadership, the correlation of class forces within civil society, pressures from outside by transnational capital, etc. Pragmatics, not ideology, must shape strategy.

It is important to recognize that such popular struggles are not solely motivated by material self-interest. As we said earlier, a nation is an imagined community. As such, the image of what that community may be is crucial. How do the members of a nation understand themselves? What are the core values they share? What kind of life do they aspire to for all members of the nation? The answers to these questions define what a particular nation is. People will be motivated to struggle in defence of that image as much as, or sometimes even more than, their self interest. That is because the nation they belong to is a part of their own identity.

References

1. K. Marx, F. Engels.(1973). *Manifeste du Parti communiste*, Paris, Livre de Poche, pp 10-11.
2. N. Poulantzas. (1978). *L'Etat, le pouvoir, le socialisme*, Paris, PUF, p. 118.
3. Je reprend à mon compte les analyses de Daniel Bensaïd dans son remarquable livre *Le Pari melancolique*, Paris, Fayard, 1997.
4. N. Poulantzas. (1976). « Les transformations actuelles de l'Etat, la crise politique et la crise de l'Etat ,' in *La crise de l'Etat*, Paris, PUF, p. 48
5. Nicos Poulantzas avait eu raison, dans les années 70, de rejetter les prévisions, assez diffusées à l'époque, d'un « déclin » de l'hégémonie mondiale nord-américaine. Cf. *Les classes sociales dans le capitalisme aujourd'hui*, Paris, Seuil, 1974, pp 94-95
6. N. Poulantzas, Les classes sociales dans le capitalisme aujourd'hui, p. 89.

Bibliography

Abrams, Phillip (1988). 'Notes on the Difficulty of Studying the State.' *Journal of Historical Sociology* Vol. 1. No.1.

Adekanye, B. (1996) *Disarming Ethnic Guerrillas, Power Sharing and Transition to Democracy in Africa: Ethiopia, Mozambique, South Africa and Uganda as Comparative Cases*, Interim research report, International Peace Research Institute (PRIO), Oslo.

_______ (1999) *Power Sharing and Public Sector Reform: New Approaches to the Distribution and Management of Governmental Power*, mimeo, UNRISD, Geneva.

Ake, Claude. (1996). *Democracy and Development in Africa.* Washington, DC: Brookings Institution.

———————(1989). 'How politics underdevelops Africa.' In: J. Ihonvbere, In., *The Political Economy of Crisis and Underdevelopment in Africa: Selected Works of Claude Ake.* JAD Publishers, Lagos.

Akwetey, E., Transition to democracy and the reform of post-colonial regimes in Zambia and Ghana. in B. Beckman and L.M. Sachikonye (eds.), Labour Regimes and Liberalisation in Africa, University of Zimbabwe Press, Harare.

Alam, M. Shahid. (1999). 'Does Sovereignty Matter for Economic Growth?' In John.

Adams and Francesco Pigliaru, eds., *Economic Growth and Change.* Cheltenham, UK: Edward Elgar.

Amin, Samir. (1973). .*Neo-Colonialism in West Africa.*

New York, Monthly Review Press.

Altvater, Elmar; Kurt Hubner; Jochen Lorentzen, et al, eds. (1991). *The Poverty of Nations: A Guide to the Debt Crisis — From Argentina to Zaire.* Zed Books, London.

Bangura, Y. (1998) Democratization, Equity and Stability: African Politics and Societies in the 1990s, Discussion Paper No. 93, UNRISD, Geneva.

Barber, Benjamin and Schulz, Andrea. (1996). *Jihad versus McWorld: How the Planet is Both Falling Apart and Coming Together.* New York: Ballantine Books.

Bartels, D. & A. (1988). 'Are Siberian native people part of a 'Fourth World." *Dialectical Anthropology* 12:245-252.

Barzun, Jacques . *(1965). Race, A Study in Superstition.* New York, N.Y., Harper & Row.

Barry N. Schwartz and Robert Disch. (1970).*White Racism: Its History, Pathology and Practice.* N.Y., Dell Book.

Bates, R. (1981) *Markets and States in Tropical Africa: The Political Basis of Agricultural Choices*, University of California Press, Berkeley.

Batley, R.A. (1996). 'Public and private relationships and performance in service provisioning,' *Urban Studies*, 33(4-5), pp 489-505.

Bayart, Jean-Francois. (1993). *The State in Africa.* NY: Longman. From a similar analytical perspective, Chabal and Daloz make an even stronger argument for rooting these networks of 'asymmetrical reciprocity' in African social structures. See Patrick Chabal and Jean-Pascal Daloz, *Africa Works* (Bloomington, IN: Indiana University Press, 1999).

——————(1989). Civil society in Africa. In: P. Chabal, ea., *Political Domination in Africa.* Cambridge University Press, Cambridge.

——————(2005). *The Illusion of Cultural Identity*, London: Hurst

Ferguson, James. (2006). *Global Shadows: Africa in the Neoliberal World Order*, Duke University Press.

Beckman, B. (1982). 'Whose state?: State and capitalist development in Nigeria', *Review of African Political Economy*, No. 23.

_______ (1988a). 'The post-colonial state: Crisis and reconstruction', *IDS Bulletin* 19(4).

_______ (1988b). 'Comments on Hyden's State and nation under stress,' in *Recovery in Africa: A Challenge for Development in the 1990s*, Ministry of Foreign Affairs, Stockholm.

_______ (1992). 'Empowerment or repression: The World Bank and the politics of African adjustment', in P. Gibbon, Y. Bangura and A Ofstad (eds.), Authoritarianism, Democracy and Adjustment: The Politics of 24 UNRISD Discussion Paper No. 113 Economic Reform in Africa, Scandinavian Institute of African Studies, Uppsala with UNRISD, Chr. Michelsen Institute and FANTOFT.

Berman, Yaniv (April 1, 2004), *Exclusive - Al-Qa'ida: Islamic State Will Control the World*, The Media Line<http://web.archive.org/web/20040610173219/http://www.themedialine.org/news/news_detail.asp?NewsID=5420>. Retrieved on 6 July 2008 .

Blake, W.O. (1858). *History of Slavery and Slave Trade.* J. and H. Miller Co.

Blom Hansen, Thomas and Finn Stepputat (eds.) (2001). States of Imagination. *Ethnographic Explorations of the Postcolonial State. Durham:* University of Duke Press.

Bolnick, B. (1997). 'Establishing fiscal discipline: The cash budget in Zambia.' in M.S. Grindle (ed.), *Getting Good Government: Capacity Building in the Public Sectors of Developing Countries*, Harvard Institute for International Development, Harvard University, Cambridge.

Bond, Patrick. (2006). *Looting Africa: The Economics of Exploitation.* London: Zed Books, p. 2.

Boutros-Ghali, B. (1994). 'Foreword,' in *Voice of indigenous peoples: Native people address the United Nations.* Edited by A. Ewen, pp 9-15. Santa Fe, New Mexico: Clear Light Publishers.

Bracking, Sarah and Graham Harrison, *'Africa: imperialism goes naked,' Monthly Review*, Nov, 2003.

Brough, M. 1989. *Indigenous social movements: A theoretical perspective.* Bachelor of Arts with Honours, Department of Anthropology and Sociology, Brisbane: University of Queensland.

Bryne, D. (1982). 'Class and the local state.' *International Journal of Urban and Regional Research* 6(1): 61-82.

Buchanan ,Patrick, J.(January 1, 2002), *Say Goodbye to the Mother Continent*, <http://www.theamericancause.org/patsaygoodbye.htm>. Retrieved on 21 May 2008 .

——————— (May 23, 2006). *The Death of the Nation State*, <http://www.theamericancause.org/print/052206_print.htm>. Retrieved on 21 May 2008 .

Burke, Edmund. 2000. *On Empire, Liberty and Reform: Speeches and Letters.* ed. David Bromwich. New Haven: Yale University Press.

Bushman, Richard Lyman. (1998). 'Markets and Composite Farms in Early America,' *William and Mary Quarterly*, 3d ser., 55.

Campbell, Horace. (1987). *Rasta and Resistance.* Trenton, NJ: Africa World Press.

Camilleri, J. and Falk, J. (1992), *The End of Sovereignty?: The Politics of a Shrinking and Fragmenting World*, Edward Elgar, Aldershot.

Capps, Gavin (2005). 'Redesigning the Debt Trap,' *International Socialism* 107, June 27, 2005, http://www.isj.org.uk/index.php4?id=116issue=107), accessed 08/30/09.

Carlson, J. (1998) Foreign Aid, Macro-Economic Governance and State Capacity in Crisis States: The Impact of Swedish Aid, mimeo, UNRISD, Geneva.

Chapin, M.(1991). 'The practical value of ecodevelopment research,' in *Biodiversity: Culture, nature and ecodevelopment.* Edited by M. Oldfield and J. Alcorn, pp 237-247. Boulder, Colorado: Westview Press.

Chazan, N. (1988). 'Ghana: Problems of governance and the emergence of civil society.' in L. Diamond et al. (eds.), *Democracy in Developing Countries: Africa*, Vol. 2, Lynne Rienner, Boulder.

Cheikh Anta Diop.(1987). *Precolonial Black Africa: A Comparative Study of the Political and Social Systems of Europe and Black Africa, from Antiquity to the Formation of Modern States.* Translated by Harold J Salemson. Contributor Harold J Salemson. Published by L. Hill, 1987. Original from the University of Michigan.

Chomsky, Noam.(2000). 'Control of Our Lives,' lecture at Albuquerque, New Mexico, February 2000. The World Bank Annual Report 2000. Economic Commission for Africa, *Transforming Africa's Economies: Overview,* April 2001.*Eliminating World Poverty: Making Globalization Work for the Poor*, White Paper on International Development Presented to the Parliament of the United Kingdom by Command of her Majesty, December, 2000. 'Debt and Sustainable Development,' Technical Advisory Paper # 4, MDGD, Bureau for Development Policy, UNDP, May 1999.

Christopher Chase-Dunn.(1989). *Global Formation: Structures of The World-Economy. New York: Basil Blackwell.*

————————————(1975). 'The effects of international economic dependence and inequality: a cross-national study,' *American Sociological Review* 40: 720-738. Reprinted in John W. Meyer and Michael T. Hannan (eds.). (1979). *National Development and the World System*, Chicago: University of Chicago Press.

————————————(1981). 'Interstate system and capitalist world-economy: one logic or two?' *International Studies Quarterly* 25, 1:19-42, March. Reprinted in *World System Structure: Continuity and Change*, edited by W. Ladd Hollist and James Rosenau. Beverly Hills: Sage, 1981 and in Joseph Grieco (ed.) The International System and the International Political Economy, London: Edward Elgar, 1993.

————————————and Richard Rubinson. (1977). 'Toward a structural perspective on the world-system.' *Politics and Society* 7, 4:453-76.

—————————— and Joan Sokolovsky. (1983). 'Interstate systems, world-empires and the capitalist world-economy,' *International Studies Quarterly* 27, 3.

——————————and Thomas D. Hall.(eds.). (1991). Core/ Periphery Relations in the Precapitalist Worlds. Boulder: Westview Press.

Chomsky, Noam.(1995). *What Uncle Sam Really Wants.* Berkeley, CA: Odonian.

Clark, J. F. (2005, Sep) '*The Contribution of Flawed Elections to State-Reformulation in Sub-Saharan Africa: Evidence from Several Cases*' *Paper presented at the annual meeting of the American Political Science Association, Marriott Wardman Park, Omni Shoreham, Washington Hilton, Washington, DC* Online <PDF> Retrieved 2006-10-05 from http://www.allacademic.com/meta/p40399_index.html

Clinton, William. (2003). '*Civil Society' - An Agreed Definition* (2003) available from http://pages.britishlibrary.net/blwww3/3way/civilsoc.htm; Internet.

Clinton, William 'Remarks to the 49th General Assembly of the United Nations, 26 September 1994.' In Joseph Nye, *Understanding International Conflict*, 4th ed. (New York: Longman, 2003), 48.

Cohen, I. L. and A. Arato. (1990). *Civil Society and Political Theory.* MIT Press, Cambridge, Mass.

Conrad, Earl. (1967). *The Invention of the Negro.* Paul S. Eriksson, Inc.: New York.

Coombs, Norman. (2008).*The Black Experience in America: The Immigrant Heritage of America.* IndyPublis: New York

Cox, Oliver C. (1970). *Caste, Class and Race* (Modern Reader paperbacks, published by Monthly Review Press, New York, N.Y.

Corrigan, Philip Richard D., and Derek Sayer. (1985). *The Great Arch: English State Formation as Cultural Revolution.* Oxford: Blackwell.

Churchill, W. and G. Morris. (1987). Between a rock and a hard place - left-wing revolution, right-wing reaction and the destruction of indigenous people. *Cultural Survival Quarterly* 11(3):17-24.

Clarke, W.C. (1990). 'Learning from the past: Traditional knowledge and sustainable development.' *The Contemporary Pacific* 2(2):223-53.

Colchester, M. (1994). 'Sustaining the forests: The community-based approach in south and south-east Asia.' *Development and Change* 25:69-100.

Connor, W. (1978). 'A nation is a nation, is a state, is an ethnic group is a ....' *Ethnic and Racial Studies* 1(4):377-400.

Cooper, F. (1997). 'Africa and the World Economy,' in Fred Cooper, et. al., eds., *Tensions of Empire: Peasants, Labour and the Capitalist World System in Africa and Latin America*, Berkeley, California: University of California Press.

Cronin, David. (2007). 'African countries fight EU for survival,' *IPS*, May 22.

Curtin, Philip D. (1969). *The Atlantic Slave Trade: A Census*. Madison, WI: University of Wisconsin Press.

Dallam, H.E. (1991). The growing voice of indigenous peoples: Their use of storytelling and rights discourse to transform multilateral development bank policies. *Arizona Journal of International and Comparative Law* 8(2):1117-148.

David Brion Davis and Steven Mintz. (1998). *The Boisterous Sea of Liberty: A Documentary History of America from the Discovery through the Civil War.* New York.

Davidson, Basil. (1961). *Black Mother: The Years of the African Slave Trade* (Boston, Mass., Little Brown and Company, 1961), Chapter I, and pp 1–25.

——————1973. *Africa in Modern History*, Penguin: London.

Diamond, Larry.(1995). *Promoting Democracy in the 1990s: Actors and Instruments, Issues and Imperatives,* report to the Carnegie Commission on Preventing Deadly Conflict, December 1995, 48.

Dijk, J.A.G.M. van (1993b). 'Communication Networks and Modernization.' *Communication Research, 20*(3), 384 407.

Dijk, Jan van (1991/1999). *De Netwerkmaatschappij, Sociale aspecten van nieuwe media.* Houten: Bohn Stafleu en van Loghum/ London, Thousand Oaks, New Delhi: Sage Publications.

Donzelot, Jacques. (1984). *L'invention du social: Essai sur le déclin des passions politiques.* Paris: Arthème Fayard.

Doornbos, M. (1990). 'The African state in academic debate: Retrospect and prospect.' *Journal of Modern African Studies* 28(2): 179-198.

Duncan, S. S. and M. Godwin. (1982). 'The local state and restructuring social relations: Theory and practice.' *International Journal of Urban and Regional Research* 6(2): 157-185.

Duhaylungsod, L. and D. Hyndman. (1993). 'Where T'boli bells toll: Political ecology voices behind the Tasaday hoax.' *Document No. 73*, Copenhagen: IWGIA

Dyck, N. (1985). 'Aboriginal peoples and nation-states: An introduction to the analytical issues,' in *Indigenous peoples and the nation-state: 4th world politics in Canada, Australia and Norway*. Edited by N. Dyck, pp1-26. St. John's, Newfoundland, Canada: Memorial University of Newfoundland.

Elford, D. (1995). *Conservation by self-determination in Central America: A critical ethnography*. Bachelor of Arts with Honours, Department of Anthropology and Sociology, Brisbane: University of Queensland.

Escobar, A. (1988). 'Power and visibility: Development and the invention of management in the Third World.' *Current Anthropology* 3:428-443.

Ejigiri, Damien. (1991). 'The Lagos Plan: Nigeria's Readiness to Implement the Delinking Strategy for Economic Development,' *International Journal of Public Sector Management*,Vol.(4).No.1

Ekeh, Peter P. (1975) 'Colonialism and the Two Publics in Africa: A Theoretical Statement.' *Comparative Studies in Society and History*, 17:91-112.

——————————(1983). *Colonialism and social structure: University of Ibadan Inaugural Lecture 1980*. Ibadan University Press, Ibadan.

——————————(1992). The constitution of civil society in African history and politics. In B. Caron, E. Gboyega, & E. Osaghae (Eds.), *Democratic transition in Africa*. CREDU, University of Ibadan, Ibadan, pp 83–104.

——————————(1994). Historical and cross-cultural contexts of civil society in Africa. Paper present at the USADI workshop on Civil Society, Democracy and Development in Africa, Washington, DC.

——————————(1995). *Kingship and civil society in post-colonial Africa*. Mimeo.

Elkins, Stanley. (1997). *Slavery : A Problem in American Institutional and Intellectual Life*. Chicago: University of Chicago Press.

Eric, Toussaint.(2005). *Your Money or Your Life: The Tyranny of Global Finance* .Chicago: Haymarket Books. P. 279.

Fabian, J. (1983). *Time and the other: How anthropology makes its object*. New York: Columbia University Press.

Fatton, R., Jr. (1992). *Predatory Rule: State and Civil Society in Africa.* Lynne Rienner Publishers, Boulder, Colo., and London.

Field, A. (1984). The indigenous peoples' network. *Cultural Survival Quarterly* 8(4):66-67.

Ferlie, E., A. Pettigrew, L. Ashburner and L. Fitzgerald (1996) The New Public Management in Action, Oxford University Press, Oxford.

Fanon, Frantz. (1963). *The Wretched of the Earth.* Translated by Constance Farrington. New York: Grove Press. Originally published in French, 1961.

Fine, R. (1992). Civil society theory and the politics of transition in South Africa. *Review of African Political Economy 55:* 71-83.

Floyd, Barry. (1979). *Jamaica: An Island Microcosm.* New York, NY: St. Martin's Press.

Fox, Jonathan and Luis Hernandez.(1989). 'Offsetting the Iron Law of Oligarchy: The Ebb and Flow of Leadership Accountability in a Regional Peasant Organization,' *Grassroots Development* 13:2 (1989): 8-15.

Frank, A. G. (1970), 'The Development of Underdevelopment,' *Monthly*

*Review Press,(*18). 4; pp17-31.

Franklin, John Hope and Alfred A. Moss, Jr., (2000). (*From Slavery to Freedom: A History of African Americans.* 8th ed. New York: A.A. Knopf.

Frazier, E. Franklin. (1965). *Race and Culture in the Modern World.* Beacon Press: Boston.

Gallagher, Buell G. (1946). *Color and Conscience.* Harper & Bros.: New York.

Giddens, A. (1991a). *The Consequences of Modernity.* Stanford (Cal): Stanford University Press, Oxford: Basil Blackwell, Cambridge: Polity Press.

——————(1991b). *Modernity and Self Identity; Self and Society in the Late Modern Age.* Cambridge: Polity Press.

Godelier, M.(1970). *Sur les Sociétés Précapitalistes.* Paris, Editions Sociales.

GRABURN, N.H.H. (1981). 1,2,3,4... Anthropology and the Fourth World. *Culture* 1(1):66-70.

Gorringe, Timothy. (1999). In his *Fair Shares: Ethics and the Global Economy*, London: Thames and Hudson.

Gossett, Thomas F. (1965). *Race … The History of an Idea in America.* Schocken Books: New York.

Gouws, A. (1993). Political tolerance and civil society: The case of South Africa. *Politikon: The South African Journal of Political Studies* 20(1): 15-31.

Gowan, Peter. (1999). *The Global Gamble: Washington's Bid for World Dominance.* London: Verso.

——————————(2003). 'U. S. Hegemony Today.' *Monthly Review*, 55:3, 30–50.

Gramsci, Antonio. 1971. *Selections from the Prison Notebooks.* New York: International.

Green, David. (1993). *Reinventing Civil Society: the Rediscovery of Welfare Without Politics.* Institute of Economic Affairs, London

GRIGGS, R. (1992). Background on the term 'Fourth World.' *Fourth World Documentation Project reprint,* 28 May 1995, ftp://ftp.halcyon.com/FWDP/fourthw.txt.

——————. (1994a). Geopolitics and the Fourth World in Europe. *Fourth World Bulletin* 3(3):1, 4-7.

——————. (1994b). Ethnicity vs nationalism - the European nations. *Research and Exploration.* 10(3):259-263.

——————. ND. 'The breakdown of states.' *Fourth World Documentation Project reprint,* 16 July 1995, ftp://ftp.halcyon.com/FWDP/statebrk.txt.

———————(1994). 'Ethnicity vs nationalism - the European nations.' *Research and Exploration.* 10(3):259-263.

Grosfoguel, Ramón . (1996). 'From Cepalismo to Neoliberalism: A World-System Approach to Conceptual Shifts in Latin America,' in: *Review*, 19 (2): 131-154.

————————————— (2002). 'Colonial Difference, Geopolitics of Knowledge and Global Coloniality in the Modern/Colonial Capitalist World-System,' in *Review* Vol. 25 No. 3: 203-24.

Gruffydd Jones, Branwen(ed.). (2006). *Decolonising International Relations: Imperatives, Possibilities and Limitations.* Rowman & Littlefield. New York

Hameso, Seyoum. (1999). Global Power, Democracy and Profit in Africa, The Sidama Concern, 4, 3 [online] URL: http://www.sidamaconcern.com/articles/globalisationtion.html

Hansen, Thomas Blom. (2001). 'Governance and State Mythologies in Mumbai.' In *States of Imagination: Ethnographic Explorations of the Postcolonial State,* edited by Thomas Blom Hansen and Finn Stepputat, 221–256. Durham: Duke University Press.

Harbeson, J. W. (1992). Civil society and state reformation in Africa. Paper presented to the International Conference on Civil Society in Africa, 5-10 January, Jerusalem, mimeo.

——————& Rothchild, D. (2000) (ed). *Africa In World Politics: The African State System In Flux*. Boulder, Colorado: Westview Press.

Hart, Bushnell. (1969). *Slavery and Abolition, 1831–1841*. London: Greenwood Press Reprint (April 30, 1969).

Harvey, cited in David Harvey and Giovanni Arrighi, (1994). The Long Twentieth Century: Money, Power, and the Origins of our Times, *Verso*.

Hashim, Y. (1994) The State and Trade Unions in Africa, Ph.D. dissertation, Institute for Social Studies, The Hague.

Henwood, Doug. (2003). *After the New Economy*. New York: The New Press.

Hernton, Calvin C. (1965). *Sex and Racism in America*. Doubleday & Co: New York .

Hopkins, A. G. (1973). 'Economic History of West Africa,' Columbia University Press.

Hilferding, Rudolf. 1981 (1910). *Finance Capital: A Study of the Latest Phase of Capitalist Development*. London: Routledge.

Hitchcock, R.K. (1994). International human rights, the environment, and indigenous peoples. *Colorado Journal of International Environmental Law and Policy* 5:1-22.

HOBART, M. (1993). *An anthropological critique of development: The growth of ignorance*. London: Routledge.

Horowitz, D.L. (1985) *Ethnic Groups in Conflict*, University of California Press, Berkeley.

Houseal, B., C. Macfarland, G. Archibold and A. Chiarl.(1985). 'Indigenous cultures and protected areas in Central America.' *Cultural Survival Quarterly* 9(1):10-19.

Hutchful, E. (1997) *The Institutional and Political Framework of Macro-Economic Management in Ghana*, Discussion Paper No. 82 UNRISD, Geneva.

————————&A. Bathily (1998) *The Military and Militarism in Africa*, CODESRIA, Dakar.

Hyden, G. (1983) No Shortcuts to Progress: African Development Management in Perspective, Heinemann, London.

Hyndman, D. (1988). 'Melanesian resistance to ecocide and ethnocide: Transnational mining projects and the Fourth World on the island of New Guinea,' in *Tribal Peoples and Development Issues: A Global Overview.* Edited by J.H. Brodley, pp 281-298. California: Mayfield Publishing Company.

—————. (1991). Organic Act rejected in the Cordillera: Dialectics of a continuing Fourth World autonomy movement in the Philippines. *Dialectical Anthropology* 16:169-184.

—————. (1994a). *Ancestral rain forests and the mountain of gold.* Boulder, Colorado: Westview Press, Inc.

—————. (1994b). Conservation through self-determination: Promoting the interdependence of cultural and biological diversity *Human Organisation* 53(3):296-302.

Ibrahim, J. (1998) Civic Culture and the African Religious Sphere, paper presented at the conference on Civil Society, Authoritarianism and Globalisation, Stockholm University (Stockholm, 18-20 September).

IIDEA (1997) The International IIDEA Handbook of Electoral System Design; International Institute for Democracy and Electoral Assistance, Stockholm.

IMF (1998). Fiscal Reforms in Low-Income Countries Experience Under IMF-Supported Programmes, by a Staff Team led by George T. Abed, Washington, DC.25 New Directions in State Reform: Implications for Civil Society in Africa

IMF. (1998).Prospective Link With EMU Poses Challenge For CFA Franc Zone IMF Survey January 12, 1998, 15-16.

Jackson, Robert H. and Carl G. Rosberg.(1982). 'Why Africa's Weak States Persist: The Empirical and the Juridical in Statehood', *World Politics* 35

———————(1990). *Quasi-States: Sovereignty, International Relations, and the Third World*, Cambridge: Cambridge University Press.

Johnson, C.S., Bitter Canaan.(1987). *The Story of the Negro Republic.* New Jersey: Transaction Books

Jonah, Gindin. (2005). 'Chavistas in the Halls of Power, Chavistas on the Street,' *NACLA Report on the Americas*, Vol. 38, No. 5 (March-April 2005), pp 27-29.

Kabah, A.T. (1998). Broadcast to the Nation on Peace and Security, Freetown, Sierra Leone, 2 September.

Kauffman, D., Kraay, A.& Mastruzzi, M. (2005). 'Governance Matters IV: Governance Indicators for 1996-2004', World Bank Policy Research Working Paper Series No. 3630, World Bank, Washington.

Keane, J. (1988). Civil Society and the State, Verso, London.

Keohane, Robert O. & Holzgrefe, J. L. (2003). *Humanitarian intervention* : ethical, legal, and political dilemmas / *edited by J.L. Holzgrefe and Robert O.* Cambridge: Cambridge University Pres.

Kohn, Margaret, and Daniel I. O'Neill. (2006). 'A Tale of Two Indias: Burke and Mill on Empire and

Slavery in the West Indies and America,' *Political Theory*,Vol.34,No.2.

Klein, Herbert S.(1999). *The Atlantic Slave Trade.* New York: Cambridge University Press.

Kohn, Margaret and O'Neill, Daniel. (2006). 'A Tale of Two Indias: Burke and Mill on Racism and Slavery in the West Indies.' *Political Theory* 34: 192-228.

Kovel, Joel. *(1970). White Racism: A Psychohistory.* Pantheon Book: New York.

Larbi, G. (1999). The New Public Management Approach and Crisis States, Discussion Paper No. 112, UNRISD, Geneva.

_______ (1998). Institutional constraints and capacity issues in decentralising management in public services: The case of health in Ghana., Journal of International Development, No. 10.

Lenin, V.I. (1939). *Imperialism: The Highest Stage of Capitalism, A Popular Outline* (New York: International Publishers.

Lerner, D. (1958). *The Passing of Traditional Society: Modernizing the Middle East.* Glencoe ILL.: The Free Press.

Leurdijk, J. (1986), *Intervention in International Politics*, Eisma BV, Leeuwarden, Netherlands.

Lewis Killian & Charles Grigg. (1964). *Racial Crisis in America* (Prentice-Hall, Inc.: Englewood Cliffs.

Lewis, Peter. (1992). 'Political Transition and the Dilemma of Civil Society in Africa,' *Journal of International Affairs* 27 (Summer 1992); 31-54.

Lewinson, Paul. (1963). *Race, Class and Party.* Russell and Russell: New York.

Leys, Colin.(1975). *Underdevelopment in Kenya, the Political Economy of Neo-Colonialism, 1964-1971.* Heinemann Educational Books, London.

Lipsehutz, R. D. (1992). Reconstructing world politics: The emergence of global civil society. *Millenium: Journal of International Studies* 21(3): 389-420.

Lipietz Alain. (1982). Towards Global Fordism? New Left Review I/132, March-April 1982

Lonsdale, John.(1994). 'Moral Ethnicity and Political Tribalism' in P. Kaarsholm & J. Hultin eds. *Invention and Boundaries: Historical and Anthropological Approaches to the study of Ethnicity and Nationalism*, Occasional Paper No. 11, Roskilde: IDS

Mabogunje, A. L. (1990). Urban planning and the post-colonial state in Africa: A research overview. *African Studies Review* 33(2): 121-203.

Mackintosh, M. (1997). New public management and social exclusion: UK lessons., *Insight*, No. 23.

Mamdani, M. (1996). *Citizen and Subject: Contemporary Africa and the Legacy of Late Colonialism.* Princeton University Press, Princeton.

———————— -& E. Wamba-dia-Wamba, eds., *African Studies in Social Movements and Democracy.* CODESRIA Books, Dakar.

————————(1995a). Introduction. In: M. Mamdani and E. Wamba-dia-Wamba, eds., *African Studies in Social Movements and Democracy.* CODESRIA Books, Dakar.

————————(1995b). A critique of the state and civil society paradigm in Africanist studies. In: M. Mamdani and E. Wamba-dia-Wamba, eds., *African Studies in Social Movements and Democracy.* CODESRIA Books, Dakar.

Mandel, Ernest (1969),*Marxist theory of the state*, With an introduction by George Novack. Downloaded on 09/26/09 with thanks from the Mandel Archive at www.angelfire.com/pr/red/mandel/

Manley, Michael. (1975). *The Politics of Change: A Jamaican Testament.* Washington, D.C.: Howard University Press.

Manuel, G. and M. Posluns. (1974). *The Fourth World: An Indian reality.* New York: The Free Press.

Margaret E. Keck and Kathryn Sikkink .(1997)..*Activists Beyond Borders: Advocacy Networks in International Politics.* Ithaca, N.Y.: Cornell University Press, 1997.

Marx, Karl.(1853). 'The Future Results of British Rule in India,' *New York Daily Tribune,* January 22.

——————————(1972). *On Colonialism: Articles from the New York Tribune and other writings.* New York: International Publishers.

————————— (1954). Capital, Vol.I, London, Lawrence and Wishart, Ch.XXVI, p.667 London, Lawrence and Wishart, Ch.XXVI, p.667 and Ch.XXXI, p.703.

—————————(1967). 'Capital,' New York International Publishers.

Mazrui, Ali Amin. 2001.On the Atlantic slave trade, see John Thornton, *Africa and Africans in the Making of the Atlantic World, 1400-1800* (Cambridge: Cambridge University Press, 1998) and Hugh Thomas, *The Slave Trade: The Story of the Atlantic Slave Trade, 1440-1870* (New York: Simon and Schuster, 1997), quoted in Ali Amin Mazrui, First of three lectures on the general theme of 'PAN-AFRICANISM IN THE ERA OF GLOBALIZATION' given on August 3,2001, at the W.E.B. Du Bois Memorial Centre for Pan-African Culture, Accra, Ghana.

——————————_(2005). UHURU BADO KIDOGO: AFRICA'S CONDITION OF 'NOT YET UHURU'; THE BALANCE SHEET, **lecture given at the invitation of the Jaramogi Oginga Odinga Foundation and delivered in Nairobi, Kenya, on Friday, July 15, 2005.**

McElroy, Wendy.(2005). 'West Africa and Colonialism' In *Freedom Daily,* January 11.

McNally, David. (2006). *Another world is possible: globalization and anti-capitalism.* Arbeiter Ring Pub., Winnipeg.

Manning, Patrick. (1990). *Slavery and African Life: Occidental, Oriental, and African Slave Trades.* New York: Cambridge University Press.

Mbaku, John Mukum & Julius Omozuanvbo Ihonvbere.(1998). Multiparty Democracy and Political Change: Constraints to Democratization in Africa. Association of Third World Studies (U.S.). Meeting. Ashgate. London.

McCall, G. (1980). 'Four worlds of experience and action,' *Third World Quarterly* 2(3):536-545.

McMichael, Philip (2000). *Development and Social Change: A Global Perspective.* Thousand Oaks, CA: Pine Forge Press, 2nd edition.

McCourt, W. (1999). *Pay and Employment Reform in Developing and Transitional Societies,* mimeo, UNRISD; Geneva.

McClintock, Anne. (1992). 'The Angel of Progress: Pitfalls of the Term 'Post-Colonialism,' *Social Text* 31/32: 84-98.

McQuail, D. (2000). *McQuail's Mass Communication Theory, 4th Edition, /* London, Thousand Oaks, New Delhi: Sage Publications.

Mehta, Uday. (1999). *Liberalism and Empire: A Study in Nineteenth-Century British Liberal Thought.* Chicago: University of Chicago Press.

Menchu, R. (1994). 'Preface,' in *Voice of indigenous peoples: Native people address the United Nations.* Edited by A. Ewen, pp 16-18. Santa Fe, New Mexico: Clear Light Publishers.

Mentan, Tatah. (1999). 'Globalisation, Democratization, Exploitation and the State in Africa: The Final Conquest?' *Anthropology of Africa and the Challenges of the Third Millennium- Ethnicity and Ethnic Conflicts*, PAAA / APA, 1999.Online:

http://www.ethnonet-africa.org/pubs/p95mentan.htm

—————(2004). *Dilemmas of Weak States: Africa and transnational terrorism in the twenty-first century. London:* Ashgate.

—————*(2007a). Held Together by Pins: Liberal Democracy Under Siege in Africa*, Trenton, N.J.: Africa World Press.

—————*(2007b). With Neither Guns nor Bullets : Recolonisation of Africa Today*, Global Publishers, New Delhi.

—————(2009). Autocracy? Myths and Realities in *Africa Today.* Mankon: Langaa Publishers.

Meyrowitz, J. & J. Maguire.(1993). Media, Place and multiculturalism. *Society 30*, (5): 41-8.

Mill, John Stuart. (1963) and (1861). 'Considerations on Representative Government.' *Collected Works XIX*: 371-577.

Mkandawire , Thandika. (1998). 'Thinking about developmental states in Africa' United Nations Conference on Trade and Development African Development in a Comparative Perspective. Project (Geneva). Development United Nations Conference on Trade and Development (Published by UNCTAD, 1998)

Polanyi, Karl. (1944). *The Great Transformation: The Political and Economic Origins of Our Time. Beacon Press: Boston.*

Montagu, Ashley. (1963). *Race, Science and Humanity* (Princeton, N.J.: Van Nostrand Insights Books.

———————(ed.).(1969). *The Concept of Race.* Collier Books :London .

Moore, Richard B. 1960. *The Name Negro: Its Origin and Evil Use.* New York, N.Y., Afro-American Publisher, Inc.

Morris, G.T. (1992). International law and politics: Toward a right to self-determination for indigenous peoples. *Fourth World Documentation Project reprint,* 15 July 1995, ftp://ftp.halcyon.com/FWDP/int.txt.

Miliband, Ralph (1969). *The State in Capitalist Society.* New York: Harper Books.

Mkandawire, T. (1995). .Fiscal structure, state contraction and political responses in Africa. in T. Mkandawire & A. Olukoshi (eds.), *Between Liberalisation and Oppression: The Politics of Structural Adjustment in Africa,* CODESRIA, Dakar.

_______ (1997). Social sciences in Africa: Breaking local barriers and negotiating international presence. The Bashorun M.K.O. Abiola distinguished lecture presented to the 1996 African Studies Association Annual Meeting., *African Studies Review,* 40(2), pp 15-36.

_______ (1999). 'The political economy of financial reform in Africa,' *Journal of International Development,* No. 11.

Muana, P.K. (1997). 'The Kamajoi militia: Violence, internal displacement and the politics of counter-insurgency,' *Africa Development,* XXII(3 and 4).

Muthu, Sankar. (2003). *Enlightenment Against Empire.* Princeton, NJ: Princeton University Press.

Mutunga,W. & Al Amin Mazrui. (2002). *Rights Integration in Institutional Context: The Experience of the Kenya Human Rights Commission,* 8 BUFF.HUM.RTS.L.REV. (2002) 123-145, at145. Authors warn of 'the misappropriation of grassroots organizations to advance the interests of middle and other class bodies…' and thus see the need for the more direct involvement of… KHRC in stimulating the formation of grassroots structures and participating in their organization, management and mobilization

Nicholas, Tracy. (1996). *Rastafari.* Chicago, IL: Frontline Distribution International.

Meyrowitz, J. & J. Maguire.(1993). 'Media, Place and multiculturalism.' *Society 30,* (5): 41-8.

Nietschmann, B. (1985). Fourth World nations: Conflicts and alternatives. *Fourth World Documentation Project reprint,* 28 May 1995, ftp://ftp.halcyon.com/FWDP/4th_wrld.txt.

____________ (1986). Economic development by invasion of indigenous nations. *Cultural Survival Quarterly* 10(2):2:12.

——————. (1987). The third world war. *Cultural Survival Quarterly* 11(3):1-16.

——————. (1991). Conservation through self-determination. *Research and Exploration* 10(3):372-373.

——————(1992). The interdependence of biological and cultural diversity. (Occasional Paper No. 21). Kenmore: Centre for World Indigenous Studies.

——————(1994). 'The Fourth World: Nations versus states,' in *Reordering the world: Geopolitical perspectives on the twenty-first century*. Edited by G.J. Demko and W.B. Wood, pp 225-242. Boulder, Colorado: Westview Press.

Nkrumah, K. (1965). *Neo-colonialism: the last stage of imperialism*. New York: International Publishers.

Nugent, David (1994). 'Building the State, Making the Nation: The Basis and Limits of State Centralisation in 'Modern' Peru'. *American Anthropologist* 96,:333-69.

Offe, C and Ronge, V. 'Theses on the Theory of the State', in Giddens, A and Held, D. (eds) (1982) *Classes, Power, and Conflict. Classical and Contemporary Debates*, London: the Macmillan Press Ltd.

Okolo, A. (1982). 'The role of International trade in thc African political economy,' in Shaw/Ojo (ed.), *Africa and the International Political System*. University Press of America.

Oldfield, M. and J. Alcorn. (1991). 'Conservation of traditional agroecosystems,' in *Biodiversity: Culture, nature and ecodevelopment*. Edited by M. Oldfield and J. Alcorn, pp 37-58. Boulder, Colorado: Westview Press.

Onimode, Bade. (1982). .*Imperialism and Underdevelopment in Nigeria: The Dialectics of Mass Poverty* . London: Zed Press.

Osofsky, Gilbert.(1968). *The Burden of Race*. Harper Torchbook, Harper & Row.

Rawley, James: www.complete-review.com/reviews/ghistory/rawleyj.htm - 18k - Retrieved on Sept.19,2006.

Pagden, Anthony. (1990). *Spanish Imperialism and Political Imagination*. New Haven, CT: Yale University Press.

——————(1995). *Lords of All the World: Ideologies of Empire in Spain, Britain, and France, c. 1500–c. 1800*. New Haven, CT: Yale University Press.

Pambazuka News 175 - http://www.pambazuka.org/ retrieved on 07/15/09.

Patrick, Stewart. (2007). 'Failed' States and Global Security: Empirical Questions and Policy Dilemmas.' *International Studies Review* 9: 644–662. Blackwell Publishing. 1079-1760.

Parajuli, P. (1991). Power and knowledge in development discourse: New social movements and the state of India. *International Social Science Journal* 127:173-190.

Pieterse, J.N. (1991). Dilemmas of development discourse: The crisis of developmentalism and the comparative method. *Development and Change* 22:5-29.

Pitts, Jennifer. (2005). *A Turn Toward Empire: The Rise of Imperial Liberalism in Britain and France.* Princeton and Oxford: Princeton University Press.

Putnam, Robert D. (2000). .*Bowling Alone.* New York: Simon and Schuster.

Quijano, Aníbal.(2000). 'Coloniality of Power, Ethnocentrism, and Latin America,'

Nepantla Vol. 1, No. 3: 533-580.

Rice, S. E. (2006). 'Global Poverty, Weak States, and Insecurity' Brookings Institution, Washington, available at www.humansecuritygateway.info/data//item 245743606/view.

Robinson, William I. (2004).*Production, Class and State in a Transnational World.* Baltimore : John Hopkins University Press.

——————————(2004). *A Theory of Global Capitalism.* Baltimore, Maryland: Johns Hopkins University Press. Otberg

Robert I.2002. 'The New Nature of Nation-State Failure,' The Washington Quarterly, XXV (2002).

————————————(2003). *Transnational Conflicts: Central America, Social Change, and Globalization*, *Verso*, 2003, p. 274.

Shore, Chris (2001). Nation and State in the European Union. In R. Kiss and A. Paládi-Kovács (eds.), *Times, Places, Passages. Ethnological Approaches in the New Millennium.* Plenary Papers 'of 7th SIEF-Conference, Budapest.

Rakodi, C. (1986). 'State and class in Africa: A case for extending analyses of the form and functions of the national state to the urban local state.' *Society and Space* 4: 419-446.

Rakoy, S. B. (2008). The diminished role of trade unions as agents of social political transformation in Africa is markedly different from their exalted position at the independence period. NGOs too are not escaping the allurements of state largess. See e.g., Sebastian Bue Rakov, *Democratization and Constitutional Review in Kenya: A descriptive and Explanatory Analysis of Democratization in Kenya in the case of the Constitution Review Process in Between the General Elections of 2002 and 2007* (Unpublished PhD thesis, University of Aalborg, Denmark, 2008).

Rawley, James A.(written 1981,rev.2005). *The Transatlantic Slave Trade.* University of Nebraska Press; 2nd Revised edition (31 Jul 2005).

Rodman, M. (1992). 'Empowering place: Multilocality and multivocality.' *American Anthropologist* 94:640-654.

Rodney, Walter. (1974). *How Europe Underdeveloped Africa.* Washington, D.C.: Howard University Press.

Rogers, E.R. (1962). *The Diffusion of Innovations.* Glencoe, ILL: The Free Press.

Ruggie, John.(1994). 'Third Try at World Order? America and Multilateralism after the Cold War.' *Political Science Quarterly*, 109, 4, 553-70.

Rupert, M and H. Smith (eds.). *(2002). Historical Materialism and Globalization.* London and New York: Routledge

Ruther Benedict, 1964. *Race … Science and Politics.* Compass Books edition, Viking Press: New York

RYSER, R. (1985). 'The rules of war and Fourth World nations,' *Fourth World Journal* 1(1):53-72.

——————. (1986). States, indigenous nations, and the great lie. *Fourth World Documentation Project reprint,* 28 May 1995, ftp://ftp.halcyon.com/FWDP/greatlie.txt.

——————. (1992). From 'balance of power' to democratising international relations: Balancing relations between nations and states in a new era. *Fourth World Documentation Project reprint,* 28 May 1995, ftp://ftp.halcyon.com/FWDP/balance.txt.

——————. (1993). Toward the coexistence of nations and states. *Fourth World Documentation Project reprint,* 16 July 1995, ftp://ftp.halcyon.com/FWDP/moscow93.txt.

—————— (1994). State craft, nations and sharing governmental power. *Fourth World Documentation Project reprint,* 16 July 1995, ftp://ftp.halcyon.com/FWDP/statcrft.txt.

————————(1996). *Fourth World geopolitics, coexistence and the new international political order.* Doctorate of Philosophy in International Relations, Cincinnati: Graduate School of The Union Institute.

Sachs, Jeffrey, D., Aaron Tornell, and Andres Velasco. (1995). 'Financial Crisis in Emerging markets: The Lessons from 1995.' *Brookings Papers on Economic Activity*, 1:1996.

Said, Edward. (1979). *Orientalism.* New York: Vintage.

Schramm, W. (1964). *Mass Media and National Development, The role of information in developing countries.* Urbana: University of Illinois Press.

Scott, James C. (1998), *Seeing like a State: How Certain Schemes to Improve the Human Condition Have Failed*, London: Yale University Press

Seymour-Smith, C. (1986). *Dictionary of anthropology.* Boston: G.K. Hall and Co.

Sills, M.A. (1993). 'Political interaction between states and indigenous nations,' in *Indigenous peoples' politics: An introduction - volume 1.* Edited by M.A. Sills and G.T. Morris, pp 5-22. Denver: Fourth World Centre for the Study of Indigenous Law and Politics, University of Colorado.

Simone, A. M. and E. Pieterse. (1993). Civil societies in an international Africa. *Social Dynamics* 19(2): 41-49.

Smith, A.D. (1986). *The ethnic origins of nations.* Oxford: Basil Blackwell Ltd.

——————————(1991). *National Identity,* London: Penguin

Snyder, Louis L. (1962). 'Race and History,' *The Idea of Racialism* (Princeton, N.J.: Van Nostrand.

Spicer, E. (1971). Persistent cultural systems: A comparative study of identity systems that can adapt to contrasting environments. *Science* 174:795-800.

————————. (1992). The nations of a state. *Boundary 2* 19(3):26-48.

Spivak, Gayatri. (1988). 'Can the Subaltern Speak?' in C. Nelson and L. Grossberg, eds. *Marxism and the Interpretation of Culture.* Urbana: Univ. of Illinois Press. pp 271-313.

Stoddard, Lothrop. (1922). *The Rising Tide of Color Against White World-Supremacy.* Charles Scribner's Sons.: New York.

Tauli-Corpuz, V. (1993). An indigenous peoples' perspective on environment and development. *IWGIA Newsletter* 1:3-17.

THE NATIVE AMERICAN COUNCIL OF NEW YORK CITY. (1994). 'Introduction,' in *Voice of indigenous peoples: Native people address the United Nations.* Edited by A. Ewen, pp 19-27. Santa Fe, New Mexico: Clear Light Publishers.

Tocqueville, Alexis. (2001). *Writings on Empire and Slavery.* ed. and trans. Jennifer Pitts. Baltimore, MD: Johns Hopkins University Press.

Todaro, M. P.(200). *Economic Development in the Third World, 7th edition (Addison Wesley.* Longman: London.

Trouillot, Michel-Rolph (2001). 'The Anthropology of the State in the Age of Globalization,' *Current Anthropology*, Vol. 42, No. 1.

Tucker, Robert ed., (1978). *The Marx-Engels Reader, 2nd ed.,(New York: W.W. Norton,);* Robert Heilbroner, *Marxism For and Against* (New York: W.W. Norton, 1980) and Paul Sweezy. *Four Lectures on Marxism* (New York: Monthly Review, 1981); Lloyd Hogan, *Principles of Black Political Economy* (Boston: Routledge and Kegan Paul, 1984), chapter 5 for the centrality of both the slave trade and slave labour in the development of U.S. and European capitalism; C.L.R James, *The Black Jacobins* (New York: Vintage, 1963) for an outstanding Marxist study of the importance of slavery in the development of capitalism in France in the 18th century; James Geschwender, *Racial Stratification in America* (Dubuque, Iowa: Wm. C. Brown, 1978), Chapter 6; Robert Miles, *Racism* (London: Routledge, 1989). See Ronald Takaki, *A Different Mirror: A History of Multicultural America* (Boston: Little, Brown and Company, 1993).

UNDP, (2000). 'Globalization and the State: an Overview,' Report of the 15th Meeting of Experts on the United Nations Programme in Public Administration and Finance, April 2000. 'Is Globalization Civilizing, Destructive or Feeble? A Critique of Five Key Debates in the Social Science Literature,' Mauro Guillen, Research Centre: Regional H. Jones Centre for Management Policy, Strategy and Organization, January 2000.

UNDP Human Development Report 1999.

Victoria, Franciscus de. (1917). *On the Indians Lately Discovered.* ed. E. Nys. Washington: Carnegie Institute.

Volker Bornschier, Christopher Chase-Dunn and Richard Rubinson. (1978). 'Cross-national evidence of the effects of foreign investment and aid on economic growth and inequality: a survey of findings and a reanalysis,' *American Journal of Sociology* 84, 3:651-83. Reprinted in Pp 187-210 in A. Seligson. *The Gap Between Rich and Poor.* Boulder: Westview Press, 1984.

Wallerstein, I. (1974). *The modern world-system: Capitalist agriculture and the origins of the European world-economy in the sixteenth century*. New York: Academic Press.

Watts, M.J. (1993). Development I: Power, knowledge, discursive practice. *Social Research* 61:257-272.

————————(2003). 'Economies of Violence: Governable and Ungovernable Spaces in an Oil Nation [Nigeria]', paper delivered to the Comparative Politics Workshop, University of Chicago, November 18th 2003, cas.uchicago.edu/workshops/cpolit/papers/watts.doc (accessed online 23/11/2007).

————————(2006). 'Empire of oil: Capitalist Dispossession and the scramble for Africa,' *Monthly Review*, September, 2006.

Walzer, Michael. (1991). 'The Idea of Civil Society: A Better Vision.' *Dissent* 38 (Spring):293-304.

Weinstein, Lena. (2008). 'Questioning authority: Interview with Robert Calderisi,' May/June 2006, In *International Socialist Review,* July-August.

Welch C.E. (1997).The NGO Revolution in PROTECTING HUMAN RIGHTS IN AFRICA: ROLES AND STRATEGIES OF NON GOVERNMENTAL ORGANIZATIONS. 'Current Africana 1995',*Review of African Political Economy*,24:73,405 — 491.

Weyler, R. (1984). *Blood of the land.* New York: Vintage Books.

Williams, E.(1966). 'Capital and Slavery,' Capricorn Books: Chapel Hill.

————————. (1970). *From Columbus to Castro: The History of the Caribbean, 1492-1969.* Harper & Row, Publishers, New York and Evanston.

————(1944). *Capitalism and Slavery*, 1964(1944), London, Andre Deutsch.

————————(1966). 'The Origin of Negro Slavery,' *Capitalism and Slavery* (Capricorn paperback. For a recent and especially thought-provoking view, see Richard Lyman Bushman, 'Markets and Composite Farms in Early America,' *William and Mary Quarterly*, 3d ser., 55 (July 1998): 351–74. See also Peter Linebaugh and Marcus Rediker. (2000). *The Many-Headed Hydra: Sailors, Slaves, Commoners, and the Hidden History of the Revolutionary Atlantic.* Boston, Mass. Beacon.

Williams, Robert. (1990). *The American Indian in Western Legal Thought.* New York and Oxford: Oxford University Press.

W.E.B. DuBois, (1945). *Color and Democracy* (New York, N.Y., Harcourt, Brace & Co., Inc.,

Wilmer, F. (1993). *The indigenous voice in world politics.* Newbury Park, California: Sage Publications, Inc.

Wilson, Record. (1964). *Race and Radicalism.* Cornell University Press: Ithaca.

Wolf, Eric. (1988). 'Inventing Society.' *American Ethnologist* 15: 752–61.

Wood Ellen Meiksins. (2003). *Empire of Capital, Verso*, 2003, p. 157.

World Bank. (1997). *Private Capital Flows to Developing Countries.* New York: Oxford University Press.

WORLD COUNCIL OF INDIGENOUS PEOPLES (WCIP). (1979). Environmental values of indigenous peoples. *Fourth World Documentation Project reprint,* 22 May 1996, ftp://ftp.halcyon.com/FWDP/indigeco.txt.

Worsley, P. (1984). *The three worlds: Culture and development.* London: Weidenfeld and Nicolson.

Young, Crawford. (1994).*The African Colonial State in Comparative Perspective.* Yale University Press

Retrieved from 'http://en.wikipedia.org/wiki/M._Crawford_Young'

Young, Robert. (2001). *Postcolonialism: An Historical Introduction.* Oxford: Blackwell.

Zghal, A. K. 1995. The 'bread riot' and the crisis of the one-party system in Tunisia. In: ——————& Z. Krichen. (1995). The Islamic fundamentalist movement in Tunisia, 1970-1990: History and language. In: M. Mamdani and E. Wamba-dia-Wamba, eds., *African Studies in Social Movements and Democracy.* CODESRIA Books, Dakar.

Zuckoff, Mitchell.(2005). *Ponzi's Scheme: The True Story of a Financial Legend (Random House: New York.* The Ponzi Scheme is a more famous U.S. fraud involving postage stamps some 86 years earlier, in 1920, by Charles Ponzi – the man who bequeathed his name to history in the form of Ponzi pyramid scheme. He is reported to have arrived in Boston in 1903 with only $2.50. Not speaking much English, he took menial jobs. Fired as a waiter for shortchanging customers, he moved up to Montreal and became an assistant teller in an Italian immigrant bank. It grew rapidly by paying double the normal 3 percent rate of interest on savings accounts, but failed when its real estate loans began to go bad. The bank's attempt to give the impression of solvency seems to have given Ponzi the idea of paying interest out of new deposit inflows rather than actual earnings.\